Public
Relations

Public Relations

Tom Kelleher
University of Florida

New York   Oxford
OXFORD UNIVERSITY PRESS

Oxford University Press is a department of the University of Oxford.
It furthers the University's objective of excellence in research, scholarship,
and education by publishing worldwide. Oxford is a registered trade mark
of Oxford University Press in the UK and certain other countries.

Published in the United States of America by Oxford University Press
198 Madison Avenue, New York, NY 10016, United States of America.

For titles covered by Section 112 of the US Higher Education
Opportunity Act, please visit www.oup.com/us/he for the
latest information about pricing and alternate formats.

Library of Congress Cataloging-in-Publication Data

Names: Kelleher, Tom (Thomas A.), author.
Title: Public relations / Tom Kelleher, University of Florida.
Description: New York, NY : Oxford University Press, [2018]
Identifiers: LCCN 2016022597 | ISBN 9780190201470
Subjects: LCSH: Public relations.
Classification: LCC HD59 .K45 2018 | DDC 659.2–dc23 LC record
    available at https://lccn.loc.gov/2016022597

9 8 7 6 5 4 3 2 1

Printed by LSC Communications, United States of America

*Each of six provisions for conduct in the PRSA Code of Ethics are covered.

Contents

Contents

Contents

SECTION IV CONTEXTS

CHAPTER 11 Legal 275

CHAPTER 12 Issues and Crises 302

Contents

Preface

Changes.

Many things changed in the course of writing *Public Relations*, not the least of which was the passing of David Bowie. On that January morning when I learned of his death, I created my own David Bowie station on Pandora and blasted his music in my car on the way to work. Stopped at a red light, I looked around at all of the other drivers with their windows up. For a moment, I wondered if anyone was listening to the same station as me, hanging on the same notes and lyrics at the same time. It's a game I used to play growing up—looking out the backseat window and trying to figure out who was listening to the same station. Who was sharing the same experience? *Then the loud sound seemed to fade.* My station was my own, personalized for me and nobody else.

The light changed, and I drove on, contemplating yet another round of chapter revisions for *Public Relations*. In particular, I thought about how I'd better add something on personalization to Chapter 10 on multimedia and mobile.

It's not surprising that Bowie's fame trended across all channels as the day progressed, but I was shocked by how many of my friends, colleagues and students shared memories on social media. So many of them were listening to the same music, watching the same videos and recalling the same lyrics. The personalized media that had me feeling very still and alone in the morning reassured me with connectedness in the afternoon. It's an apparent paradox, and *Public Relations* is full of them.

Understanding digital media means understanding how they can be highly personalized and private at the same time that they are extremely amplified and social. In the same way, understanding the field of public relations means understanding how the interpersonal concept of human relationships can be extended to large organizations and broad publics. Public relations requires one-way and two-way communication, mass and interpersonal media, quantitative and qualitative research, advocacy and accommodation, controlled and uncontrolled information, global and local strategy, etc.

If you get these big ideas, you'll be able to manage all of the technological change just fine.

Turn and face the strange.

APPROACH

Writing this book has made me as mindful as anyone of how fast the field is changing. New technologies, new news, new cases, new faces—I've tried to keep the content fresh with all sorts of cases ranging from student experiences and small-but-meaningful exchanges between organizations and publics to incidents of international diplomacy and global crisis. More importantly, however, I've tried to make sure the underlying concepts are sound so that the lessons can be applied to the next big app, meme, crisis or event to fill our ceaseless newsfeeds.

As anyone listed in the acknowledgments section that follows can attest, I write slowly. I first pitched the idea for this text more than four years ago:

> *I am now looking to write an introductory text that aligns in both content and format with the new and changing landscape for public relations while still offering students a sound foundation in the body of knowledge of public relations on which most college curricula build.*

One thousand, five hundred and forty-eight days have passed between that email and my writing this preface. But it's not just me. Academic publishing in general moves slowly. I've learned to accept that as a blessing. Time forces us to check how our *understanding* of the concepts and the lessons from yesterday's cases and examples can be *applied* in the present, and how we can use that knowledge to *analyze* unfolding trends and news. Unlike a status update, snap, tweet or post, the content of this text has to be *evaluated* on the knowledge it delivers more so than on the momentary trends it taps.

Look at the citations and links in the references. There are hundreds of referrals that lead to countless additional resources—almost all of it freely available on the internet. My goal has been to offer a structure to work with so students can climb the pyramid of Bloom's taxonomy from recall to understanding to application to analysis to evaluation. For the most part, I've left the top of the taxonomy—*creation*—to students and their professors. Courses in public relations writing, multimedia production or campaigns will focus more on that part, and students will turn to other texts, trainings and online resources as they delve deeper into creating public relations tactics and programs on their own.

In any case, I am grateful for the time I've had to tweak the material and test its resilience. In a way, each of the case studies and examples is a little test. Does the moral of the story still resonate? Does the key point still hold? I have no doubt that some of the examples will eventually crack under the pressure of history as the field changes, and I look forward to adapting. But my highest hope for *Public Relations* is that it offers a cohesive enough foundation, such that teachers, students and professionals can explore the changing world of public relations with mutual understanding and a common vocabulary.

ORGANIZATION

Public Relations has four sections: (I) Foundations, (II) Strategy, (III) Tactics, and (IV) Contexts.

The Foundations section starts with Chapter 1, "Principled Public Relations," which presents classic definitions of public relations alongside the crowdsourced PRSA definition. Arthur Page's principles of public relations management provide a framework for introducing ethical practice. Professional organizations and codes of ethics are also introduced. The rest of the Foundations section identifies concepts that have always been core to good public relations and discusses how many of these concepts have become more pronounced with the rise of social media. Chapter 2, "Public Relations Models Through the Ages," covers public relations history with Grunig and Hunt's models and Lamme and Russell's taxonomy of goals of public relations. The next two chapters, "Convergence and Integrated Communication" (Chapter 3) and "Relationship Management" (Chapter 4) outline hot topics for today's newsfeeds, but they build from a long tradition of scholarship.

The Strategy section includes all of the elements of the traditional four-step RPIE process. The section starts with "Research" (Chapter 5) and includes a discussion of formative and summative research to highlight the cyclical nature of strategy. Next is "Planning" (Chapter 6), followed by "Implementation" (Chapter 7), which covers action and communication in strategic programs and campaigns. The last chapter in the Strategy section, "Evaluation" (Chapter 8), returns to the importance of research with a focus on measurement and metrics for success in digital communication.

The Tactics section includes three major skill and technology areas covered in two chapters: "Writing" (Chapter 9) and "Multimedia and Mobile" (Chapter 10).

The Contexts section (Chapters 11–14) addresses the forces influencing the practice of public relations as emerging sociotechnical trends challenge public relations people to confirm, rethink or in some cases abandon past practices and ideas. Chapter 11, "Legal," discusses law and policy. Chapter 12, "Issues and Crises," covers the issues life cycle and cases of conflict and crisis management. Chapter 13, "Global," covers global contexts that are broadening today's practice of public relations. Finally, Chapter 14, "Careers," delves into public relations careers, addressing different areas of specialization, different types of employers and the progression from entry level to senior management.

PEDAGOGICAL FEATURES

Every chapter of *Public Relations* showcases an outstanding set of features and pedagogy. These include: learning outcomes aligned with key Universal Accreditation Board (UAB) competencies, case studies, ethics topics mapped to the PRSA Code of Ethics, In Case You Missed It practical tips, Q&As with professionals and scholars, bulleted summaries, discussion questions and key terms defined in the margins.

Learning Outcomes

In addition to learning outcomes specific to emerging media, each chapter opens with public relations learning outcomes aligned with the

UAB groupings of competencies (see Appendix A for the complete list). This ensures *Public Relations* is professionally relevant.

Case Studies

Every chapter includes at least one extended run-in case study embedded in the text, and some chapters contain two or even three.

Ethics Topics Mapped to the PRSA Code of Ethics

Ethics are integral to the first chapter and discussed in every chapter thereafter. Each of the six provisions for conduct in the PRSA Code of Ethics is covered.

In Case You Missed It (ICYMI)

End-of-chapter boxes summarize some of the most useful tips covered in the chapter, particularly as they pertain to social media use.

Voices from the Field Q&As with Professionals and Scholars

Each chapter includes a Q&A with a practitioner or scholar offering additional from-the-field perspectives and insights into concepts and cases presented in the chapters.

Captions

Queries included at the end of most photo and figure captions prompt critical thinking about the highlighted examples.

Bulleted Summaries

Summaries organized around the learning outcomes identified at the start of each chapter reinforce the key takeaways.

Discussion Questions

Suggested questions at the end of each chapter encourage students to demonstrate learning outcomes by discussing personal and professional experiences or by analyzing and evaluating online resources. Instructors can easily deploy these in face-to-face or online teaching as writing assignments or discussion starters that connect student learning outcomes with current events and technologies.

Marginal Glossary

Key terms are defined in the margins of the text where they are first bolded, to reinforce key concepts.

ACKNOWLEDGMENTS

Thanks to God for blessing me with wonderful parents, family, teachers and friends.

Thanks to my wife Robin and sons Henry and Miles. On good writing days, the research and writing flowed easily, but so too did the hours. Robin and the boys were supportive and patient as dad stared at screens and tapped on keyboards from Honolulu to Gainesville. They put up with my fretting about details and deadlines on the bad days too.

Thanks to everyone at Oxford University Press. Thanks to Acquisitions Editor Toni Magyar and her predecessor Mark Haynes, for seeing the value in this project at the outset. Along with Assistant Editor Paul Longo, Toni was instrumental in converting a prospectus and a handful of draft chapters into the fully developed learning resource you're reading now.

I won the lottery when Lisa Sussman agreed to serve as development editor. There's not a paragraph in this text that Lisa didn't make better in some way—sometimes through four or five iterations. Thank you, Lisa!

Thanks to Dr. Karen Freberg of the University of Louisville for carefully crafting the Dashboard assessments, Dr. Susan Waters of Auburn University for her diligent work on the Test Bank, Dr. Cayce Myers of Virginia Tech University for his authoring of the Instructor's Manual, Dr. Shirley Carter of the University of South Carolina for her effort in making the open access materials, and Dr. Jocelyn DeAngelis for producing the PowerPoint lecture slides.

Many thanks to all of the following reviewers for their useful comments:

P. Anne Baker	*Oakland University*
Vincent Benigni	*College of Charleston*
Kati Berg	*Marquette University*
Julie A. Cajigas	*The University of Akron*
Christopher Caldiero	*Fairleigh Dickinson University*
Michelle Carpenter	*Old Dominion University*
Lolita Cummings Carson	*Eastern Michigan University*
Shirley S. Carter	*University of South Carolina*
Jennifer Chin	*University of North Carolina–Wilmington*
Rochelle R. Daniel	*Bowie State University*
Jocelyn DeAngelis	*Western New England University*
John DiMarco	*St. John's University*
Jeff Duclos	*California State University–Northridge*
James Everett	*Coastal Carolina University*
Michele E. Ewing	*Kent State University*
Patricia Fairfield-Artman	*University of North Carolina at Greensboro*
Barry Finkelstein	*Luquire George Andrews*
Robert French	*Auburn University*
Mark Grabowski	*Adelphi University*
Chris Groff	*Rutgers University*
Karen L. Hartman	*Idaho State University*
Christine R. Helsel	*Austin Peay State University*
Amy Hennessey	*Ulupono Initiative*
Corey A. Hickerson	*James Madison University*
Randy Hines	*Susquehanna University*
Sallyanne Holtz	*University of Texas at San Antonio*
Brad Horn	*National Baseball Hall of Fame and Museum*
Nathan Kam	*Anthology Marketing Group*

Natalie Kompa	*Ohio Dominican University*
Thomas A. Lamonica	*Illinois State University*
Keith Lindenburg	*Brodeur Partners*
Lisa Lundy	*University of Florida*
Sufyan Mohammed	*University of Scranton*
Aaron Moore	*Rider University*
Lisa H. Newman	*University of Cincinnati*
Dana Alexander Nolfe	*Bryant University*
Susan Pahlau	*Colorado Christian University*
Veronika Papyrina	*San Francisco State University*
Heather Radi-Bermudez	*Florida International University*
Kyle F. Reinson	*St. John Fisher College*
Risë J. Samra	*Barry University*
Jean K. Sandlin	*California Lutheran University*
Kathleen Stansberry	*Cleveland State University*
Marlane C. Steinwart	*Valparaiso University*
Robin Street	*University of Mississippi*
Dustin W. Supa	*Boston University*
Kaye D. Sweetser	*San Diego State University*
Philip Tate	*Luquire George Andrews*
Richard Waters	*University of San Francisco*
Susan E. Waters	*Auburn University*
Cynthia Wellington	*Webster University*
Quan Xie	*Bradley University*
Alissa Zito	*Loyola Marymount University*

Mahalo to all my students, colleagues and friends in Hawaii, where this project was born. The public relations community welcomed me from my first days on the job there when I joined PRSA and began advising the University of Hawaii Chapter of PRSSA in 1999. They taught me how public relations can be taught and practiced with aloha.

This book doesn't exist without my first public relations teachers at the University of Florida. Linda Hon and Mary Ann Ferguson have been chief architects in building the body of knowledge this book attempts to cover. They both mentored me as a graduate student. How cool is that? And when I returned to UF 20 years after starting graduate school here, I joined a number of the field's other most influential voices. You'll see names like Kathleen Kelly and Rita Linjuan Men as key contributors to the knowledge on these pages too.

Thank you to UF College of Journalism and Mass Communications Dean Diane McFarlin, Executive Associate Dean Spiro Kiousis, Associate Deans Debbie Treise and Mike Weigold, and all of my colleagues in the Department of Advertising who took a chance on hiring me here two years ago, and then supported me as I juggled all the new responsibilities with getting this book done. Go Gators!

CHAPTER 1
Principled Public Relations

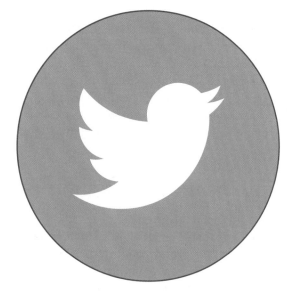

"A little bird told me . . ." What kinds of disclosure issues arise
when a public relations professional is asked to tweet for a client?

KEY LEARNING OUTCOMES

1.1 Define public relations in terms of organizations, publics and the relationships between them.

1.2 Explain how public relations can serve as a management function.

1.3 Recognize key principles and values for ethical conduct in public relations.

1.4 Understand the importance of ethics in public relations.

1.5 Apply systematic ethical decision-making for public relations.

1.6 Identify international professional associations and become familiar with codes of ethics.

RELATED UNIVERSAL ACCREDITATION BOARD COMPETENCY AREAS

2.1 INTEGRITY • **2.2** ETHICAL BEHAVIOR • **3.3** COUNSEL TO MANAGEMENT
4.3 KNOWLEDGE OF THE FIELD • **5.5** LEADERSHIP SKILLS

Among Publix's publics are frequent shoppers, fans and coupon clippers including the mother of two who developed the "I Heart Publix" website at http://www.iheartpublix.com/.

Are you part of a public for Publix?

Engagement. Conversation. Influence. Transparency. Trust. These concepts pepper workshops, seminars, articles and online discussions of what social and digital communication technologies mean for public relations. While essential for professional practice today, they have been at the heart of good public relations since long before Facebook, Twitter and Snapchat.

This chapter introduces classic definitions of public relations as well as a modern description crowdsourced by the Public Relations Society of America (PRSA). By and large the crowdsourced, social-media-era definition matches the classics that have been used in the teaching and practice of public relations for decades. While keywords like *publics*, *organizations*, *communication* and *relationships* may not be buzzworthy, they have stood the test of time as key components in any sound definition of public relations.

Defining Public Relations

Publics—it's not a term you hear every day outside of classrooms and strategy meetings. I still recall vividly the first day in my very first public relations course. The professor started right in discussing the importance of relationships between organizations and publics. For a moment, I was confused about why we would spend so much time talking about relationships between organizations and *Publix*, the prominent southern U.S. supermarket chain ("Where shopping is a pleasure!"). Of course, he was talking about the plural of the term *public*, which did turn out to be important to our first lesson in public relations. In public relations, **publics** are groups of people with shared interests related to organizations.

General public—now here's a term, referring to everyone in the world, you probably do hear every day. How is the general public responding to today's news events? What's the best way to get our message out to the general public? Can we engage the general public on this issue? The first two questions are nearly impossible to answer, and the answer to the third question is probably "no." That is the problem with the general public. For all practical purposes the general public doesn't help us with strategy, and it doesn't help us identify any real people with whom we want to communicate.

Engaging in public relations means communicating with people who are part of specific groups with specific interests. Some of these publics are groups that have an effect on the **organizations** for which we work. These include large corporations, small businesses, nonprofits, schools, government agencies, **nongovernmental organizations (NGOs)** organized at the local, national, or international level, and even clubs and student groups—pretty much any group of people organized to pursue a mission. Others are people who are affected by our organizations. Most publics fit both criteria in that the influence is mutual.

The American Red Cross (organization) sets up a Twitter list to promote resources for tornado victims in Oklahoma (public) following a deadly twister. That's public relations. Representatives of a Public Relations Student Society of America (PRSSA) chapter (organization) make an announcement in an introductory communications class to recruit new members (public). That's public relations. The Japan National Tourism Organization (organization) posts photos and videos to its "Visit Japan" Facebook page and interacts with commenters (public) on the page. That's public relations. Hewlett-Packard Co. (organization) posts a news release announcing that quarterly profits have slipped and hosts a live audio conference call for media contacts (public) and investors (another public) in order to satisfy Securities and Exchange Commission (SEC—yet another public) regulations. That's public relations too. Notice that in none of these cases have the organizations set out to engage the general public. Instead, Oklahoma tornado victims, new communication majors, Facebook commenters, media contacts, investors and the SEC are identified as specific publics.

The labels for publics and organizations are sometimes interchangeable. If executives from Hawaiian Electric Co. (organization) visit homes of community leaders in the neighborhood of proposed new power lines (public) to discuss options for meeting increased energy demand, that's public relations. And if neighbors in the community organize a coalition (organization) to oppose the electric company (public) at government hearings, that's still public relations.

Completing a full definition of **public relations** requires more than just identifying organizations and publics. We still have to understand the second part of the term *public relations*—the relations.

The American Red Cross used its Twitter feed immediately after devastating tornadoes swept through Oklahoma.

Who were the Red Cross's key publics?

> To define public relations, consider organizations, publics and the relations between them.

Textbook Definitions

Perhaps the most commonly cited definition of public relations is the one written by James Grunig and Todd Hunt in their classic 1984 public relations text *Managing Public Relations*: "the management of communication between an organization and its publics."[1] There's a lot to this business of managing communication, which is why so many other definitions of public relations abound. Another classic definition from another classic public relations text, *Cutlip and Center's Effective Public Relations*, defines public relations as "the management function that establishes and

Public relations
Management of communication between an organization and its publics, or the strategic communication process that builds mutually beneficial relationships between organizations and their publics.

TV shows like "Scandal," which features Kerry Washington as crisis management consultant Olivia Pope, present an entertaining view of "PR."

What messages do shows like this send about the field of public relations?

maintains mutually beneficial relationships between an organization and the publics on whom its success or failure depends."[2]

Naturally, people are wary, even skeptical, of textbook definitions. Ask people outside of the field of public relations what public relations is and you'll get quite different answers. Even communication students, many of whom intend to go into "PR," may surprise you. Rather than risking miscommunication about Publix on the first day of discussing public relations in my introductory classes, I play the word association game.

"Quick! Tell me the first thing that comes to your mind when I say public relations." I call on a student.

"Damage control." I call on another.

"Spin." Another.

"Scandal!" The class laughs, but the answer resonates.

ABC's *Scandal* is one of several television shows that features "PR" agents as key characters. Olivia Pope, the protagonist of ABC's hit political drama, is a former White House communication director who runs her own Washington, D.C., crisis consulting firm. She "fixes" all sorts of political crises with clever deception and slick execution. Actress Kerry Washington, who plays Pope on the show, describes the character as glamorous but seriously flawed. "She's an entrepreneur, she's very smart, she has an amazing closet, and those are all things that I think are worthy of admiration," says Washington. "But she is nobody's role model."[3]

So what do we make of this disconnect between public relations as professors and professionals want to define it and public relations as *Scandal* viewers, students, critical bloggers, our parents and so many others see it? It is tempting to just ditch the name and call it something else. Many organizations have done that, or they have never called the function public relations in the first place. Instead, they have departments of public affairs, corporate communications, community relations and so on. Some organizations have really exercised their creativity in naming the roles of people who manage communications between them and their publics. Dane Cobain of South Africa's Memeburn website highlighted 21 ridiculous job titles.[4] Among them are social activationist, community data guerrilla, senior social media capability architect and the dreaded social media guru.

Crowdsourcing a Definition

The negative connotations and confusion over job titles have not been lost on those in the profession. In late 2011 and early 2012, PRSA set out to tackle the definition of public relations.

"Public Relations Defined" is an initiative to modernize the definition of public relations. Through an open and collaborative effort, PRSA and its industry partners are providing a platform for public relations, marketing

What does it really mean when someone claims to be a social media guru?

and communications professionals to add their voice to a new definition of public relations.[5]

The effort included consultation with 12 allied organizations including the Canadian Public Relations Society, PRSSA, the National Black Public Relations Association, the Hispanic Public Relations Association and the Word of Mouth Marketing Association. The advent of social media was certainly a factor, as reported by Stuart Elliot in *The New York Times*:

Perhaps the most significant changes have occurred most recently, as the Internet and social media like blogs, Facebook and Twitter have transformed the relationship between the members of the public and those communicating with them. A process that for decades went one way— from the top down, usually as a monologue—now goes two ways, and is typically a conversation.[6]

Given the circumstances, PRSA's use of a blog and its comments from readers (http://prdefinition.prsa.org), Twitter (#PRDefined), and an online form for submitting candidate definitions seemed appropriate. It was an exercise in crowdsourcing. Oxford Dictionaries defines the verb **crowdsource** as "obtain (information or input into a particular task or project) by

Crowdsource
To obtain information or input into a particular task or project by enlisting the services of a number of people, either paid or unpaid, typically via the internet.

enlisting the services of a number of people, either paid or unpaid, typically via the internet."[7] And that's exactly what PRSA did. In this case the help was unpaid. By day 12 of the open submission period, the top 20 words submitted as part of suggested definitions for public relations were:

organization (mentioned in 388 submissions)
public (373)
communication (280)
relationship(s) (260)
stakeholders (172)
create (170)
mutual (158)
understand (153)
build (152)
audiences (147)

inform (144)
management (124)
brand (119)
company (116)
business (112)
people (100)
engages (94)
client (92)
awareness (88)
maintain (81)[8]

The task force soon had narrowed the field of definitions down to three finalists, opened a public comment period online, hosted a second "Definition of Public Relations Summit" with partner organizations, revised the three definitions, and held a public vote to select the new definition. And the winner was . . . "Public relations is a strategic communication process that builds mutually beneficial relationships between organizations and their publics." You may have noticed that the crowdsourced and modernized definition of public relations isn't all that different from the classic definitions.

Principled Public Relations Management

Regardless of how you define it, good public relations requires excellent management. When an organization's communication is focused more on image and less on what the organization is actually doing, negative connotations like **spin** and damage control become unfortunately accurate descriptions.

The problem with communication strategies based on image and fluff, however, is that publics can see right through them. Sometimes they will play along for the fun of it. This is common in sports and entertainment. Sensationalism, snafus, ballyhoo and bombast are all part of what keep people interested in Miley Cyrus' wardrobe choices or Mike Tyson's celebrity antics well beyond their talents for acting, singing or boxing.

But publics are ready to call you on it if you try to promote your organization in ways inconsistent with how your organization is managed. It is easier than ever for people to call out businesses for such inconsistencies. **Greenwashing** is a great example. Many organizations try to present

Spin
Disingenuous strategic communication involving skewed interpretation or presentation of information.

Greenwashing
When an organization spends more resources claiming to be "green" through publicity, advertising and marketing than actually implementing practices that minimize environmental impact.

Sites like http://www.greenwashingindex.com make it easy for publics to share opinions about organizations.

How should public relations people engage such publics?

themselves as eco-friendly to appeal to environmentally conscious publics. EnviroMedia Social Marketing has partnered with the University of Oregon School of Journalism and Communication to promote a "Greenwashing Index."

> *Everyone's heard the expression "whitewashing"—it's defined as "a coordinated attempt to hide unpleasant facts, especially in a political context." "Greenwashing" is the same premise, but in an environmental context. It's greenwashing when a company or organization spends more time and money claiming to be "green" through advertising and marketing than actually implementing business practices that minimize environmental impact. It's whitewashing, but with a green brush.*[9]

If your efforts at communication and promotion are not consistent with how your organization is managed, your organization will be seen far closer to the "bogus" end of the greenwashing index than the "authentic" end. Sites like http://www.greenwashingindex.com make it easy for people to collect and share their experiences. "If you've seen an ad promoting the environmental qualities of a product or company, post it here, rate it, then come back to see what other users say."[10]

Of course, publics have been discussing businesses and their **authenticity** since long before the internet. Arthur Page, longtime vice president of

Authenticity
The degree to which one communicates reliably, accurately and true to his or her own character and the character of the organization that he or she represents.

Arthur W. Page was an early proponent of authenticity and transparency in American public relations.

Do Page's principles apply any more or less in the digital age?

Transparency
Deliberate attempt to make available all legally reasonable information for the purpose of enhancing the reasoning ability of publics.

AT&T Inc., worked at the company from the 1920s through the '30s and '40s and into the '50s. Page was one of the first public relations people to reach that level of management in an organization of that magnitude. He articulated and practiced principles of public relations management that apply as well now as they did in the mid-20th century.

1. Tell the truth.
2. Prove it with action.
3. Listen to the customer.
4. Manage for tomorrow.
5. Conduct public relations as if the whole company depends on it.
6. Remain calm, patient and good-humored.
7. Realize the company's true character is expressed by its people.

Tell the Truth

It's one thing to not lie; it's another to proactively tell the truth. This principle can be equated with the idea of **transparency**.[11] Public relations researcher and ethicist Brad Rawlins has defined it as the opposite of secrecy:

Transparency is the deliberate attempt to make available all legally reasonable information—whether positive or negative in nature—in a manner that is accurate, timely, balanced, and unequivocal, for the purpose of enhancing the reasoning ability of publics and holding organizations accountable for their actions, policies, and practices.[12]

Even in cases that necessitate secrecy, tell the truth about what information your organization is protecting and why.

Arthur Page realized that large organizations like AT&T were particularly susceptible to public mistrust and suspicion when they overzealously protected secrecy. Governments, schools, churches, NGOs and nonprofits are all in danger of breeding fear, apprehension, dislike and distrust when they shirk transparency. Of course, there are times when secrecy makes sense to publics, such as in times of national security crises or when businesses want to protect proprietary information to compete in markets, but even in those cases, organizations can still "tell the truth" about what they are keeping secret and why.

Prove It with Action

Good public relations is based much more on what an organization does than on what it says.

You might call it the 90-10 rule. Page said that 90 percent of good public relations should be determined by what an organization does, and about 10 percent by what they say. Publicity is important, but only if it follows action. Disneyland is the happiest place on earth. Ajax is stronger than dirt. 3M is innovation. Levi's quality never goes out of style. These are among the 40 most powerful slogans for brands, according to the Advergize website,[13] but think about how much work goes into making the slogans resonate. The slogans are hollow if the organization isn't managed in such a way as to make the words ring true.

You won't see BP's "Beyond Petroleum" slogan on the list. In 2000, BP introduced a new logo as part of a major re-branding campaign by its agency Ogilvy & Mather. The bright, new—and of course green—sunburst logo was a textbook example of branding. Literally. In Pavlik and McIntosh's *Converging Media* textbook, the authors defined branding as "the process of creating in the consumer's mind a clear identity for a particular company's product, logo, or trademark." To illustrate the concept in the second edition of that text, the logo was captioned "British Petroleum has successfully re-branded its company with a new logo and a public image as being environmentally friendly."[14] (And I'm the first to admit I used it as an example in my own classes!)

But according to contributors on the PR Watch website, "BP's investment in extractive oil operations dwarfed its investment in renewable energy."[15] Critics immediately began to question the campaign. Then in the summer of 2010, when BP's Deepwater Horizon rig exploded leading to one of the worst manmade environmental disasters in history, BP was just hammered on social media. Online contests were introduced to see who could design the best logo mocking BP's green sunburst. A YouTube video portraying clumsy BP executives botching an attempt to clean up spilled coffee went viral, getting 10 times more views than BP's official YouTube channel headliner following the accident. More than 160,000 Twitter users followed a fake BP Twitter account spoofing the company.

Later, BP did make some commendable efforts as part of its continuing road to recovery. They used Twitter to send important information out as fast as possible when media inquiries were overwhelming their media relations staff. But in terms of action, BP soon became seen as "A Textbook Example of How Not to Handle PR," at least according to an NPR story title. After interviewing experts, journalist Elizabeth Shogren concluded that BP "failed to communicate the three key messages the public needed to hear: That BP was accountable for the disaster, was deeply concerned about the harm it caused and had a plan for what to do."[16] Not only were they not able to communicate well, they also weren't ready to prove it with action.

Listen to the Customer

Listening, or paying attention to and processing what others are communicating, is at the heart of **two-way communication**. For organizations with large publics, listening requires an investment in systematic research. It also requires management to be responsive to what the media and employees have to say. The press may pick up on public sentiment, and employees often have a very good sense of what people outside the organization think. In both technical terms and everyday language, listening is more than just hearing. While those managing an organization may hear what's being said about the organization in the news, at the water cooler, online

BP's sunburst logo was designed to highlight the company's commitment to the environment.

What comes to your mind when you see the BP logo?

Following the BP oil spill, web users competed to design the best mock logo for the company.

Why do you think it was so easy to mock BP after the oil spill?

Listening
Deliberately paying attention to and processing what others are communicating. In public relations and organizational communication, this means processing feedback.

Two-way communication
When both parties send and receive information in an exchange, as opposed to the one-way dissemination of information from an organization to its publics.

Feedback
Information returned from the environment in response to an organization's action or communication that can be used for continuous adjustment and improvement of the organization.

Proactive
A management style that is anticipatory, change-oriented and self-initiated to improve the organization's environment and its future.

Reactive
A management style that mainly responds to problems as they arise rather than anticipating them and averting them.

To effectively listen in public relations, participate in and monitor online communities, in addition to using traditional research.

or out on the street, real listening means considering what the **feedback** means for the organization and what can be done about it. Page saw listening as an important part of public relations, and he saw the public relations person's role as one of keeping upper-level management and others inside an organization informed about public sentiment.

Counting headlines, Facebook likes, Twitter followers, phone calls, YouTube views or keyword mentions gives some indication of what people are thinking and talking about, but good listening requires more careful and deliberate attention to what is being said and what that means for your organization and how it is managed. You can't manage a business on buzz alone.

Manage for Tomorrow

Be **proactive**. That's easy enough to say, but harder to do. After a crisis hits, it is much harder to engage in thoughtful dialogue with publics about what an organization can and should be doing. When public relations people are called in after a major screw-up to clean up the mess, their role is mostly **reactive**, limited to damage control, at best, or spin, at worst, unless they can report that the organization is taking real action to correct whatever problems have occurred. While even the very best-managed of organizations are susceptible to surprise crises, some organizations simply miss opportunities to stave off disasters because they are not listening well to what is going on in their environment and considering the ethical implications. This kind of listening today requires traditional research as well as participation in and monitoring of online communities and forums.

Page's proactive public relations—managing for tomorrow—means building goodwill, avoiding business practices that will lead to unfavorable business conditions, and anticipating how publics will respond to business decisions that will have negative consequences. This concept of proactive public relations is based on two big assumptions. First, public relations people have a role in managing the operations and policies of an organization. Second, public relations people are in a position to sense when major opportunities arise or when trouble is brewing.

Page acknowledged that the purpose of public relations isn't to try to answer every little complaint "because you can't run around and put salve on every sore that appears in the world." This is good news for those monitoring online product reviews! Rather, proactive public relations is tied to a broader strategy. University of Florida Professor Emeritus Robert Kendall (the one who taught me about publics in my very first public relations course) defined proactive public relations as a "philosophy of public relations that takes the initiative in planning the nature of the relationships desired with publics and executes programs, campaigns, or activities designed to achieve the desired ends."[17] Strategic public relations is proactive.

Conduct Public Relations as if the Whole Company Depends on It

Page saw public relations as a **management function**, but he also realized that top managers were not the only ones responsible for public relations. In discussing leadership, he described how the role of a company president is "first to have the company intend to do the right thing by the public" and then to "get everyone in the company to do his part in carrying out the policy, effectively, reasonably and politely."

Employees have always been spokespeople for organizations, whether that was in their job titles or not. If we want to know what is going on with the big manufacturing plant in our community, we may read about it in the newspaper, but we also won't be afraid to ask our neighbors who work there. Airline ticket agents and flight attendants may be our windows into the workings of the larger airline. The mail carrier may be our source on the postal service. Public relations depends on all of these people, and all of these people depend on public relations.

No one wants to be part of an organization that is dreaded in his or her own neighborhood. We want to go to schools, volunteer for nonprofits and join civic and religious organizations that are respected in our communities. We want to work for organizations that are managed well and proactive in public relations, and of course we want them to stay solvent and avoid crises too. To the degree that public relations supports these goals, we all depend on it even if we aren't officially working in public relations.

Remain Calm, Patient and Good-Humored

I love this one. Page reminds us not to forget the importance of being good-natured, even in dealing with stressful day-to-day situations and larger organizational crises. Publics resent organizations with rude people representing them and, all else being equal, are more forgiving of those that are pleasant. It's human nature.

Throughout the ages, good public relations people have known how important it is to maintain good relationships with reporters. "Never pick a fight with someone who buys ink by the barrel," the old saying goes. The same idea applies in this era of digital publishing and consumer-generated media (CGM). Review sites like Yelp, Google Places, Angie's List and TripAdvisor give all sorts of consumers a voice. No barrels of ink required.

In fact, the human element is even more important as publics are more likely to turn to peers online as sources of information about large organizations than they are to listen to major media institutions. In annual surveys of public trust conducted by the public relations firm Edelman, respondents report that people "like me" are more trustworthy than major media sources. CEO Richard Edelman attributes this shift to "the dispersion of authority" that comes with social media and advises public relations people to include all members of their organizations in their communication strategies. "Smart businesses will talk to employees first, because citizens now trust one another more than they do established institutions."[18]

Management function
Part of an organization involved in its overall leadership and decision-making, guiding how the organization operates in its environment, rather than merely following the instructions of others.

The popular "Keep Calm" meme was derived from a World War II public safety poster in Great Britain.

What do you think drives the popularity of this meme?

Conversational voice
An authentic, engaging and natural style of communication that publics perceive to be personable.

Flaming
Hostile communication among internet users.

Academic research bears out Page's principle as well. In surveys and experiments, my colleagues and I have found that a variable called **conversational voice** is important in maintaining good relationships with publics online. This "voice" is gauged by asking people how much they agree with statements about how an organization communicates. Organizations with communicators who are perceived as making communication enjoyable, using a sense of humor, admitting mistakes, and even providing links to competitors, rank higher on the conversational-voice scale. And that conversational voice correlates with public relations outcomes such as satisfaction and commitment, as well as trust.[19]

PCWorld's Robert Strohmeyer offered sound advice in writing about how to deal with Yelp disasters:

> I like to think that most people are generally sensible, but the Internet has an uncanny knack for transforming rational adults into raving, infantile morons. Yelp, doubly so. Once you accept this basic tenet, you can begin to view your online critics as the reasonable minds they probably are, rather than the juvenile half-wits they appear to be.

He discourages hostile communication or **flaming** of critics or trying to sue them. Instead, he recommends working within the Yelp toolset by signing up for a business account, which lets you claim your business's Yelp page. Once you've done that you can both encourage positive reviews (but don't insist on them!) and respond constructively and politely to critics, the same way you would if they were at your service counter or reception desk. Moreover, says Strohmeyer, "Have fun with it."

Respond constructively and politely to critics online, the same way you would if they were at your service counter or reception desk.

Sometimes the best way to handle tense situations is to stay engaged with the community and keep a sense of humor.

Would you be inclined to dine at this restaurant?

Realize the Company's True Character Is Expressed by Its People

Effective integrated communication means that publics form their beliefs and attitudes about organizations based on all their points of contact with an organization. Organizations are made up of people, and these people themselves are the most powerful points of contact that others have with the organization. "I am quite certain that the general body of our employees can be trained to represent the company effectively even on complicated subjects," said Page.[20] As Harold Burson, founding partner of Burson-Marsteller, put it, "The thinking goes like this: public relations should permeate every corporate transaction—literally involving almost every employee—from the receptionist to the person at the check-out counter, those who sell the product and those who service it." In other words, "Public relations is now everybody's job."[21]

Social media have only amplified this idea. Managing relationships between organizations and publics means managing organizations in ways that encourage constructive relationships to arise from the countless interpersonal interactions online and offline between all the people who represent the organization and all those with whom they communicate in that role. While the idea of managing for effective **integrated communication** that is consistent across organizational functions goes way back before the internet, social media have changed the game with new management challenges in an era in which people "like me" are becoming more influential, while mainstream media and large institutional sources are struggling for credibility. Particularly in online contexts, this requires managing **distributed public relations**, in which public relations responsibilities are shared among a broad cross section of an organization's members or employees. People look for authenticity in online communication. They still read and view news stories told by journalists about organizations, but more and more, publics communicate directly with all sorts of people from organizations online. When that happens, there is an opportunity for the organization to communicate its true character.

Ethics

Page's principles of public relations make sense on a practical level. It is not hard to understand why he had such a long and successful career. But these principles also show the importance of moral philosophy and ethics in public relations. Truth, action, empathy and character give meaning to the day-to-day work of public relations. Put bluntly, damage control and spin are lame. Who wants to do that for a living? There are many good reasons to put ethics at the center of your thinking about good public relations.

Reasons for Studying Ethics

You'll feel better about yourself. **Ethics** are moral principles that govern behavior and are deeply personal. You'll wake up in a much better mood every morning if you know you are going to work for an organization with values

Integrated communication
Communicating with publics consistently across organizational functions including public relations, advertising, marketing and customer service.

Distributed public relations
Intentional practice of sharing public relations responsibilities among a broad cross section of an organization's members or employees, particularly in an online context.

Ethics
Moral principles that govern a person's or group's behavior.

congruent to your own. Strategic public relations means that the public relations tactics you perform are derived from solid goals and objectives, and that those goals and objectives serve the broader mission of your organization. This doesn't mean that you have to agree with every single action the organization takes. In fact, the very nature of ethics is dealing with competing values and gray areas. You may agree wholeheartedly with the mission of a nonprofit that employs you, but that doesn't mean you agree with the way they go about pursuing that mission. Sometimes you have to take a stand in your own organization to make your case when you disagree, and you should feel empowered to do so. The important thing is that you can practice public relations in a way that feels right to you and in a place where you don't feel like you are selling your soul to get the job done every day. In a field like public relations, which year after year is listed among the most stressful career options you can choose, your sanity may well depend on how you and those you work with handle ethical dilemmas and gray areas.

Of course, ethics aren't all about gut feelings. Good people make bad decisions all the time. Resolving ethical problems is a matter of the heart, but it is also an intellectual activity. As public relations practitioners move up in their careers, and as they earn more and more respect in management, the importance of their ethical decision-making becomes more important to the organizations they represent, and, ideally, they get better at ethics. This is why it is essential to study principles and systems for ethical reasoning now and to continue to brush up on your ethics throughout your career, which leads to the next point.

You'll be better at your job. Many ethical dilemmas arise out of interactions with reporters, clients, colleagues and members of various publics. Solid relationships with reporters are built on trust, consistency and mutual understanding of professional roles and responsibilities. Retaining clients and attracting new ones requires a reputation for fairness and integrity. Loyalty and expertise are among the keys to positive and productive relationships with colleagues. And transparency is essential in dealing with online communities when strategic communication is the essence of your job. Developing a solid ethical framework that you can explain to others will help you in all of those relationships, and those relationships are the stuff of which successful, fulfilling careers are made.

You'll be more important at work. As Shannon Bowen puts it, communication professionals must pay attention to ethics before they desperately need to. "Once a crisis of conflicting ethics or high media interest befalls the organization it is too late to begin searching for ethical guidance."[22] Bowen is a professor, ethicist and member of the Arthur W. Page Society. In her research she has found that spotting ethical dilemmas is key to resolving issues before they become crises. Beyond just identifying ethical dilemmas, public relations people must be able to discuss the issues with members of their organization's dominant coalition. **Dominant coalition** is a term used to describe the group of people with the greatest influence in how an organization operates, including CEOs, presidents, board members, top managers, vice presidents and so

Dominant coalition
Group of people with the greatest influence in determining how an organization operates and pursues its mission.

on. The dominant coalition may or may not include public relations executives. However, these are the people who steer the organization at the highest levels, and a public relations person who is well versed in rational, defensible, ethical decision-making will be in the best position to inform this group in handling public relations issues before they become crises.

Competing Duties

Working in public relations means serving many masters. In their book *Public Relations Ethics*, Philip Seib and Kathy Fitzpatrick highlight the source of many ethical dilemmas as individual practitioners face them.[23] That source is competing duties. If you work in public relations, you have a duty to: (1) yourself, (2) your client, (3) your employer, (4) the profession, (5) the media and (6) society. I'm willing to bet that there are vegetarians who work in public relations agencies that represent steakhouses. I'm sure there are people who are deeply annoyed by cable news channels, but who still work hard to accommodate their TV producers prior to interviews. I even know a certain textbook author and professor who criticizes Walt Disney Co.'s massive media empire and then happily takes his kids to Walt Disney World. None of these folks are necessarily sellouts. The vegetarian may welcome the restaurant to his community to boost the economy while providing jobs, not to mention the business for his own agency, which supports his own financial stability. The public relations practitioner arranging the cable news interview may weigh the importance of free speech and vigorous debate as much more important in society than her opinion of the particular station's host and format. And your textbook author doesn't think a personal boycott of a major media conglomerate is a requisite for educating others about issues of media consolidation in society. On the other hand, there are times when public relations practitioners must say no to reporters. There are times when agencies should decline clients. There are times when a potential paycheck is not worth the dissonance it creates.

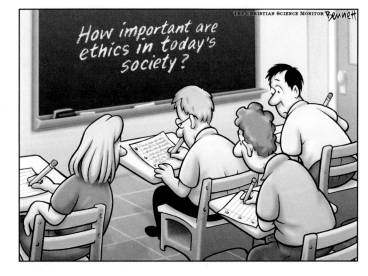

Learning (and practicing!) ethics has value well beyond the classroom.

What do you see as the major benefits of studying ethics before working in public relations?

A Guide for Decision-Making

Addressing these apparent dilemmas ethically requires careful thinking. Fitzpatrick offers the following guide for public relations practitioners:

1. Define the specific ethical issue/conflict.
2. Identify internal/external factors (e.g., legal, political, social, economic) that may influence the decision.
3. Identify key values.

4. Identify the parties who will be affected by the decision and define the public relations professional's obligation to each.

5. Select ethical principles to guide the decision-making process.

6. Make a decision and justify it.[24]

In many ways, social media have made ethical communication easier. We get to speak in our own voices in forums in which direct, informal communication is valued. Social media give us means for discussing and resolving our professional issues with easy access to others' opinions and views. We get to experiment in mixing our personal and professional identities. This can lead to a heightened sense of awareness of our consistencies and inconsistencies. At the same time, however, this breaking down of clear divisions between our personal and professional communication raises new dilemmas, and digital media technologies introduce new opportunities for deception.

Case Study

"Tweeting Under False Circumstances"

Todd Defren runs SHIFT Communications, a public relations firm that specializes in digital and social media that has served clients including McDonald's, Salesforce.com, TechCrunch, H&R Block and Tyson Foods. Defren is also a highly influential blogger with a large number of readers of his *PR Squared* blog.[25] Defren has highlighted some new dilemmas unique to social media.

Let's use Fitzpatrick's process to walk us through one of Defren's cases, "Tweeting Under False Circumstances."[26] (Quoted material is from Defren's blog post.)

DEFINE THE SPECIFIC ETHICAL ISSUE/CONFLICT

A client asked Defren and his associates to tweet for him at a trade show from the client's Twitter account. The client was adept at Twitter and prominent in his field. He had a significant number of loyal followers on his account who were used to hearing directly from him via that channel.

He posts regularly, sometimes several times a day. He "gets" Twitter; he finds value in the dialogue and his followers appreciate that a well-placed exec from a Big Company is engaged with them online.

Now, a big industry tradeshow is coming up. He'll be very active there, as a speaker and organizer. The executive wants his tweetstream to reflect his activity at the show, and to highlight other happenings at the conference, as well. He's very concerned that he won't be able to support this many to-do's.

IDENTIFY INTERNAL/EXTERNAL FACTORS

A big part of the appeal of Twitter as a form of social media is that followers have access to interesting and influential people with whom they otherwise would not be able to interact. The culture of social media is an external factor that must be considered, and the executive's commitment to authenticity in this environment is an internal factor.

> *You can see how this request comes from a "good place." This executive's commitment to online engagement is so fierce, he doesn't want to abandon it even for an important event. He knows his followers would understand his absences, but he thinks there is going to be real value in tracking what's happening at the conference, and in responding to folks online throughout.*

IDENTIFY KEY VALUES

Loyalty, transparency, expertise and independence are among the key values in this case. Not only does Defren have to weigh his loyalty to the client, but he also must consider the loyalty and trust that the client's Twitter followers may have in the executive. This loyalty brings transparency to the forefront because if those followers expect the executive to write all his own tweets and if he is planning on changing that without telling them, they may be deceived. The behind-the-scenes change would mean a lack of transparency. The client means no harm—his request comes from a good place, as Defren said—but part of what he is paying Defren and his firm for is expertise in knowing the lay of the land in social media and counseling on exactly this type of situation.

> *While it's true he is asking us to misrepresent ourselves, he feels that it would still be authentic because of his trust in us.*

IDENTIFY THE PARTIES WHO WILL BE AFFECTED

This is where those competing duties to various people come into play. This case appears to be a doozy because Defren has a duty to pretty much everyone in Seib and Fitzpatrick's list: (1) himself, (2) his client, and (4) the profession, (5) the media and (6) society.

- **DUTY TO SELF:** As is pretty clear from his blog, which includes detailed analysis of ethical dilemmas like this one, Defren invests his own intellect, hard work and time in his strategic communication practice. If he botches this, it could damage his reputation and lead to personal disappointment. There also could be financial consequences for him personally.

- **DUTY TO CLIENT:** Defren's firm has been hired to do a job. Yes, a big part of that job is to communicate for the client, but he also owes the client solid independent counseling based on his expertise and knowledge of social media.

- **DUTY TO THE PROFESSION:** Not only will botching this job with poor ethical decision-making discredit Defren, it also may reflect poorly on the whole field of public relations. Unfortunately, examples of misrepresentation and deception in public relations are not hard to find, as these cases tend to get called out and told and re-told online. Mentioning public relations and ethics together in the same sentence will lead to rolled eyes and snarky responses in many circles. The only way to combat this is with performance.

- **DUTY TO THE MEDIA:** The media in this case are mostly social media, Twitter users in particular. Just as relationships with reporters, editors and producers are critical to effective communication via magazines, newspapers, radio and television, relationships with Twitter users are the essence of effective tweeting. If Defren disappoints his client's followers, he's not only undermined his client's credibility and effectiveness, but he will also have taken something away from the utility of the medium as a whole.

- **DUTY TO SOCIETY:** Social media have the potential to facilitate meaningful democratic dialogue and healthy economies by affording publics the opportunity to engage organizations in the honest exchange of ideas, currency, products, services and social capital. Social media also can provide a haven for misinformation, deceit, mistrust, cynicism and generally shattered expectations. I'm guessing Defren wants to contribute to the former and not the latter.

SELECT ETHICAL PRINCIPLES TO GUIDE THE DECISION-MAKING PROCESS

At this stage of the analysis it becomes fairly clear that openness, honesty, trust, transparency and authenticity are at stake. **Deontological ethics** are systems of decision-making that focus on duties or rules. To the degree that the principle of duty is central to the decision on how to act in this case based on moral obligations to each of the parties, you could say that it guides our thinking. Of course, other principles apply too, and we will look at some of those in cases in the chapters that follow.

MAKE A DECISION AND JUSTIFY IT

So what did Defren do?

> So we suggested a compromise. . . . Yes, we would tweet from his account, but with the following conditions:
>
> Prior to the event, he must tweet, "During the show some of my tweeting will be supplemented by our extended team."
>
> A reminder to that effect would go out, regularly, throughout the conference, i.e., every 10th tweet would remind followers that someone besides the executive might be "at the controls" of his Twitter account.
>
> When character spaces permitted, we'd add a #team hashtag to denote that the tweet was not published by the exec—but honestly, this attribution fell away more often than not; we largely relied on the "every 10th tweet" approach to cover our ethical backsides.

Deontological ethics
System of decision-making that focuses on the moral principles of duty and rules.

In the end, the solution seemed easy, but this was largely due to Defren's expertise and careful ethical thinking. He was able to serve the client well with a compromise that didn't require compromising his ethics or causing harm to his business, his profession or society. Defren and his client experienced no "pushback" from the tweets. Interestingly, Defren still had some ethical concerns and questions (about whether some people would still be duped despite the every-10th-tweet approach), and was courageous enough to post the whole case as well as his follow-up concerns in a very public blog entry inviting feedback. When I checked last, there were more than 150 comments on the post, and the vast majority of them were constructive and supportive. The very act of airing his case and concerns for open discussion honors the spirit of social media while also reinforcing Defren's commitment to ethical practice—in the sense of the word *practice* that means that we are all always working to improve in this area.

Voices from the Field

Kathy Fitzpatrick

Kathy Fitzpatrick is a professor and senior associate dean in the School of Communication at American University. She is a member of the Arthur W. Page Society, whose members are corporate, agency and academic leaders in the field of public relations. She served as head of the Educators Academy of PRSA, is a former president of the Dallas Chapter of PRSA, and was a member of the task force that developed the current PRSA Code of Ethics.

In general, do you think public relations is moving toward higher ethical standards?
Yes, I believe that higher ethical standards in public relations are more commonplace, partly due to the globalization of society and changes in technology that require a higher level of openness and transparency in organizational communications. Also, there is

increased emphasis on ethical standards among industry groups. With its new code of ethics in 2000, PRSA took a big step toward becoming the ethics standard bearer in the United States. I believe the code—and promotion of the code—has heightened awareness of ethical standards in the field. Many public relations firms also have developed extensive codes of ethics and operating standards for staff members. Globally, the International Public Relations Association, the Global Alliance for Public Relations and Communication Management and other leading associations stress ethical principles and practices as well.

What kinds of ethical issues are entry-level public relations people likely to face?
Deceptive practices are a big issue. For example, a situation might occur in which a boss (whether in a

continues

continued

corporation, non-profit or firm) asks an entry-level practitioner not to disclose certain information that the practitioner believes should be revealed. Activities such as greenwashing—to make a company look more socially responsible than it really is—come to mind here as well.

In addition, conflicts may surface when a practitioner's own values and beliefs are incongruent with the culture of an organization. For example, a philosophy of doing "anything to win" creates a tense operating environment for professionals who want to uphold ethical standards. Also, if an organization is promoting a cause or idea with which a practitioner disagrees, this creates internal dissonance that can result in a lot of stress. Thus, new practitioners must decide what types of organizations they are willing to represent and what they will do for them.

What kinds of new ethical dilemmas have come up with the growth of social media?

Issues related to honesty and transparency top the list here. For example, it's easy to be deceptive online. If you work for a hotel and your boss asks you to post a positive review of your accommodations on travel websites, what do you do? If you are tweeting about a new product or service offered by your company, do you identify yourself as an employee of the company?

In what ways have new media contexts reinforced or challenged classic principles?

The fundamentals of ethical public relations practice have not changed. They simply must be applied in new contexts and platforms.

How much can ethics be taught and learned in public relations, and how much does it just depend on the person's individual values?

At the end of the day, ethical decision-making is a personal matter with individual accountability. Whether you raise your hand at work to question a particular issue you see as unethical depends to a great extent on your personal and professional courage to do the right thing. Having said that, ethics education can have a tremendous impact in helping students and practitioners recognize ethical issues and dilemmas, better understand the implications of unethical practices and develop guidelines and processes for resolving them. Graduates of public relations programs must be equipped with the special expertise and skills required for successful practice in public relations, but they also need an understanding of the professional standards and social obligations of public relations professionals.

What is the most important guide that a public relations practitioner might use in trying to make ethical decisions?

Public relations professionals should always consider whether they are contributing to—or interfering with—informed decision-making on the part of publics affected by an organization's decisions or actions. This really is the bottom line when practicing public relations ethically in a democratic marketplace of ideas.

Codes of Ethics

Most organizations of communication professionals offer codes of ethics to articulate their values and to guide their members. While it is debatable whether or not pubic relations is technically a profession, codes of ethics certainly encourage professionalism. One major factor keeping public relations from being recognized as a profession like law or medicine or architecture is licensure. You do not need a license to practice public relations. Any quack can call him- or herself a PR person. This is unfortunate, but the alternative, according to those opposed to professional licensing, would be a violation of our right to free speech. Imagine if you were not allowed to speak on matters of public concern in an official capacity because you did not have a license.

Criticisms of Codes

Lack of enforceability is one criticism against codes of ethics. If a member acts within the law, but outside of the code of ethics, revocation of the person's membership is the most the association can do in response. The good news is that it doesn't happen very often (in fact, it never happened in five decades of PRSA's original code[27]).

However, this leads to a second criticism of codes of ethics, which is that they simply are not effective or even necessary as means of policing behavior. Most members of these professional organizations practice public relations with good intention, and those few who do run blatantly afoul of the codes can probably take advantage of the subjective nature of interpretation and the relatively weak mechanisms of enforcement to evade any institutional consequences.

A third criticism is that codes of ethics can be vague and lack internal consistency. By definition, ethical dilemmas involve competing choices. Loyalty may run up against independence. Confidentiality may come at the expense of transparency. When codes of ethics call for all of the above, the member may be put in a pickle. PRSA updated its code in 2000, and one big change from the prior code was that its emphasis on enforcement was eliminated, which leads to some of the positives of codes of ethics.

Advantages of Codes

First, codes of ethics help communicate the professional standards of an association's membership to both internal and external parties. Many of you reading this book may not pursue public relations as a career. You may go into advertising, marketing or journalism. Or you may become a dentist, deep-sea diver or deputy sheriff. But if you read the codes of ethics or discuss them with anyone who knows them, you will come away with a much better idea of what members of these organizations do and what values they embrace. For better or worse, everyone is exposed to public relations in democracies like ours, and the more people understand what makes for good, ethical public relations the better.

Review and discuss organizations' codes of ethics to better understand the values that members embrace.

Second, codes offer carefully articulated and professionally agreed-upon guidelines for decision-making and action. For example, the PRSA Code of Ethics is designed "to be a useful guide for PRSA members as they carry out their ethical responsibilities" and "to anticipate and accommodate, by precedent, ethical challenges that may arise."[28] The PRSA values form a foundation

Accredited in public relations (APR)
Credential awarded by PRSA and other UAB affiliates to those who have demonstrated competency in the knowledge, skills and abilities required to practice public relations effectively.

Accredited business communicator (ABC)
Credential awarded by IABC to recognize communicators who have reached a globally accepted standard of knowledge and proficiency in their chosen field.

for ethical conduct (see Appendix A). The PRSA Code of Ethics also outlines six provisions of conduct. In Chapters 2–14 of this book, each of these provisions will be discussed in the context of at least one case of ethics.

Third, there are practical and reputational advantages to knowing and working with established codes of ethics. Professional communication associations such as the Universal Accreditation Board (UAB) and the International Association of Business Communicators (IABC) offer voluntary accreditation, which allows practitioners to distinguish themselves among others in the field with a professional designation. UAB grants the designation of "**Accredited in Public Relations**" (**APR**), and the professional credential for IABC is "**Accredited Business Communicator**" (**ABC**). Criteria include demonstrated professional experience, and evidence of knowledge, skills and abilities, including ethics. For APR, ethics and law make up 13 percent of the exam.

Professional Associations

The UAB includes several affiliates including PRSA, the Agricultural Relations Council, Asociación de Relacionistas Profesionales de Puerto Rico, Florida Public Relations Association, National School Public Relations Association, Religion Communicators Council and the Maine Public Relations Association. Dozens of established organizations with codes of ethics serve members all over the world, including the African Public Relations Association, the Public Relations Consultants' Association of Malaysia (PRCA Malaysia), the Public Relations Institute of Ireland (PRII) and the Mexican Association of Public Relations Professionals/Asociación Mexicana de Profesionales de Relaciones Públicas (PRORP). Membership (even without seeking accreditation) usually requires formally acknowledging and agreeing to abide by the standards set forth is such codes. Interestingly, the main values identified in the codes share more commonalities than differences across cultures, including common moral principles such as fairness and honesty.

For comparison to the PRSA Code of Ethics, the International Public Relations Association (IPRA) Code of Conduct is included (see Appendix B). This code, adopted in 2011, represents a consolidation of three prior international codes (the 1961 Code of Venice, the 1965 Code of Athens and the 2007 Code of Brussels). You'll notice many consistencies between the IPRA code and the PRSA code, but it is also interesting to note the IPRA focus on human rights and dignity. The IPRA code also includes some language specific to online media and issues of trust, credibility and privacy.

Regardless of whether you call it a field, a practice or a profession, *public relations* can be defined best by both words and actions. While there is no denying the existence of poor public relations and shady practice, professional organizations stand to help bring our body of knowledge together with ethical and effective practice for the benefit of students, practitioners and society.

In Case You Missed It

If you tell people you're studying public relations, they may not know what you mean. Here are a few tips from the chapter to help you think about what public relations people do, just in case anyone asks!

- To define public relations, consider organizations, publics and the relations between them.

- Even in cases that necessitate secrecy, tell the truth about what information your organization is protecting and why.

- Good public relations is based much more on what an organization does than on what it says.

- To effectively listen in public relations, participate in and monitor online communities in addition to using traditional research.

- Respond constructively and politely to critics online, the same way you would if they were at your service counter or reception desk.

- Review and discuss organizations' codes of ethics to better understand the values that members embrace.

SUMMARY

1.1 Define public relations in terms of organizations, publics and the relationships between them.
According to a recent PRSA task force, "Public relations is a strategic communication process that builds mutually beneficial relationships between organizations and their publics."

1.2 Explain how public relations can serve as a management function.
When public relations is practiced as a management function, practitioners proactively communicate with an organization's publics, carefully consider what feedback means for the organization, develop strategy and work with the organization's leadership to implement and evaluate both actions and communication.

1.3 Recognize key principles and values for ethical conduct in public relations.
Arthur Page's principles for public relations management (e.g., tell the truth; prove it with action) are as relevant today as they were in his time. Codes of ethics also articulate common values that have been vetted by professionals. Classic ethical principles and frameworks, such as duty, can be applied in public relations just as they are in other areas of life.

1.4 Understand the importance of ethics in public relations.
Ethical public relations practitioners can work with a cleaner conscience, but they also can work with a clearer sense of how to handle difficult situations with reporters, clients, colleagues and various publics. In turn, ethical public relations practitioners are more valuable to the organizations that depend on them. Value to organizations results in greater job opportunities.

1.5 Apply systematic ethical decision-making for public relations.
Step-by-step guides such as Fitzpatrick's "Ethical Decision-Making Guide," cases like Defren's client tweeting example, and codes of ethics all offer good guidance for practicing ethical decision-making offline and online.

1.6 Identify international professional associations and become familiar with codes of ethics.
PRSA and IPRA are two major professional organizations offering codes of ethics, but they are not the only ones. See online resources for many more.

DISCUSSION QUESTIONS

1. Describe the job of one public relations person you've seen in media (real or fictional). How does that job description compare to the formal definition of public relations presented in this chapter?

2. Name an organization that you have worked for or had direct experience with that does some form of public relations. Would you say that public relations is part of that organization's management function? Why or why not?

3. What would Arthur Page like most about Facebook?

4. Some people describe public relations as the conscience of an organization. Do you think that is a good way to define public relations? Why or why not?

5. Search online for another communication-related code of ethics such as one for journalism, filmmaking, blogging or marketing. How are the values expressed in that code different from the values expressed in the PRSA code?

KEY TERMS

CHAPTER 2

Public Relations Models Through the Ages

It took much more than a stroke of luck for tobacco companies to convince women to smoke in the 1930s. Were the tactics they used ethical?

KEY LEARNING OUTCOMES

2.1 Analyze public relations models on one-way/two-way and asymmetrical/symmetrical dimensions.

2.2 Demonstrate knowledge of key figures in public relations history.

2.3 Integrate knowledge of social history with knowledge of public relations.

2.4 Identify common motivations for strategic communication in history.

2.5 Apply knowledge of history to analyze modern public relations practices.

2.6 Distinguish public relations from journalism.

2.7 Discuss the ethics of transparency, objectivity and advocacy.

RELATED UNIVERSAL ACCREDITATION BOARD COMPETENCY AREAS

2.2 ETHICAL BEHAVIOR • **4.1** PUBLIC RELATIONS MODELS AND THEORIES
4.3 KNOWLEDGE OF FIELD • **6.1** RELATIONSHIP BUILDING • **6.2** REPUTATION MANAGEMENT

n the opening pages of *Managing Public Relations*, right before defining public relations as the management of communication between an organization and its publics, Grunig and Hunt reflected on the problems of the times (early 1980s). They described public relations as a "young profession" with "roots in press agentry and propaganda, activities that society generally holds in low esteem."[1] They then charted a historical progression of public relations to frame the maturation of the profession by outlining four models of public relations in history: (1) press agentry/publicity, (2) public information, (3) two-way asymmetrical and (4) two-way symmetrical.

While the formal treatment of public relations as a field of study and practice may have been a 20th century development, historians have traced elements of public relations back through recorded history. Modern communication historians make the case that public relations activities are as old as religion, education, business and politics.

Public Relations Models in History

Generations of public relations students have learned about the field's development through the lens of Grunig and Hunt's four models of public relations. However, these models also have been criticized for oversimplifying public relations and its history. What public relations people do doesn't fit neatly into four boxes, some say. This is exactly why Grunig and Hunt used the term *models*:

> *We've chosen the term 'models' to describe the four types of public relations that we believe have evolved through history, in order to emphasize that they are abstractions. In scientific usage, a model is a representation of reality . . . if we construct models of public relations behavior by observing the most important components of that behavior, then we can make some sense out of the many diverse communication activities we call public relations.*[2]

In the first two models, press agentry/publicity and public information, the communication is primarily one-way. In the second two models, two-way asymmetrical and two-way symmetrical, the communication is two-way (Figure 2.1).

Press Agentry/Publicity

Born in Madagascar in 1674, Joice Heth arrived in America in her youth and was a slave to one Augustine Washington, father of George Washington. Heth was

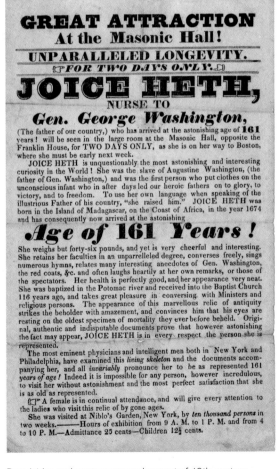

Broadsides and posters were a key part of 19th-century publicity tactics.

Do you see tactics like this used today?

Publicity/press agentry	Organization ↘ Publics	Communication is mostly one-way, initiated by an organization with little concern for accuracy or completeness
Public information	Organization → Publics	Communication is mostly one-way, initiated by an organization to inform publics with truthful and accurate information
Two-way asymmetrical	Organization ↘↘ Publics	Communication is two-way but unbalanced, with the organization using research/feedback in an effort to persuade publics to change attitudes or behaviors
Two-way symmetrical	Organization ⇄ Publics	Communication is mostly balanced, with the organization as likely to change attitudes or behavior as its publics

Figure 2.1 Four Models of Public Relations

the first one to put clothes on the future father of America, and she basically raised the boy. In 1836, Heth was 161 years old and retained astonishingly good health, singing hymns, laughing heartily and telling stories of the boy Washington . . . Or so potential patrons were told in the billing of an attraction that began the press agentry career of showman extraordinaire P.T. Barnum.[3]

That not everyone bought the story about Joice Heth did not bother Barnum. On the contrary, he relished the attention that controversy brought.

> *At the outset of my career, I saw that everything depended on getting the people to think, and talk, and become curious and excited over and about the "rare spectacle." Accordingly, posters, transparencies, advertisements, newspaper paragraphs—all calculated to extort attention—were employed, regardless of expense. My exhibition rooms in New York, Boston, Philadelphia, Albany, and in other large and small cities, were continually thronged and much money was made.[4]*

Press agentry/publicity model
Model of public relations in which communication is mostly one-way, initiated by an organization with little concern for accuracy or completeness in order to gain the attention of publics.

Barnum will forever be associated with the **press agentry/publicity model**. Propaganda, attention getting and less-than-accurate information (if not downright lies) are hallmarks of the press agentry model, which is as alive in this millennium as it was then.

In December 2015, KFC invaded an annual TV awards show in Hong Kong (the TVB awards—the equivalent to the Emmys in the United States) by delivering boxes of fried chicken wings to the elegantly dressed celebrities in attendance. *Brandchannel's* Abe Sauer described the stunt as garish: "Hong Kong's TV royalty awkwardly accepted the greasy boxes thrust upon them and proceeded to gracelessly gnaw at fried chicken wings while the award show went on."[5] The stunt was reminiscent of the Oscars the year before when Ellen DeGeneres ordered pizza to be delivered for all the stars in attendance. DeGeneres's pizzas, however, were from a local Los Angeles pizza place called Big Mama's and Big Papa's, and the slices of pizza were much easier to serve and eat in formal attire than the KFC wings in Hong Kong. Big Mama's and Big Papa's franchise owner estimated a 500 percent increase in sales following the Oscars.[6]

Case Study

The Reality of "The Situation": Gaining Attention in the Marketplace of Ideas

Publicity stunts, and the publicity/press agentry model in general, would not still be around if there wasn't some payoff in their use. In August 2011, clothing retailer Abercrombie & Fitch offered via a **news release** to pay *Jersey Shore* reality TV star Mike Sorrentino (aka "The Situation") and his co-stars to *not* wear Abercrombie & Fitch clothing.

> *We are deeply concerned that Mr. Sorrentino's association with our brand could cause significant damage to our image. . . . We have therefore offered a substantial payment to Michael "The Situation" Sorrentino and the producers of MTV's* The Jersey Shore *to have the character wear an alternate brand. We have also extended this offer to other members of the cast, and are urgently waiting a response.*[7]

MTV responded in an e-mail, "It's a clever P.R. stunt, and we'd love to work with them on other ways they can leverage 'Jersey Shore' to reach the largest youth audience on television."[8] *CNN*, *Forbes*, and *The New York Times* picked up the exchange, and of course entertainment media like *US Weekly* and Hollywood.com jumped on the story, along with countless associated blogs. The echoing internet chatter reverberated far and wide, and Abercrombie & Fitch Chief Executive

News release
A statement of news produced and distributed on behalf of an organization to make information public. Traditionally news releases (aka press releases) have been issued to news media with the intent of publicizing the information to the news organization's readers, listeners or viewers.

Michael Jeffries described the whole stunt as "a lot of fun."[9] Was this effective public relations? It would be hard to argue that it was not *if* you define public relations as merely generating publicity.

Undoubtedly less fun for Abercrombie & Fitch, however, was a viral YouTube video made by Greg Karber in 2013 in response to Abercrombie & Fitch's refusal to sell XL or XXL clothing to women and their generally "exclusionary" marketing strategies. In a 2006 interview quote that was widely re-circulated on the internet, Jeffries had said:

> *In every school there are the cool and popular kids, and then there are the not-so-cool kids. Candidly, we go after the cool kids. We go after the attractive all-American kid with a great attitude and a lot of friends. A lot of people don't belong [in our clothes], and they can't belong. Are we exclusionary? Absolutely.[10]*

Karber's video, titled "Abercrombie & Fitch Gets a Brand Readjustment" with the **hashtag** FitchThe-Homeless, features him buying Abercrombie & Fitch clothes at thrift stores and taking them to Los Angeles' skid row to give to homeless people. He encourages viewers to gather all their Abercrombie & Fitch clothes and their friends' and neighbors' Abercrombie & Fitch clothes and to donate them to homeless shelters. Then he asks viewers to post what they are doing on social media. *Mashable* reported that Karber's video had nearly 400,000 hits on May 14, 2013 (it was posted on May 13), and within a couple of weeks had more than 7 million views. Karber said his goal was to make Abercrombie & Fitch "the world's number one brand of homeless apparel."

"I was really upset by the Abercrombie & Fitch CEO's comments, and I wanted to do something to turn that negative energy into a positive social good," Karber told a *Mashable* reporter in an e-mail.[11]

Once again, we can ask whether this is good public relations. If 7 million YouTube hits and a slew of resulting news coverage in less than two weeks isn't evidence of effective showmanship and publicity, what is? But the campaign still has been criticized for its shortcomings. According to some critics and advocates, Farber overlooked the interests of one public that was undeniably central to his campaign—the homeless. While he definitely put his message out to Abercrombie & Fitch and millions of internet users, it is unclear how much he really communicated with or worked to understand the perspective of the homeless. In criticizing the campaign, Los Angeles

When Abercrombie & Fitch offered to pay MTV reality show star Mike Sorrentino (aka "The Situation") not to wear A&F clothing, the stunt created a lot of buzz for both organizations.

Who benefited?

Hashtag
A word or phrase (with no spaces) preceded by the hash symbol (#) that users can include in posts to categorize information online. Many social media platforms allow users to search or filter news feeds for information identified with the tag.

social worker Rachel Karman wrote, "It seems to say: I won't wear this garbage, but they should, in order to prove my point because they fit the proper stigma to do so."[12] She showed the video to several homeless people on skid row and recorded their responses.

"It doesn't look like he is explaining what he is doing to anyone he is giving clothes to. That's not right," said one of the people Karman interviewed.

Another said, "Why isn't he talking to people when he gives them the clothes? I hate it when people who think they are do-gooders act like that."

On one hand, #FitchTheHomeless goes to show that publicity can serve many interests in society, not just the Pizza Huts and Abercrombie & Fitches of the world that make for such easy targets for public relations critics. On the other hand, the marketplace of ideas is a noisy place where thoughtful strategy sometimes gets lost in the quest for attention.

Departing from Grunig and Hunt's four models, University of Amsterdam Professor Emeritus Betteke van Ruler studied communication management internationally and identified several typologies. Typologies help us classify things into general categories based on their common characteristics. Archaeologists use typologies to classify artifacts. Van Ruler developed typologies to classify types of public relations practitioners. One of those typologies is the town crier. Like the press agent/publicist, van Ruler's town crier is mostly seeking to be heard in the marketplace with little concern for listening to others outside of his organization. You can almost hear the echoes of "Hear ye! Hear ye!" in the way Jeffries and Karber communicate their messages. There's nothing wrong with working to gain attention in a crowded marketplace, but there is a point of diminishing returns in simply turning up the volume without stopping to listen to others. Sometimes even the best-intentioned voices do more to add to the cacophony than they do to bring clarity or understanding on the important issues they wish to discuss.

Public Information

Long before Bill Gates and Mark Zuckerberg dropped out of Harvard, Ivy Ledbetter Lee left graduate school at Harvard in the late 19th century, largely for financial reasons. Whereas Gates and Zuckerberg eventually changed the nature of personal media as we know them with Microsoft and Facebook, Lee started the nation's third public relations agency and went on to become the man many refer to today as the founder of public relations.

Before his stint at Harvard, Lee had graduated cum laude from Princeton in 1898 and had worked as a stringer for the Associated Press, the *Philadelphia Press* and the *Chicago Record*.[13] And prior to starting the public relations agency Parker & Lee in late 1904 with George Parker,[14] he

Ivy Lee began his career as a journalist, and he carried journalistic values into his work for corporate clients.

How was Lee's work in public relations different from journalism?

Public information model
Model of public relations in which communication is mostly one-way, initiated by an organization to inform publics with truthful and accurate information.

worked for *The New York Journal, The New York Times* and *New York World*.[15] Parker & Lee's credo heralded a journalistic background: "Accuracy, Authenticity, and Interest,"[16] and it very much distinguished Lee's brand of public relations from Barnum's press agentry.

While the Parker & Lee agency only lasted a few years, Ivy Lee went on to represent some of the biggest names of the day in corporate America, including the Pennsylvania Railroad and the Rockefellers. While Lee's legacy is complex—he also counseled I.G. Farben, the German dye trust, on how to improve relations with Americans after the Nazis took control of the trust—his name is deeply associated with the **public information model** of public relations in which communication is mostly one-way, initiated by an organization to inform publics with truthful and accurate information. When he sent materials to the press, Ivy Lee was known to include his "Declaration of Principles," which stated:

> *This is not a secret press bureau. All our work is done in the open. We aim to supply news. . . . Our matter is accurate. Further details on any subject treated will be supplied promptly, and any editor will be assisted most cheerfully in verifying directly any statement of fact. . . . In brief, our plan is frankly, and openly, on behalf of business concerns and public institutions, to supply the press and public of the United States prompt and accurate information concerning subjects which it is of value and interest to the public to know about.*[17]

Transparency is a value we hear much of in the age of social media. Although it is debatable to what degree Lee was walking the walk, he was talking the talk of transparency a good century before the internet. As Clive Thompson put it in *Wired* in 2007, "Transparency is a judo move. Your customers are going to poke around in your business anyway, and your workers are going to blab about internal info—so why not make it work for you by turning everyone into a partner in the process and inviting them to do so?"[18]

In the early 1900s, railroad accidents were not uncommon, and railroad companies would generally do what they could to keep the bad news under wraps. But when the Pennsylvania Railroad had a wreck near Gap, Pennsylvania, Ivy Lee did a little informational judo:

> *Instinctively the railroad management put its news suppression machinery into motion. Just as quickly, Lee reversed it. Reporters were invited to travel to the scene of the accident at the railroad's expense. Lee promptly set up facilities for reporters and photographers.*[19]

The resulting coverage was better than usual, and the Pennsylvania Railroad was later compared favorably to railroads that refused to adopt such an open-access policy.

Rather than working to obstruct reporters, Ivy Lee encouraged them to cover accidents.

Why would a public relations practitioner want to communicate openly about an organization's crises?

Today, most public relations departments within organizations spend at least part of their time serving the public information function. Even when organizations are not seeking to gain extra attention, they still often need to get messages out accurately and reliably. In many cases, public communication is actually required by law. For example, publicly held corporations, which are organizations that have offered shares for trading in stock exchanges or other public markets, are obligated to file certain reports and to make public certain information that may affect investors' decisions. The regulatory agency governing such activity in the United States is the Securities and Exchange Commission (SEC), and the information that could affect investors' decisions is called **material information**, which we cover in more detail in Chapter 11 dealing with legal issues. Annual reports and quarterly profit/loss statements are examples of material information that must be released in a timely, accurate and fair manner. So even if Nestlé or United Airlines have a bad quarter and don't meet their earnings goals, they still have to report that information in a way that ensures that anyone interested in buying or selling shares is properly informed as a result.

Public information is also a common practice in government work. In fact, the job title of **public information officer (PIO)** is most commonly associated with government jobs. The Federal Emergency Management Agency (FEMA), which is part of the U.S. Department of Homeland Security, offers a public information office awareness course as part of its Emergency

> Organizations must get messages out accurately and reliably, even when they are not seeking to gain extra attention.

Material information
Any information that could affect investment decisions related to a particular security such as stock in a publicly traded company.

Public information officer (PIO)
A public relations person, commonly working in a government position, whose job focuses on the dissemination of information to appropriate publics in an accurate and timely manner.

Management Institute. The first module in the web-based course describes the role of their public information officers:

> They tell the public about services and programs that can affect their lives, like information about staying healthy, fire safety, and changes in community college tuition. They also tell people how they can prepare for a disaster, and protect themselves when disaster strikes. PIOs get their message out by communicating directly with the public, working through the traditional news media and through new media.[20]

Notice that the role focuses on one-way communication: PIOs "tell the public about," "tell people how" and "get their message out." Public information and publicity/press agentry are both one-way models of communication, but the essence of the public information is quite different in character from press agentry in that the goal is much more focused on providing accurate information than attention-getting. Public affairs officer (PAO) is a more common title in military jobs. Military PAOs can be uniformed or civilian. As we'll see in Chapter 14, the U.S. Department of Defense is one of the largest employers in the world.

Case Study

Edward Bernays' "Torches of Freedom"

Picture this. On the crowded streets of one of the world's busiest cities, a group of influential young people does something carefully planned but also unexpected by the crowds around them. Behind-the-scenes organizers have worked social networks and even mainstream media to maximize coverage, and the perfectly choreographed event draws the attention of onlookers. Some are shocked. Some are delighted. But it becomes apparent that the event was staged for more than just shock value or entertainment. Some see it as the start of a social movement.

No, this isn't a reference to "Frozen Grand Central" in early 2008, when 207 agents of the group Improv Everywhere stopped in their tracks and froze in place for five minutes in the midst of Grand Central Station, later garnering more than 30 million YouTube hits. It's also not about the "World-wide Pillowfight Day" **flash mobs** organized a few months later for fun and entertainment in dozens of cities from Atlanta to Zurich. Nor is it part of the infamous Facebook-driven, iPod-wearing, disco-dancing mob that shut down a London train station in 2009.

Instead, the event described was the "Torches of Freedom" march; the "influentials" were New York debutantes; and the site was an Easter parade on Fifth Avenue in New York. The date, however, was 1930 and the man

Flash mob
When a group of people plans and executes a surprise public event or performance that is usually organized via electronic media and unanticipated by those who are not participants.

Long before carefully orchestrated surprise street events were termed "flash mobs," Edward Bernays organized the Torches of Freedom event as part of a sophisticated persuasive campaign.

How did Bernays link smoking a cigarette with women's fight for equality?

behind the scenes was Edward Bernays. Bernays competes with Ivy Lee for the legacy of being known as the father of public relations. Oh, and about those "torches of freedom," they were cigarettes marketed to women.

Bernays coordinated the Torches of Freedom event on behalf of his client George Washington Hill, president of the American Tobacco Company. Here is how Bernays recalls the project in his memoir *Biography of an Idea*:

> Hill called me in. "How can we get women to smoke on the street? They're smoking indoors. But, damn it, if they spend half the time outdoors and we can get 'em to smoke outdoors, we'll damn near double our female market. Do something. Act!"
>
> "There's a taboo against such smoking," I said. "Let me consult an expert, Dr. A.A. Brill, the psychoanalyst. He might give me the psychological basis for a woman's desire to smoke, and maybe this will help me."
>
> "What will it cost?"
>
> "I suppose just a consultation fee."
>
> "Shoot," said Hill.
>
> [Bernays was no stranger to psychoanalysis. His uncle was Sigmund Freud.]
>
> Brill explained to me: "Some women regard cigarettes as symbols of freedom," he told me. "Smoking is a sublimation of oral eroticism; holding a cigarette in the mouth excites the oral zone. It is perfectly normal for women to want to smoke cigarettes. . . . But today the emancipation of women has suppressed many of their feminine desires. . . . Feminine

traits are masked. Cigarettes, which are equated with men, become torches of freedom."

In this last statement I found a way to help break the taboo against women smoking in public. Why not a parade of women lighting torches of freedom—smoking cigarettes?[21]

Bernays called friends at *Vogue* magazine to get a list of debutantes. Then he had his secretary, Bertha Hunt, sign and send a personalized telegram to each one. Think direct-messaging, 1930s style:

In the interests of equality of the sexes and to fight another sex taboo I and other young women will light another torch of freedom by smoking cigarettes while strolling on Fifth Avenue Easter Sunday. We are doing this to combat the silly prejudice that the cigarette is suitable for the home, the restaurant, the taxicab, the theater lobby, but never no never for the sidewalk. Women smokers and their escorts will stroll from Forty-Eighth Street to Fifty-Fourth Street on Fifth Avenue between Eleven-Thirty and One O'Clock.[22]

It worked. Bernays reported that the event made front-page news in both photos and text and opened editorial debates in the weeks that followed in publications from coast to coast. As evidence of his success he cited newspaper reports in Massachusetts, Michigan, California and West Virginia that women were smoking on the streets.* "Age-old customs, I learned, could be broken down by a dramatic appeal, disseminated by the network of media."[23] While Bernays' strategy was mostly intuitive and his reasoning was mostly theoretical, the case illustrates the power of public relations tactics as powerful tools for persuasion.

---

*Bernays' claims about the impact of national publicity resulting from the Torches of Freedom event were later called into question by historians.[24]

Two-Way Asymmetrical Communication

Bernays is also credited (or *blamed*, depending on your perspective) with getting Americans to consume more bacon for breakfast. Bernays researched breakfast diets of his fellow Americans in the early 20th century and found that for the most part Americans ate light breakfasts of "coffee, maybe a roll, and orange juice."[25] So he consulted with his doctor about the benefits of a heavier breakfast and, lo and behold, he found that "a heavy breakfast was sounder from the standpoint of health than a light breakfast because the body loses energy during the night and needs it during the day." He then asked that doctor to write to thousands of other doctors to confirm the benefits of a hearty breakfast. When about 4,500 of the 5,000 doctors to whom they wrote concurred with the conclusion, Bernays publicized the finding nationally.

Interestingly, the resulting news coverage not only headlined the benefits of a hearty breakfast as broadly endorsed by thousands of doctors, but also "many of [the newspapers] stated that bacon and eggs should be embodied with the breakfast, and as a result sales of bacon went up." How did Bernays know that bacon sales went up? Bartlett Arkell, founder and president of the Beech-Nut Packing Company, wrote him and told him as much. Arkell would know because bacon was one of Beech-Nut's primary products. And Beech-Nut was one of Bernays' clients.

What distinguishes Bernays' work from other publicity stunts is the use of research to understand publics, develop strategy and even to evaluate the results. Bernays applied the social science of the times. He saw the role of the public relations counselor as interpreting publics to clients as well as interpreting clients to publics. He saw public relations as a two-way street.

Today's public relations professionals have access to more scientific research and ridiculous amounts of online data to help them understand publics and to gauge the success of their efforts. Surveys, e-mail responses, Twitter comments, usability studies and focus groups are examples of ways organizations get to know their publics these days, as are less obtrusive sources of data that you as a consumer/internet user may provide without even knowing it. Just check your web browser's cookies!

The torches-of-freedom stunt and bacon-and-eggs "study" had all the trappings of press agentry and publicity, but behind the scenes was evidence of a clever two-way model of communication designed to sell more cigarettes and bacon by leveraging an understanding of desires, diets and deference to authority. The communication may have been two-way in that sense, but it was also clearly not balanced. As Grunig and Hunt put it, both Bernays and Lee "stressed the importance of communicating the public's point of view to management," but in actual practice, "both did much more to explain management's view to the public."[26] This two-way **asymmetrical model** of communication describes much of the work that modern public relations professionals practice as they advocate and work to persuade publics on behalf of organizations. Bernays may be criticized for promoting tobacco as liberating and bacon as healthy, but his idea of using two-way communication and research to persuade publics can (and is) just as likely to be applied by organizations with quite different perspectives such as the American Cancer Society or the American Heart Association.

Bernays later regretted promoting tobacco, a sentiment he expressed plainly in his memoirs, claiming that the dangers of tobacco were not understood at the time. Historians, and Bernays himself, also made it clear that his work was produced in partnership with his wife Doris Fleischman, who retained her last name throughout her career. They worked together for 58 years from their marriage in 1922 until her death in 1980. Bernays lived until 1995 when he died at the age of 103.

Professionals today have access to more scientific research and online data to help them understand publics and to gauge the success of public relations efforts.

Edward Bernays used research and persuasive tactics to sell bacon.

Was this any more or less ethical than his use of research and persuasion to sell cigarettes?

Asymmetrical model
Model of public relations in which communication is two-way but unbalanced, with the organization using research/feedback in an effort to persuade publics to change attitudes or behaviors.

Doris Fleischman and Edward Bernays worked together for 58 years from the time they were married until her death.

How might this sort of relationship have influenced their work?

Symmetrical model
Model of public relations in which two-way communication is mostly balanced, with the organization as likely to change attitudes or behavior as its publics.

Bernays is associated with the unbalanced two-way asymmetrical model in the same way that Ivy Lee has been associated with the public information model and P.T. Barnum has been associated with the publicity/press agentry model. Each has been painted with broad strokes here mostly for the purposes of providing colorful illustrations of models of public relations. It's worth noting that Edward Bernays himself is largely responsible for framing the history of public relations as a mostly 20th-century progression from press agentry to a sophisticated two-way management function that helps corporations understand public interests. Among the benefits of Bernays' longevity in life and career was that he had decades to write and promote his take on the history of the field he helped define in his earlier years.

Two-Way Symmetrical Communication

Symmetry is balance. In a two-way **symmetrical model** of communication, organizations are just as likely to change as their publics. Historical examples are out there, but are not as easy to come by as splashy stories of press agentry and persuasion. In the epilogue to his nearly 800-page authoritative volume on the history of public relations, *The Unseen Power: Public Relations, A History*, Scott Cutlip suggested that Earl Newsom's work on behalf of Ford Motor Company may fit the bill for an example of two-way symmetrical communication.[27] As principal of his own firm, Earl Newsom and Company, Newsom counseled some of America's largest and most powerful corporations of the mid-20th century such as Standard Oil, Merrill Lynch, Trans-World Airlines, CBS and Ford Motor Company. According to Cutlip, Newsom did not consider himself an "agent" for clients, responsible for publicity and promotion. Rather, Newsom saw himself as a counselor first and foremost, advising clients on management issues of public interest.

In the mid-1950s, Ford Motor Company, along with the rest of America's auto industry, was taking heat for automobile safety, or lack thereof. Newsom counseled Ford to launch a safety campaign. The campaign, however, was much more than a publicity stunt or sales drive. It included a Ford-sponsored national safety forum attended by safety researchers, auto industry engineers and law enforcement officials. Henry Ford II announced a $200,000 grant to Cornell University for the specific purpose of researching highway safety and injury prevention. The campaign also included short movies illustrating the research and development of dashboard crash padding, safety door latches and more safely designed steering wheels. While much of Ford's reputation for safety unraveled in the decades that followed, the effort to use research and two-way communication between an organization (Ford) and its key publics (researchers, safety experts, engineers and ultimately automobile owners) to the mutual benefit of both the organization and its publics illustrated the idea of two-way symmetrical communication. To the extent that Ford changed its operations and vehicle design in the interest of its publics, the relationship was more symmetrical than if they had just kept their research and development closed to outside influence and feedback and used the campaign only to promote later sales.

Arthur Page, whose principles for ethical management of public relations are outlined in Chapter 1, is also seen as an example of an upstanding practitioner with a symmetrical worldview. He saw winning public approval, confidence and trust as essential to successful management. In his words, "All business begins with the public permission and exists by public approval."[28]

Cornell Aeronautical Labs, Liberty Mutual Insurance and Ford Motor Company partnered to develop the 1957 Cornell-Liberty Safety Car as one of the first auto concepts developed from crash testing.

Would you characterize the relationship between Ford and its publics as symmetrical?

Yet, if there is a name associated with the two-way symmetrical model of public relations, it is not a public relations man, but a theorist, or actually two theorists. James and Larissa Grunig are emeritus professors at the University of Maryland. Together with many colleagues, the Grunigs developed and executed a decades-long program of research on excellence in public relations. Among the main ideas to emerge from these studies was that "using the two-way symmetrical or a combination of the two-way symmetrical and two-way asymmetrical model (called the mixed-motive model) almost always could increase the contribution of public relations to organizational effectiveness."[29] This line of research and theory, which started in the 1970s and 1980s, continues today.

Although we may not find any one contemporary organization or practitioner to serve as a model of pure and continuous symmetry in public relations, we do see plenty of examples of engaging public relations in which the engagement is fueled by moments of good, balanced communication between two or more interested parties. Many of these examples come from nonprofits and public utilities.

Public utilities have unique relationships with their publics. Whereas consumers may exercise some power in dealing with many corporations by way of their purchasing decisions, competition for market share is less of a factor than governmental regulation and community responsiveness in how public utilities are managed.

As a consumer you don't get to choose your electric company or water treatment facility the way you choose your brand of light bulb or kitchen water filter. Sure, you may feel rather powerless when you get your electric bill and find out that your rates are going up, but before those rates go up, they must be approved by some sort of regulatory agency or board. And if

The upper Wa'ahila ridge of Manoa Valley is still mostly free of power lines after key publics in the community voiced opposition to the idea.

Why are utility companies often inclined to practice two-way symmetrical communication?

your electric company proposes a new power plant in your community, you and your neighbors may be quite motivated to find out how that regulation works and voice your position on the issue.

There are many different models for regulating utilities depending on the location, government structure and nature of the service being provided, but the basic idea is that in exchange for getting to operate without normal market competition, public utilities should be able to show that they are serving public interests in good faith. This situation sets the stage for public utilities to come to the table of two-way symmetrical communication with their publics fairly often.

Robbie Alm served for more than a decade as a vice president of Hawaii's largest public utility, Hawaiian Electric Co. (HECO), first as vice president of public affairs and later as executive vice president. In those roles he directly counseled the president and CEO on controversial matters such as the construction of new transmission stations, power plants, wind farms and a generating station on Oahu that was billed as the world's largest combustion turbine fueled by 100 percent biodiesel.[30]

Alm practiced what he calls community-based problem-solving, and it wasn't all rainbows and trade winds. Proposing giant wind mills on the serene, small-town island of Lanai to generate power for neighboring Oahu, running power lines across scenic mountain ridges, or building massive power plants anywhere will lead to some major controversy. "I think we're terrible listeners as a society," he said, speaking from experience with so many hotly contested issues. "You can have a desired outcome, and that can be taken into account, but you have to let the community guide the process in order to see it through."

This isn't to say that public approval is a foregone conclusion. That would be all asymmetrical. In fact, those power lines across the Wa'ahila ridge behind the University of Hawaii at Manoa never were built, and the hillsides of Lanai are still without windmills. Other projects, however, have proceeded with public consent, and Alm earned respect in Hawaii for the symmetry and humility in his style. "If you really try to hold on to your positions no matter what, they're almost guaranteed to slip away," he says, "but if you're really doing the right things, people feel that and they'll work with you."[31] While still working at HECO, Alm joined an independent, nonprofit-funded program called Collaborative Leaders Network (CLN), where he is pursuing his philosophy in working with political, corporate, nonprofit and community leaders in Hawaii on strategies to solve problems of mutual concern.

A Broader Social History of Public Relations

Historical portraits of Barnum, Bernays and even Lee are colored with a tint of infamy. But Barnum served as a mayor of Bridgeport, Connecticut, and founded Bridgeport Hospital. Bernays applied his expertise to promote the NAACP, Thomas Edison's invention of electric lighting, and the field of public relations itself. Ivy Lee worked for the American Red Cross. Indeed, a different sample of cases and clients sets a different tone for the history of public relations. The tactics that each man helped develop can, like any other instrument of communication, be used for good or evil.

Moreover, a broader, more inclusive, social history of public relations reveals that effective public relations was around long before the rise of 20th-century business in America. Historians have debunked the "Big Bang Barnum" narrative as a comprehensive accounting of the birth of public relations.[32]

Historians Margot Opdyke Lamme at the University of Alabama and Karen Miller Russell at the University of Georgia culled through decades of literature on the history of public relations and found more than 70 articles, chapters and books that focused on history prior to the 20th century.[33] Besides business, they found public relations to have a rich heritage in three "deep veins" of history: religion; education, nonprofit and reform; and politics and government.

> Effective public relations was around long before the rise of 20th-century business in America.

Religion

Lamme and Russell highlighted evidence of public relations as early as the first century. Although I wouldn't go so far as to say that St. Paul was a PR guy, at least one public relations historian identifies Paul as "one of the most influential communicators in history." "In the contemporary language of public relations, he played all its roles: writer-technician, liaison, manager and strategist," wrote Robert E. Brown of Salem State University with an admitted sense of anachronism in making the case.[34] In addition to authoring much of the *New Testament*, St. Paul deftly segmented his publics (Jews and early Christians), tailored his rhetoric for his audiences, visited churches, and was effective enough in spreading his message to change the course of religion and world history.

Religious leaders and organizations remain adept at both traditional and emerging public relations tactics. The Religion Communicators Council (RCC), which was chartered in 1929 and promotes "faith perspectives in public discourse," claims to be the oldest public relations professional organization in the United States.[35] Current RCC members include public

St. Paul has been referred to as one of the most influential communicators in history.

Was St. Paul practicing public relations?

A Year Of...
ISLAMO
GRAPHIC.COM

5660
Fans

402 000+
Page Views

1020
Followers

1661
Followers

351
Followers

Top 10 Islamographics

1. Fiqh of Marriage → Alia Nadhirah
2. How to be a Better Muslim → Aneesah Satriya
3. 7 Things your Muslim Wife Won't Tell You → Passant Muhammed
4. The 10 Commandments and Islam → Khalil Aleker
5. 5 Ways to Control you Tongue → Khalil Aleker
6. Advantages of Wearing the Hijab → Khalil Aleker
7. Surah Al-Fatihah – A Dialogue with Allah → Aneesah Satriya
8. How to Gain Tranquility in Salah → CanvasDawah.com
9. Did you know this about the Quran? → Khalil Aleker
10. 6 Steps to get closer to Allah → Zaakir Hoosen

Visit Islamographic.com - Islam is Beautiful

Religious organizations remain among the most spirited in public relations.

Why do you think that is?

relations practitioners representing Baháʼí, Christian, Hindu, Jewish and Muslim faiths.

Examples of religions using social media are everywhere. Rabbi Josh Yuter was celebrated by the National Jewish Outreach Program as a top-ten Jewish influencer for his use of social media: "Yuter is not only a pulpit rabbi. He's a popular blogger, tweeter, and podcaster (his Jewish-themed podcasts were downloaded more than 20,000 times last year.)"[36] The website Islamographic.com offers Islamic education through infographics.[37] Even the pope has a Twitter page: @Pontifex.

Education

College commencements are a time of great pomp and circumstance. Graduation ceremonies are also annual fundraising campaign kickoffs. As university foundation officials stand at podiums across the globe in caps and gowns each year and plead with new graduates to remember their alma maters as they move on and start earning larger paychecks, these school officials hope that commencement acts as the start of a beautiful friendship. While we may not know exactly when this practice started, Harvard College is known to have begun fundraising campaigns as early as 1641 when college representatives were sent to England to emphasize how the college was educating American Indians as part of a pitch for donations.[38] In the 1700s Princeton and Columbia (at the time named King's College) both used news releases to publicize their commencement ceremonies.[39]

Politics and Government

Lamme and Russell found examples of public-relations-type activity dating back to Alexander the Great in the fourth century B.C. Tutored by Aristotle (speaking of rhetoric!) as a boy, Alexander went on to become not only a great warrior, but also a great war reporter, or at least he saw to it that others sent stories of his exploits in battle back to Macedonian courts. Early American history is also chock-full of classic public relations strategies and tactics such as sloganeering ("Give me liberty or give me death!"), **pseudo-events** organized primarily for media coverage (Boston Tea Party), and opinion-editorial writing (*The Federalist Papers*).[40]

In 2009, a new political tea party emerged in high-profile public events, TV news, print headlines and online news feeds. Brendan Steinhauser was among the organizers of the Taxpayer March on Washington that helped

Pseudo-event
An event organized primarily for the purpose of generating media coverage.

propel the modern tea party movement into a nationally recognized political force. Steinhauser was later recognized by *Time* magazine as one of its "40 Under 40" and a "rising star" in American politics. *Time* credited his success in part to his effectiveness in training others in "the mechanics of social networking, voter outreach, and grass-roots organizing."[41]

Of course, political communicators and strategists on the other side of the political spectrum have also been effective in advocating for their ideas and candidates in the raucous arena of American politics. Democratic presidential candidate Howard Dean has been called the godfather of modern social media campaigning. In 2004, Dean's campaign used the internet to raise money like no one had ever done before at that level of politics, racking up loads of small online donations that added up to compete with the numbers generated by more traditional large donations.[42] Dean didn't win the election, but he reset the stage for political campaign financing. Many analysts see this shift in strategy as a major factor in President Barack Obama's two subsequent election victories.

Pseudo-events are organized primarily for media coverage.

Was the Boston Tea Party a public relations stunt?

Major Motivations for Public Relations

Lamme and Russell's broader view of public relations history reveals several major motivations for public relations throughout the ages. These include recruitment, legitimacy, agitation and advocacy, in addition to profit.

Recruitment

St. Paul recruited for the Christian Church. The Sons of Liberty recruited fellow colonists for their revolutionary activities like the Boston Tea Party. Today, public relations practitioners are involved in the recruitment of volunteers for nonprofits, new members for political organizations, new hires for corporations, and, of course, new students for colleges and universities.

While the timeless tactics of face-to-face visits, meetings and events are still the backbone of many recruiting efforts, today's recruiters are just as likely to use social networking sites and other forms of social media to carry out their work. In a survey of more than 1,400 people on a registered list of human resources and recruiting professionals conducted by *Jobvite* in 2015, 92 percent of recruiters reported using social media to support recruiting efforts. Eighty-seven percent said they used LinkedIn, 55 percent said Facebook, and 47 percent of those polled reported using Twitter.[43]

In a study of university officials, San Diego State University Professor Kaye Sweetser and I found that those communicators working in admissions and recruiting were among the most enthusiastic adopters of social media for public relations work. As one participant in the study put it, there's a "competitive advantage" in using social media "to attract and maintain a younger demographic, which is adept and attuned to social media." Another said, "If [students] are there and that is where they naturally are, then you have to go to [that] market. . . . We need to be there."[44]

<aside>
Today's recruiters are just as likely to use social networking sites and other forms of social media to carry out their work as they are more traditional tactics.
</aside>

Legitimacy

Öffentlichkeitsarbeit means "work for the public sphere" in German.[45] Scholars have found *Öffentlichkeitsarbeit* to date back as far as the 10th century when Austrian monarchs and statesmen disseminated coins, pictures and pamphlets to legitimize their positions.[46] Lamme and Russell also highlighted studies showing how early Christian churches sought legitimacy, and later how members of the church were used to enhance the legitimacy of others' efforts.

In the 18th century when James Oglethorpe, who founded the American colony of Georgia, was looking to promote the settlement of Savannah, he leveraged the endorsement of the Archbishop of Canterbury. "Oglethorpe and his associates were well aware of the value of the staged event to attract public attention—the *pseudo-event* is *sine qua non* of today's promotion," wrote Scott Cutlip in one such historical recounting. Oglethorpe traveled to England to "rally for support" and brought an Indian chief and some of his warriors with him. To boost legitimacy, Oglethorpe's itinerary included a staged meeting with the Archbishop of Canterbury. The visit of Oglethorpe and the Indians generated lots of publicity, and Oglethorpe's travel party upon his return to Georgia included two shiploads of new colonists.

In the 20th century, communication researchers identified a function of mass media that they called **status conferral**. Paul Lazarsfeld and Robert Merton wrote in 1948 that "the mass media bestow prestige and enhance the authority of individuals and groups by legitimizing their status."[47] For this reason, many public relations practitioners would consider it a crowning achievement to get their client or organization (or themselves) featured on the *Today* show, in *Time* or the front page of their major metropolitan newspaper. That type of coverage, provided it's positive, means instant legitimacy.

Today, Google, Yahoo, Bing and other major news and search sites confer legitimacy by way of algorithms that take into account what users

<aside>
Status conferral
When media pay attention to individuals and groups and therefore enhance their authority or bestow prestige to them.
</aside>

are searching for and linking to. In a sense, they crowd-source search results. Rather than a small group of editors acting as gatekeepers for what gets covered, decisions about what gets the top billing in organic search results depend on automated calculations. **Organic search results** are those that are not paid for as advertising or sponsored links. An entire field of practice known as **search engine optimization (SEO)** has sprouted, and public relations practitioners are among the most interested in sharpening their skills. The goal of SEO is to make your links rank as highly as possible in the results when someone does a keyword search for your client's name, products or services. Having a client show up on the first page of Google results for their business's keywords is for many as much of a professional win as making the cover of a magazine or newspaper.

Internet power players confer legitimacy in other ways too. In November 2012, over the objections of Israel and the United States, the United Nations General Assembly voted to recognize the state of Palestine, upgrading its U.N. membership from "observer entity" to "nonmember observer state." Legitimacy was implied. But that legitimacy was bolstered significantly five months later in May 2013 when Google changed the name on www .google.ps from "Palestinian territories" to simply "Palestine." As noted in a follow-up story by NPR's Emily Harris, "Google didn't announce the name change, but it didn't have to. In a place where small gestures can carry great symbolism, Palestinians noticed right away."[48]

Agitation

Getting people fired up has long been a motivation of strategic communicators. For example, scholars have studied how Napoleon used the press to cultivate hatred of England and how the Female Moral Reform Society in America in the 19th century went as far as to purchase a newspaper and build its circulation as part of the organization's organized efforts to eradicate sexually transmitted diseases and prostitution.[49]

Organized agitation evolved into new forms with the rise of the internet. On January 18, 2012, Wikipedia went dark in protest of the Stop Online Piracy Act (SOPA) and the Protect Intellectual Property Acts, which were bills pending in U.S. Congress. The legislation was written to crack down on the pirating of copyrighted and trademarked material online, but opponents believed it would stifle internet freedom, innovation and creativity. Reddit and thousands of smaller websites coordinated service blackouts as well. Google promoted and hosted an online petition, which was signed by more than 7 million people before the bills' sponsors in Congress postponed pursuing the legislation in response to the public outcry.[50]

Google
Palestine

strokeluck of   Google search

English :Scale Google.ps Available languages

Google confers status.

Why do you think Google recognition matters so much?

Major news and search sites confer legitimacy by way of algorithms that take into account what users are searching for and linking to.

Organic search results
Search engine results that are generated because of their relevance to the search terms entered by users and not resulting directly from paid placement as advertising.

Search engine optimization (SEO)
Process of improving the position of a specific website in the organic search results of search engines.

SOPA protestors offered web users an image to put on their websites to censor their own logo as a statement of protest.

How effective do you think online activism is when compared with in-person activism?

Promoting a cause also means supporting a mission, which requires strategy beyond mere awareness.

Advocacy
Public promotion of a cause, idea or policy.

Propaganda
The spread of information used to promote or support a particular point of view. In modern use, the term usually refers to false, misleading or exaggerated information.

A similar movement of agitation was staged by European activists in protest of the international Anti-Counterfeiting Trade Agreement (ACTA). The petition in this case was hosted by avaaz.org: "Avaaz—meaning 'voice' in several European, Middle Eastern and Asian languages—launched in 2007 with a simple democratic mission: organize citizens of all nations to close the gap between the world we have and the world most people everywhere want."[51]

Advocacy

On the flip side of agitation is **advocacy**, which is the very first professional value listed in the PRSA Code of Ethics. Whereas agitation has been used in history in opposition efforts, advocacy in the history of public relations has meant promoting persons, organizations and nations. As an example of one of the longest-running promotional campaigns in history, Lamme and Russell highlight the Catholic Church's "1,000-year public relations campaign." Featuring St. James as a patron saint to Spain, it promoted both the church and Spanish nationalism in the ninth and 10th centuries.[52] The very term **propaganda** derives from the work of the Catholic Church to propagate faith. Prior to the world wars of the 20th century, the word did not carry the negative connotation it has today.

Advocacy and promotion are easy to spot. Colored ribbons are prime examples. Pink ribbons for breast cancer awareness, yellow ribbons to support troops, red to support the fight against AIDS and HIV, even periwinkle to support research on stomach and esophageal cancers. Each ribbon is a symbol of a cause with organizations working on behalf of the cause. Of course, mere awareness is only part of the process of advocacy. Promoting a cause also means supporting a mission, which requires strategy beyond mere awareness. Successful propagation of the faith may be evidenced in church membership numbers, attendance and institutional partnerships. Fighting cancer requires money for research, physician involvement, preventive behavior and early detection of treatable conditions.

Profit

Of course, generating revenue has been a major motivator for public relations throughout the ages, and not just for big corporations. Even "nonprofits" such as churches, governments, foundations, schools, nongovernmental organizations and foundations have sought to raise money as seen in the examples discussed in this chapter. That said, one of the largest roles for

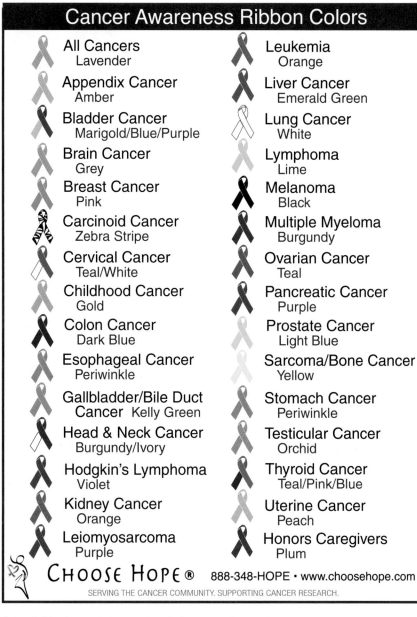

Cancer Awareness Ribbon Colors

All Cancers Lavender		**Leukemia** Orange	
Appendix Cancer Amber		**Liver Cancer** Emerald Green	
Bladder Cancer Marigold/Blue/Purple		**Lung Cancer** White	
Brain Cancer Grey		**Lymphoma** Lime	
Breast Cancer Pink		**Melanoma** Black	
Carcinoid Cancer Zebra Stripe		**Multiple Myeloma** Burgundy	
Cervical Cancer Teal/White		**Ovarian Cancer** Teal	
Childhood Cancer Gold		**Pancreatic Cancer** Purple	
Colon Cancer Dark Blue		**Prostate Cancer** Light Blue	
Esophageal Cancer Periwinkle		**Sarcoma/Bone Cancer** Yellow	
Gallbladder/Bile Duct Cancer Kelly Green		**Stomach Cancer** Periwinkle	
Head & Neck Cancer Burgundy/Ivory		**Testicular Cancer** Orchid	
Hodgkin's Lymphoma Violet		**Thyroid Cancer** Teal/Pink/Blue	
Kidney Cancer Orange		**Uterine Cancer** Peach	
Leiomyosarcoma Purple		**Honors Caregivers** Plum	

CHOOSE HOPE® 888-348-HOPE • www.choosehope.com

SERVING THE CANCER COMMUNITY. SUPPORTING CANCER RESEARCH.

Colored ribbons are prime examples of advocacy and promotion.

How many of these colors would you recognize? What are the benefits of this type of awareness?

public relations has been and always will be working in conjunction with advertising and marketing to promote the sale of products, services and ideas. Chapter 3 will cover the differences, and perhaps more important, the integration of public relations with related functions such as marketing and advertising.

Voices from the Field

Karen Miller Russell

UNIVERSITY OF GEORGIA Professor Karen Miller Russell studies and teaches media history with an emphasis on public relations. Dr. Russell served as editor of the *Journal of Public Relations Research* from 2010 to 2015 and is author of *The Voice of Business: Hill and Knowlton and Postwar Public Relations* as well as numerous articles for communication and public relations journals. A former public relations writer for the Wisconsin Department of Transportation, public relations specialist for the American Camping Association and former photography and publicity assistant for Common Wealth Development, Dr. Russell is also interested in social media, globalization and corporate social responsibility initiatives.

Many textbooks have presented well-known historical events like the Boston Tea Party as examples of early public relations, even though no one at the time would have thought to call it PR. Do you have concerns about that as a historian?

The Boston Tea Party and other pre-20th-century events may not have been "public relations" as we know it today, but they definitely belong in PR history. Many scholars have assumed that PR started in the United States around the turn of the 20th century, but I'd argue that it started long before that in politics, religion and reform movements. These groups developed the strategies and tactics that eventually became institutionalized in corporate public relations practice, and that's a legitimate subject for study.

The UAB and other accrediting bodies include knowledge of history as part of their criteria for accreditation. How does that kind of knowledge benefit practitioners beyond helping them get the credential?

There are three good reasons for studying PR history. First, we can always learn from seeing what worked and didn't work in the past, especially if you can pinpoint the reasons behind success or failure. Second, although times have changed, basic principles of public relations remain the same. You may be communicating on a different platform, but you're still trying to share information, manage a reputation, advocate and build relationships, just as people have been doing over the ages. Third, studying history provides context for understanding what's happening today. For example, I studied business responses to the 1950s Civil Rights Movement with co-author Margot Opdycke Lamme, and we learned that although U.S. corporate executives often sincerely wanted to help bring about social change, their commitment to it slackened when public pressure died down. Seeing how that happened and what it meant to both organizations and activists can help us understand what's happening in race relations today.

How has America's history shaped differences between U.S. public relations and public relations in other countries? How has the U.S. "imported" or "exported" public relations as a practice?

Natalia Salcedo, a Spanish historian, argues that the development of public relations varies in different countries because of the history and culture of each nation. It makes sense that public relations in Eastern European countries that were behind the Iron Curtain during the Cold War would be quite different from public relations in North America and Western Europe, to take just one example. But there has also been a great deal of cross-pollination within companies operating multinationally or among politicians and diplomats watching what their counterparts are doing in other countries. The United States certainly exported some aspects of PR practices after World War II, but no doubt American executives also learned from working in Asia, Europe and South America during the same time period.

If you could sit down with Edward Bernays and Doris Fleischman for an interview right now, what would you ask them?

I actually met Edward Bernays once and briefly chatted with him about the research I was conducting on the New York agency Hill and Knowlton. What a character! I would love to meet Doris Fleischman, though, and I would ask her to talk about her role in their agency, campaigns she developed for the NAACP and other organizations, and what it was like to be a professional woman during a time when that was discouraged. I have a feeling that she played a much larger role than we realize in the success of their firm.

What's the most important lesson from public relations history that a student can take into the job market?

Be ethical: the truth always comes out eventually.

Ethics: Transparency, Objectivity and Advocacy

Disclosure and dissemination of information is a cornerstone of public relations ethics. Media ethicist Patrick Lee Plaisance argues that transparency is ethical not because of its strategic outcomes (e.g., reputation for doing the right thing), but because it is essential to human dignity.[53] He cites philosopher Immanuel Kant in building a case that the best reason to be transparent is respect for other people. By making available all relevant information, we respect others' autonomy in informed decision-making. Grunig and Hunt painted Ivy Lee as an exemplar of the public information model of public relations: "Lee viewed the public as made up of rational human beings who, if they are given complete and accurate information, would make the right decisions."[54]

As a former journalist, like many of today's public relations practitioners, Lee embraced the general idea of **objectivity**. I say "general idea" here because objectivity is a philosophically elusive concept. Oxford Dictionaries define the adjective "*objective*" as "not influenced by personal feelings or opinions in considering and representing facts."[55] But journalists, or any other human beings for that matter, struggle with total removal of feelings and opinions in selecting, interpreting and reporting facts. You won't find objectivity specifically stated in the Society of Professional Journalists (SPJ) Code of Ethics, but that doesn't mean they have abandoned the idea of pursuing truth. "Journalism does not pursue truth in an absolute or philosophical sense, but it can—and must—pursue it in a practical sense," according to the Pew Research Center's principles of journalism.[56]

Whereas Lee identified with journalists (and many journalists identified with Lee), Edward Bernays made it a point to define public relations as much more than a journalistic function. Bernays embraced advocacy, and in doing so unabashedly distinguished public relations from journalism.

Objectivity
State of being free from the influence of personal feelings or opinions in considering and representing facts.

Today, there is little debate about advocacy's place in public relations as opposed to journalism.

Advocacy is a value in the PRSA Code of Ethics: "We serve the public interest by acting as responsible advocates for those we represent. We provide a voice in the marketplace of ideas, facts, and viewpoints to aid informed public debate."[57]

Advocacy is a no-no in the SPJ Code of Ethics, where journalists are advised to "distinguish between advocacy and news reporting." "Analysis and commentary should be labeled and not misrepresent fact or context. Distinguish news from advertising and shun hybrids that blur the lines between the two."[58]

The case has even been made that Edward Bernays did more to advance the ethical evolution of public relations than Ivy Lee because Bernays embraced advocacy and encouraged writing it into a code of ethics rather than trying to act as a journalist while on the payroll of a non-news organization. Genevieve McBride wrote in the *Journal of Mass Media Ethics* in 1989 that public relations' struggle toward professionalism would benefit from a view of history that embraces Bernays' "disassociation from the journalistic perspective" rather than Lee's "dysfunctional standard of objectivity."[59]

Whether you practice public information with a journalistic set of values or advocacy with a penchant for persuasion, the principle of transparency is critical. In a democracy, it is OK to advocate, as long as you are transparent about what you're doing, meaning that you respect others' autonomy in informed decision-making.

Transparency also offers a useful lens for studying public relations history. In what ways was Bernays' work for Beech-Nut ethical? Unethical? How about Ivy Lee's work with Nazis in Germany? Should Lee be let off the hook because he was transparent? Lee could (and did) argue that his work in counseling Germans in the late 1930s was consistent with his respect for rational human decision-making. He said he was working to improve mutual understanding between Americans and Germans. In a congressional hearing in 1934, Lee testified that he counseled German propaganda minister Joseph Goebbels and other German leaders that "they would never in the world get the American people reconciled to their treatment of the Jews."[60] The same hearing revealed that Lee was receiving $25,000 a year from the German dye trust for his public relations counsel. Assuming Lee was upfront about his business arrangement, was his work ethical?

The principle of transparency is critical whether you practice public information with a journalistic set of values or with advocacy.

In Case You Missed It

While public relations tactics have
been around since the dawn of
civilization, our body of knowledge
about the field has come a long way
in the past few decades. Here are
some time-tested truths, along with
a slightly new perspective.

- Organizations must get messages out accurately
  and reliably, even when they are not seeking to
  gain extra attention.

- Professionals today have access to more scientific
  research and online data to help them understand
  publics and to gauge the success of public
  relations efforts.

- Effective public relations was around long
  before the rise of 20th-century business in
  America.

- Today's recruiters are just as likely to use social
  networking sites and other forms of social media to
  carry out their work as they are to use more
  traditional tactics.

- Major news and search sites confer legitimacy by
  way of algorithms that take into account what users
  are searching for and linking to.

- Promoting a cause also means supporting a
  mission, which requires strategy beyond mere
  awareness.

- The principle of transparency is critical whether
  you practice public information with a journalistic
  set of values or with advocacy.

ICYMI

SUMMARY

2.1 Analyze public relations models on one-way/two-way and asymmetrical/symmetrical dimensions.

One-way models of public relations are all about getting information
out and, in the case of press agentry, getting attention. The public
information model is one-way too, but it is more concerned with
accuracy. Two-way models range from asymmetrical, in which
organizations use research and feedback to persuade publics, to
symmetrical, in which organizations and publics exhibit more mutual
communication and change.

2.2 Demonstrate knowledge of key figures in public relations history.

Barnum, Lee and Bernays are often associated with press agentry,
public information and scientific persuasion, respectively. But a
fuller history recognizes the contributions of many other innovative
communicators and strategists. These include historical figures
with household names like Alexander the Great, St. Paul or Alexander
Hamilton. Twentieth-century public relations also owes its development
to figures like Doris Fleischman, Arthur Page and Earl Newsom.

2.3 Integrate knowledge of social history with knowledge of public relations.

Business, religion, education, politics and government are intertwined with public relations throughout history inasmuch as organizations and publics have communicated, persuaded and adapted to each other over time.

2.4 Identify common motivations for strategic communication in history.

While the term *public relations* may not have existed in common use prior to the 20th century, its functions and tactics have been applied in pursuit of recruitment, legitimacy, agitation, advocacy and profit throughout human history.

2.5 Apply knowledge of history to analyze modern public relations practices.

Seemingly modern phenomena such as flash mobs, internet activism and radical transparency were preceded in history by events and actions built on the same general principles (e.g., publicity stunts, propaganda and declarations of principles like Ivy Lee's).

2.6 Distinguish public relations from journalism.

Public relations values advocacy. Journalism values objectivity—or balance of coverage if objectivity isn't possible.

2.7 Discuss the ethics of transparency, objectivity and advocacy.

Edward Bernays and Ivy Lee can be compared. Lee pursued journalistic integrity, but he still worked on the payroll of specific organizations to which he was loyal. Bernays embraced advocacy.

DISCUSSION QUESTIONS

1. Some say that real-life public relations is better described with a mixed-motive model in which one-way and asymmetrical communication are used by the same organizations that are also practicing symmetrical communication. Describe a relationship that you have as an individual that could be seen as mixed-motive.

2. Both Ivy Lee and Edward Bernays have been called the "father of public relations." Do either one of them deserve that title? Why or why not?

3. Name a major historical event not mentioned in this chapter in which public relations played a key role, and explain how public relations was involved (even if it wasn't called public relations at the time).

4. How would P.T. Barnum use social media? Provide some specific examples.

5. Find an example of a blogger or social media influencer doing journalism, and describe how that is different from public relations.

6. Asymmetrical public relations is much more common in everyday practice than symmetrical. Does that mean most of the field is inherently unethical? Why or why not?

KEY TERMS

CHAPTER 3

Convergence and Integrated Communication

Is Red Bull an energy drink company that produces media content, or a media company that produces energy drinks?

KEY LEARNING OUTCOMES

3.1 Define different forms of convergence.

3.2 Analyze how convergence affects public relations.

3.3 Discuss how functions of advertising and marketing may be integrated with public relations.

3.4 Distinguish public relations from advertising and marketing.

3.5 Discuss public relations' role in the free flow of information in society.

RELATED UNIVERSAL ACCREDITATION BOARD COMPETENCY AREAS

1.6 AUDIENCE IDENTIFICATION • **2.2** ETHICAL BEHAVIOR • **4.3** KNOWLEDGE OF FIELD
5.6 ORGANIZATIONAL SKILLS • **6.5** NETWORKS

Admit it. One of the very first things you do in the morning is check your media device. If not, then you are a better person than I! I watch the apps update. I check my social network sites to see what clever memes my friends are propagating. I check media-business news and see how the latest round of mergers and acquisitions affects the products and services I use. Whether I realize it or not through the blur of my just-opened eyes, the world delivered to me by my bundled talk, text and data plan has continued to converge and re-converge as I slept. Your new smartphone can undoubtedly handle many more functions than your last smartphone. There's a good chance many of your favorite TV shows, movies, music and news sources are owned by the same big company. Your cultural interests increasingly overlap with people from all over the planet. This is the world you, your organization and your publics inhabit. And, it's ever more technologically, culturally and economically converged every time you upload, download, like, snap, submit, share or agree to yet another end-user license agreement.

Communication firms are merging and converging with one another in the global marketplace of ideas, while professional communicators continue to weigh the pros and cons of integrating public relations with advertising and marketing. Making sense of all this convergence and integration and what it means for public relations requires an understanding of the multiple dimensions of convergence, an appreciation for the workings of integrated communication, and a respect for classic principles of public relations that apply steadily as times and technologies change.

Black box fallacy: Multipurpose devices have not simplified life as much as some have hoped.

Why do you think that is?

Convergence

Convergence is a concept that can be difficult to understand, in part because it has different meanings in different contexts. USC Professor Henry Jenkins recommends thinking about multiple processes of convergence.[1] Convergence can be a technological process, but convergence also describes cultural, economic and professional processes.

Technological Convergence

We may be seduced by the idea that one day all of our media needs will be met with one elegant device. Jenkins calls it the **black box fallacy**. "Sooner or later, the argument goes, all media content is going to flow through a single black box into our living rooms (or, in the mobile scenario, through black boxes we carry around with us everywhere we go),"[2] but as he points out, it just doesn't work out that way.

For me it was the iPhone 3GS. I was one stoked customer walking out of the Apple store in the summer of 2009 with my brand new device. In my hand I held a phone, a compass, a GPS, a camera, a calculator, a news reader,

An interactive multimedia kiosk at the Johnson Museum at Cornell University.

In what ways are kiosks like this one a product of technological convergence?

a video recorder, a voice recorder, an audio player, a TV and an app store that would let me turn the thing into my own portal to Twitter, Facebook, LinkedIn or any other social network service I wanted. My mediated life was going to be simple and uncluttered. Or not. As the years go by, my family and I seem to be losing the war against technoclutter. Old tablets, phones, earbuds, cameras, wires, flash drives, charging wires, game consoles, iPods, Bluetooth devices, routers, printers, monitors and remote controls litter our home, car and office.

Make no mistake. **Technological convergence** is real. Technological convergence brings together formerly separate technical capabilities. As multiple forms of media content get digitized, opportunities for mixing and mashing them increase. "When words, images and sounds are transformed into digital information, we expand the potential relationships between them and enable them to flow across platforms," wrote Jenkins in *Technology Review* in 2001.[3] We see technological convergence everywhere—on our smartphones, TVs, car dashboards, kids' games and public kiosks.

But human uses, needs and desires for media vary widely from person to person. There's no single solution for everyone. And there's no single media solution for any one person across every situation. This is why that magical black box doesn't exist, and it also is why public relations people must understand other dimensions of convergence beyond the technological ones.

> Public relations people must understand other dimensions of convergence beyond the technological ones.

Cultural Convergence

Just as technological convergence presents an apparent paradox (media are combining at the very same time that media technologies are proliferating), so too does **cultural convergence**. On one hand, we are witnessing vast cultural hegemony. Hegemony—now here's a term usually reserved for the most critical approaches to public relations.

Stemming from Marxism, cultural hegemony occurs when a ruling class imposes its social, political or economic ideals on subordinate groups in society at the expense of cultural diversity. Public relations people are rarely portrayed as the good guys in these scenarios. "Americanization" or "McDonaldization" are examples, with "an increasing convergence on specific forms of artistic, culinary, or musical culture—usually, but not exclusively, moving from the United States, via newly global media, to the rest of

Technological convergence (aka digital convergence)
When information of various forms such as sound, text, images and data are digitized, affording communication across common media.

Cultural convergence
When various forms of culture are exchanged, combined, converted and adapted. On a global scale, this phenomenon has accelerated with the growth of digital media.

the world," writes Yale Law Professor David Singh Grewal.[4] On the other hand, clearly, "cultural borrowing" increasingly works in other directions. McDonald's restaurants in India serve chicken and fish as well as curry-infused options.

To the degree that successful public relations entails changes in human attitudes, knowledge and behavior, public relations people must work toward an enlightened understanding of their organizations' roles and their own personal roles in cultural exchanges. Jenkins describes cultural convergence as "both a top-down corporate-driven process and a bottom-up consumer-driven process."[5] Public relations people work where the two meet. They must understand and communicate from the standpoint of their organization's cultural values while understanding and interpreting their publics' cultures back to the organization as well. Participating actively and transparently in public forums—constructively engaging **participatory culture**—is an important part of managing relationships, particularly in media environments characterized by cultural convergence.

Cultural convergence works in two directions for McDonald's, which exports mainstream American culture but also adopts local tastes.

Is this a balanced exchange? What are some ramifications of this type of cultural convergence?

Economic Convergence

Ketchum is a huge public relations agency with offices and affiliates in 70 countries. Ketchum represents consumer-brand clients ranging from FedEx to Ikea to Kleenex to IBM. Ketchum and its subsidiaries also have served government agencies like the IRS and the Department of Education in the United States and international clients including the government of Russia.

If Ketchum is huge, Omnicom is huger. Omnicom acquired Ketchum as a subsidiary in 1996.[6,7] Omnicom is a global advertising, marketing and communication services conglomerate that owns firms providing services in advertising, strategic media planning, digital marketing, direct marketing and, of course, public relations. Omnicom serves 5,000 clients in more than 100 countries.[8] The vastness of this network entails not just public relations, but advertising, marketing, lobbying and emerging digital and social media services as well. This is **economic convergence**.

As with technological and cultural convergence, economic convergence presents a contradiction. At the same time that agencies are diversifying

Participatory culture
A culture in which private citizens and publics are as likely to produce and share as they are to consume; commonly applied in mediated contexts in which consumers produce and publish information online.

Economic convergence
When various media organizations and functions are merged under a single ownership structure. This form of media convergence is different from the term economists use to describe trends in world economies.

services, building networks and opening global offices to serve geographically unique clients and publics in almost every corner of every continent, the overall number of major corporate players is dwindling. The Ketchum family tree is just one example that illustrates the size and scope of economic convergence in strategic communication. Omnicom, along with global conglomerates Interpublic and WPP, top the list of holding firms ranked by revenues from public relations operations.

If you watched Super Bowl 50 in 2016, you saw Peyton Manning's last game as he and the Denver Broncos took down Cam Newton and the Carolina Panthers 24-10. But you also likely saw the most expensive advertising event of that year, in which $4.6 to $5 million was spent on each 30-second paid spot.[9] You might remember the Advil "Distant Memory" ad with a grandma doing yoga, or the NFL "Super Bowl Babies Choir," featuring fans born about nine months after their parents' favorite team won the big game.[10] The NFL also aired a "No More" ad against domestic violence. These three ads were products of the Grey New York advertising agency. Grey is owned by the holding company WPP. Or you may remember commercials for Colgate (owned by Colgate Palmolive), Butterfinger (owned by Nestlé) or Heinz (owned by Kraft Heinz Co.). These ads also came from agencies owned by WPP.

While public relations doesn't have a Super Bowl of its own, the case illustrates some of the pros and cons of economic convergence. Big companies have the capacity to produce excellent work. They have global networks that provide top-notch technical, creative and strategic expertise to clients ranging from very specialized and localized organizations to mainstream companies reaching the widest possible audiences and publics. At the same time, the number of voices in the marketplace, when defined by corporate ownership, is shrinking.

For Super Bowl advertising, much of the marketplace is for commodities like candy bars, ketchup and toothpaste. For public relations, which operates more in the marketplace of ideas than in the marketplace of commodities, the stakes may even be higher. We may not lose sleep after learning that competing brands of sodas and chips may be represented by agencies that are owned by the same parent companies. But what if the clients are different national governments? How do you feel about a single communication firm representing both tobacco companies and healthcare organizations? How do you feel about the NFL partnering with a nonprofit organization to air anti-abuse ads during the Super Bowl? Economic convergence at the corporate level requires extra attention to public relations' role in society at large.

Professional Convergence

We can add **professional convergence** to the dimensions of convergence that matter most in public relations. One of the benefits of converged, multiservice agencies is that they can integrate communication functions strategically. Publicity and advertising can be used to support the marketing of consumer products. Marketing tactics can be used to support public relations. Public affairs and government relations benefit from good public relations with an organization's stakeholders. Healthy employee relations help customer service and sales. And so on, and so on.

The architects of multibillion-dollar mergers are not the only ones who must understand how all the functions go together. Each person working for each client must also understand how the functions integrate in order to manage, communicate and counsel most effectively. From the intern to the account executive to the CEO, agencies operate best when everyone has a good sense of how their job fits into the larger mission and service to any particular client. Someone who places a hashtag in a paid TV advertisement should know what is going to happen when TV viewers jump platforms from their TVs to other screens. When the communication goes online, the company representatives monitoring the hashtag conversation should be in tune with the management of the organization hosting the exchange. The account executive, the media buyer, the advertising creative, the social media strategist, the online host and the executives of the organization itself all need to work in concert.

Revlon promoted #LOVEISON with this video display in New York's Times Square.

What types of employees and media people have to collaborate to make a campaign like this work?

If you place a hashtag in a TV ad, you should know what will happen when TV viewers jump platforms from their TVs to other screens.

Integration raises one more apparent paradox of convergence. Successful integration of functions of communication requires an understanding of, and respect for, the unique goals and contributions of each. This doesn't just apply to the big players on the world stage. Integration is equally important for in-house communications teams and for small organizations employing only a single communication specialist. In fact, if you are working alone communicating for a small business or nonprofit, you have no choice but to think through how all your communication and management functions gel together for a common purpose. Good public relations means recognizing both the differences and commonalities of advertising, marketing and public relations.

Divergence

Using the term *paradox* to describe convergence sheds light on apparent contradictions, but philosophically it is not really that hard to reconcile ideas like professional diversity and integration. Divergence and convergence go

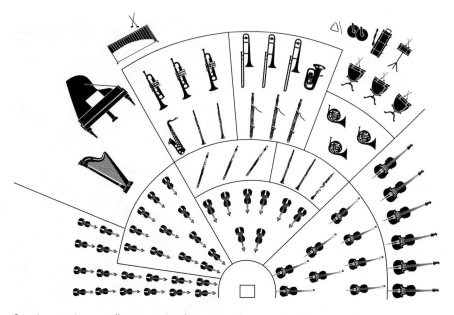

Symphony orchestras offer a metaphor for integrated communication.

How is a conductor's role different from that of a town crier?

Before diving headfirst into integration, understand how public relations differs from advertising and marketing in its goals.

hand in hand. The best chefs know the unique flavors of their individual ingredients well before they mix them together to serve the perfect dish. Chemists understand elements, compounds and mixtures. Music directors know how each instrument plays in their ensemble. Betteke van Ruler, whose "town crier" typology of a public relations practitioner was introduced in Chapter 2, also identified a "conductor" type of public relations person. The conductor is tasked with orchestrating different communication activities in much the same way that one leads a symphony. Before diving headfirst into integration, understand what exactly is being integrated and how public relations is fundamentally different in its goals from advertising and marketing.

Advertising

Despite the explosion of innovation and change in media industries in recent decades, most media business models still rely on advertising dollars as a primary source of revenue. In traditional mass media, **advertising** is the paid media space that sponsors use to persuade audiences. The media space in broadcast media is measured based on time—for example a 30-second radio or TV ad. Sponsors generally pay more for prime-time and wide-audience programming events like the Super Bowl, and less for time in local programming at off-peak times with smaller audiences. In print media, the space is often sold based on column inches. If you look at a printed newspaper or magazine, you'll see that each page has space for a certain number of columns across and a certain number of inches in length up and down. If an organization wants

Advertising
Media space purchased by sponsors to persuade audiences; or the practice of planning and producing this service.

to buy ad space that is three columns wide and six inches long, the buyers would pay for 18 column inches. Or buyers may pay for the space based on the portion of the pages used. You can look through magazines to find one-third-page ads, half-page ads, two-page spreads, and so on.

Advertisement pricing formulas include not just the amount of time or space, but also the estimated audience size, the demographics and influence of that audience, contract arrangements between the organization and the media outlet, and the context for placement and timing of the ad. For example, in 2016, the global circulation of *The Wall Street Journal* (including U.S., Asia and Europe editions) was estimated at 1,437,863 copies. The standard rate for a 1/7-page (18 column inches) black-and-white ad was $45,088, while a full-page (126 column inches) color ad cost $409,601. That's about $3,250 per column inch. Meanwhile a local ad in *The Daily Tar Heel* student-run newspaper at the University of North Carolina at Chapel Hill, with a circulation of 14,000 copies, was priced at $14.20 per column inch. It makes a lot more sense for the local yogurt shop to advertise in *The Daily Tar Heel*. However, for a private jet charter company, it may make more sense to advertise in *The Wall Street Journal*.

One metric for calculating advertising value is **cost per thousand (CPM)** (the *M* in CPM is the Roman numeral for 1,000). A three-column-inch ad in the student newspaper costing $42.60 to reach a circulation of 14,000 would yield a CPM of $42.60/14 = 3.04, or $3.04 per thousand readers. Public relations people sometimes use these calculations to figure an equivalent value for publicity when an organization is covered in the unpaid column inches of news and editorial content. This metric, known as **advertising value equivalency (AVE)**, has been widely discredited as a measure of effective public relations. Proper evaluation of public relations requires much more careful thinking about the effects of communication than simply figuring what media coverage would have cost if you paid for it. The AVE issue will be discussed further in Chapter 8 on evaluation.

While newspapers and magazines make some money from subscriptions and single-copy sales, the majority of their revenue comes from advertising in the form of print advertising and online advertising paid for by marketers. (Some publications like student newspapers are free and depend almost entirely on advertising for their budgets.) Online advertising revenues are growing, while print advertising revenues are dropping.

For the price they pay, marketers get to choose the placement of their messages and design the message as they see fit for their purposes (within reason). Marketers hire advertising firms to strategically plan the precise words they want in the copy. The firms select fonts and colors that will work best. They choose the models and frame the pictures. In audio and video, they carefully design and produce the material to their own exact standards. In short, marketers buy not only media space, but the ability to control the content of that space.

Online, advertisers can buy **banner ads**, which display ads on a portion of web pages. Another option is **pre-roll advertising**, which is a

Cost per thousand (CPM)
A measure of advertising reach that represents the cost of an advertisement relative to the estimated size of the audience.

Advertising value equivalency (AVE)
A calculation of the value of news or editorial coverage based on the cost of the equivalent amount of advertising space or time.

Banner ads
Advertisements on web pages designed to encourage users to click to reach an advertiser's site.

Pre-roll advertising
A commercial ad is displayed as online video before the desired video is shown.

Banner ads and pre-roll ads are criticized for being annoying and ineffective.

What kind of evidence would it take to convince you these ads have value?

Analytics help track behavior as users move from initial exposure to some target behavior, such as making an online purchase.

commercial ad displayed for a few seconds as online video before the desired video is shown.

The CPM metric is commonly used with banner ads. Calculated based on the cost per thousand web page viewers, CPM is most similar to traditional advertising metrics for value. Of course, there are a lot more data that can be tracked online than with traditional mass media. **Click-through rate** is the percentage of users who view an ad and actually click on it. If a thousand people view a banner ad on a web page, and 15 of them click on the banner, the click-through rate is 1.5 percent.

Newer media enterprises rely on advertising for revenue too. Yahoo, Bing and Google sell sponsored results that appear when users search for certain keywords. So if you search for "yogurt," you'll find yogurt ads and links prominently displayed at the top of your results. **Search advertising** is a good deal for advertisers because they reach people who are searching for specific keywords related to their business, and the pricing is tied more closely to the behavioral results of the ad (e.g., clicking) than to the number of people assumed to be in the audience exposed to the ad. Even beyond clicking on the initial links, Google Analytics and similar services help track user behavior as they move from initial exposure to some target behavior such as making an online purchase or setting up an appointment to talk to a

Click-through rate
Percentage of users who view an ad on the web and click on it to reach an advertiser's site.

Search advertising
Paid placement of advertising on search-engine results pages. Ads are placed to appear in response to certain keyword queries.

sales representative. **Analytics** is a term used to describe researching online data to identify meaningful patterns.

Media space also can be sold in the form of pop-up ads on mobile apps, promoted tweets on Twitter, banners towed behind airplanes, product placements in TV shows or movies, videos in Facebook news feeds, real billboards on the highway, virtual billboards on the highway in your video game, the hoods of NASCAR race cars, or the decks of skateboards, snowboards and surfboards.

Organizations buy advertising to reach audiences, most commonly to persuade people to buy products or services. Effective advertising sparks a desire in people. It piques interests and persuades. People who buy an organization's products and services are certainly an important public with whom to build and maintain relationships.

But beyond seeking profit, advertising can also be used to recruit employees and members, advocate and agitate for causes, and legitimize organizations and their missions. As such, advertising is an important tool for public relations. Likewise, public relations efforts can work to support advertising.

Marketing

Of course, advertising is a tool for **marketing** too. The American Marketing Association defines marketing as "the activity, set of institutions, and processes for creating, communicating, delivering, and exchanging offerings that have value for customers, clients, partners, and society at large."[11] In a classic text first published in 1960, Professor E. Jerome McCarthy introduced a handy way to learn the basics of what he called the marketing mix.[12] McCarthy's four P's include *product*, *price*, *place* and *promotion*.

PRODUCT

The product is the thing to be sold. Very often it is a tangible item like a car or a serving of yogurt or an electric toothbrush. Or the "product" can be a less tangible item like downloadable computer software or a service like a mobile voice, text and data plan. Ideas and behaviors such as preventing skin cancer or registering to vote can also be marketed. Marketers are involved with the development and branding of products and product families, and they analyze product life cycles. A new product will be marketed differently from a "mature" product. Kwikset, the lock company, marketed its Bluetooth-enabled "Kevo" deadbolt—"Users can simply touch the deadbolt while the authorized

Three-time ASP Women's World Tour Champion Carissa Moore delivers a dynamic medium for paid sponsorship.

How many ads do you see?

Analytics
Researching online data to identify meaningful patterns. In strategic communication, analytics often focus on how web traffic leads to behavioral results such as sharing information or making online purchases.

Marketing
Business of creating, promoting, delivering and selling products and services.

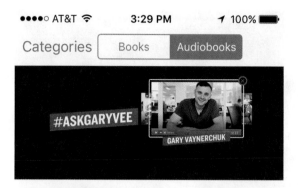

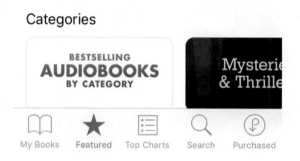

Books Made into Movies   See All >

Zootopia (Unabridged) — Disney Press
The Taliban Shuffle: Str... — Kim Barker
The Choice (Unabridged) — Nicholas Sp...
Alle Div... Ver

Categories

BESTSELLING AUDIOBOOKS BY CATEGORY

Mysteries & Thrille

My Books · Featured · Top Charts · Search · Purchased

With digital media, the point of sale is often the same as the medium used to consume the media, such as music or audiobooks purchased on a smartphone.

How have digital media changed the way music, videos and books are marketed?

Market skimming
Marketing strategy that starts with higher prices for early adopters of unique products and services and then lowers prices later to sell to a broader base of consumers when competitors enter the market.

Marketing mix
Combination of product, price, place and promotion strategies in support of profitable exchange.

smartphone remains in their purse or pocket to unlock the door"—differently from a mature product like one of their standard key-operated deadbolts. As a consumer, I found out about the new Kevo device because it was listed as a "Product of the Year" on the *Electronic House* website, which "serves discriminating consumers who enjoy the elegance, simplicity and fun afforded by integrated home technology."[13] Whether or not I can afford a $200 door lock is another issue!

PRICE

Price is obviously an important consideration, as it determines the revenue a company receives from sales, and therefore the company's profits. Pricing is sophisticated business. A product must be priced somewhere in line with customers' perceived value and affordability. If a product is priced too low, the company will not make a profit, and moreover, the product may be perceived as "cheap" in the negative sense of the word. Higher pricing may give the product some prestige, but if the product is not affordable, no one will buy it.

Understand that this is a gross oversimplification of pricing strategies. Many, many other factors come into play. For example, one pricing strategy is called **market skimming**, in which consumer products are priced higher at first when eager early adopters are willing to pay a premium for a new and unique product, but then priced lower later to appeal to broader, thriftier markets once the product is more mature in its life cycle and when similar competitors have likely entered the market. If Kwikset uses this strategy, they eventually may bring down the price of a Kevo into a more affordable range, especially as more lock companies start competing for business with similar products. Understanding pricing strategy requires knowledge of psychology and economics among other social sciences. Like public relations, marketing involves research and theory to understand people and how they communicate with organizations and respond to their offerings.

PLACE

If you think of markets as places where buyers and sellers meet, you get a good sense of why distribution is such an important part of the **marketing mix**. You still can't download a pineapple or a pair of running shoes. Marketers have to figure out the best way to get products like these to their consumers. Produce has to be canned, frozen or kept fresh during harvesting, packing and shipping. Many stores and their shoppers now demand

According to an analysis conducted by SMG Delta, an agency that tracks television advertising, Donald Trump spent less money on paid advertising than his biggest competitors in the 2016 U.S. presidential campaign primaries, but he received far more "free" media publicity.

Why was Trump so successful in gaining publicity? And what other costs may have been associated with obtaining the coverage?

organic and locally grown foods, which means the logistics of packing and shipping interact with the appeal of the product itself. Food items are also marketed to restaurants and not just end consumers. Runners can order running shoes on Zappos, and they can return them for free, but many still prefer to go to an actual bricks-and-mortar store to try the shoes on and get personal advice from store staff before making a purchase.

That said, the internet has opened many new markets, and dramatically transformed others. Where do you buy music (if you buy music at all)? Probably not at a record store. At one time most music was purchased in the form of tapes and disks, and people went to record stores to buy albums. Now most music is purchased digitally. This has changed the entire economic system of the music industry, and it has changed how music is marketed too. Rather than focusing on how many CDs to burn and how to get the right number of those disks to the right stores where they will sell and to the right DJs who might play them on the radio, modern music marketers pay closer attention to online downloads, playlist apps and subscription streaming services. With digital media, the point of sale is most often online through sites like Amazon, iTunes or eBay.

In marketing, like public relations, selecting the right channels is an important skill. Marketers choose channels of distribution to support their sales efforts. For media products like music, movies, books and news, the channels for delivery and the channels for communication are often one

Publicity
Unpaid media coverage, or the practice of deliberately planning and producing information and activities to attract this coverage.

Third-party credibility
Assumption that information delivered from an independent source is seen as more objective and believable than information from a source with a vested interest in persuasion.

and the same. You may use an e-book reader such as a Kindle or iPad to find your next novel, purchase it and read it.

PROMOTION

If channels of distribution are the key to *place* in the marketing mix, channels of communication are the key to *promotion*. Ask a marketer what he thinks of public relations, and he will probably say he loves it as long as public relations people are not competing for control of his budget. From a marketer's perspective, public relations, like advertising, is a great tool for promotion.

Through the sales-focused lens of the marketing mix, public relations is sometimes reduced to tactics such as **publicity**. As a tool for both marketing and public relations, publicity can be defined broadly as activity designed to draw media attention. Publicity can be compared to advertising in three major ways: cost, control and credibility.

In terms of *cost*, advertisers pay to guarantee media space, while publicity entails unpaid media coverage. Publicity happens when an organization, person, product or service is covered as part of a news story, editorial, feature article, interview or any other news format in broadcast, print or online media. In this sense, publicity is "free," but there are many other costs in gaining good publicity including staff salaries, production of multimedia content, planning and hosting special events, and managing an organization in a way that makes it newsworthy in the first place.

Advertisers get to *control* the message that they present in the media space that they buy. Promoters using publicity cede that control to editors, TV producers, journalists, analysts, bloggers and any other third parties who bring news to audiences and publics.

Promoters promote. Advocates advocate. Salespeople sell. That's what they are supposed to do. Independent journalists, on the other hand, are expected to consider other perspectives on the story. If you send a tech writer a sample of your new smartphone-enabled door lock with a news release about the product launch, she may rave about it in her column or on her blog. Or she may test it against competing devices and report that your product stinks in comparison. Or—and this is probably the most common response to attempts at publicity—she may just ignore you altogether. This is all part of media relations, which will be discussed more in Chapter 5.

Because advertisers pay to communicate the message, they may appear to have less *credibility*. One reason for giving up control of the message is that good publicity benefits from **third-party credibility**. If you (first party) are trying to persuade a potential customer (second party) to buy your product, the independent reporting of a third party may help your case. Of course you think your product is great, and if you buy ad space you're going to use it to say so! Consumers understand that. But when independent sources—such as tweeters, magazine columnists or newspaper reporters—present your product in a positive light as part of a tweet, column or news story, their opinions might carry more weight for the very reason that they don't come from the same party who is trying to profit from product sales.

Third-party credibility is not necessarily a law of nature. Research has shown that publicity isn't always more persuasive than advertising, but the general idea stands that publicity brings something to the mix that advertising doesn't. Even though publicity is not free, there are times when it is certainly more economical in reaching customers than advertising, and good publicity has the added benefit of being delivered by a source *independent* of your organization.

Marketers also use **word-of-mouth promotion**. The Word of Mouth Marketing Association (WOMMA) keeps its definition simple: "any business action that earns a customer recommendation."[14] The third-party idea applies here too, except with word of mouth, the third party is more likely to be someone the customer knows and trusts on a more personal level. When you get information on a product or a brand from your friends chatting in class or posting on Instagram, that's word of mouth. When you turn around and share that information with others, you become the third party. WOMMA advocates word-of-mouth marketing that is:

1. *Credible:* Marketing messages flow from businesses to customers and from customers to other customers and are honest and authentic.

2. *Respectful:* Businesses are transparent and earn consumer trust regarding privacy matters.

3. *Social:* WOM marketers encourage and engage in conversations about their products by actively listening and responding online and offline.

4. *Measurable:* WOM programs are well-defined, monitored and evaluated in gauging success.

5. *Repeatable:* A business repeats its WOM success over and over again to the point where it becomes a "truly talkable brand."[15]

Integration

Professional communicators must understand the differences among communication functions. As media systems converge, however, the lines between public relations, advertising and marketing—as everyone else sees them—blur.

Is the Lowe's pinboard on Pinterest a tool for marketing or public relations? If Sam's Chowder House in Half Moon Bay, California, pays to promote its Facebook posts and sees a 19 percent increase in restaurant

Word-of-mouth promotion
Passing of information and recommendations from person to person.

Word-of-mouth marketing should be credible, respectful, social, measurable and repeatable.

guests as a result, is that advertising or public relations?[16] When American Eagle's lingerie and apparel brand Aerie launched "The Real You Is Sexy" campaign to promote positive body images and encouraged users to post to Instagram or Twitter using #aeriereal to be featured on the brand's sites, was that public relations or marketing?[17] What about paying a Kardashian to retweet your content? Or the LEGO YouTube channel—do you consider that a tool for public relations or marketing?

These may be important questions for the sponsoring organizations as they budget for specific departments, but from a consumer's perspective, a brand should speak with one consistent voice. As consumers, we may understand that an organization is responsible for the communication, but we usually don't spend much time thinking about whether the communication is coming from an advertising or marketing or public relations department, or even from other consumers. This consistency and seamlessness in the minds of consumers and publics is a key outcome of effective integrated communication.

Integrated Marketing Communication

As a customer, you probably have a pretty clear idea how you feel about, say, your local grocery store. This feeling, or attitude, is based on your points of contact with the store, its products and its brand. Sure, you're influenced by your previous shopping trips there, but also the coupons they mail you, advertisements you've seen on TV, the prices they charge, conversations with friends who worked there, a donation they made to your club, events they have sponsored, the way they let little leaguers sell candy bars out front, whether or not they buy produce from local farmers, their new app for your smartphone, and their membership card program. Whether or not you shop at the store depends on your beliefs and attitudes about the store, and in your mind that "clear idea" of how you feel is based on countless factors. As a customer, you don't lose sleep over what was public relations, marketing or advertising. But for the people promoting the store and its sales, a major challenge is to coordinate all of these points of communication as smoothly and effectively as possible.

In generating sales revenue, **integrated marketing communication** is key. At times public relations tactics may be applied in support of advertising, marketing or sales promotion. At other times, the tools of advertising and marketing may be used as tools for public relations. In either case, effective convergence of organizational communication and management functions means smooth integration from the perspective of the organization's publics.

In the early 1990s, at the dawn of this digital age of participatory media, Bob Lauterborn called for a shift of thinking about the functions of advertising, marketing and related communication functions. Lauterborn, a former advertising executive for industry giants like General Electric and International Paper Co. was an early proponent of integration. He recognized how the shifting landscape of media was changing the nature of communication between organizations and their customers: "In the days of

Integrated marketing communication
Strategic coordination of communication functions such as marketing, advertising and publicity to achieve a consistent concept in consumers' minds.

'Father Knows Best,' it all seemed so simple. The advertiser developed a product, priced it to make a profit, placed it on the retail shelf and promoted it to a pliant, even eager consumer."[18] With the rise of digital media, consumer options for interaction with organizations increased. Communicators needed to think differently about the people with whom they were attempting to communicate. Those pushing for integrated communication advocated an outside-in approach that started with people rather than products. In response to the four P's, Lauterborn introduced the four C's.

CONSUMER

Consumer wants and needs should replace "product." "You can't sell whatever you can make any more. You can only sell what someone specifically wants to buy. The feeding frenzy is over; the fish are out of school," Lauterborn wrote in *Advertising Age* in 1990. The rise of mass media in human history accompanied the rise of mass production and consumption. As innovations of the Industrial Revolution made it easier for manufacturers to produce massive quantities of products (picture automobile assembly lines or truckloads of cases of identical cans of beer) mass media provided appropriate channels for promoting those goods (picture high-speed newspaper presses or Super Bowl–sized TV audiences). Henry Ford's famous quote sums up the relationship between the mass producer and his publics: "Any customer can have a car painted any colour that he wants so long as it is black."[19]

Of course mass production and mass communication still define much of our world, but what Lauterborn and others noticed about the role of consumers changing in the 1980s and 1990s has only accelerated in this millennium.

Mass production led to mass promotion via mass media during the Industrial Revolution.

How has the relationship between organizations and the consumers they market to changed?

COST

Cost to satisfy wants and needs should replace "price." Beyond just dollars and cents that people pay for goods and services are many other costs. What are they giving up to make the purchase? How much time does it take? Psychological factors come into play too. Lauterborn mentioned the costs of conscience and guilt. The dialogue of the satirical TV series *Portlandia* presents the polar opposite of Henry Ford's example in modern-era markets:

> *Waitress: If you have any questions about the menu, please let me know.*
> *Female diner: I guess I do have a question about the chicken. If you can just tell us a little more about it?*
> *Waitress: The chicken is a heritage breed, woodland-raised chicken that's been fed a diet of sheep's milk, soy and hazelnuts.*
> *Male diner: And this is local?*
> *Waitress: Yes, absolutely.*
> *Male diner: I'm going to ask you just one more time, and it's local?*
> *Waitress: It is.*
> *Female diner: Is that USDA Organic, or Oregon Organic, or Portland Organic?*
> *Waitress: It's just all-across-the-board organic.*
> *Male diner: The hazelnuts, these are local?*
> *Female diner: And how big is the area where the chickens are able to roam free? . . .*

The questioning continues until the waitress leaves and comes back with the chicken's papers. ("His name was Colin.")[20] The humor in this sketch comes from its kernel of truth about the increasing level of responsiveness to and understanding of consumer wants and needs required to compete in modern consumer-centered marketplaces.

CONVENIENCE

Convenience to buy should replace "place." Our concept of marketplaces has followed a similar historical cycle as media and manufacturing. The local food movement is a throwback to times before the Industrial Revolution. Back then, if you didn't raise your own chickens or grow your own vegetables, you probably interacted with the farmer who did. People bought shoes from cobblers and not mall outlets. The Industrial Revolution added convenience in some ways, but most of that convenience was driven from the supply side. Supermarkets and big-box stores stand as evidence of that. Nonetheless, there are limits to what you as a consumer can find by going to a bricks-and-mortar Walmart, Gap or Target store, and driving there to see what's available seems more and more inconvenient. "People don't have to go anyplace anymore," said Lauterborn, describing the era of catalogs, credit cards and phone orders in 1990 that would soon become the era of Zappos and Zillow, eBay and Etsy.

COMMUNICATION

Communication should replace "promotion." Perhaps this is the most profound change suggested. In *The Cluetrain Manifesto: The End of Business as Usual*, internet visionaries Doc Searls and David Weinberger painted a nostalgic picture of early markets as real places "filled with people, not abstractions or statistical aggregates" that were alive with interpersonal conversations. Those conversations, they argued, were interrupted by the industrial era. Searls and Weinberger welcomed a return to richer, less promotional, interaction between people afforded by the internet and social media, "where markets are getting more connected and more powerfully vocal every day."[21] With the growth of social media, other hybrids of journalism and marketing-related functions have arisen.

Hybrid Functions

It is no secret that one of the most common career paths for public relations people leads through a newsroom of some sort—a career track that dates back to Ivy Lee (Chapter 2). Some of the most skilled and influential people working in public relations have worked as journalists, and many college programs in public relations share academic space and curricula with journalism. Experience working with and training alongside journalists helps tremendously with the media-relations aspect of public relations.

You know those harsh deadlines and ridiculous penalties for factual errors in your writing assignments in school? Those really do help train you for the "real world" of public relations. If you take a news writing class or work at your college newspaper or intern at a TV news station, you are also making contacts and building working relationships with people in the media who may help you throughout your career. Learning the news business and its core values and ethics gives you a tacit sense of where the line between journalism and public relations is drawn. Yet, even if you never work in the news media—and many of the best public relations people have not—understanding newsworthiness and practicing storytelling are important for success in your job in public relations.

The most effective public relations people have always been good storytellers. Good stories, told well, make complex organizations and ideas understandable. That kind of communication helps build and maintain relationships between organizations and publics. Advertisers and marketers have always endeavored to tell stories too, but their channels have been constrained to scarce paid space, and their focus has traditionally been tied to sales and customer loyalty. The concurrent trends of integrated communication strategy and increased channels for communication have set the stage for some interesting hybrids.

In **content marketing**, organizations develop media content to attract audiences and interact with publics. The content may be narrative

Content marketing
Development and sharing of media content to appeal to consumers as part of an indirect marketing strategy in which consumers are drawn primarily to media content instead of directly to the product being marketed.

Good stories, told well, make complex organizations and ideas understandable.

stories, videos, photo memes, blogs, statistics or infographics, but the idea is to make it interesting and engaging enough that people will seek it, consume it, and share it for its own information or entertainment value rather than see it as an interruption to some other media experience. People are bombarded with unrequested advertising and marketing messages all day every day, and they work hard to avoid and ignore them with DVR fast-forwarding, spam filters and ad blockers. Content marketing is a counter-tactic, but not an adversarial one. Instead of being pushier, content marketers work to draw people to them on their own accord; this is also called **inbound marketing**. According to the Content Marketing Institute, "The essence of this content strategy is the belief that if we, as businesses, deliver consistent, ongoing valuable information to buyers, they ultimately reward us with their business and loyalty."[22]

By most definitions, the goal of content marketing is still pretty much straight marketing. The "targets" are still labeled customers, buyers and audiences, but the fact that content marketing involves organizational storytelling and communication engagement that likely reverberates well beyond sales makes it an important point of integration in an organization's communication efforts. Red Bull is a prime example. As *Mashable* tech writer James O'Brien put it, "Red Bull is a publishing empire that also happens to sell a beverage."[23]

Case Study

Red Bull's Content Marketing Strategy

I'm trying to write a book here, and Red Bull is making it really hard for me to stay focused. I just opened www.redbull.com to do some research, and I found myself seven minutes into a video of snowboarder Jeff Moore, watching him pull a front-side 360 off a three-story parking garage before being chased away by the building's security crew. I even had to skip an "ad" for Microsoft OneDrive to get to the video "content" on Red Bull's embedded YouTube channel. I can't tell the video series from the advertising from the marketing from the public relations. They've got fantastic photography, incredible videos, sharply written feature stories and inspiring blogs by extreme athletes. Not only do they have the obligatory Facebook, Twitter, Google+, Instagram, YouTube and Pinterest buttons, but the content is actually something I might want to share with my friends on these networks (or in my book-writing as with the picture of surfer Carissa Moore). From a strategy standpoint, though, the most interesting part is that there is *no mention whatsoever* of the Red Bull beverage product unless I seek it out. In the far upper-right corner of the web page there are two small links for "Products and company" and "Shop." That's content marketing.

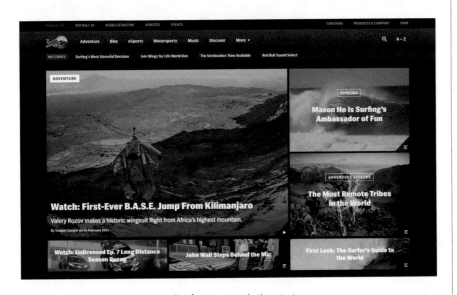

Red Bull's website is a prime example of content marketing strategy.

How does the website help sell their energy drink? Is that the website's main purpose?

The term **brand journalism** describes a similar strategy, but as the name indicates, the primary focus is on journalistic skills. Critics of content marketing are concerned that the practice will lead to backlash as the mad dash to provide content in support of sales will lead to poorer quality content and strategy. According to Christopher Penn of SHIFT Communications, "As content marketers struggle to keep up with the demands of creating content all the time that's high quality, increasingly they'll look to professionals who can maintain that pace without breaking a sweat—journalists."[24]

Chrysler Group LLC followed this strategy when it hired Ed Garsten, a veteran journalist with 20 years at CNN as correspondent, bureau chief, anchor and producer, and experience as a national auto writer at the Associated Press and General Motors beat writer for *The Detroit News*. As head of Chrysler Digital Media, Garsten led a team that handled the Chrysler media website, broadcast communications, social media and video production. "Most of us on the 8-person team have had actual television news and/or production experience giving us the background and skills to launch an in-house video operation for Chrysler Communications," blogged Garsten in describing the operation.[25] While Garsten and his team clearly brought journalistic talent to the job, the broader strategy is still one of marketing and public relations.

Brand journalism
Application of journalistic skills to produce news content for an organization to communicate directly with its publics without going through a third-party news organization.

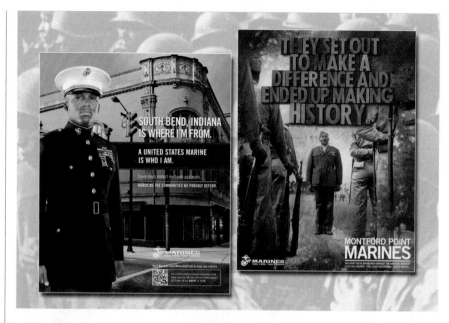

Sometimes ads are purchased to do more than sell goods or services.

How do these advertisements serve a public relations function?

How Public Relations Is Different at Its Core

In Chapter 1, we defined public relations as the management of relationships between an organization and its publics. In Chapter 2, we saw how public relations differs from journalism in that public relations people ethically advocate on behalf of their organizations, while journalists seek to report without bias favoring any one particular organization. In this chapter, we find that advertising and marketing overlap considerably with public relations. Many of the same tools and skills apply to all three endeavors, and all three work to promote an organization and its products, services and ideas, but public relations differs in at least three ways: in its organization, publics and relationships—the three main components of its core definition.

Organization (Beyond Offerings)

Marketing and advertising are primarily concerned with promoting an organization's offerings, and most often those offerings are products and services that the organization sells or exchanges to remain profitable. Public relations also promotes an organization's offerings, but more important, *public relations promotes the organization as a whole*. There are exceptions to this general rule such as institutional advertising, which is paid advertising space that promotes an organization more than any of its specific products or

When an ad serves an institutional goal beyond sales and marketing, it is acting as a tool for public relations.

services. However, when an ad serves an institutional goal beyond sales and marketing, it is acting as a tool for public relations.

Publics (Beyond Audiences)

In this chapter's discussion of advertising and marketing, you may have noticed that the groups of people who are targeted for advertising and marketing are referred to as audiences and not publics. The term **target audience** implies a carefully identified group of people who are chosen in strategy development for their propensity to buy an organization's products, services or ideas. Marketers pay for advertising in the newspaper to reach readers who might buy yogurt or lease private jets. They buy ads on FM radio, Pandora or Spotify to reach listeners who may purchase software. They sell insurance to Facebook users and medicine to TV news viewers. Readers, listeners, users and viewers are all best described as audiences in this context because their primary relationship to the organization is one of financial exchange.

In advertising and marketing, organizations want to persuade audiences to buy stuff. These groups also fit the definition of publics because customers and consumers certainly have an effect on organizations, and organizations certainly have an effect on them. However, public relations people are responsible for building and maintaining relationships with publics even when the publics may never buy or sell anything from or to the organization. Neighbors, legislators, employees, students, volunteers, competitors, voters, taxpayers, disaster victims, veterans, beachgoers and bicyclists may all be publics for certain organizations in circumstances in which no financial exchange is involved. The term *public* implies a more balanced two-way relationship than the term *audience*—one that is not predicated on the probability of a direct profit.

Relationships (Beyond Sales)

In advertising and marketing, relationships are a means to an end, and that end is usually sales. In public relations, *maintaining relationships is an end in itself to the degree that an organization's success or failure depends on healthy working relationships with all sorts of publics* beyond customers and those in the product supply chain. Media relations is a good example. Public relations people nurture relationships with journalists and editors in local, national and global media. Yes, favorable publicity is a common goal, but the scope and duration of the relationship is much greater than any one promotional strategy. Because publicity in reputable news outlets cannot be bought like advertising, public relations people have to work to understand journalists and their interests in order to understand how to provide useful information to journalists as they do their work. Public relations people also need to build trust with the media.

Publicity isn't always welcome. During crises, public relations people work under great stress to preserve their organization's interests and resolve

> **Target audience**
> Group of people strategically identified for their propensity to consume an organization's products, services or ideas.

> Building and maintaining relationships with publics is essential, even if they never buy from or sell anything to your organization.

> The greater the trust between public relations people and journalists, the better each party will be able to perform during tense times.

problems, while reporters are out to report what the organization has done wrong. Their roles are at odds, yet they still rely on each other. Public relations practitioners need journalists to help them communicate with their publics. Journalists need the public relations people to help them understand what happened. The greater the amount of mutual trust, the better each party will be able to perform during tense times. As we'll see in later chapters, trust is one important dimension of relationships, and news media are just one type of public with whom public relations people must maintain relationships.

Voices from the Field

Bill Imada

BILL IMADA is founder, chairman and chief collaboration officer of the IW Group, a fully integrated marketing communications firm that specializes in the growing multicultural markets in the United States. With more than 25 years of experience in marketing, public relations, advertising and training, Imada and his company continue to represent some of the top brands, including American Airlines, The Coca-Cola Company, Godiva Chocolatiers, McDonald's USA, MetLife, Nissan North America, Pacific Gas & Electric Company, Toyota, Walmart Stores, Walt Disney Imagineering, Warner Bros. Pictures, Verizon and many others. The IW Group also represents a number of prominent governmental agencies and nonprofit organizations.

How do you feel about the merging of agencies into bigger and bigger conglomerates? Are clients being served better?

Mergers and acquisitions have occurred for decades, and we will continue to see agencies of all sizes consolidate and reposition themselves regularly. IW Group was approached more than a decade ago by all of the major communications and marketing conglomerates. I opted to go with True North who agreed to allow me to maintain a controlling interest and to manage and operate the agency as a smaller,

niche-focused firm. Not long after I sold a minority stake in IW Group, Interpublic Group purchased True North. To IPG's credit, they continue to allow me to run the agency independently.

Are clients better served by bigger and more complicated conglomerates?

Yes and no. For large, multinational companies, having one entity manage, direct and fulfill their needs in regions around the world can be more efficient and effective. Yet, many of these global firms don't always deliver on good customer service, and offices tend to run autonomously, which may discourage collaboration.

How about smaller firms or in-house communication operations? What kinds of challenges do they face in an age of convergence?

Smaller firms must deal with rising labor costs, rapidly changing digital and social media platforms, and a more demanding workforce. Although smaller firms offer greater flexibility and mobility, it has been difficult to match the salaries, benefits and extra perks a larger and better financed firm can provide. Smaller firms also have to compete with other communications and marketing firms, in-house agencies, nimble two-person boutiques, short-term contractors and student-inspired on-campus agencies that have lower operational and overhead costs. As a result, the smaller agencies have to offer their employees an experience they cannot get at a larger firm: for example, working with a more intimate team of colleagues on different accounts covering a wider array of industries, ensuring a closer and more direct working relationship with agency clients, and offering the opportunity for co-workers to create strong emotional bonds.

Do you see public relations as fundamentally different from marketing and advertising?

No. The lines blurred years ago. In today's world, advertising agencies have PR and marketing teams and vice versa. Advertising agency leaders, who once turned their noses up whenever public relations was discussed as a legitimate profession, now realize they must have a public relations and marketing strategy folded into everything they do. And, more and more clients expect agencies to do PR, marketing and advertising. IW Group was established 25 years ago as a PR-focused agency. We realized after two years that we needed to diversify our business. Today, if we were to silo PR at our agency, it would only represent 15 percent of our business portfolio.

Do you see cultural convergence [when various forms of culture are exchanged, combined, converted and adapted] as a positive in global societies? What's public relations' role in cultural convergence?

Cultural convergence to me is like saying: "We need to level the playing field." The playing field will never be level; at least not in my lifetime. Every person on this planet will retain some aspect of his or her cultural heritage regardless of what happens in the world. Our agency is multicultural and includes people of different races, ethnicities, views and mindsets. Although we initially focus on life's many intersections that bring us together (e.g., food, music, entertainment, etc.), as PR and advertising professionals, we also see our individual and cultural uniqueness as one of our core value propositions. The growth of digital media hasn't changed this; rather, it has placed an accent on them. Today, it is cool to be unique.

Brand journalism and content marketing—are they anything new?

No. This has been going on for more than a decade. An example of content marketing includes "advertorials." And we have been using forms of brand journalism for years. In places such as Asia, there has always been an imaginary line between journalism and branding.

If you were invited to speak to a public relations class, what would you most want to discuss?

Diversifying diversity would be one. Diversity isn't just about race and gender; rather, it includes diversity of heart and mind, spirit, regional immersion, viewpoints, sexual orientation, socio-economic conditions and so much more. I also like to talk about "changing the conversation." We have a tendency to use idioms and sayings to guide our thinking, such as: "We shouldn't reinvent the wheel," or "We should think outside of the box." But, sayings like these tend to inhibit our ability to grow, innovate and push the boundaries that we are forced to live in at work and in many of our communities. It is critical for students and faculty to really push intellectual curiosity, including curiosity of people, places, experiences, ideologies and more.

Any specific advice for the next generation of public relations practitioners?

"Taste the street." A young woman, many years ago, asked me what I thought about the name of her new Vietnamese restaurant: "Taste of Saigon Street." Saigon, once the capital of South Vietnam and today known as Ho Chi Minh City, is very crowded, noisy and chaotic with the grit and grime of any city in the region. When I first heard this restaurant name, I thought to myself: "No American diner would ever want to eat a meal in a restaurant named after a dirty thoroughfare in a place like Saigon." When I shared this concern, the young woman said: "Mr. Imada, I grew up on the streets of Saigon. I remember fondly the smells, sounds, banter and life along the busy streets of my home country. The street represents my values and my soul. I want to bring those flavors to the people of America." There are many ways to advance PR. Clearly, one way is to get a flavor for all that is around us. Sometimes we miss that taste without even realizing it.

Ethics: Free Flow of Information

On September 11, 2013, *The New York Times* published an opinion-editorial letter by Russian President Vladimir Putin. "Recent events surrounding Syria have prompted me to speak directly to the American people and their political leaders," he wrote. "It is important to do so at a time of insufficient communication between our societies." This was intercultural communication at the highest level. After outlining Russia's perspective on how to respond to the crisis of chemical weapons use in Syria, Putin wrote,

> *My working and personal relationship with President Obama is marked by growing trust. I appreciate this. I carefully studied his address to the nation on Tuesday. And I would rather disagree with a case he made on American exceptionalism, stating that the United States' policy is "what makes America different. It's what makes us exceptional." It is extremely dangerous to encourage people to see themselves as exceptional, whatever the motivation.*[26]

Putin's sentiments, particularly the part about American exceptionalism, immediately provoked responses from across the United States via mainstream media and social media alike. U.S. Senator and Chair of the Senate Foreign Relations Committee Robert Menendez said in an interview on CNN, "I almost wanted to vomit." The video clip was posted on CNN's "The Lead" blog where the video could be retrieved as digital information just like Putin's words themselves could spread from www.nytimes.com to anywhere in the world.

The convergence of media technology and culture was at the center of this international exchange, and public relations people played a direct role. As revealed on a BuzzFeed politics page, Ketchum public relations had placed the Putin letter in *The New York Times*. American public relations firms commonly represent foreign governments in the marketplace of ideas, and the Putin letter certainly carried a voice in that marketplace, but Ketchum's role still raised eyebrows. *ProPublica*, a nonprofit, public interest news website, had investigated Ketchum's business relationship with Russia less than a year before the Putin letter and found that Ketchum had "placed pro-Russia op-eds in American publications by businesspeople and others without disclosing the role of the Russian government." They reported that Ketchum was paid $1.9 million to represent Russia for a six-month period ending in May 2013.[27]

Transparency is certainly an issue to be discussed in the context of convergence. It presents yet another apparent paradox. On one hand, convergence has made identifying original sources of information a more complicated task. On the other hand, the distributed nature of communication makes transparency more of an imperative for effective relationship building. If there is a single word to describe how the culture of emerging media differs from traditional mass media, it is *participation*.

Participatory media allow people to not only consume information but to report and disseminate it as well. Blogging journalists who interact and collaborate with their readers as sources are taking advantage of the participatory nature of social media to do their research and to tell their stories. Cultural convergence in a digital media environment means that people from around the world can work together to participate in the news cycle by pooling resources to investigate stories. Public relations in this era means engaging participatory culture rather than fighting it.

When a huge public relations firm represents one of the largest nations on Earth as its client, economic convergence is definitely part of the story. Cultural convergence is too. In this case cultures clashed on two levels: first, the tension between U.S. and Russian views of America's role in world politics as expressed by each country's leaders; second, the friction between layers of media. It is not at all unusual for public relations agencies to serve as liaisons between mainstream news media like *The New York Times* and those with important opinions like President Putin, while on social media there is more of an expectation that people will speak directly on their own behalf without hidden parties in the mix.

"We've kind of hit a wall," President Barack Obama said on his way to Russia in September 2013 referring to differences of opinion on chemical weapons issues in Syria.

What sort of conflicts of interest may arise when public relations firms represent national governments?

When asked directly, *The New York Times* did not deny or try to cover anything up: "The op-ed came through the PR firm (Ketchum) and went through the normal editing process," answered *New York Times* spokesperson Eileen Murphy when questioned by the online site *BuzzFeed*.[28]

In response to *ProPublica*'s inquiry, Ketchum's Jackie Burton said the action was normal: "Consistent with Ketchum's policies and industry standards, we clearly state that we represent the Russian Federation."

As discussed in Chapter 2, advocacy is the very first item listed in the PRSA Code of Ethics under professional values: "We serve the public interest by acting as responsible advocates for those we represent. We provide a voice in the marketplace of ideas, facts, and viewpoints to aid informed public debate."[29] But the PRSA code also calls for disclosure of information: "Open communication fosters informed decision making in a democratic society." Both ideas are central to the *free flow of information* in society. In 2015, Ketchum stopped representing the Russian Federation in the United States and Europe "amid continuing tensions between the country and Western governments."[30] But should Ketchum have done more to proactively disclose their work for Putin when they had Russia as a client?

Other provisions of conduct in the PRSA code besides the free flow of information may apply too: *competition*, *conflicts of interests* and *enhancing the profession* (see Appendix B). Did Ketchum run afoul of any of these? Have social media and online news sites like *ProPublica* and *BuzzFeed* changed standards for disclosure, or simply made disclosure more achievable?

In Case You Missed It

To fully understand public relations, you have to be able to zoom in on specific strategies and tactics and then zoom out to see the big picture of convergence and integration. Here are some snapshots from the different focal points in this chapter.

- Public relations people must understand other dimensions of convergence beyond the technological ones.

- If you place a hashtag in a TV ad, you should know what will happen when TV viewers jump platforms from their TVs to other screens.

- Before diving headfirst into integration, understand how public relations differs from advertising and marketing in its goals.

- Analytics help track behavior as users move from initial exposure to some target behavior, such as making an online purchase.

- Word-of-mouth marketing should be credible, respectful, social, measurable and repeatable.

- Good stories, told well, make complex organizations and ideas understandable.

- When an ad serves an institutional goal beyond sales and marketing, it is acting as a tool for public relations.

- Building and maintaining relationships with publics is essential, even if those publics never buy from or sell anything to your organization.

- The more trust between public relations people and journalists, the better each party will be able to perform during tense times.

SUMMARY

3.1 Define different forms of convergence.
Rather than being a single trend, convergence is better thought of as a number of processes that can be defined separately, including technological, cultural, economic and professional convergence.

3.2 Analyze how convergence affects public relations.
Technological convergence affects the communication tools and tactics public relations people use. Cultural convergence means that understanding the interaction of organizational cultures and public cultures is an increasingly important task with more global contexts than ever before. As firms merge, economic convergence affects services on both a local and global level. Professional convergence is what happens when those services (and the jobs of the people who provide them) are integrated.

3.3 Discuss how functions of advertising and marketing may be integrated with public relations.

When integration is done right, advertising and marketing support public relations, and vice versa. In the minds of publics, an organization's management and communication efforts should be consistent.

3.4 Distinguish public relations from advertising and marketing.

Public relations is different from advertising and marketing in that it focuses on the overall relationship between the whole organization and many of its publics. Products are only part of what is promoted. Customers are only one public. Relationships are about much more than sales and profit.

3.5 Discuss public relations' role in the free flow of information in society.

Public relations practitioners advocate for organizations in the marketplace of ideas. Advocacy is a central value in democratic societies, but public relations people must remain transparent about their role and purpose.

DISCUSSION QUESTIONS

1. Do you have more or fewer media devices now than you did two years ago? How has technological convergence changed your day-to-day media use?

2. Search for a familiar brand's website or social media presence as it appears in another country (for example, "McDonald's India," "McDonald's Facebook India," "Red Bull Japan" or "Greenpeace Argentina"). What evidence of cultural convergence do you see? Is the cultural sharing working in both directions?

3. Describe an advertisement you've recently observed that does not seem to be selling a particular product or service. Who is the ad "marketing" to and why?

4. Would you rather work for a public relations agency/department or an integrated communication agency/department? Explain your preference.

5. Do you think a public relations firm in one country should represent the foreign government of another country during times of conflict between the two nations? Discuss your ethical reasoning.

KEY TERMS

CHAPTER 4

Relationship Management

As Kermit the Frog sang, "It's not easy being green." How does Coca-Cola balance its main business of selling soda with efforts to promote healthy living?

KEY LEARNING OUTCOMES

4.1 Apply knowledge of interpersonal relationships to organization-public relationships.

4.2 Discuss the concept of relationships as central to public relations.

4.3 Identify broad categories of stakeholders with whom public relations people build and maintain relationships.

4.4 Define different areas of public relations practice by identifying the publics with

whom relationships are built and maintained.

4.5 Evaluate corporate social responsibility as a strategy for balancing the interests of diverse publics.

RELATED UNIVERSAL ACCREDITATION BOARD COMPETENCY AREAS

1.7 DIVERSITY • **2.2** ETHICAL BEHAVIOR • **6.1** RELATIONSHIP BUILDING
6.3 INTERNAL STAKEHOLDERS • **6.4** MEDIA RELATIONS

Congratulations! You made it. You're the vice president of public relations. You're seated in a bright glass conference room, taking in a sweeping view of the city skyline with your counterparts in legal, accounting and marketing. You've earned a coveted seat at the proverbial management table. But the mood darkens a bit when the CEO enters, takes a seat with the sun at her back and says she needs to trim some expenses. She then asks everyone to justify their budgets.

The general counsel (legal) explains how his unit is winning lawsuits and keeping the organization in compliance with various laws to avoid costly penalties. The chief financial officer (CFO) presents impressive budget figures and forecasts. The chief marketing officer (CMO) draws a direct link between his department and sales revenue.

It's your turn. What do you say?

This is somewhat of a trick question because much of what you do in public relations is done in collaboration with the others. Excellent public relations helps resolve disputes before they become crises or end up in litigation. The CFO relies on public relations for help communicating in a timely and accurate manner with all financial stakeholders, including shareholders, employees and analysts. And as we saw in Chapter 3, public relations and marketing work together in support of sales and profit. But what does public relations do in its own right? In public relations, you manage the relationships that all of the other departments depend upon. This is your time to shine.

This chapter builds on a broader definition of public relations as the *management of mutually beneficial relationships with publics*. Relationships built around news, commerce and contentious issues are all part of the field, and this chapter discusses jobs in those areas of public relations. At the highest levels of organizational management, however, relationships with all of an organization's stakeholders must be managed simultaneously and in balance. Corporate social responsibility is one strategy for reaching that balance, and this chapter includes an illustrative case from one of the world's largest companies. But regardless of the size or mission of your organization, the ethical, harmonious and simultaneous management of all those relationships may be one of the toughest jobs there is.

Managing Relationships

If we want to understand organization-public relationships and explain how those relationships are beneficial, we have to think about real people and how they interact with one another. Starting in the 1980s, public relations educators and practitioners began to turn their focus from publicity to relationships. In 1984, the same year that Grunig and Hunt published *Managing Public Relations*, Professor Mary Ann Ferguson presented a key paper calling for public relations scholars to focus on relationships as the central idea for the field.

In the decades that followed, organization-public relationships became a more prominent topic for research and for understanding public relations in general. In 2000, Professors John Ledingham and Stephen Bruning published *Public Relations as Relationship Management*, a text that advocated turning away from the idea of public relations as mainly "a means of generating favorable publicity" and embracing "the notion that relationships ought to be at the core of public relations scholarship."[1] The ensuing shift in thinking rose concurrently with the rise of new ways for publics to communicate with organizations. Social media emerged as alternatives to mass media at the same time that we moved from seeing public relations as an overwhelmingly mass-mediated phenomenon to a more conversational, relationship-building one.

In heralding the rise of **participatory media**, social media enthusiasts welcomed a return to the more direct way of communicating that was common before industrialization and mass communication drove a wedge between organizations and their publics. They refocused on the importance of conversations in the marketplaces where organizations and publics meet.

For some insights on how to understand relationships between organizations and publics, scholars turned to interpersonal communication research. They sought to discover if what worked in relationships between spouses or between doctors and patients, for instance, might help us better understand the strategies that would succeed in organization-public relationships.

This illustration by Felipe Dávalos is of an Aztec marketplace.

How might relationships in digital marketplaces be similar to relationships in ancient marketplaces?

Taking Care of Relationships

Professors Dan Canary and Laura Stafford have studied interpersonal relationships for decades. In the early 1990s they catalogued a number of successful **relational maintenance strategies**, which included the following:

- *Positivity:* expressing favorable attitudes, and interacting with partners in a cheerful, uncritical manner.

- *Openness:* self-disclosure and directly discussing the nature of the relationship including its problems, and willingness to listen.

Participatory media
Media in which publics actively participate in producing and sharing content.

Relational maintenance strategies
Ways of building and sustaining mutually beneficial relationships between organizations and publics.

Exchange relationships
Relationships in which each party gives benefits to the other with the expectation of receiving comparable benefits in return.

Communal relationships
Relationships in which each party gives benefits to the other and a primary motivation for each is the other's benefit.

- *Assurances:* covertly and overtly communicating the importance of the relationship and a desire to continue with the relationship.

- *Social networking:* relying on the support of mutual friends and common affiliations.

- *Sharing tasks:* performing one's responsibilities including routine tasks and chores; in a marriage or partnership, this may include cooking, cleaning and managing finances.

In research reports for the Institute for Public Relations, Professors Linda Hon and James Grunig took these strategies and recommended a shift to focus on public, rather than interpersonal, relationships.

- *Openness* would include disclosures about the nature of the organization and information of value to its publics.

- *Assurances* would include communication that emphasized the importance of publics in the relationship.

- *Social networking* would involve an emphasis on common affiliations between the organization and publics—on social network sites, these links might take the form of shared Twitter followers, LinkedIn connections or mutual likes on Facebook.

- *Sharing tasks* would include things like asking for public support or offering support when appropriate—as when an organization voices its backing for a cause, encourages employees to volunteer, or makes a donation.

Laverne Cox spoke to fans at the Global Citizen Festival, promoting global goals (and raising funds) to protect the environment and end extreme poverty.

What type of relationship between the publics—in this case the Global Citizen organization and festival attendees—does this event support?

Key Outcomes of Relationships

Depending on the specific goals and objectives of organization-public relationships, mutually beneficial relationships may come in many forms. The benefits may come as the result of **exchange relationships**, as when a customer buys a product or service. If the transaction goes well, the company earns sales revenue and the customer receives something of value in return. In investor relations, a publicly held corporation secures capital, and investors get a return by way of dividends or increased value of the shares they own. In contracts and legal actions, specific terms for exchanges are spelled out in detail.

According to Hon and Grunig, **communal relationships** are equally important, if not more important, to public relations people in the long run. "In a communal relationship, both parties provide benefits to the other because they are concerned with the welfare of the other—even when they get nothing in return."[2] Hon and Grunig highlighted four key outcomes of good organization-public relationships:

- *Control mutuality:* although it may be unrealistic to expect steady and perfect symmetry, each side should have some sense of control and be comfortable with the balance of influence.

- *Trust:* Hon and Grunig identified three dimensions of trust: "*integrity:* the belief that an organization is fair and just . . . ; *dependability:* the belief that an organization will do what it says it will do . . . ; and *competence:* the belief that an organization has the ability to do what it says it will do."

- *Satisfaction:* in satisfying relationships both parties have positive expectations and feel like those expectations are being met.

- *Commitment:* is the relationship worth continuing? This question can be asked as a matter of time and effort or in terms of the emotional investment. How much does each party value the relationship relative to competing relationships?

Research has shown that these long-term relational benefits correlate with shorter-term communication effects like the achievement of specific strategic goals and objectives that may be on the table in a meeting with a CEO. That is, the better the long-term relationships you cultivate between your organization and its publics, the more likely you are to be able to achieve your daily, monthly and annual goals. Pursuing communal relationships may not on its own be enough to sustain most organizations in their missions, but when excellent public relations builds and maintains solid relationships in coordination with other organizational units doing their jobs well, the whole organization thrives. Healthy long-term relationships can save organizations money by reducing costs of strikes, boycotts, lawsuits and lost revenues from dissatisfied customers who take their business elsewhere. On the positive side, strong relationships help garner support from donors, legislators, consumers, employees, volunteers and shareholders.

> The better the long-term relationships between your organization and publics, the more likely you are to achieve your goals.

St. Jude Children's Research Hospital has some of the most loyal "fans" of any organization.

With which publics do they maintain relationships? What are some of the outcomes of these relationships?

Organizational-public relationships have many parallels to interpersonal relationships.

How are your relationships with organizations on social media similar to your relationships with friends on social media?

There are two ways to think about interpersonal relationships and organization-public relationships. First, we can think of the interpersonal relationship as an analogy for the organization-public relationship. Relationships between organizations and publics are *like* relationships between individuals. Both require effective communication and mutual understanding. The same kinds of strategies work in both, and the outcomes sought are similar too. These relationships can be observed by asking people about their experiences with an organization as a whole.[3]

Second, we can think of interpersonal relationships *as components of* organization-public relationships. The relationship between the two groups of people is made up of all the interpersonal interactions involved when individuals in organizations communicate with individuals in publics. For example, individuals may *trust* specific people in an organization with whom they've interacted. They may be *satisfied* with the interpersonal exchanges and *committed* to continuing conversations as long as they feel a sense of *mutual control* in the relationship.

Professor Elizabeth Toth pointed out early in the relationship-management literature that interpersonal communication is the foundation for analyzing organization-public relationships. She recommended a focus on relationships between public relations people and all of an organization's constituencies within various contexts.[4] For example, the context of media relations would call for looking at relationships with journalists and editors; the context of internal communications would mean looking at relationships with employees and members; and the context of issues management might mean thinking about communication with individual advocates and activists. Three major contexts for organization-public relationships are news-driven relationships, commerce-driven relationships and issues-driven relationships.

News-Driven Relationships

Sharing news has and always will be an important part of public relations. Whether it is editing a company newsletter, blogging about your organization's current events or working to get coverage in national or international outlets, news is very much the currency of public relations practice.

Media Relations

Think about the term *media*, "the main means of mass communication (especially television, radio, newspapers, and the internet) regarded collectively," according to Oxford Dictionaries.[5] When people speak of the *news media*, they are generally referring to the people who use these channels to write, produce and deliver news—the journalists, bloggers, analysts, editors and producers who report news. Relationships with these people are at the heart of media relations. Sometimes news media come to an organization for information, and other times the organization goes to the news media to get stories out. Over the course of a career in public relations, you will likely find yourself in both situations, often with the same people. The same person whom you pray will attend your organization's groundbreaking today may call you a year from now when your new building has a gas leak.

As public relations executive Peter Himler observed in a 2014 blog post for PRSA, despite the increase in channels for communicating directly with publics, "One look at any PR job board will reveal that media relations remains the single-most sought-after competency by agencies of all stripes and most in-house communications departments."[6] Understanding modern media newsroom operations and the jobs of reporters, editors, bloggers and TV producers is as much a key for career advancement in public relations as it has ever been.

Pitching

Pitching is when public relations practitioners encourage the news media to cover stories involving their organizations. To keep up with industry trends, I subscribe to several e-mail and trade publication lists for public relations. Scarcely a week goes by when one of these sources doesn't include some form of advice on pitching—"Seven Ways to Think Like a Reporter," "Five Reasons Your Pitch Stinks," "How to Pitch TV News Reporters," "Pitching a Broadcast Story? Think Visual," "How NOT to Write a Pitch Letter" and "The Dos and Don'ts of Pitching Journalists on Social Media" are just a few examples. Pitching is one of the most common and challenging tasks that public relations practitioners face. A few themes emerge from these types of advice columns.

KNOW NEWSWORTHINESS

Journalists have to make decisions every day about what qualifies as news. Depending on the size of their news organization and its audience, journalists may receive dozens if not hundreds of pitches for every one news story they actually cover. Although much of the news you see in newspapers, on the web and over the airwaves results from pitches made to journalists, much of it also happens without pitching. A public information officer for the National Park Service may spend a lot of time talking to reporters covering a wildfire, or a sports information director for a university may answer a sports reporter's request to interview a head football

Pitching
When a public relations person approaches a journalist or editor to suggest a story idea.

TABLE 4.1 **ELEMENTS OF NEWSWORTHINESS**

TIMELINESS	We care about "new" news more than "old news."
PROXIMITY	We are interested in stories and events that happen when they are local or hit "closer to home."
CONFLICT AND CONTROVERSY	We are drawn to problems or differences within a community.
HUMAN INTEREST	We relish stories of people overcoming great challenges or rising to the occasion to achieve amazing feats. We also pay attention when cute animals, funny kids or gross facts affect our emotions.
RELEVANCE	We depend on pertinent and applicable information to help us make decisions.

Newsworthiness
Standard used to determine what is worth covering in news media.

coach about a big win. A wildfire or a big win for the hometown team are both *newsworthy*.

Whether journalists find the stories themselves or become aware of them with the help of people working in public relations, **newsworthiness** is the criterion they use to determine what is worth covering as news and what is not. PBS's *Student Reporting Labs* program for aspiring journalists lists these five key elements of newsworthiness: timeliness, proximity, conflict and controversy, human interest and relevance (see Table 4.1).[7] Others include novelty, shock value, impact or magnitude and superlatives such as the first, largest, longest, oldest or most expensive of some category.

Looking at stories in the news media and identifying what makes them newsworthy is usually pretty easy. What's trickier is understanding which news from your organization is newsworthy *from the perspective of journalists and their audiences*. If your CEO adopted three new puppies, it may be timely (happened yesterday), proximal (he is bringing them into the office), controversial (some office staff are allergic to dogs), interesting (they are *soooo* cute!) and relevant (new policy—everyone can bring their pets to work one day a week). By all

When University of Missouri graduate student Jonathan Butler went on a seven-day hunger strike to bring attention to issues of racism at Mizzou, massive social media movements ensued (e.g., #ConcernedStudent1950); the Mizzou football team and coach threatened to go on strike in support; and eventually the University of Missouri system president Tim Wolfe resigned.

Which elements of newsworthiness led to so much media attention in this case?

means, put it in your employee newsletter or tweet about it for your personal networks. But does this "news" belong on tonight's local TV news or in the daily newspaper? How about national news?

The puppy story is a bit of a silly example, but look at the news releases streaming on international services like PRNewswire.com or BusinessWire.com and you'll likely find examples that are even less newsworthy. A medical care management company was nominated for an award in workers' compensation case management,[8] an employee of a "healthy lifestyle company" achieved the rank of "2-star ambassador" within his own organization[9] and a wood composite company announced that it was extending warranty coverage for its decking and railing materials up to five years. All of these news releases were pushed out over international media services in a 20-minute period on a Thursday afternoon.

Of course context is important. If your CEO adopted the puppies as part of the launch of a major new partnership with your local Humane Society, the story may be newsworthy in your community beyond your organization. Likewise, the medical care award, the employee recognition and the extended warranty may be newsworthy in some limited contexts. Newsworthiness is in the eye of the beholder. When you know a journalist and her beat, and you have newsworthy information to present in good form that is important to her readers (viewers, listeners, etc.), you will be set up for a win-win—the mutual benefit of helping the journalist with her job while benefiting your organization by getting its story out. But if you mismatch your news with the journalist, at best you will be ignored and at worst you will lose credibility and damage the relationship for the future.

EMPATHIZE WITH REPORTERS

Finding an appropriate outlet for any story means really understanding the person to whom you are sending the news, and just as important, understanding his or her audience. A famous quote from Sun Tzu's *The Art of War* says, "To know your enemy, you must become your enemy." At the risk of framing the relationship between public relations practitioners and journalists as hostile (it shouldn't be!), we may apply the same general idea. To know the news media, you must become the news media.

Advice from the trade press tells us to consider journalists' deadlines, to understand their business and to answer questions such as "Why do I care?" and "Why now?" from their perspective. In other words, put yourself in their shoes. Experience working in newsrooms certainly helps. But even if you have never worked as a journalist, you can still empathize with what it's like to work on deadline and make an effort to understand the people to whom the journalist delivers the news. Read their news stories, watch their programs and follow their social media accounts; all of these things will help you to better understand their style and the type of news they cover.

Before pitching to reporters, read their news stories, watch their programs and follow their social media accounts to better understand their style and the type of news they cover.

MAKE YOURSELF USEFUL

Good journalists do a tremendous amount of research, and public relations specialists are in a unique position to help with access to an organization's people and information. If you work for a school board, you may be one of the most important sources for information for an education reporter. You may be asked for information on test scores or teacher salaries even when those are not the stories you are hoping to communicate. Knowing what information you can share, and what information you are legally obligated to share, will help you help journalists. Even when you have to decline to share information, for example because it is private personnel data or student information, being open about your constraints will help. Again, there may be no immediate benefit to you or your organization when you work with a journalist on a tough story, but building and maintaining a relationship will likely pay off in the long run with fair coverage and greater receptiveness when you do have positive news to share.

Another way to make yourself useful is to direct reporters to other people within your organization who can help as sources. Don't be offended if journalists want to skip right over you as a source. Remember: Put

Online services like this one help initiate source-reporter relationships.

How might relationships started from "media catching" be different from relationships started with pitching?

yourself in their shoes. If you were writing a news story about school district test scores, would you rather interview a public relations representative or a school board member, principal or teacher?

Interviews and source-reporter relationships can also be initiated more proactively. Many universities maintain experts databases that catalog professors and researchers based on their areas of expertise and their willingness to work with journalists on related stories. The internet has facilitated this on a global level with services like PR Newswire's ProfNet or Vocus's HARO (Help a Reporter Out) that connect reporters with sources. This practice has been called **media catching**.[10] It reverses the traditional flow of pitching from sources to reporters. Instead of public relations people pitching stories to journalists, journalists can post queries online to which any registered user with relevant information or expertise can respond.

While relationships are key to media relations, depending on the nature of your organization or clients, many if not most of your relationships with journalists may be best characterized as exchange relationships. You exchange information or access for news coverage. Especially early in your career, you may not have longstanding relationships with many of the journalists you pitch. Nonetheless, in situations where you haven't worked with a journalist before, knowing newsworthiness, empathizing and making yourself useful will not only help your chances of **story placement**, it also may set the stage for a longer-term professional relationship.

Commerce-Driven Relationships

As we saw in Chapter 3, many of the relationships in public relations are driven by dollars. The most obvious examples are business-to-consumer relationships. Other important relationships driven primarily by commerce include business-to-business relations, employee relations and investor relations.

B2C

B2C, or business to consumer, can describe software, types of organizations, or the relationships between organizations and publics. B2C software usually means e-commerce platforms in which an end user can initiate and complete a transaction online. If you buy an airline ticket from an airline website, order a pair of shorts from a retail store online or purchase software to download, you are working with B2C applications. In the context of the rise of e-commerce as a major sector in world economies, B2C is used to describe companies that sell products or services directly to consumers online. Prior to the dot-com boom, people probably wouldn't have thought to refer to their local bookstore as "B2C," but when Amazon.com rose to success selling books and other products directly to consumers via the internet, the business model was seen as innovative. Amazon, along with countless other companies that have entered the direct-to-consumer market online, are referred to as B2C companies.

Media catching
When journalists post queries online inviting public relations people or others with relevant information or expertise to respond. Public relations people "catch" these opportunities rather than "pitching" story ideas to journalists.

Story placement
The outcome of a successful pitch, when a story involving a public relations practitioner's organization or client is covered in the news media.

Business to consumer (B2C)
The relationship between a business and the end users or consumers of its product or services.

Mobile technologies have changed the nature of many consumer purchases.

How is your relationship with online retailers different from your relationships with retailers that have physical stores? Where do you like to shop more often?

The term B2C also highlights the relationships between businesses and their customers. The four C's of integrated marketing communication (consumer, cost, convenience and communication) highlight important dimensions of those relationships. But, as any businessperson knows, financial success depends on relationships with a number of different publics in addition to customers. By definition, public relations people have an important role to play in maintaining relationships with any group of people on whom the organization's success or failure depends. In business these publics include other businesses, employees and investors.

B2B

B2B stands for business to business. Like B2C, B2B is often used to describe technologies such as the platforms that businesses use to perform online transactions with each other. B2B also refers to the relationships between business people from different companies or organizations. For example, when a business hires another business for a service such as management consulting or accounting services, that's a B2B relationship. In the context of marketing, the supply chain from raw materials to manufacturers to wholesalers to retailers involves many B2B relationships before products ever make it to consumers. If you purchase a new smartphone, think of all the transactions that are involved before the device ever reaches the palm of your hand. Silicon is mined or extracted from sand and purchased to make microchips. Microchips are assembled with touch screens, microphones, optical devices and so on. The computer is then programmed with software including multiple apps that enable multiple services and functions. For every one smartphone that is sold, there are countless prior business transactions involving the raw materials, buying and selling of component parts, assembly, delivery, intellectual property and so on.

Besides the sheer volume of transactions involved, a major difference between B2C and B2B is the nature of the buyers. B2B buyers shop as part of their job. The individuals and committees that make decisions about where to buy raw materials from for manufacturing products or which package delivery service to contract with are normally well-informed buyers. They are hired, retained and promoted for their expertise in understanding the market and for making rational, highly informed purchasing decisions based on all the data available to them. They use computers and software programs to help them, but, like journalists in media relations, they are still people who make decisions in the context of interpersonal relationships.

Research from Google and the Corporate Executive Board (CEB) supports this point. In a 2013 survey of 3,000 B2B buyers across 36 brands and seven categories, researchers found that "B2B buying is highly personal—even more so than B2C buying—due to the level of personal risk buyers feel." They found that 40–70 percent of customers reported an emotional connection to B2B brands such as Cisco, Oracle, Accenture, SAP and Deloitte, compared with 10–40 percent for brands like McDonald's, Nordstrom, Target and CVS.

Business to business (B2B)
The relationship between a business and other businesses.

Public relations people play a role in B2B relationships using many of the same tactics and channels of communication used for relationships with other key publics. Next time you walk through an airport, pay attention to the display ads and billboards. You'll notice that it's not just coffee and neck pillows being promoted, but also IT systems and consulting services.

Likewise, you've probably seen ads for B2B companies on TV, online and in magazines, particularly if you pay attention to the same news and events as businesspeople. Naturally, the *Wall Street Journal* or Bloomberg.com will carry B2B news and advertising, but businesspeople also watch sports, go on vacations and attend music festivals, which is why you may notice many events (e.g., the FedEx Cup) and venues (e.g., Oracle Arena) bearing the name of B2B companies.

The Austin Convention Center is packed with exhibitors pitching emerging technology, new websites, games and startup ideas at the South by Southwest (SXSW) Interactive Festival trade show.

How are B2B relationships similar to B2C relationships?

Social media provide additional vehicles for B2B communication. In a blog entry for Social Media Today, Jennifer Hanford identified many good examples.

- E-mail marketing company Constant Contact maintains more than 100 Pinterest boards subscribed to by more than 20,000 followers featuring photos and images that communicate "'intangible' solutions on this visual platform by tapping into their creativity."[11]

- Global cloud computing company Salesforce.com uses its Facebook page to post company links, pictures and news. They use the main Facebook page to respond to followers who comment and ask questions and to link to the other Facebook pages for the company's various divisions. They also include product demos and news on industry trends.

- Inbound marketing company HubSpot uses Twitter to strike "a good balance between tweeting content and audience engagement." With tens of thousands of followers, their social media team not only posts news but also asks questions of their followers to start conversations. They answer questions as well.

- Cisco Systems uses its YouTube channel to post videos for its tens of thousands of subscribers that "engage, educate and inform without overtly selling."

- Dell uses LinkedIn groups to post company news, career information and links to job openings, as well as to host business and product-specific discussions.

B2B companies use social media too.

Who do you think follows Cisco on Instagram?

Healthy relations with internal publics, such as employees, are prerequisites for healthy relations with external publics.

Internal publics
Groups of people with shared interests within an organization.

External publics
Groups of people with shared interests outside of an organization. These groups either have an effect on or are affected by the organization.

Employee Relations

Internal publics are an important part of public relations. If we're talking about businesses and commerce-driven relationships, the internal publics are employees. Perhaps nowhere else in public relations are the relational outcomes of trust, satisfaction, commitment and control mutuality so apparent. Trusting, satisfied, committed and empowered employees are sure to be more productive and more attuned to and invested in the organization's mission. Moreover, in a world where employees are often the first line of communication with **external publics**, healthy internal relations are prerequisites for healthy external ones.

Internal trust is essential to the operating climate of most businesses, and that trust works both ways. When employees trust the organization and the organization's management trusts the employees, everyone benefits. On the employees' side, most indices of "best places to work" include trust as a central component. When *Fortune* partners with the Great Place to Work Institute to pick the 100 best companies to work for, two-thirds of the score is based on the results of a trust index survey.[12] On the business side, Nan Russell writes in *Psychology Today* that organizational benefits of workplace trust include the following:

- Greater profitability

- Higher return on shareholder investment

- Decreased turnover of top performers

- Increased employee engagement

- Heightened customer service

- Expanded staff well-being

- More collaboration and teamwork

- Higher productivity

- Enhanced creativity and innovation[13]

Establishing and maintaining trust isn't always easy. In fact, it's really hard to foster a trusting workplace when the relationship isn't already positive to begin with. Many variables come into play as part of the over-arching organizational culture. Some of these, such as the personalities of the people involved, are outside of the scope and control of public relations, but others, particularly communication and policy, may be areas in which public relations people can offer some help.

In the digital age, BYOD (bring your own device) policies are a good example. Intel Corp. has such a policy, and allows employees to use their own mobile devices to access the company's internal IT system. According to one report, about 30,000 employee devices are logged in daily.[14] This policy requires Intel's senior management to trust employees to properly handle and protect sensitive corporate information. It also requires employees to trust the company to keep their information private. The issue with BYOD policies, labeled a "trust gap" by researchers, is that employees often don't understand just how much personal information the employer can retrieve.

Intel Corp. handles the trust gap issue with communication. They post answers to frequently asked questions on their intranet, they train IT help desk employees to discuss BYOD monitoring and they operate a 24/7 telephone support system. The results are mutually beneficial. On one side, employees get to use the devices with which they are most comfortable—in a one-year period the number of employees using their own devices at Intel increased from about 3,000 to about 17,000. On the other side, organizations get more productivity—Intel estimated that employees using their own devices produced an average of 57 more minutes of work a day than they would have otherwise.

Professor Linjuan Rita Men surveyed more than 400 employees of U.S. companies across several industries to see which channels of internal communication were most effective. She found that e-mail and direct face-to-face communication in traditional meetings and with direct managers facilitated information exchange, listening and conversation. Social media, including social network sites, blogs, instant messaging, wikis and streaming audio and video channels were less commonly used, but they served to improve the organizational climate by boosting employee engagement: "In other words, the more often companies use social media to connect with employees, the more engaged employees feel. When employees are engaged, they feel empowered, involved, emotionally attached and dedicated to the organization, and excited and proud about being a part of it."[15] Print media such as newsletters, brochures, reports and posters, though still important for disseminating information, had less of an effect on employee engagement in Men's study.

Investor Relations

If you use salary data as a measure of organizational importance, **investor relations** is one of the most valued functions among job titles that include the word "relations." In 2016, the median salary for an investor relations manager in the United States was more than $120,000, and top IR officers

Investor relations
Management of relationships between an organization and publics in the financial community—for example, investors, analysts, regulators.

IR managers are familiar with companies like Standard & Poor's, which offers stock market information resources such as the S&P 500 index.

How is investor relations different from other areas like media relations or consumer relations?

While financial information is tightly regulated, investor relations managers use many of the same channels of communication as any other public relations person.

at corporations make between $200,000 and 250,000.[16] Even though investor relations managers are just as likely to come from backgrounds in business management, accounting or finance as they are to come from communications or public relations, investor relations is very much a public relations function. The National Investor Relations Institute defines investor relations as "a strategic management responsibility that integrates finance, communication, marketing and securities law compliance to enable the most effective two-way communication between a company, the financial community and other constituencies, which ultimately contributes to a company's securities achieving fair valuation."[17]

Professor Alexander Laskin has researched investor relations as a subfunction of public relations. When Laskin interviewed investor relations managers, he found they overwhelmingly agreed that building relationships with investors and analysts is one of the most important things they do. Most cited the importance of good relationships in building trust that the company can do what it says. This leads to financial publics giving the company and its management the benefit of the doubt during times when they might otherwise second-guess their investments. In his panel study, Laskin developed the following statement on relationship building in investor relations, which the participants endorsed.

The rewards of this relationship can be significant. Value gaps tend to diminish because investors believe management can accomplish what it says. Positive events and development earn higher stock gain rewards. A flat or down quarter isn't an automatic sell signal. . . . Patience is more likely to be accorded.[18]

While financial information is tightly regulated, as discussed in Chapter 11, investor relations managers use many of the same channels of communication as any other public relations person. These include face-to-face meetings, conference calls, press conferences, news releases, brochures, periodic (e.g., quarterly or annual) reports, websites, blogs and online video.

Issues-Driven Relationships

Social and environmental issues are big concerns for even the most profit-focused organizations. Relationships with customers, employees, investors and other businesses may be driven by money, but they are also driven by where the organization stands on issues that affect human and natural resources. Some organizations, however, exist for the very purpose of addressing social or environmental issues. They focus specifically on issues for the sake of making a difference, with a much less direct link to any commercial motive.

Nonprofit Organizations

The Nature Conservancy's mission is "to conserve the lands and waters on which all life depends." The American Heart Association exists "to build healthier lives, free of cardiovascular diseases and stroke." AARP's mission statement reads, "To enhance quality of life for all as we age. We lead positive social change and deliver value to members through information, advocacy and service." With mission statements like these, nonprofit organizations define themselves by a commitment to some sort of environmental or social benefit besides profit.

Of course, this doesn't mean nonprofits don't need to generate revenue. They still need money to pursue their missions, but the relationships that they maintain with their publics are centered on the issues. Among the most important publics for nonprofit organizations are volunteers and donors. Both support the missions of nonprofits. Donors donate money, and volunteers donate time.

Volunteers and donors are among the most important publics for nonprofit organizations.

VOLUNTEERS

Managing relationships with volunteers involves a mix of external and internal communications. Recruiting volunteers means reaching out into the community and other organizations to find and initiate relationships with people who are likely to help your organization by volunteering time and effort. When college public relations campaign classes take on nonprofit organizations as clients, a common initial goal for the campaigns is to recruit volunteers. Another common goal, which often emerges after students do some initial research, is *retaining* volunteers.

DONORS

Although nonprofits do make money from fees for services and goods, government grants, and other sources, they also depend on donors for revenue. Issues-driven organizations must work just as hard as—if not harder than—commerce-driven organizations to meet their financial goals. That said, those financial goals should not be confused with the greater social benefits the organizations exist to support. The money is only a means to an end. Thus, the most fruitful donor relationships are long-term and based on mutual commitment to the organization's mission. Research and practice both bear out the idea that "fundraising is less about raising money and more about

A volunteer at a Berliner Stadtmission shelter for refugees gives out clothing donated by Japanese brand Uniqlo. Germany took in more than a million migrants and refugees in 2015, mostly from Syria and Iraq.

What sustains the relationships between the charity that runs this shelter, its volunteers, its donors, and the migrants and refugees it serves?

building relationships."[19] PRSA Fellow, former fundraising executive and professor of public relations Kathleen Kelly recommends stewardship as a key practice for success in nonprofit public relations management. Four elements of stewardship have been found to influence how donors perceive their relationships with nonprofit organizations. Kelly's four R's are reciprocity, responsibility, reporting and relationship nurturing.

- *Reciprocity:* When donors support an organization, the organization should respond with appreciation. This may be as simple as a handwritten thank-you note or recognition in a member magazine. In cases where someone has made a tax-deductible contribution, the organization can reciprocate with a written thank-you and confirmation that will help the donor file for a deduction.

- *Responsibility:* If you make a donation to aid disaster victims, or to help feed local families in need, you want to be able to trust that the organization is using your donation for that specific purpose. Nonprofits have a responsibility to do what they promise to do. However, all nonprofits use at least a small part of their budgets for administrative functions, so nonprofit executives need to work hard to make sure that donations are managed properly. Public relations people can serve to make sure that donors' wishes are clearly understood, communicated and honored in the management of funds.

- *Reporting:* The web has made it much easier for organizations to share tax forms, financial plans, audit information and detailed information about programs and services that demonstrate social accountability as well as financial accountability.[20] The best nonprofits are readily transparent.

- *Relationship nurturing:* This final "R" echoes the idea of communal relationships in which financial exchanges take a back seat to mutual respect and recognition. One measure of relationship nurturing is how often donors hear from an organization when they are *not* being asked for money.[21] As Kelly puts it, the best way to nurture a long-term relationship is simple: "Accept the importance of previous donors and keep them at the forefront of the organization's consciousness."[22] Include donors on e-mail lists. Network with them on social networking sites. Send them copies of breaking news releases that are going to news media. Invite them to events. All of these are ways to keep them in the loop and in the organizational "consciousness."

When Publics Are Organizations and Organizations Are Publics

An **issue** is any important topic or problem that is open for debate, discussion or advocacy.[23] If products, services, stocks and money are the stuff of exchange in regular marketplaces, issues are what fuel exchange in the marketplace of ideas. When groups of people are organized on more than one side of an issue, the terms *organization* and *public* become interchangeable.

Issue
An important topic or problem that is open for debate, discussion or advocacy.

ACTIVISTS

Larissa Grunig defines an *activist public* as "a group of two or more individuals who organize in order to influence another public or publics through action that may include education, compromise, persuasion, pressure tactics or force."[24] In issues management and crisis management, activists are often defined from the perspective of one organization, but in thinking about two-way relationships, organizations themselves may be activists. Many nonprofits and NGOs are just as organized, sophisticated and effective in their public relations strategies as the other organizations with which they interact.

Take Chicago surfers, for example. Yes, real surfers—not the kind who browse websites but the people who ride freshwater waves in Lake Michigan. For the City of Chicago and the Chicago Park District, surfers did not constitute a public to be concerned with until 2008, when a surfer was arrested for surfing in Lake Michigan. At that point, surfing in Lake Michigan became a recognized *issue*.

Then a *public* emerged. By 2009, "a group of local surfers, watermen, and assorted activists, many of whom had never met," had organized enough to get the attention of city and park district officials.[25] City officials met with this new public and communicated with them in a two-way process that resulted in the lifting of the surfing ban with some restrictions, which were outlined in a 2009 document titled "Non-Motorized Water Sports Information and Safety Awareness," published by the Chicago Park District.[26]

But instead of seeing their collective action as a one-time deal and dissolving their affiliation once the matter was temporarily settled, the group of surfers and activists started the Chicago chapter of the Surfrider Foundation. In doing so, the *public* became a bona fide *organization*. When in January 2012 another surfer was arrested for surfing in Lake Michigan, the organization, now part of a 50,000-plus-member 501(c)(3) nonprofit environmental organization, was ready to act. They activated a network of supporters around the country, including 11-time world champion Kelly Slater, who did an interview with the *Chicago Sun-Times* ("It's unbelievable. It's just a body of water. What's with the regulations?") and expressed his solidarity with the arrested surfer on Twitter for his hundreds of thousands of followers ("Say what?! Maybe a few of us should attend court with him").[27]

GOVERNMENT AGENCIES

Organizations of all types practice advocacy. For example, Allstate insurance company advocates issues related to federal insurance regulation. In this case, a for-profit company is advocating a position on an issue that directly affects its business interests. For this purpose, Allstate pays for **lobbying** activity to influence legislation ($3,190,000 in 2015 according to OpenSecrets .org[28]). This type of activity might also be called **legislative relations** or **government relations** because it involves relationships between the

The Chicago chapter of Surfrider Foundation was founded partly in response to an issue in which a surfer was arrested for surfing in Lake Michigan.

When did this group become more of an organization than a public?

Lobbying
Working to influence the decisions of government officials on matters of legislation.

Legislative relations
Management of relationships between an organization and lawmakers, staffers and others who influence legislation.

Government relations
Management of relationships between an organization and government officials who formulate and execute public policy.

Members of the Boston Children's Hospital's government relations team attend an event at the Massachusetts State House to meet with elected officials and advocate for legislation.

Are they acting as an organization, a public, or both?

Public affairs
Management of policy-focused relationships between an organization, public officials and their constituents.

Corporate social responsibility (CSR)
Companies' commitment of resources to benefit the welfare of their workforce, local communities, society at large and the environment.

Ethically balancing loyalties is one of the toughest jobs of public relations managers.

organization and the government entities that regulate the organization's business environment.

Chapter 11 covers some key regulatory agencies with which public relations practitioners should be familiar, and Chapter 2 discusses politics and government as part of the heritage and contemporary practice of public relations. One of the primary functions of government **public affairs** is the dissemination of information *to* constituents (i.e., public information). Another key function is advocating *for* those constituents.

In this chapter, and throughout the text, we see how the idea of building and maintaining relationships applies in the public sector. A government agency may be seen as either an organization or a public depending on your perspective. In the school board example for media relations, we saw the public school board as an organization with a public relations person who was responsible for communicating with news media and other publics. With the Chicago surfer example, we saw how the case could be framed with Surfrider Foundation as the organization and the city park service as a public.

Ethics: Corporate Social Responsibility and Loyalty

Corporate social responsibility (CSR) refers to a company's commitment to allocate resources to benefit society and the environment. The contributions may come in the form of financial donations, employee time or socially beneficial business practices. While nonprofit organizations exist primarily to make a positive difference in their communities and the natural environment, for-profit businesses and corporations exist primarily to make money. If they don't make money, they eventually will not exist at all and cannot benefit anyone.

Nobel Prize–winning economist Milton Friedman took this logic to an extreme in a famous 1970 article published in *The New York Times Magazine* titled "The Social Responsibility of Business Is to Increase Its Profits." Whether you agree with Friedman or not, he raises interesting ethical questions about how for-profit companies balance their need to make money with their responsibilities as corporate citizens. At the heart of the matter are competing loyalties. Companies may have loyalties to their communities and the natural environment, but they also must be loyal to their shareholders and employees who

Voices from the Field

Heather Harder

HEATHER HARDER is a public relations professional with experience in speechwriting, media relations, content marketing and more. She served as PRSSA national president from 2014 to 2015, earned a B.A. in strategic communications from Elon University and frequently volunteers her time to PRSA and to mentoring and speaking at PRSSA events.

I'm guessing you were taught that public relations can be defined as relationship management. How does that definition square with what you're doing now as an account executive?

Relationships mean everything to agency work. I've discovered it's not just the relationships you have with your clients and that your clients have with their communities. It's the relationships you have with your coworkers, the relationships you have with your local PR community and so much more. Essentially, public relations is a relationship building and management function, but that applies in a broader sense than students may realize.

Do you work on any CSR [corporate social responsibility] projects now? What kinds of challenges and rewards does that bring in terms of relationship management?

I have worked with two corporate foundations, one of which recently won a PR News CSR award that I helped with. The biggest challenge is establishing natural initiatives that the public sees as authentic and not simply as "PR ploys." You have to work with clients to get them to understand this. If the public doesn't trust that your CSR initiatives are deeply integrated into company culture and not just for show, your efforts will be futile.

In what ways have you seen social media help or hinder public relations people manage professional relationships as individuals?

Social media moves quickly. I think the people who keep up with the latest apps are not only good at building professional relationships, but also at bringing new ideas to their clients and businesses. I think LinkedIn is the best way to professionally network and that people should use it as a conversation-starter. Twitter can also be effective for meeting new people and recognizing their work by sharing it and tagging them.

At the organizational level have you noticed any innovation in how organizations manage relationships with publics?

The latest buzz term I've heard is "influencer marketing." I think companies are getting smart at finding advocates who are connected to various groups and communities and tapping into those people to get an "in" and build trust. I've also seen companies being more personable and sharing their employees' and customers' stories on social media. Essentially, companies are finding innovative ways to build third-party credibility.

What advice do you have for students as they manage the transition from classroom learning to professional careers?

Once you leave the classroom, you become much more responsible for your own learning. See everything as a learning opportunity. Don't just focus on learning the hard skills, which you can easily do by practicing often and participating in webinars, trainings and more. Focus on learning the ins and outs of things like conversation and persuasion. Observe talented leaders in the office, figure out how to get people on board with your ideas and learn the art of client and stakeholder relations.

rely on them to remain profitable. Ethically balancing loyalties in a company's relationships with publics as diverse as environmentalists, government agencies, unions, employees and stockholders is one of the toughest jobs of public relations managers.

Case Study

Coca-Cola and Corporate Social Responsibility

Coca-Cola's position atop the branding world hasn't come easily, and its future there isn't guaranteed. In 2013, Coca-Cola slipped to third place behind Apple and Google on Interbrand's list of best global brands.[29]

In recent years sugary drinks have been identified as culprits in the fight against obesity. Now being the number one soda brand in the world carries with it the risk of also being labeled as public enemy number one in the fight against obesity, particularly in America. How can a company that relies on sales of sugary drinks that lead to obesity, diabetes and tooth decay make a compelling case that it also cares deeply about the health of consumers?

Elon University student and PRSSA president Heather Harder won the 2014 Arthur W. Page Society case study competition with her analysis of how Coca-Cola has managed its precarious position. She summarized the company's strategy as one of corporate social responsibility. "By acknowledging the obesity issue and spending millions of dollars on anti-obesity efforts, Coca-Cola is demonstrating corporate social responsibility—if not in its products, then at least in its community involvement."[30]

In late 2012 and early 2013, Coca-Cola launched a campaign called "Coming Together" that included a theme that "all calories count." The theme emphasized logic that consumers should balance the number of calories taken in with the number of calories they burn, and that calories from Coke products are essentially the same as calories from any other source. Coca-Cola used a variety of tactics to support the theme including:

- videos aired on mainstream media (CNN, Fox, MSNBC)

- a crowdsourced effort that invited consumers to e-mail comingtogether@coca-cola.com with personal stories

- online video via http://www.coca-colacompany.com/coming-together/

- the announcement of several "commitments to fighting obesity" including

  - offering low- or no-calorie options in every market
  - more prominently displaying calorie information on product labels
  - funding physical activity programs worldwide

Coca-Cola's brand faces threats as sugary drinks are seen as a public health problem.

How can a soda company promote its main product while simultaneously working to be socially responsible?

- adopting more responsible marketing practices that avoid targeting children under the age of 12.[31]

The PRSA Code of Ethics features loyalty as a core value. "We are faithful to those we represent, while honoring our obligation to serve the public interest." In this case, those working in public relations for Coca-Cola must balance their loyalty to their employer with their loyalty to many publics with varying interests.

According to Harder, "The challenge is for Coca-Cola to find a way to be taken seriously as a player in anti-obesity efforts while simultaneously increasing sales and offering consumers the products they love." Harder's conclusion highlights the importance of relationships with several key publics in defining the success of the CSR efforts.

CRITICS AND ACTIVISTS

Perhaps the most vocal opposition in this case is the Center for Science in the Public Interest (CSPI), a nonprofit organization that seeks "to educate the public, advocate government policies that are consistent with scientific evidence on health and environmental issues, and counter industry's powerful influence on public opinion and public policies."[32] The essence of CSPI's criticism was captured in the brevity of a single tweet on May 8, 2013. "Coca-Cola is desperately trying to disassociate itself with #obesity. Too bad the core product causes it."[33]

CONSUMERS

Let's face it. People don't drink Coke for their health these days. If you work for Coca-Cola, you can be loyal to your consumers in a lot of ways with a lot of different products, but it would be a stretch to imply that your signature cola equates to healthier food options. That said, research shows that consumers pay attention to CSR. In 2015, Nielsen surveyed more than 30,000 consumers in 60 countries. Sixty-six percent of them said they would be willing to pay more for goods and services from socially responsible companies, up from 55 percent in 2014 and 50 percent in 2013.[34]

INVESTORS

To preserve excellent investor relations with its thousands of shareholders around the world, Coca-Cola must maintain a profitable business model. Can you imagine what it would mean to shareholders—and even entire economies—if Coca-Cola just stopped selling soda because the product was unhealthy? The **golden mean** is an ethical principle in Aristotelian, Buddhist and Confucius philosophies, which holds that the most ethical course of action lies

Coca-Cola has begun offering more low-calorie options including Coca-Cola Life, which is made with stevia, a plant-based sugar substitute.

To which publics is Coca-Cola loyal in this marketing effort?

Golden mean
Ethical doctrine holding that the best courses of action are found between extremes.

 CSPI
@CSPI

Follow

Coca-Cola is desperately trying to disassociate itself with #obesity. Too bad the core product causes it.

The Center for Science in the Public Interest (CSPI) sent this tweet in May of 2013.

How can Coca-Cola balance loyalty to its shareholders and employees with loyalty to the consumers represented by organizations like CSPI?

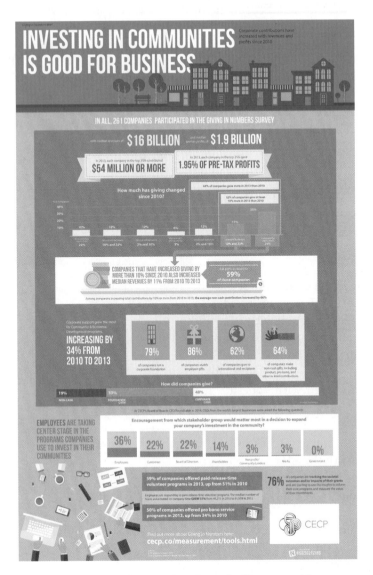

CECP is a coalition of CEOs who believe that societal improvement is an essential measure of business performance. In 2014, they released this infographic highlighting trends in corporate societal engagement.

Is there a causal relationship between corporate giving and increased revenue? Why or why not?

between extremes. A golden CSR strategy for Coca-Cola undoubtedly lies somewhere between shuttering its flagship product line to allay the concerns of its critics and ignoring its critics altogether with an uninhibited drive for profit. In fact, CSR may help with profitability, as is evident in research suggesting a link between charitable giving and corporate revenues.[35]

EMPLOYEES

Positive relationships with employees are an important part of the equation linking social responsibility with profitability. It is not hard to imagine how companies with satisfied, committed, trusting and empowered employees (i.e., those with excellent relational outcomes) are more likely to profit in business. CSR trends include programs that encourage employees to participate in service such as pro bono work or paid release time to volunteer in their communities.

POLICYMAKERS

Legislative relations also come into play, and Coca-Cola invests strategically in its own advocacy. The company lists corporate taxation, environmental policy and product-specific policies including taxes and regulation as areas for investment. Product-specific policy was made more salient when former New York Mayor Michael Bloomberg proposed a ban on the sale of sugary drinks larger than 16 ounces. In its relationship with regulators and legislators, Coca-Cola "advocates for choice and opposes discriminatory tax policies that single out certain beverages."[36] The New York City Board of Health fought for years to impose the policy, but in 2014, the New York State Court of Appeals ruled that the attempted big-soda ban exceeded the scope of the city's regulatory authority.[37]

Managing an organization requires managing relationships with all sorts of publics. Ethical issues arise when loyalty to any one public risks damage to mutually beneficial relationships with others. Those who work in public relations for Coca-Cola, like people in organizations of all sizes all over the world, face ethical challenges in remaining faithful to those they represent while honoring their obligation to serve the public interest. Corporate social responsibility can be both a strategy for and an outcome of careful relationship management in public relations.

In Case You Missed It

Effective public relations means managing relationships between an organization and its publics. Social skills and business skills both come into play, as highlighted in some of the key takeaways from this chapter.

- The better the long-term relationships between your organization and publics, the more likely you are to achieve your goals.

- Before pitching to reporters, read their news stories, watch their programs and follow their social media accounts to better understand their style and the type of news they cover.

- Healthy relations with internal publics, such as employees, are prerequisites for healthy relations with external publics.

- While financial information is tightly regulated, investor relations managers use many of the same channels of communication as any other public relations person.

- Volunteers and donors are among the most important publics for nonprofit organizations.

- Ethically balancing loyalties is one of the toughest jobs of public relations managers.

SUMMARY

4.1 Apply knowledge of interpersonal relationships to organization-public relationships.
Many of the same relationship strategies that work in personal relationships—positivity, openness, assurances, social networking and sharing tasks—also work in maintaining relationships between organizations and their publics. The outcomes are similar too: trust, satisfaction, commitment and a sense of mutual control.

4.2 Discuss the concept of relationships as central to public relations.
Relationships between organizations and publics can be thought of at the group level where the relationships between one group of people

(organization) and other groups (publics) are analogous to interpersonal relationships. These relationships can also be thought of as the aggregate of all the interpersonal interactions between individuals in the organization and individuals in publics. Either way, managing the relationships for mutual benefit of all parties is at the heart of public relations.

4.3 Identify broad categories of stakeholders with whom public relations people build and maintain relationships.

Public relations people build and maintain relationships with media (journalists, editors, producers, bloggers, etc.), financial publics (investors, analysts, regulators, etc.), internal publics (employees, members, etc.) and an array of external publics including consumers, donors, government officials, community leaders and activists, including those who oppose the organization.

4.4 Define different areas of public relations practice by identifying the publics with whom relationships are built and maintained.

One way to categorize the different areas of public relations is news-driven, commerce-driven and issues-driven. Although there is much overlap, common jobs in public relations align with these categories. Media relations and publicity are news-driven. Investor relations, marketing communication, customer relations and employee relations are mostly commerce-driven. Public affairs, legislative relations and issues management are mostly issues-driven.

4.5 Evaluate corporate social responsibility as a strategy for balancing the interests of diverse publics (stakeholder analysis).

The Coca-Cola case illustrates how one company has attempted to balance the varying interests of investors, employees, consumers, activists, lawmakers and global communities. The CSR strategy involves committing resources to benefit society and the environment while also seeking profits. The question for analysis is how effective the company is in building and maintaining simultaneous relationships with a range of stakeholders with very different interests.

DISCUSSION QUESTIONS

1. Relationships can be complicated. Discuss a love-hate relationship that you have with a particular organization. What does that organization do well in the relationship? What does that organization do that causes frustration?

2. Describe another organization for which you think of yourself as a key public (for example, as a student at a university, as a taxpayer in a state, as a customer for a business or as a volunteer for a nonprofit).

What is the role of public relations in the relationship? Do the people performing that role have different titles than "public relations"?

3. Search for an advertised public relations job (public affairs, investor relations, etc.) at an organization where you'd like to work. From the job ad, what publics does it appear you would work with most in that position?

4. Name a for-profit company that you admire as socially responsible. What do they do that makes you admire them? How do you think their socially responsible activities help or hurt their profits?

KEY TERMS

CHAPTER 5

Research

Are you active, aware or just meh on the issue of net neutrality?

n politics, it is sometimes said that a new campaign starts the day after Election Day. Although we hope that our elected officials will focus more on getting their new job done than on getting reelected, there is quite a bit of truth here for campaign strategists. An election is like a survey of voters, and fresh election results yield all sorts of new data to kick off planning for future campaigns.

Strategic planning is a cyclical process. Whether a college student is planning one semester's budget based on the prior semester's spending, a volleyball coach is reviewing last season's performance to plan for the next season, or a campaign strategist is analyzing the results of one campaign to plan for the next one, the process is similar. Successful planning begins, ends, and begins again, with research (Figure 5.1). In between are planning (Chapter 6) and implementation (Chapter 7). This chapter explains how strategy starts with research. Public relations campaigns and programs with research-based goals and objectives lend themselves to proper evaluation (Chapter 8). Proper evaluation helps you make a case for the value of your work. Being able to demonstrate the value of your work gets you hired and promoted.

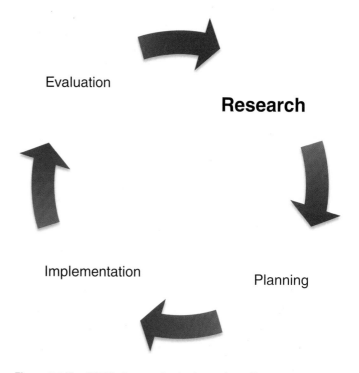

Figure 5.1 The RPIE Cycle campaign begins, ends, and begins again, with research.

What are some of the very first questions campaign planners should ask, and what kind of research helps answer them?

Research in the RPIE Cycle

For years, public relations students studying for exams and practitioners reviewing for accreditation interviews have referred to the four-step process of researching, planning, implementing and evaluating programs. RPIE and acronyms that start with "R" have served as trusty mnemonic devices. RACE,[1] ROPE[2] and ROSIE[3] are three common examples. RACE stands for research, action, communication and evaluation. ROPE stands for research, objectives, programming and evaluation. ROSIE includes research, objectives, strategies, implementation and evaluation. Not only do they all start with an "R," but they all end with an "E" for evaluation, which is a type of research in and of itself.

If we think of strategic public relations as a dynamic and cyclical process, it makes sense that the evaluation of one action, program or campaign feeds back into the next. In fact, evaluation can happen at any point in a strategic program, not just at the end.

Evaluation can happen at any point in a strategic program, not just at the end.

"I must say, your hindsight on this project was far more accurate than his foresight."

Evaluation of one project can serve as insight for the next one.

How does public relations research help turn hindsight into foresight?

Formative Research

When research comes at the beginning of the planning process, or during the implementation of a plan, it is known as **formative research**. The information acquired during formative research helps you formulate your program or campaign and its components, including goals, objectives, strategy and tactics. On one hand, formative research, or formative evaluation, can be casual and unscientific. If you call a few reporters to pitch a news story idea and they all decline abruptly, you may want to step back and re-formulate your approach based on that information before you call anyone else. That's *informal* formative evaluation. However, informal trial and error on its own does not constitute strategic public relations.

On the other hand, formative research and evaluation can be carefully planned and sophisticated. Public relations professionals may begin campaigns or programs with detailed web **analytics**, carefully collected survey data on key publics or formally designed interviews. They also may continue to track those analytics, re-administer the surveys and interview people for the duration of the campaign or program, using the live feedback to make corrections to strategy.

Summative Research

Summative research is when you've reached an end or stopping point in your campaign and you want to answer the question, "Did it work?" One way to differentiate between a campaign and an ongoing program is that a campaign has a defined beginning and end. A political campaign ends with an election. A year-end fundraising campaign ends on December 31. A product-launch campaign ends when the product is fully available in the market, or at some specific date determined by the campaign's planners. In identifying an end-date for a campaign, planners make themselves accountable for specific outcomes at a specific point in time. Yes, those summative results can and should inform ongoing work and future campaigns, but as final evaluations, they answer the question of whether and to what extent the campaign achieved its goals (e.g., won the election, raised the target amount of money or met sales projections for a new product).

Formative research
Research conducted at the beginning of the planning process, or during the implementation of a plan.

Analytics
A field of data analysis used to describe, predict and improve how organizations communicate with publics; commonly refers to tracking of website traffic and resulting behavior.

Summative research
Research conducted at the end of a campaign or program to determine the extent that objectives and goals were met.

When the "E" is placed at the end of an acronym like RACE or ROPE, it suggests summative evaluation. Remember, however, that research and feedback are important throughout the entire process of public relations work. This chapter focuses mostly on research as part of the planning process. Chapter 8 delves into specific methods for measurement including evaluation research designed to quantify results of campaigns. One method to begin planning is to organize research into three major areas: (1) situation, (2) organization and (3) publics.

Situation

Good public relations cases read like good stories, and good stories rely on an interesting setting. The setting provides the context for the problem or opportunity from which the public relations goals arise. At the very beginning, the situation may be only vaguely stated or implied (e.g., "We need to raise awareness"), but with research the situation can be analyzed more carefully to initiate strategic planning. Public relations case studies and write-ups for public relations case competitions such as PRSA's Silver Anvil awards normally include a **situation analysis** at the beginning. Table 5.1 provides some examples of situation analysis starters from 2015 PRSA Silver Anvil winners.[4]

Each of the cases described in Table 5.1 begins with a narrative presentation of the situation. The impetus for a public relations effort is either a problem, an opportunity or some combination of the two. And, getting started means doing research to first identify the problem or opportunity and then to understand it well enough to create a narrative.

An effective situation analysis leads to a clear, concise **problem or opportunity statement** on which the client or organization and the team representing them agree. In their text *Strategic Communications Planning*, Brigham Young University's Laurie Wilson and Joseph Ogden write that a core problem statement can be written in a single sentence.[5] Others recommend a paragraph or two. Because it captures the essence of the situation and determines the scope and value of your proposal, your core problem or opportunity statement may well be one of the most carefully constructed sentences or paragraphs you write in all of your work in public relations. Distilling a vague, complex and ambiguous context down to a brief statement that everyone involved can agree upon requires careful analysis.

AT&T mounted the "It Can Wait" campaigns to curb smartphone-distracted driving.

What kind of research could they do to know if the campaign efforts worked?

Situation analysis
A report analyzing the internal and external environment of an organization and its publics as it relates to the start of a campaign or program.

Problem or opportunity statement
A concise written summary of the situation that explains the main reason for a public relations program or campaign.

CAMPAIGN	SITUATION
KETCHUM'S "DRIVING ON HYDROGEN—LAUNCHING HYUNDAI'S TUCSON FUEL CELL VEHICLE"	"What if I told you there was a technology that combined the best of gasoline and battery-electric vehicles? A car that produces zero emissions, runs on the most abundant element on the planet, and has a similar range and refueling time to a gasoline car. This technology exists, but skeptics have convinced the public it's not a viable solution to end our dependence on fossil fuels. . . ."
MSLGROUP, LEO BURNETT TORONTO AND SMG'S "ALWAYS #LIKEAGIRL: TURNING AN INSULT INTO A CONFIDENCE MOVEMENT"	"When a new Always-sponsored survey found that the start of puberty and first periods mark the lowest moments in confidence for girls, Always determined that empowering girls during this critical life stage should become our mission. We discovered that somewhere between puberty and adulthood, women had internalized the phrase 'like a girl' to mean weakness and vanity. So, we took 'like a girl' and transformed its negative power to mean 'downright amazing.' . . ."
GOLIN'S "AN INSPIRED MISSION: TAKING HEART ON THE ROAD" FOR PETSMART	"PetSmart? Petco? To consumers, they're one in the same. But for one retailer, its mission went beyond sales . . . beyond the cash register. Its focus was on a larger imperative and embarked on a journey to define what is truly special—truly different—about itself, and reach the heart of its customers. What they found was their belief: Pets make us better people, and formed its defining mission: Creating more moments for people to be inspired by pets. . . ."
LDWWGROUP'S "CARNIVAL CORPORATION: NAVIGATING THE WORLD'S LEADING CRUISE COMPANY TO SMOOTHER WATERS"	"A series of high profile incidents in 2012 and 2013, including the sinking of the Costa Concordia resulting in the deaths of 32 passengers and the infamous Carnival 'poop cruise,' shook consumer confidence in Carnival Corporation and its nine cruise lines. Not surprisingly, bookings dropped, revenue sagged and the reputation of the corporation and its brands suffered after the incidents with brand perception dropping by as much as 50 points. A new leadership team was put in place and the corporation brought in long-time PR professional Roger Frizzell to help tackle head on the recovery of the company's reputation. . . ."

SWOT ANALYSIS

One common approach for structuring the analysis is the **SWOT analysis**. SWOT stands for strengths, weaknesses, opportunities and threats.

Strengths are factors internal to your organization or client that will help you reach your goals or fulfill your mission. If your client is the faculty of a local college, some strengths might be a range of faculty projects that benefit local communities or a record of faculty involvement in community

SWOT Analysis
Description and discussion of an organization's internal strengths and weaknesses and its external opportunities and threats.

organizations as part of their professional service. It would take research to learn what these projects and organizations are and understand who benefits.

Weaknesses are internal factors that make it harder for your organization or client to do what it wants to do. In the college example, weaknesses may be a lack of training or professional incentive for faculty to communicate their scholarship outside of their peer groups. Or, perhaps there is a gap in communication between college faculty and the professional communicators representing the school. Again, it would take research to obtain an accurate sense of the internal communication environment.

Opportunities and threats are external variables. A relatively close-knit college town where there are few degrees of separation between citizens and the people working in the college could be an opportunity for word-of-mouth communication. A decreasing revenue projection that will put greater scrutiny on the college's budget may be a threat.

As with strengths and weaknesses, opportunities and threats are often two sides to the same coin. Greater scrutiny of an organization's budget may be perceived as a threat. Programs could be cut or jobs could be at risk. But at the same time, close attention to an organization's budget may provide an opportunity to communicate the value of the organization's work. In addition to educating students, colleges and universities employ thousands of people, generate revenue in patents and licenses and provide launching pads for start-ups. Discovering strengths, weaknesses, opportunities and threats and listing them in a table is an appropriate start, but the actual analysis of that information requires closer examination and discussion. Prioritizing the most relevant information, deciding what *not* to focus on, and understanding how different factors relate to one another and to your organization's mission are all part of the work you do in getting ready to tell the story.

SWOT ANALYSIS

	Helpful	Harmful
Internal origin	**S** Strengths	**W** Weaknesses
External origin	**O** Opportunities	**T** Threats

SWOT analyses help you identify key factors in planning for public relations.

How might researching factors of internal origin (strengths and weaknesses) be different from researching factors of external origin (opportunities and threats)?

Gaining a deeper understanding of a situation requires digging for information of substance beyond an internet search.

RESOURCES FOR SITUATION RESEARCH

In all likelihood, situation research starts with an internet search and conversations with the clients. However, gaining a deeper, more analytic and more nuanced understanding of the situation than what the client already knows from their own quick Google search requires digging deeper for information of substance. Here are some potential resources for researching the situation:

- Summaries of relevant media coverage, including stories placed in print, broadcast or online media. The organization may already have reports on file or may subscribe to media monitoring services (see Chapter 8) that generate such reports.

- Copies of any organizational documents related to the problem that the client is willing to share, including policies, reports, archived correspondence and web or intranet material.

- Collateral material from prior campaigns and programs (brochures, web content, product information, etc.), news releases and ads.

- Any available statements, reports or information from or about the organization's competitors that is relevant to the situation.

- Calendars or schedules of related events.

- Copies of relevant laws, regulations, budgets or pending legislation that are publicly available through government web pages or upon request from government agencies.

- Any research already conducted and reported (surveys, interviews, content analyses, communication audits, message testing and usability studies, etc.).

- Web analytics reports, which track website traffic such as the number of unique visitors to a site, the number of page views, how much time people spend on a site, the percentage of people who leave after seeing only one page (bounce rate) or indicators of other objectives such as the number of registrations or downloads (see Chapter 8).

- Prior marketing, advertising and public relations plans.

As a cohesive narrative analysis of the situation comes together, and as that brief problem or opportunity statement begins to take shape, it's crucial to stay in touch with the client or organization's management to ensure you are on the right track. For example, consider the problem/opportunity statement for Ogilvy Public Relations Worldwide and DuPont's "Welcome to the Global Collaboratory" campaign:

> DuPont was challenged by its "chemical company" reputation, despite being a long-time global contributor to food production, nutrition and safety. It also confronted a landscape with a chief competitor, Monsanto, espousing a strong, public POV [point of view] that biotechnology is the primary answer to the problem. DuPont retained Ogilvy to develop a campaign to showcase to the global food influencer community its commitment to bringing together key audiences who can create solutions to ensuring global food security.[6]

An organization and its publics are embedded in the situation and must, therefore, be researched concurrently. Although practitioners may start with a general background and broad context for strategic public relations efforts, delving deeper makes apparent the need for research specifically focusing on the organization and its publics.

Organization

Perhaps the best place to start understanding an organization is its mission. The mission is the organization's steady, enduring purpose. For example, a college or university's mission may entail research, teaching and service. Even if you are working **in house** or are already familiar with a client, you may still find it useful to review the organization's **mission statement** if one is available.

MISSION STATEMENTS

A for-profit corporation's mission may be quite different from the mission of a nonprofit or NGO. For example, compare Trader Joe's mission statement:

> *The mission of Trader Joe's is to give our customers the best food and beverage values that they can find anywhere and to provide them with the information required to make informed buying decisions. We provide these with a dedication to the highest quality of customer satisfaction delivered with a sense of warmth, friendliness, fun, individual pride, and company spirit.*[7]

to the four-word mission statement of the American Humane Society, which packs a punch:

> *Celebrating Animals, Confronting Cruelty.*

Not all organizations publish a mission statement, but you can still find evidence of an organization's broadest guiding principles and philosophy in key publications such annual reports, or even the "About Us" section of a website or app.

These resources also give researchers a sense of the organization's values and culture. Given the amount of effort and levels of review that these major organizational statements often require before being published, they should be taken seriously as indicators of the reason the organization exists and deeper purpose of why people work there.

RESOURCES FOR ORGANIZATION RESEARCH

Other written documents to seek in learning about an organization may include the following:

- Any written history

- The organization's charter and bylaws

In house
When public relations people are employed directly within an organization rather than working for an external agency or contracted as independent consultants.

Mission statement
A formal statement of an organization's steady, enduring purpose.

- A flow chart or other description of the organizational structure

- Product or service descriptions

- Biographies of or interviews with key executives and board members

- Summary budget reports, and other summary data on staffing, profits, stock values and so on

- Social media account profiles, posts and networks including individuals and other organizations

- Organizational communication policies and social media policies if available

- Any prior research reports or audits of internal communication channels or programs

Of course, researchers cannot rely on formal written material alone to understand what makes an organization tick. Reviewing a company's webpage, publications and archives is not sufficient to gain tacit knowledge of something as intangible as **organizational culture**. Designing a public relations campaign with an appreciation for organizational culture in the context of a particular situation (or a situation in the context of an organizational culture) requires astute observation of not just written evidence but of people and their behavior.

Publics

In conducting research on the situation and organization, you gain a good understanding of the benefits that an organization seeks from public relations campaigns and programs. Public relations professionals use that research, along with research on publics, to develop goals and objectives that serve the organization's broader mission. But remember that the best relationships are mutually beneficial. This means you have to work to understand not just the interests of your own organization, but also the interests of your publics. What are *they* going to get out of the relationship? This kind of understanding requires thinking about research as part of a larger process of two-way communication. The RPIE process is very much a cycle of interactive communication between organizations and their publics. Just as your richest interpersonal communication happens when you listen as much as you talk, organization-public relationships flourish when public relations people spend as much energy trying to understand publics as they do trying to get their messages out.

> Organization-public relationships flourish when you spend as much energy trying to understand your publics as you do trying to get your message out.

INTERNAL AND EXTERNAL
Publics can be either internal or external to the organization, and that designation may depend on the context. Employees and members are almost always thought of as internal publics, and as such they can be reached via

internal channels such as face-to-face meetings, company e-mail lists, hallway bulletin boards, intranets and even the organizational grapevine. To the degree that these channels are used for gaining feedback, they can be used for research and evaluation.

While an organizational chart may offer a relatively simple map for reference when identifying internal publics, it is important to think about the definition of a public when identifying and prioritizing internal publics. Remember, publics are groups of people with shared interests who have an effect on an organization or whom the organization affects. Most people internal to an organization will fit both these criteria, but specific situations will mean prioritizing internal publics differently. If a university is working to gain funding based on its faculty research and community service, faculty members will be a key internal public. In a campus nighttime safety campaign, university police and resident assistants may be more important. Alumni, who share an identity with the school, may be considered internal or external, depending on the situation.

Police officers and firefighters participated in an organized event to protest Greek government austerity measures and pension reform.

In this situation, were the protestors internal or external publics for the government?

External publics are outside of the organization and are generally reached via channels such as mass media, direct mail and the web. Each of these channels also can serve as a resource for feedback and research. Even though mass media such as TV, newspapers and radio are mostly one-way forms of communication, audience data from services like Nielsen TV ratings, responses to radio promotions, coupon codes from print ads or traffic data from web pages can all be useful in researching external publics.

Of course, there are limitations on how precisely publics can be segmented based on the media they use. The most massive of mass media will certainly reach internal publics. You can bet employees are as affected by a Super Bowl commercial for their company as their global customers are—hopefully in a positive manner. Favorable cable news coverage or a front-page story in the news may have a similar effect. For internal publics, a well-received, big-time mass media hit may provide a boost in morale or give employees extra confidence that people have heard of their company when they pursue a sales lead or introduce themselves at a meeting.

Likewise, even the most interpersonal channels can reach external publics. This has always been the case with word-of-mouth communication, and it is more pronounced with social media.

Online, the lines between internal and external communication are increasingly blurring. In 2006, when corporate blogging was becoming a trend of interest for public relations research, I surveyed a sample of people who had read and commented on blogs posted by people who worked at Microsoft and found that more than 30 percent of the commenters also

External publics
Groups of people that exist mostly outside of an organization and have a relationship with the organization.

When Yahoo CEO Marissa Mayer rolled out a new work-from-home policy, the company received more feedback than it anticipated or likely wanted when it was forwarded externally.

How do social media blur the lines between an organization's internal and external communications?

Social media blur the lines between an organization's internal and external communications.

worked at Microsoft. The blogs were clearly channels for both internal and external communication. In this case, the effects looked to be beneficial because the respondents reported high levels of trust and satisfaction in their relationship with the organization.[8]

But it can go the other way too. When Yahoo CEO Marissa Mayer wanted to roll out a new rule discouraging Yahoo employees from working remotely, HR director Jackie Reses sent out an internal memo introducing the new policy. It was marked "PROPRIETARY AND CONFIDENTIAL INFORMATION— DO NOT FORWARD."[9] The memo was immediately forwarded anyhow, and within hours the story was all over social media and mainstream media alike. Yahoo management certainly received way more feedback than they sought.

LATENT, AWARE, ACTIVE

According to Kurt Lewin, a pioneer in social and organizational psychology, "There is nothing so practical as a good theory."[10] A good example of practical theory in public relations is James Grunig's situational theory of publics. The theory applies easily to practice, in that it helps us identify and strategize about publics in the context of a situation analysis and the planning that follows. The situational theory of publics basically says that publics range from latent to aware to active based on their levels of involvement, problem recognition and constraint recognition.

Case Study

Situational theory of publics
Theory that the activity of publics depends on their levels of involvement, problem recognition and constraint recognition.

Net neutrality
When data transmitted on the internet is treated equally by governments and service providers in a way that does not slow down, speed up or manipulate traffic to create a favorable business environment for some organizations or users over others.

Applying the Situational Theory of Publics: Net Neutrality

The case of net neutrality offers an example of how the **situational theory of publics** can be applied. **Net neutrality** "means that Internet service providers may not discriminate between different kinds of content and applications online," according to Free Press's "Save the Internet" Campaign at www.savetheinternet.com. The issue, as described by the group is this:

The biggest cable and telephone companies would like to charge money for smooth access to web sites, speed to run applications, and permission to plug in devices. These network giants believe they should be able to charge

Web site operators, application providers and device manufacturers for the right to use the network. Those who don't make a deal and pay up will experience discrimination: Their sites won't load as quickly, and their applications and devices won't work as well. Without legal protection, consumers could find that a network operator has blocked the Web site of a competitor, or slowed it down so much that it's unusable.[11]

The Free Press organization advocates for net neutrality, and in doing so opposes Federal Communications Commission (FCC) regulations that would allow for a tiered system supported by telecommunications companies. In 2014, the FCC considered adopting a rule that would allow internet service providers to offer a "fast lane" on the internet for companies that are willing and able to pay for it. Under this rule Netflix might have paid Comcast or AT&T to improve streaming speeds of its video material relative to other content providers. There was certainly more than one side to this issue, and the legal, technological, economic and societal issues underlying the debate were rather complex. For example, Netflix's CEO actually strongly supported net neutrality for "democratizing access to ideas, services and goods," and also because ISP interconnection fees will ultimately lead to "a poor consumer experience," he blogged in 2014.[12] Were you part of a latent, aware or active public for the issue? The answer depends on three questions.

PROBLEM RECOGNITION

How often do people stop to think about the issue? If people haven't detected an issue, they won't think about it much. This doesn't mean they aren't affected or don't have a say. They may well still be part of a key public. They just don't realize it. Think of all the Netflix viewers, YouTube uploaders, and online gamers who never stopped to think about net neutrality before 2014. These are **latent publics**, because even though they can be defined as a public, they themselves don't recognize it. Once they do recognize the issue—**problem recognition**—and start thinking about it, they become **aware publics**. Most strategic public relations efforts involve not just mere awareness, but some level of understanding of the issue, and, beyond that, behavior.

LEVEL OF INVOLVEMENT

How connected do people feel to the issue? A key factor in whether people will become **active publics** on an issue is their **level of involvement**. People who used the internet primarily for low-bandwidth activities like checking e-mail or occasional light web browsing may have been aware of the net neutrality issue, but they just didn't see a strong enough connection between the issue and their personal situations to get active on the issue. From a public relations planner's perspective, research on demographics and psychographics is useful in identifying involved publics. Research on **demographics** answers questions like how old these people are and where they live. Research on **psychographics**, on the other hand, answers

Latent publics
People who are affected by a problem or issue but don't realize it.

Problem recognition
When people detect a problem or situation in their environment and begin to think about it.

Aware publics
People who recognize that they are affected by a problem or issue in their environment.

Active publics
People who behave and communicate actively in response to a problem or issue.

Level of involvement
The degree to which people feel or think that a problem or issue affects them.

Demographics
Data describing objective characteristics of a population including age, level of income or highest educational degree obtained.

Psychographics
Data describing psychological characteristics of a population including interests, attitudes and behaviors.

The goal of this message that made the rounds on Facebook and other social media sites appears to be to move publics from latent to aware or from aware to active.

What types of research do you think led to this tactic?

questions about variables such as the personality types of heavy internet users and their preferences for online content. The psychographic profile of a potential active public in the net neutrality debate is one of a heavy data user who combines personal and social use of bandwidth.

CONSTRAINT RECOGNITION

What, if anything, can people do about the issue? Let's say your public now really understands net neutrality and they're good and mad about it being taken away (high problem recognition) because of how badly that change will mess up their internet experience if they are not willing to pay more to access high-quality content (high level of involvement). What are they going to do about it? The answer depends on **constraint recognition**, and a smart public relations plan will have a response to that question ready for publics at this stage. Free Press told web users they had options. "Share this page to spread the word to stop them from selling out Net Neutrality!" was one option. Signing an online petition to the FCC was another.

In 2015, instead of adopting rules providing for a fast lane, the FCC sided with millions of people who took an active stance on the issue. The FCC adopted rules to protect the open internet: "America's broadband networks must be fast, fair and open—principles shared by the overwhelming majority of the nearly 4 million commenters who participated in the FCC's Open Internet proceeding."[13] The Free Press organization called the decision the "biggest victory for the public interest in the FCC's history."[14]

Urgent: sign this petition to save the open Internet

Despite massive growing resistance, the FCC just voted to advance rules that could slow down and censor the Internet by allowing ISPs to discriminate when they deliver content. Everyone needs to take action right now.

Don't let Comcast and AT&T control the future of the Internet

"Dear FCC, we need real net neutrality. Protect internet users from monopolistic ISPs and don't let companies censor, slow down, or block websites while requiring other sites to pay for faster service. Please stand up for all internet users and our right to communicate."

Email   Sign Petition

Fight for the Future and Center for Rights will contact you about future campaigns. Privacy Policy

Like our page or donate to help on future campaigns to protect our basic rights:

FFTF Fight For The Future
Like Page   152K likes
Follow @fightfortheftr

Fight for the Future is a nonprofit organization that creates civic campaigns including this one advocating for net neutrality.

How many specific ways can publics become active from this web page?

OTHER WAYS OF SEGMENTING PUBLICS

Depending on the context, public relations strategists may choose to segment publics in a number of other ways. For clear prioritization, publics may be labeled as primary, secondary and tertiary. Suppose you are planning a community park cleanup. You may decide that young volunteers are your **primary public**. According to the Useful Community Development website (http://www.useful-community-development.org), you could recruit local children: "At age 3 and up, they can pick up trash," and "Teenagers can be drawn in, especially if you provide a good-looking T-shirt. . . ." In planning, you would also want to develop strategy to communicate with their teachers and parents, especially if some of your recruits are only three years old! Parents of small children would also be primary publics, but you might decide to label parents of older teenagers and teachers who might encourage participation as **secondary publics**. Additional groups, known as **tertiary publics**, could include city officials, sponsors or private waste removal companies as well as other park users who will benefit.

In cases involving competition or divisive issues, publics may be segmented into proponents, opponents and uncommitted. Campaign strategy, especially in political campaigns, often focuses on the uncommitted. While it is important to reinforce the attitudes of supporters, and occasionally those opposed to your candidate or position may be won over in an election, the greatest gains in many campaigns come from undecided or independent voters. The same logic applies outside of politics. Some people will support your efforts even without a public relations program, and others will never get involved; however, you can make progress with publics that are somewhere in between, moving them from latent to aware to active.

Sometimes it makes sense to segment publics based on their role in the communications process. For example, you may want to think about the sources for your messages such as employees or members of your organization, the intermediaries such as reporters, community leaders or social media influencers, and the target publics who will receive and respond to the message. Keep in mind that in two way-communication, senders and receivers will have interchangeable roles. For example, company representatives may be expected to send information out, but having those same people positioned to receive and respond to feedback is important too.

RESOURCES FOR RESEARCH ON PUBLICS

The following are useful resources for conducting research on publics:

- *Results of prior surveys.* These may be either conducted by the organization or by others who have sampled from populations that overlap significantly with key publics.

- *Publicly available databases, including census data.* Funded by the government, U.S. Census data are free to access, and www.census.gov allows for

Planners need to consider many publics that will be involved in various ways with an event like this park clean up in Detroit.

Can you name some primary, secondary and tertiary publics for this event?

Some people will support your efforts without a public relations program, and others will never get involved, but you can make progress with publics that are somewhere in between.

Primary publics
Groups of people identified as most important to the success of a public relations campaign or program.

Secondary publics
Groups of people who are important to a public relations campaign or program because of their relationship with primary publics.

Tertiary publics
Groups of people who indirectly influence or are indirectly affected by a public relations campaign or program.

Census data are freely available at www.census.gov.

How might these type of data be useful in a public relations program?

searching and analysis based on geography, demographics and topics such as education, economy, health and business.

- *Market research reports.* These generally cost money if you want data tailored to your specific questions about key publics, but they can be useful and fascinating if your budget permits them. For example, the Strategic Business Insights' VALS™ (values, attitudes and lifestyles) system offers demographic and psychographic profiles of consumers.

- *Media lists.* These include journalists and other opinion leaders (e.g., columnists, editors, commentators) and influencers online (e.g., bloggers and other actively engaged social media users).

- *News stories or online reports about key publics.* For example, if you search for "Sacramento park cleanup" you'd find information from the city of Sacramento about volunteer programs, a nonprofit organization called American River Parkway Foundation that coordinates cleanup activities, and news and information about "Creek Week" including its past sponsors and Facebook group ("First we clean . . . then we celebrate!"). More controversial situations will more likely have been covered in news reports including descriptive information about proponents and opponents. News stories or prior research reports may also include perspectives gained from interviews that offer richer perspective than is available from statistical reports.

- *Social media accounts of representatives of key publics.* Blogs, Twitter accounts, public Facebook groups and Instagram accounts can offer a better understanding of a public's motivations, concerns and general culture from a first-person perspective.

- *An organization's past communication records with key publics.* Look around for collections of comment cards, e-mail folders with public feedback, archived comments or replies to social media posts, minutes from public meetings, guest lists for special events and even logs of incoming phone calls (including complaints). As a customer, I actually like it when I'm told that my call to a company "may be recorded." It gives me hope that my concern will be taken seriously (though somehow I doubt those call recordings are listened to very often!).

Quantitative Research

When numbers and statistics accompany the results of research, it is considered **quantitative research**. In a blood drive, quantitative data could include demographic statistics on blood donors and non-donors in a county, the number of e-mail accounts that are known to have received an invitation, the percentage of people who click on a link in an e-mail invitation, the number people who respond to a Facebook invitation, the number

Quantitative research
Research that results in numerical or statistical data and analysis.

of retweets of a Twitter announcement, other more sophisticated analytics of the pattern of social media activities, the number of people who make an appointment to donate blood, the number of people who actually board the bloodmobile on a given day, and perhaps most important, the amount of blood actually donated. Surveys and experiments are common methods for quantitative research.

Surveys

Questionnaires that are administered online, on printed paper or face-to-face allow researchers to gather data from respondents that can be presented in quantitative form. Reports can include the number or percentages of people who answered questions in certain ways (yes, no, maybe, strongly agree, etc.) and more sophisticated statistics such as correlations, and tests of the significance of interactions between variables.

For example, researchers who surveyed a sample of Polish university students with questionnaires administered in lecture rooms found that 19 percent had considered blood donation and that 37.9 percent had not decided about donating blood or had never even thought about it. They also reported that religious obligation (measured with a numerical scale of agreement with the statement "My religious beliefs encourage me to help other people") correlated with another item that measured "definite consideration of blood donation."[15] A positive correlation in this case means that people who reported stronger religious beliefs were more likely to consider donating blood.

Experiments

Experiments allow researchers to test predictions based on controlled differences between groups. For example, researchers working with the Swiss Red Cross and the Zurich Blood Donation Service sent three different invitations out to people who were registered in the blood donation service's database. Recipients of the invitations were randomly assigned to one of three groups. Members of one group, a **treatment group**, were offered a lottery ticket as an incentive to donate. A second treatment group was offered a free blood screening. The third group, known as a **control group**, was offered no special incentive. Because more than 10,000 donors were part of the study and participants were assigned to groups randomly, any difference between groups could reasonably be attributed to the different invitations and incentives. The researchers found that "offering a lottery ticket increases usable donations by 5 percentage points over a baseline donation rate of 42 percent."[16]

Content Analysis

Content analysis does not involve direct interaction or questioning of people, but rather analyzing the content of people's communication. Any type of recorded communication—from newspaper articles to TV shows to YouTube comments to Instagram feeds—can be systematically analyzed.

Treatment group
A group of subjects or people in an experiment that receive or are exposed to a treatment.

Control group
A group of subjects or people in an experiment that do not receive or are not exposed to a treatment for the purpose of comparison.

Content analysis
A systematic method for analyzing recorded information such as audio, video or text.

Social media allow countless ways for people to communicate.

What are some useful units of analysis that can be quantified in a medium like Facebook?

In planning a blood drive, it may be useful to analyze the content of comments on the organization's Facebook page, news stories that mention the organization by name, letters and e-mails written to the organization or internal communication such as memos and newsletters. University of Miami Professor Don Stacks identified four types of units of analysis that can be quantified.[17]

1. *Words or symbols.* How many times has the word *bloodmobile* been used in the local newspaper in the past year? How many times during a drive was #bloodmobile used on Instagram? How many arm selfies appeared?!

2. *Characters.* These are the people involved or the roles that they play. How often do stories include *volunteers*, *donors*, *doctors* or *recipients*?

3. *Time and space.* How many minutes of news coverage does a blood drive get on TV? How much space does the announcement get in a company e-mail newsletter?

4. *Items.* An item is the message itself. How many tweets? How many comments on a blog? Even the number of likes on Facebook could count as items.

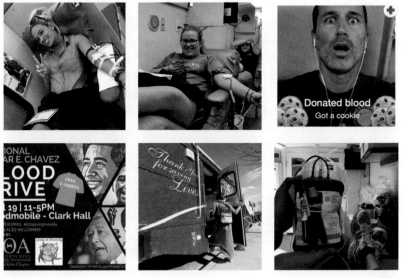

The label #Bloodmobile aggregates an interesting sample of user-generated content related to blood drives.

How might you use Instagram in the research process for planning a blood drive in your community?

Content analysis also can reveal themes and underlying messages in communication. Stacks calls this *latent* content. A careful analysis of blog entries about donating blood may, for example, reveal a theme of interpersonal influence if bloggers regularly mention key people who motivated them to donate. Convenience, guilt, safety or altruism could also show up as themes. Exploring deeper themes and meaning, however, is much more of a qualitative endeavor than quantitative. Therefore, content analysis can be quantitative or qualitative.

Qualitative Research

Qualitative research answers open-ended questions that can't be answered with numbers alone. What motivates people to donate blood? What fears, concerns or misconceptions do potential donors have? What differences have volunteers observed between one-time donors and donors who give blood repeatedly? Interviews, focus groups and direct observation give researchers and strategists a deeper understanding of human behavior.

Interviews

While it is interesting and useful to know that researchers have found a statistical correlation between religious beliefs and consideration of blood donation, much more can be learned about what potential blood donors are thinking and feeling by sitting down with them (or talking on the phone or Skype, etc.) and asking carefully considered open-ended questions. In-depth interviews allow respondents the opportunity to elaborate, sometimes revealing answers the researcher may have never even considered. Perhaps the connection between religion and blood donor attitudes has something to do with deep-seated personal values. Or maybe it's just convenience if the blood drives are organized at churches? Or perhaps it's a combination of these factors? Interviewing people is a good way to find out. Interviews enable respondents to answer questions in their own terms instead of merely agreeing or disagreeing with statements in surveys or answering questions within the constraints of short-answer questionnaire formats. Interviews can focus on facts and biographical information, beliefs, feelings, motives, behaviors, perceived norms and conscious reasoning for feelings and behavior.[18]

Focus Groups

In public relations, we are very often interested in how people think, feel and act in groups. Focus groups are essentially group interviews. Instead of sitting down with an individual, you would arrange to interview a small group of six to 12 people together. While each person may not have the opportunity to articulate his or her own insight at length the way he or she would in a one-on-one interview, the conversation among people in a focus group may yield results that more closely approximate the way people form and express ideas in social settings.

Qualitative research
Research that results in in-depth description and understanding without relying on the use of numbers or statistics to analyze findings.

Focus groups were commonly used by advertising firms in the *Mad Men* era of the 1950s and 1960s to test ad concepts, and they have been widely adopted in social sciences in recent decades.

How can public relations researchers use focus groups?

A well-moderated focus group will allow group members to explore points of agreement as well as areas in which members diverge in their attitudes, beliefs and behaviors. In his book *Focus Groups as Qualitative Research*, sociologist David Morgan wrote about how focus groups can bring to life topics that may be mundane or difficult to explore in depth with any one individual: "I once watched a marketer with a background in sociology conduct a lively demonstration focus group of professors and graduate students who discussed their use of bar soap."[19] Indeed, it would be hard to imagine sitting down with one person for an hour or so to talk about a bar of soap. Imagine what a skilled group moderator could do with the right group of people from one of your key publics discussing a topic like blood donation.

Direct Observation

Of course, what people say is not always consistent with what they do. Therefore, do not overlook direct observation as a form of research. Two types of direct observation are participant and nonparticipant observation. In **nonparticipant observation** the researcher does not interact with the people being observed. A researcher might sit unnoticed a few feet away from volunteers who are staffing a blood drive registration table or out of the way in the back of a bloodmobile and watch what people do and say. In **participant observation**, the researcher interacts with those being observed, sometimes for very long periods of time. You may have seen

Nonparticipant observation
Research method in which the researcher avoids interaction with the environment or those being observed.

Participant observation
Research method in which the researcher deliberately interacts with the environment and those being observed.

documentaries dealing with anthropologists who go to great lengths to become part of the cultures they wish to understand. Research in public relations planning likely will not require such an intense personal commitment. If your organization is a local blood bank, you could learn a lot by serving as a volunteer or by going through the blood donation process yourself while observing others.

Direct observation can also reveal important variables to measure in other types of research. For example, a blood bank may decide to do further research on factors that influence donors, such as cleanliness of facilities, the comfort of waiting areas, food and drink options and donor interaction with counselors.

Secondary and Primary Research

Many of the resources for research listed earlier would be considered **secondary research**, which is the re-use of research and data that have already been collected. When public relations strategists explore census data, read market research reports, search for blogs or news stories on the web or review research from past case studies, they are conducting secondary research. Consider how much you can learn about blood drives (situations), blood banks (organizations) and blood donors (publics) without even stepping away from your computer. In writing this chapter, every single resource on blood drives consulted was available online! But if I wanted to plan my own blood drive here in my own hometown, I would still have some specific questions that would require primary research to answer.

Primary research involves designing research and collecting your own data for communication planning. One clear benefit of primary research is that it allows you to tailor research to your own specific purposes. While I have learned that lottery tickets were an effective incentive to convince people to donate blood in Switzerland and that college students in Poland are motivated in part by religious beliefs, I may want to test other incentives with my own research.

Formal and Informal Research

As mentioned near the beginning of this chapter, research in public relations ranges from casual and unscientific to carefully planned and sophisticated. In other words, the options range from **informal research** to **formal research**. The more carefully that public relations strategists design research with clear rules and procedures for the collection and analysis of information, the more formal the research.

The U.S. Department of Health and Human Services includes an agency called the Substance Abuse and Mental Health Services Administration

Secondary research
Collection, summary, analysis or application of previously reported research.

Primary research
Systematic design, collection, analysis and application of original data or observation.

Informal research
Research conducted without clear rules or procedures, which makes the findings difficult to replicate or compare to other research or situations.

Formal research
Research designed with clear rules and procedures for collection and analysis of information.

Primary research allows you to tailor your research to your own specific purposes.

The Substance Abuse and Mental Health Services Administration (SAMHSA) spends millions of dollars on scientific research, including face-to-face survey administration, to attain good data on drug use and health issues in the United States.

Why is this research so expensive?

(SAMHSA). SAMHSA funds a national survey on drug use and health that involves interviews with a random sample of nearly 70,000 Americans aged 12 or older. The company selected to conduct the research, Research Triangle Institute, won the bid to conduct the research based on their expertise in research design, sampling and data collection, processing, analysis and reporting. This formal process has obvious advantages over less formal research. The survey is designed to "provide national and state-level estimates on the use of tobacco products, alcohol, illicit drugs (including non-medical use of prescription drugs) and mental health in the United States."[20] Goals for the research include providing accurate data on drug use and abuse, tracking national trends in the use of alcohol, tobacco and various types of drugs, studying the consequences of substance use and abuse, and identifying high-risk groups. The resulting data are of great value to SAMHSA and the organizations it serves, including state and local health departments, the U.S. Department of Education and the White House Office of National Drug Control Policy. It is easy to imagine how the research would be useful in strategic planning for anyone practicing public relations in any one of these organizations. The research yields a wealth of data on the situation and the publics with whom these organizations are most concerned.

Informal research just wouldn't provide the same value in results. The main issue with formal research, however, is that it doesn't come cheap. The SAMHSA contract award for 2014 with optional surveys running through 2017 costs U.S. taxpayers $210,301,771!

So, let's say you don't have a couple hundred million in your budget, but you still need to do some research. Informal research can be designed and conducted for practically free. If you were researching drug and alcohol issues, you could ask your friends and family about drugs and alcohol (informal interviews or focus groups), create a quick online questionnaire or Facebook poll and post it on your organization's page (informal survey), compare a few different types of brochures to see if they have different effects on people (informal experiment) or skim local newspapers for drug- and alcohol-related stories (informal content analysis).

Of course, asking some questions to a few friends and conducting a $200 million national survey represent extremes on the spectrum from informal to formal research. Deciding on research that best meets your organization's needs and budget means weighing costs and benefits. Two of the biggest factors driving decisions about research are reliability and validity.

Reliability refers to how well a particular research technique can be applied multiple times and yield comparable data. In getting ready for a long trip, I often lift my suitcase and estimate how much it weighs because I don't want to get dinged with a $25 fee for overweight luggage if my bag weighs more than 50 pounds. I zip my bag closed and lift it a few inches off the ground. "About 40 pounds," I figure. "No problem."

Two hours later, I unload my family's luggage from the car to the curb at the airport. I lean way into the back of the car to heave my bag out. "Oh no!," I think this time. "This thing has got to weigh at least 55 pounds." In reality, my bag weighs the same at the airport as it did at home, but my guestimate is not reliable.

I get to the ticket counter for the moment of truth. "Please put your bag on the scale," says the ticket agent. The digits on the display scramble and then settle in on the reading—52 pounds. "D'oh!" I take my bag off the scale, pull a jacket and a book out, and heave it back on the scale. The digits on the scale scramble again as we all wait for the new reading . . . 49 pounds. "Woohoo!" No one argues with the scale. We assume it is reliable. If you place the same bag with the same contents on the scale multiple times it should give the same reading. That's reliability. If you get a different reading on a second measure as in my case, you assume that the weight of the suitcase actually changed, not that something is wrong with the scale. Again, the assumption is that the scale is reliable.

One of the goals of the national drug use survey is to track changes in drug and alcohol use. The formal research methods employed are designed for reliability so that if the results show a year-to-year change in drug or alcohol use among a certain population, researchers can be confident that the change in results is due more to actual changes in the population than to errors in the survey as a measurement tool. Smaller (and less expensive!) research designs can be reliable too if they are designed well.

Validity refers to the accuracy of a measurement or observation in reflecting what the researcher intends to measure or observe. After the agent checks my bag at the ticket counter it rides on a conveyor belt and disappears into another part of the airport, likely to go through an X-ray machine or pass by bomb-sniffing dogs. The scale at the ticket counter may offer a reliable reading of weight in pounds, but no validity in representing the contents of the bag. From the weight scale, the agent would have no idea whether the bag contains 49 pounds of books or 49 pounds of clothes or 49 pounds of pineapples.

Validity in public relations research and social science research can be particularly tricky because we often try to measure and observe things that are much harder to define than books, clothes or pineapples. When the concepts to be measured include intangibles like attitudes toward an

Reliability
Consistency and precision of a particular research technique.

Validity
Accuracy of a particular research technique in measuring or observing what the researcher intends to measure or observe.

Validity is a big concern when trying to measure intangibles like attitudes toward an organization or involvement with an issue.

organization, involvement with an issue or behavior that is not easily observed in public, validity is a big concern. Even in a very reliable survey of alcohol use for example, we have to wonder about validity. Consider the following finding from a SAMHSA report.

"Nationally, 15.9 percent of all persons aged 12 to 20 were binge alcohol users in the 30 days prior to being surveyed. Estimates ranged from 9.2 percent in Shelby County, Tennessee, to 46.3 percent in the District of Columbia's Ward 2."[21]

Reading this report after reviewing the research methods, I am fairly confident in the reliability of the results. I'm confident that there is significantly more binge drinking in D.C.'s Ward 2 than in Shelby County, Tennessee. But I'm a little less confident in how well the data from a self-report drinking survey represents the complexity of alcohol use and abuse. The researchers carefully define binge drinking as having five or more drinks on the same occasion at least one time in the past 30 days, but people may reasonably disagree about what these self-reports actually indicate in terms of alcohol abuse.

Another example is campus crime safety campaigns. If you organize a campus safety campaign that emphasizes the importance of reporting suspicious activity, how would you feel about an increase in calls to police on your campus? Would you be disappointed because this indicates more suspicious activity? Or would you welcome the news that more suspicious activity was actually reported? Or would you need more information to draw a conclusion? This is a question of validity and requires a deeper understanding of the information available. You may obtain that information from further quantitative data (number of actual convictions or data on property loss) or you may obtain it from qualitative research (in-depth interviews with law enforcement, riding along with police on their beats, etc.).

No single research method, no matter how formal, is perfect. There are always trade-offs. The strengths of a large-scale national survey with tens of thousands of participants can become limitations in understanding deeper social phenomena. Careful observation or in-depth interviewing can reveal rich information to help you understand your organization and publics and their deeper motivations, attitudes and behavior, but reliability becomes an issue with this type of research because it would be difficult to repeat with consistent results.

A research methods course will help you design and evaluate research for reliability and validity. Even if you end up performing secondary research or hiring others to conduct research, understanding the different types of research and the strengths and limitations of your options is a critical part of planning for strategic public relations and for reporting the results of your work with confidence.

No single research method, no matter how formal, is perfect. There are always trade-offs.

Voices from the Field

Sarab Kochhar

SARAB KOCHHAR, PH.D., is associate director in APCO Worldwide's Washington, D.C., office where she serves as a strategic counsel for clients on measurement and evaluation for communication programs. Kochhar also holds the position of director of research with the Institute for Public Relations (IPR). She has worked in both public and private sectors, including with Burson-Marsteller in Bangalore, India; with the government of Chandigarh, Punjab, and Haryana where she managed the tourism function, including sports, medical, health and cultural tourism; and with the Ketchum Research and Analytics Group in New York.

Public relations research very often entails social science research. In what ways have you seen traditional social science research methods best applied in public relations?
From secondary research that helps them to strategize and plan to primary research used to measure and evaluate the campaigns, public relations professionals use traditional social science research methods extensively. For example, social science research methods are used to plan, design a campaign, ensure campaign objectives are realistic and connected to the outcome, identify and describe the relevant publics, develop and test messages and channels, monitor the progress of PR efforts and show the impact and effectiveness of programs.

We hear a lot about new methods for evaluating social media efforts with digital metrics to show results [a later chapter will focus on measurement and evaluation], but in what ways are strategists using digital resources for formative research?
Digital resources are being used to better understand customers and their behaviors and preferences. As one example, U.S. retailer Target was able to predict when one of its customers was to going to have a baby. Digital resources are also helping organizations and strategists to predict what products will sell. For example, car insurance companies understand how well their customers actually drive.

Even government election campaigns can be optimized using digital resources.

Are digital media making research cheaper and easier for public relations people?
Digital resources are certainly making the research easier for public relations professionals. Digital media has helped the public relations professional to use research in setting up objectives, developing strategy and creating tactics. The social media landscape has especially redefined the roles that engagement, interactivity and participation play in public relations. For example, organizations are using big data like social media mentions and reviews to gauge their brand's reach. Digital resources serve as competitive intelligence during the public relations and social media planning process. Yelp is one example of a company that is starting to tackle big data and taking advantage of data mining for creating better services. Yelp's log data contain the number of times ads are displayed to users, user clicks and so on. Data mining helps Yelp in designing search systems, showing ads and filtering fake reviews. In addition, data mining enables products such as "review highlights" and "people who viewed this also viewed . . ."

What specific research skills will help entry-level job candidates in the job market, and how can they acquire these skills?
Candidates entering the job market should know and understand both qualitative and quantitative research methods and how to apply those to public relations campaigns. The key elements of public relations research are being able to take research methods and apply them specifically to public relations contexts and issues. But most important is the ability to think like a researcher. Professionals should be able to look at a problem and think about the research questions, research methods, forms of data, and data analysis that would help them to both solve the research problem and/or look at a client need in a unique way.

Utilitarianism
Principle that the most ethical
course of action is the one that
maximizes good and minimizes
harm for people.

Ethics: Utilitarianism

Research helps us make informed decisions. Public relations practitioners use research not only to inform their own thinking and strategy, but also to inform and persuade their organizations and publics. Contributing to the marketplace of ideas in a way that informs citizens in democracies is one of the highest ideals of public relations. One of the most common ways that public relations professionals engage the marketplace of ideas is to present research data.

In democracies, ideas are often judged based on the question of which course of action will do the greatest good for the greatest number of people.

Research the consequences of competing actions and determine which action does the most good and the least bad. That's utilitarian ethics.

In philosophy, this approach to decision-making is called **utilitarianism**. Nineteenth-century English philosopher Jeremy Bentham and one of his students, political economist and philosopher John Stuart Mill, spelled out utilitarianism as an ethic of consequences. That is, they wrote that you can decide on an ethical course of action by determining which actions will have the best consequences. Take into account all the good and bad consequences of competing actions and determine which action does the most good and the least bad, and then you are ready to act ethically.

Ethics of consequences can be applied in everyday decision-making. In deciding how to handle media interview requests when bad news breaks, which stories to include in newsletters, what photos to pin on Pinterest and even which employee tweets to retweet, public relations practitioners think through the consequences of their actions in an effort to make the right decisions every day. But when dealing with large-scale issues of public concern, research is often brought into the mix to help organizations decide on their positions and then advocate appropriately.

Take, for example, the issue of raising minimum wages for fast-food restaurant workers. It's an interesting and difficult political and economic issue, and we have organizations with paid professionals ready and willing to help us sort out the best course of action.

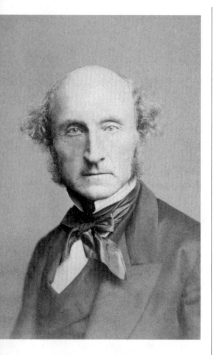

John Stuart Mill advanced the ethics of utility—making decisions based on expected consequences.

How can research help public relations practitioners practice utilitarianism?

A nonprofit organization called the Employment Policies Institute published a research report by an economics professor at San Diego State University that found that raising minimum wages actually leads to reduced employment opportunities for entry-level laborers. The study of data over two decades shows that in weak labor markets "each 10 percent minimum wage increase reduces employment for young drop-outs by over four percent."[22] John Stuart Mill would love this, right? The data show us that even though some people would benefit from raised wages, others—particularly the least skilled and least experienced employees—would suffer because there are fewer jobs. The thrust of the research posted by the Employment Policies Institute suggests that *not* raising minimum wages would do the greatest good for the greatest number of people.

Of course there is another side to this issue. The Center for Labor Research and Education at UC Berkeley published results of a study that showed "the fast-food industry costs American taxpayers nearly $7 billion annually because its jobs pay so little that 52 percent of fast-food workers are forced to enroll their families in public assistance programs."[23] If low wages hurt both the fast-food workers and taxpayers, then the utilitarian answer seems to be to raise wages. What would Mill say now?

As the minimum wage case shows, determining the most ethical answers to public-interest questions by trying to maximize positive and minimize negative outcomes can be difficult. Philosophers call it utilitarian calculus, and it has its limits. In the minimum wage case much of the confusion stems from the fact that the organizations promoting the research have very different political agendas. The data from the Berkeley study were used by a group called the National Employment Law Project, which hosts websites such as http://www.raisetheminimumwage.org and http://www.just-pay.org that advocate for higher minimum wages. On the other side, the Employment Policies Institute is closely tied with a public relations firm called Berman and Company and the website http://www.minimumwage.com. According to a report in *The New York Times*, Berman and Co. bills the nonprofit Employment Policies Institute for services of its employees, and "the arrangement effectively means the nonprofit is a moneymaking venture" for Richard Berman and his associates who actively represent and advocate for the restaurant industry.

Perhaps the moral of the story for public relations is to avoid confusing the use of research for advocacy and profit with the process of utilitarian ethics. As public relations scholars Shannon Bowen and Don Stacks point out, a primary weakness of utilitarian ethics is that the person who applies them can use them "to sanction whatever he or she wants to maximize in their *personal* good outcomes, as opposed to maximizing the greatest good for the greatest interest in the public interest."[24]

In 2012, the Institute for Public Relations measurement commission adopted a statement on ethical standards in public relations research and measurement that promotes many core values beyond utilitarianism: "All research should abide by the principles of intellectual honesty, fairness, dignity, disclosure, and respect for all stakeholders involved, namely clients (both external and internal), colleagues, research participants, the public relations profession and the researchers themselves."[25]

Workers protest for a higher minimum wage.

In what ways could reasonable people disagree about the consequences of raising minimum wages?

Both raisetheminimumwage.org and minimumwage.com use research to argue their opposing sides to an issue.

How do these two examples illustrate the limitations of utilitarianism in applied research ethics?

ICYMI

In Case You Missed It

The very first thing most of us do when we need an answer to a new question is hit the search button. But research in public relations is about so much more than online searching and "re-searching." To develop effective strategy and achieve worthwhile outcomes, we have to ask the right questions and understand the best methods for answering them. Here are some tips to consider as you get started with your programs and campaigns, maybe even before you open Google.

- Evaluation can happen at any point in a strategic program, not just at the end.

- Gaining a deeper understanding of a situation requires digging for information of substance beyond an internet search.

- Organization-public relationships flourish when you spend as much energy trying to understand your publics as you do trying to get your message out.

- Social media blur the lines between an organization's internal and external communications.

- Some people will support your efforts without a public relations program and others will never get involved, but you can make progress with publics that are somewhere in between.

- Primary research allows you to tailor your research to your own specific purposes.

- Validity is a big concern when trying to measure intangibles like attitudes toward an organization or involvement with an issue.

- No single research method, no matter how formal, is perfect. There are always trade-offs.

- Research the consequences of competing actions and determine which one does the most good and the least bad. That's utilitarian ethics.

SUMMARY

5.1 Explain the role of formative and summative research in the RPIE cycle.

Formative research is conducted before and during a campaign or program to develop and fine-tune strategy. Summative research is conducted at the end to answer the question, "Did it work?" However, one campaign or program normally leads to another, so what may be considered summative for one effort may become formative for future strategy. Research and evaluation can be thought of as connected parts of a cycle rather than the beginning and end of a linear process.

5.2 Describe the contents of a situation analysis.

In writing a situation analysis, the planner researches and reports on the strengths and weaknesses of an organization along with the opportunities and threats in the organization's environment (i.e., SWOT analysis) as they relate to the motive for a public relations program or campaign. The narrative analysis leads to a concise problem or opportunity statement that clearly articulates the reason for planning a public relations program or campaign and sets the stage for campaign goals.

5.3 Strategically segment publics.

Publics can be identified and researched on several dimensions. Some categories for segmenting publics are (1) internal and external; (2) latent, aware and active; and (3) primary, secondary and tertiary. Demographic and psychographic information can help researchers understand publics.

5.4 Compare the costs and benefits of various research methods.

Researchers must weigh the relative costs and benefits of different research options including primary and secondary research, formal and informal research, and quantitative and qualitative research. Secondary research is generally cheaper and easier than primary research, but primary research yields custom results that are directly applicable to the situation at hand. Informal research is easier than formal research, but formal research is conducted with rules and procedures that allow for more confidence in the results. Quantitative research allows for clear numerical reporting and analysis of large amounts of data. Qualitative research allows for richer description and deeper understanding of the people or content studied.

5.5 Differentiate between reliability and validity.

Reliability refers to the consistency and precision of a research technique: "Does the instrument produce the same or comparable results in repeated trials?" Validity refers to the accuracy of the technique: "Are you measuring what you think you're measuring?"

5.6 Evaluate utilitarianism as an ethical principle for public relations research.

Utilitarianism is a useful ethical principle to the extent that the person applying it makes unbiased and informed decisions based on a clear understanding of the relative harm and benefit of competing courses of action. When researchers work with a biased perspective on the data available, they tend to calculate benefit and harm in ways that support their own opinions or agendas rather than society at large.

DISCUSSION QUESTIONS

1. Recall an event or activity that you've planned and conducted in the past year. What kind of research, if any, did you do? How could evaluation of that effort help you next time you do a similar event or activity? What kind of research would you do next time?

2. Think of a public relations campaign idea that would be helpful to a familiar organization. Quickly jot down relevant strengths, weaknesses, opportunities and threats that come to mind. What kinds of research would you need to do to more formally develop your SWOT analysis for that organization?

3. Name an organization that's facing an issue trending in the news. Who are the organization's internal and external publics? Who are the latent, aware and active publics for the issue? Who are primary, secondary and tertiary publics?

4. Have you ever conducted a survey, focus group or other type of social research? Aside from cost, what are some advantages and disadvantages of doing research yourself versus paying for research services?

5. Using an example, explain the difference between reliability and validity. (Bonus if you can use your explanation to show a measure that is reliable but not valid, or valid but not reliable.)

6. Name a decision that a politician made that you don't agree with. Make a utilitarian argument for why you would make a different decision. What kind of research supports your case (and his or hers)?

KEY TERMS

Active publics   121
Analytics   112
Aware publics   121
Constraint recognition   122
Content analysis   125
Control group   125
Demographics   121
External publics   119
Formal research   129
Formative research   112
In house   117
Informal research   129
Internal publics   118
Latent publics   121
Level of involvement   121
Mission statement   117
Net neutrality   120
Nonparticipant observation   128
Organizational culture   118

Participant observation   128
Primary publics   123
Primary research   129
Problem or opportunity statement   113
Problem recognition   121
Psychographics   121
Qualitative research   127
Quantitative research   124
Reliability   131
Secondary publics   123
Secondary research   129
Situation analysis   113
Situational theory of publics   120
Summative research   112
SWOT analysis   114
Tertiary publics   123
Treatment group   125
Utilitarianism   134
Validity   131

CHAPTER 6

Planning

Convincing people to wash their hands more is a universal challenge. How do international organizations collaborate to change behavior and measure success?

KEY LEARNING OUTCOMES

6.1 Analyze strategic communication outcomes.

6.2 Map public relations strategy from mission to tactics.

6.3 Write SMART objectives.

6.4 Distinguish between outputs, outcomes and impacts.

6.5 Develop basic timelines to organize tasks in a strategic public relations program.

6.6 Identify key categories of public relations budget items.

6.7 Apply consequentialism to make ethical decisions about setting and achieving public relations objectives while enhancing the profession.

RELATED UNIVERSAL ACCREDITATION BOARD COMPETENCY AREAS

1.4 STRATEGIC THINKING • **1.5** PLANNING • **2.2** ETHICAL BEHAVIOR
4.2 BARRIERS TO COMMUNICATION • **5.2** RESOURCE MANAGEMENT

Jackpot! When the ice bucket challenge went viral in the summer of 2014, it raised ridiculous amounts of awareness for The Amyotrophic Lateral Sclerosis (ALS) Association. Facebook users posted more than 2.4 million related videos, while Instagrammers hashtagged some 37 million videos #ALSicebucketchallenge or #icebucketchallenge.[1] Many criticized the campaign for encouraging people to dump ice water on their heads to avoid making donations, but others were quick to point out that the campaign raised more than $100 million in 30 days.[2] There's no way the ALS group, or any other organization, can predict exactly how a viral campaign of this magnitude will play out. Luck played a role, no doubt, but a quote attributed to Roman philosopher Seneca puts that role in perspective: "Luck is what happens when preparation meets opportunity."

The ALS Ice Bucket Challenge went viral in the summer of 2014 and raised more than $100 million in 30 days.

What makes a campaign like this go viral? What is the role of planning?

Public relations **planning** is preparation for opportunity (Figure 6.1). Planning is the forethought about goals and objectives and the strategies and tactics for achieving them. Studying outcomes of past campaigns and programs can help us develop goals and objectives for future ones. There are a number of steps that take place between noticing ice buckets being dumped over people's heads in your Instagram feed and writing a check to support amyotrophic lateral sclerosis (ALS) research. This chapter discusses those steps as well as the key components of plans to achieve them: goals, objectives, timelines and budgets.

A Hierarchy of Outcomes

There are times when a client or organization knows they need help with public relations, but they have a hard time specifying exactly what it is that they want you to do. Your job as the public relations professional is to convert fuzzy thinking into a strategy that will lead to meaningful results for the organization.

One of the most common client requests is "Help us raise awareness." Awareness may be part of the desired results, but more often than not, awareness is only an intermediate step in a larger process to reach some other goal. Awareness of a cause, a new product or an app is only part of the process in leading people to donate, purchase or download, and to continued involvement or use beyond that.

Planning for public relations means considering a number of outcomes beyond awareness. Even in the most balanced of organization-public relationships, public relations practitioners need to think strategically about communication. That is, they need to think about the specific

Research

Planning

Evaluation

Implementation

Figure 6.1 In the RPIE cycle, planning is preceded by research (including evaluation of past programs and campaigns) and drives implementation.

How does research help planners write better goals and objectives?

Planning
Forethought about goals and objectives and the strategies and tactics needed to achieve them.

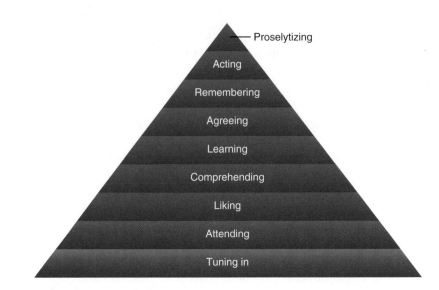

Figure 6.2 McGuire's hierarchy of effects.

Why might digital media marketers sometimes refer to this process as a funnel?

outcomes of their action and communication. Yale social psychologist William McGuire developed a hierarchy-of-effects model that outlines key steps in public communication campaigns (Figure 6.2): tuning in, attending, liking, comprehending, learning, agreeing, remembering, acting and proselytizing.

Tuning In

Before communication can have any effect at all, people must be exposed to the messages. Think of all the messages you see and hear every day: advertising, announcements, posters, fliers, email, social media posts and so on—you get the picture—even the most tuned-in media users are exposed to way more messaging than anyone can possibly pay attention to. While exposure is necessary in communication, it is only the first step in effective communication.

Attending

Attention is the next challenge. Take almost any hallway bulletin board in any college classroom or lecture hall. Watch as people walk by the posted fliers day after day. They are all exposed to the message if they even glance at the bulletin board, but how many of them actually pay attention? Next time you listen to ads on a streaming music service like Pandora or Spotify (assuming you haven't subscribed to the ad-free version), pay attention to how you pay attention. Do you notice the first ad or two more than the ones that come on after you've been listening a while?

Liking

On Facebook, we can signal our "likes" with a thumbs-up. It's one of many emotions we can express. According to McGuire, "liking" in particular is an

Awareness of a cause, new product or app is only one step in leading people to donate, purchase or download.

There's evidence of limited success with this hallway flier because some of the contact tabs have been taken.

When someone takes a contact tab, which steps to persuasion are complete? Which still remain?

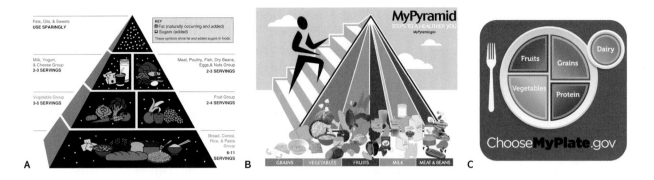

The USDA has a lot on its plate in communicating dietary guidelines in a likable and understandable way.

How is the newer message design (C) an improvement over older designs (A and B)?

important step in message processing because people must maintain interest in a message in order to process it further. In public relations, our messages are often more complex than a Facebook photo, a hallway flier announcing an event, or a streaming radio ad for tacos. Our publics may not love the idea of donating blood, eating more vegetables or joining a community discussion on a controversial issue, but if we are going to convince them to participate, our communication has to keep them engaged. If they dislike or just do not understand a message, they are unlikely to process it.

Comprehending

Sometimes people like a message, but they just don't get it. Again, in public relations, goals and objectives for communication often depend on publics understanding complex ideas or considering different sides of multidimensional issues. A clever post or credible spokesperson may get lots of "likes," but effective communication requires comprehension.

I really liked the U.S. Department of Agriculture's old food pyramid to promote balanced eating. My reading of that poster on the cafeteria walls of elementary, middle and high school was that I should carb-load like an endurance athlete and then top off with maybe a nice steak and a milkshake. In hindsight, that's probably not what the USDA was really trying to communicate. They later revised the food pyramid to emphasize more exercise and more individually appropriate choices. But that revision confused people too. Realizing that their message may have been liked but was too often misunderstood, the USDA settled on a plate graphic to illustrate the importance of a balanced diet.

Learning

Helping publics acquire relevant skills is one of the more difficult goals to achieve in public relations. Consider campaigns to get people to save for retirement, properly separate recyclables, or maintain safe privacy settings on social media accounts. Public relations basically becomes an act of

When campaign goals include helping publics acquire relevant skills, public relations basically becomes an act of teaching.

teaching. However, instead of the students sitting captive in a classroom, the primary public may be new employees who are overwhelmed in their first week on the job, tired residents taking their trash out, or distracted teenagers uploading to their Instagram accounts. Reaching and teaching each public will require different tactics. New employees may be asked to view an online video about retirement plans at their leisure before registering for benefits. Instructions for recycling might be placed right on the bins. Teens' parents may be recruited to review privacy settings before signing mobile contracts (although teaching parents may be harder than teaching their kids).

Agreeing

So let's say you've taught your public how to open a retirement account, where to dispose of pizza boxes or how to revoke access to third-party websites when posting photos on mobile apps. That still doesn't mean they will agree to do so. Attitude change is at the heart of persuasion.

Remembering

McGuire reminded communicators that publics must both store what they've learned in memory and later retrieve that knowledge and attitude at the right time. Even with the best intentions, people often forget to do what it is they learned and agreed to do. When was the last time you actually reviewed your privacy settings on your social media accounts? Would a reminder help? Building reminders into public relations campaigns makes sense.

Acting

A lot of work goes into using communication to change knowledge and attitudes, but the most important results are usually behavioral. I'm thinking of my annual flu shot. Each fall, I *view*, *read* and *hear* messages about flu season and the importance of getting a flu shot. I *pay attention* because I hate getting sick. I wouldn't say I love the messages, but they do hold my *interest* as I think about how vaccines work and the risks and benefits for individuals and communities. I *understand* what getting a flu shot entails, that I am eligible and that it will be covered by my insurance. I *learn* that all I have to do is walk in to a clinic on a Monday through Friday, sign a form and roll up my sleeve. I *agree* it's a good idea. Then I get an email *reminder* on a Tuesday afternoon when I have no other appointments. But none of this matters to me, my immune system or the general state of public health in my community if I don't actually walk into the clinic and get the shot! *Behavior* is what matters most.

Proselytizing

Some of the very best campaigns and communication efforts go beyond a two-step communication flow from sender to media and from media to receivers. They go viral like the ALS Ice Bucket Challenge. People not only learn, agree and act, but they encourage others to do likewise; this is referred to as **proselytizing**. Proselytizing may be the secret sauce of viral social media, but it also is key to the endurance of historical social movements in religion, education and politics (see Chapter 2).

Using McGuire's Hierarchy of Effects for Planning

While not every public relations program will address all nine of these outcomes, and the steps do not always happen in the same order, thinking through McGuire's list (McGuire and others have offered other steps besides these) can help your planning in a number of ways. First, the list will help you avoid the mistake of setting goals at one level (e.g., liking) when what you and your client really want is effectiveness at a greater level (e.g., acting).

Second, the list will help you identify specific objectives and tactics and remind you not to forget any key steps. The remembering step may cue you to include reminder emails or build an app feature that notifies publics when it's time to act. When you are evaluating your efforts, the list may help you diagnose what worked and what didn't. Maybe your campaign message was tremendously popular (lots of liking) but led to very low participation. You might then review whether people actually understood your key message (comprehending) and knew how to act (learning).

Third, the list serves as a reminder to be realistic about expected outcomes. Let's say you get your story placed in *The Wall Street Journal*, and it contains your key messages just how you want them. Score! The 2016 U.S. circulation figure for the global edition is 1,437,863. For simplicity, we might optimistically estimate the following:

- Nearly 1.5 million people are exposed to the message.

- A third of those who are exposed pay attention (500,000).

- A fifth of those who pay attention are interested enough to read the story (100,000).

- Most of those who read it understand the key message (75,000).

- A third of those who understand the key message acquire the skills you want them to (25,000).

- Half of those with the skills agree (12,500).

- One in 10 of those who agree remember (1,250).

- Half of those who remember finally act on the message (625).

Convincing 625 people to do something is excellent if you're leasing airplanes or seeking large donations to a nonprofit, but it may not be as meaningful if you're selling smoothies or trying to get out votes for a national

Proselytizing
When members of publics advocate or promote to others the goals and objectives of a communication strategy. Proselytizing is a key part of campaigns going viral.

Avoid setting goals at one level (e.g., liking) when what you and your client really want is effectiveness at a greater level (e.g., acting).

Fourteen different organizations, including Apple Inc., Boeing Co., Boston Consulting Group, CBS, Viacom, Walt Disney Co., Sony Corp. and United Talent Agency, were mentioned on just the front and back page of the Marketplace section of *The Wall Street Journal* on one particular day.

What kinds of outcomes might these organizations expect?

election. And in either case, 625 is a far cry from the 1.5 million **impressions**— the measure of how many people were exposed to a message—that you may be tempted to claim as a metric of success.

Digital media allow for better tracking of steps as well. For some steps, such as liking and proselytizing, subscribers can gather fairly specific data. Metrics available for online video sites like You-Tube allow subscribers to see the number of unique views, the average view duration, the number of people who shared the material or commented on it and the content of those comments. You may find that almost everyone who started a video watched it all the way through or that almost no one who clicked on it actually watched it or shared it.

Digital marketers, who are focused on sales as a final outcome, sometimes refer to the process outlined in McGuire's model as a **funnel**. The funnel represents a customer's journey from exposure to purchase (and eventually post-purchase loyalty and sharing/proselytizing). In Google Analytics, the basic process is termed a *conversion funnel*. "With this funnel in place, you can see whether users navigate from one page or screen to the next," as explained on a Google Analytics support page.[3] Any online action that can be tracked electronically then becomes a measurable step in the process. For example, a marketer might track the number of people who find their business's home page from a Google search, then the number of those people who click on a promotion, then those who fill in a form, and then the number of people who make a purchase online. Similar processes can be tracked for organizations with goals of recruiting new members, getting petitions signed or registering people for online discussion forums.

For now it's important to think specifically and realistically about the outcomes of strategic communication. Chapter 8 will delve more into measurement at various levels of outcomes.

Strategic Planning

Tactical decision-making refers to daily management and communication without consideration of the strategic objectives, goals and mission of an organization. **Strategic decision-making**, on the other hand, means

Impressions
A measure of how many people were exposed to a message.

Funnel
A model for tracking how people move from exposure and awareness to action, particularly in online marketing where the goal is to convert a large number of web page viewers to sales leads or purchases.

Tactical decision-making
Daily management and communication tactics implemented without consideration of the strategic objectives, goals and mission of the organization.

Strategic decision-making
Daily management and communication decisions made with mindfulness of the objectives, goals and mission of the organization.

that public relations tactics are planned and implemented to help an organization pursue its mission and goals.

A public relations person posting a short looping video on the microblogging service Tumblr may be doing so as part of a broader strategy. For example, General Electric (GE) curates curious Vine clips on a Tumblr page called #6SecondScience Fair (http://6secondscience.tumblr.com). Sure, this seems like a cool tactic, but as described by communications trainer and consultant Stuart Bruce on his blog, these six-second videos are part of a strategy that connects them to GE's mission at the broadest levels. Bruce lauded GE's #6secondscience fair on Vine "because the very concept embodies GE's message of science and technology."[4] GE started by posting its own Vines and then opened the forum to its publics, encouraging people to share their own short science videos on Twitter using the hashtag 6secondscience.[5]

General Electric (®)
Feb 28, 2013

What happens when you combine milk, food coloring and dish soap? #howto #6secondscience

17,720,466+ Loops

230.5K Likes   189.5K Revines   3,782 Comments

Say something nice

General Electric posts brief video clips of science experiments with #6secondscience.

What makes this tactic strategic?

If, however, you are working in public relations and you find yourself posting a video just because you think it would be cool to post a video or because it seems like a trend you should be following, your decision-making may be more tactical than strategic. In an article about using Tumblr, Neil Patel of KISSMetrics offers some questions strategic communicators should ask themselves before diving in:

> *Why do you want to create a Tumblr blog? Just because everyone else is isn't a good answer. Do you want to build awareness to your brand? Another blog? Do you want to create revenue? Do you want to educate customers? Or improve customer service relations? Your answers will help you create a sustainably successful Tumblr blog.[6]*

Tactics are the specific actions you take and items you produce in public relations. Video clips, news releases, websites, fliers, special events, press conferences, infographics, TV ads, email messages, hashtags and apps are all tactics. Indeed, public relations isn't public relations without tactics. However, absent a broader strategy, it's hard to say what value tactics have for your organization. *An example of a tactic would be: Development of an app that allows high school students to record, upload and post a running total of the amount of material they recycle.*

Objectives are the specific measurable steps that you must achieve to accomplish larger goals. Video views, people in attendance at a special event, coverage in news media of a press event, placement of recycling bins at key locations, a minimum percentage of social media followers who use a

Tactics
Specific actions taken and items produced in public relations.

Objectives
Statements that indicate specific outputs or outcomes desired. In strategic public relations, objectives are specific steps taken to achieve broader goals.

Pounds of recycled material may be used to define a campaign goal.

What kinds of public relations tactics and objectives could be used to achieve such a goal?

particular hashtag or number of app downloads all could be quantified and measured as evidence of objectives being met. Objectives are valuable to organizations when they help meet broader goals. *An example of an objective would be: To achieve 1,000 downloads and registrations of the recycling app by high school students in the Orange County school district by February 15.*

Goals are desired outcomes that directly help an organization pursue its mission. Dollars donated, percentage of the population registered to vote, products sold and pounds of waste recycled are all examples of goals that could be set at various levels to contribute in a meaningful way to an organization's mission. *An example of a goal would be: Orange County high school students will recycle ten tons of plastic by June 1.*

An organization's **mission** is the overall reason the organization exists. The mission should guide all management and communication. Finding the cure for a disease, sustaining democracy, making money or preserving the environment may be central to various organizations' missions. *An example of a mission would be: Zero waste in Orange County.*

Of course, many tactics go into achieving an objective, multiple objectives are normally required in order to attain a goal, and organizations perpetually work toward goals in pursuit of their missions (Figure 6.3). **Strategy** is the underlying logic that holds a plan together and offers a compelling rationale for why we expect a plan to work. A campaign can have one overarching strategy as well as several smaller strategies that work in conjunction to support various dimensions of success. *An example of a strategy would be: High schools will compete to see which school logs the most recycled material by the end of the school year, with progress posted online and publicized on social media, and the winner will receive a full day off for an eco fair and picnic at the end of the school year.*

Figure 6.3 In strategic public relations, a mission drives goals, goals drive objectives, and objectives drive tactics. Think about what you're doing right now (reading this book!).

Are you being strategic or tactical? If strategic, what are your own larger objectives, goals and mission?

Case Study

Global Handwashing Day: Goals, Objectives and Outcomes

Did you know that October 15 is Global Handwashing Day? The Water Supply and Sanitation Collaborative Council (WSSCC) is a global partnership organization based in Geneva, Switzerland, that is affiliated with the

United Nations. Partners include NGOs, private companies and government agencies. In its mission statement, WSSCC lays out its vision "of a world where everybody has sustained water supply, sanitation and hygiene."[7] From that mission and vision, the organization has adopted a broad strategy to contribute "substantially to global efforts to improve sanitation and hygiene for vulnerable sections of society, with a special focus on communities in Africa and Asia."

UNICEF, a key partner with WSSCC in sponsoring Global Handwashing Day, has published a toolkit for handwashing campaign planners, which outlines major goals for handwashing campaigns. These goals are derived from the larger missions of WSSCC and UNICEF and provide the strategic rationale for objectives that determine appropriate tactics. Program planners want to see behavior change. They want more people to wash their hands and to sustain that behavior. This, in turn, leads to the "ultimate goal" of public health impact, including reducing diseases such as respiratory infections and diarrhea.[8]

Specifically, the UNICEF toolkit presents the following goal: "Increase, improve and/or sustain good hand washing behaviour and form good handwashing habits."[9] This is a great goal! We should all wash our hands more. And it clearly serves the missions of WSSCC, UNICEF, government health ministries, soap companies and any other organization affiliated with Global Handwashing Day. However, campaign planners need more than a well-stated and well-intentioned goal. Success in strategic public relations means being able to demonstrate the results of your work. A goal like this can be achieved by identifying and accomplishing objectives as steps along the way.

NGOs, private companies and government agencies all partner to make Global Handwashing Day happen.

How do private companies benefit from participating?

SMART OBJECTIVES

Well-designed objectives are SMART objectives. SMART stands for **s**pecific, **m**easurable, **a**ttainable, **r**elevant, and **t**ime-bound.

Specific

Well-written objectives state exactly what the strategic communicator plans to accomplish in a way that makes the outcome clear to all who see it. A goal to improve handwashing behavior is general. It is also debatable. My 7-year-old son and I have very different opinions about what counts as good handwashing, and a trained public health worker might have advice for us both. An objective serving the goal of improving handwashing would need to be more specific about what is meant by improvement. Does improved handwashing mean people will wash their hands more often? At specific times? Using more soap? Perhaps all three of these are important outcomes needed to achieve the larger goal. In that case, each would be the basis for a separate specific objective. Multiple objectives may serve each goal.

Measurable

Can the results be observed and measured in a way that shows actual change? A clear objective sets a standard that will define success. This could be the number of times people report washing their hands in a day, the percentage of people who are observed washing their hands before meals or the pounds of soap used in a community center in a month.

Attainable

Although you want to be ambitious in setting objectives, it's important to be realistic. Research and past experience may guide planners in finding that balance between ambitious and attainable. In a hospital staffed by professional healthcare workers, it might be realistic to aim for 100 percent participation in an effort to get doctors and nurses to wash their hands thoroughly before contact with patients, but would it be realistic to try to get 100 percent of children in a remote village to wash their hands three times a day?

Relevant

Do the objectives relate clearly to the goal and mission? An objective to generate a certain number of re-blogs on a Tumblr site dedicated to handwashing may be specific, measurable and attainable. But if your goal is to increase handwashing in specific communities in Africa, you would need to be able to explain how that Tumblr blog is relevant where it matters.

Time-Bound

Timing is a critical part of strategy. Setting a deadline for accomplishing an objective adds accountability. It also aids planning, as deadlines for specific objectives become milestones for achieving larger goals in the broader campaign timeline. A goal for a certain percentage of children to wash hands in school in October may be preceded by an objective to guarantee donations of soap to the schools by the start of the school year.

Example objectives in the UNICEF toolkit include the following. Do you think they are SMART?

- "Increase knowledge about the benefits of handwashing with soap among primary school-aged children in 100 primary schools within one year."

- "Increase the number of primary school-aged children that wash hands with soap before eating in 100 primary schools within one year."[10]

In writing goals and objectives it is important to think beyond what you plan to *do* and to think about what you plan to *accomplish*. While it makes sense that a strategic plan outlines **outputs**—tasks completed—a plan without goals and objectives that specify the results of those efforts will fall short on strategy. Output objectives focus on the tangible efforts of public relations such as the number of tweets posted, news releases sent, events sponsored or schools visited by experts. As Professor Ronald Smith puts it in his text *Strategic Planning for Public Relations*, "Measure outputs if you wish. They can provide useful assessment of what has been done. But don't stop there."[11]

Beyond outputs, **outcomes** identify the results of public relations work. How many people retweeted your tweet? How many news organizations covered the story in your news release? How many schools reported participating in Global Handwashing Day as a result of invitations from health experts? How many students were observed washing their hands?

In the big picture of public relations campaigns and programs, planners may want to account for impact. **Impacts** are the broadest and furthest-reaching results of public relations efforts. They also are the hardest results to attribute to the specific efforts of a particular program. You may never know if your recycling program affects global climate change, but you may be able to at least estimate the amount of energy conserved or landfill space saved. These would be impacts beyond the outcomes of the number of people who report recycling, which may follow the output of distributing recycle bins. Here are samples from the UNICEF handwashing program:

- *Output:* Number of door-to-door visits by hygiene promoters to discuss with caregivers the role of handwashing in nurturing children.

- *Outcome:* Proportion of primary caregivers who report washing hands with soap and water at two critical times during the day.

- *Impact:* Reduced prevalence of illness among children younger than 5 years old living in the household observed.

Outputs

Tasks or work attempted and completed, including communication tactics produced. Outputs can be completed without necessarily leading to meaningful results (i.e., outcomes).

Outcomes

Observable results of public relations work.

Impacts

The broadest and furthest-reaching results of public relations efforts, often stated in terms of societal benefit.

Timelines

As outlined in the RPIE (**r**esearch, **p**lanning, **i**mplementation and **e**valuation) model, research leads to goals and objectives, which lead to strategies and tactics, which are monitored, adapted and evaluated with further research. The process is cyclical, but it also happens in a logical order, and a timeline for that order puts each step in chronological context. At the most

A good timeline determines
when to spend resources (such
as time and money) on what.

basic level of management, a good timeline determines when to spend resources (such as time and money) on what. Key steps in a public relations plan timeline include formative research, client/management meetings, implementation of management and communication tactics, production of media and communication materials, events and evaluation.

Formative Research

Once you have a general idea of your goals and how they fit into the organization's larger mission or vision, you'll want to start thinking about two types of formative research. The first is **benchmarking**. Benchmarking research defines your starting points for accomplishing goals and objectives. While it's impressive that ALS raised $100.9 million between July 29 and August 29, 2014, what gives that figure real meaning in gauging the success of the Ice Bucket Challenge is the fact that ALS had raised $2.8 million during the same time period the year before. In a handwashing campaign like the one in the UNICEF example, you would want to do research in the early stages of planning to determine the proportion of primary school-aged children who wash hands with soap prior to eating *before* you start so that you can later determine your program's success in "moving the needle," so to speak. If 75 percent of children are found to wash hands before eating in the 100 schools under observation, then that would be your benchmark, and 95 percent or even 100 percent might be a reasonable goal. If, however, you learn that only 5 percent of children currently wash hands before eating, then that would be your benchmark, and a goal of 50 percent (a 10-fold increase) might be more realistic.

In management by objectives (MBO), planners consult with their organizations and clients to determine appropriate objectives for which they will be accountable. For both social and scientific reasons, a 50 percent success rate in a handwashing campaign may or may not be a desirable outcome. Benchmarks can be used for broad program goals or at the level of any specific objective. Any of the steps in McGuire's model can work as a place to gather benchmark data for later comparison to determine the effectiveness of strategic communication.

McGuire's steps also work in formative *evaluation*. The purpose of formative evaluation is to monitor program efforts to enable corrections based on feedback; it may be used at any time in a campaign and may be built into a timeline as a periodic or ongoing effort. For example, social media analytics allow communicators to monitor real-time feedback in response to any post. Review of annual, weekly, daily or even hourly reports of social media activity can be built into program timelines. Which Facebook posts are getting the most views (tuning in)? Which tweets are "favorited" the most (liking)? Which Tumblr blog entries are re-blogged (proselytizing)? You can check if certain times of day, sources of information or types of content such as replies to others, humor, personal narrative or rational

Social media analytics allow
communicators to monitor
real-time feedback in response
to any post.

argument are working or not working well and adjust your social media strategy accordingly based on that diagnosis. Formative evaluation works for any form of communication strategy and not just social media.

Client/Management Meetings

Public relations campaigns and programs are often initiated in a meeting with a client or with management in your own organization. After that initial meeting, public relations planners forecast the timeline for their proposed project. In cases in which an agency is trying to win new business, the agency will then develop a competitive campaign proposal to try to win the business. If you've ever watched *Mad Men* or other portrayals of a client pitch, you can imagine the amount of preparation that goes into the proposal. Winning new business or management approval requires a clear articulation of strategy and mutual agreement about how that strategy will be implemented. Beyond the initial meeting and pitch, plans should include an outline of how often those implementing the campaign will meet with clients or management.

Action and Communication Tactics

Communication should be planned around organizational action. Sometimes the communication must precede action, as when an electric company consults with communities via town hall meetings prior to installing new power lines. Communication also is planned concurrently with action, as when commuters and customers are notified in real time about construction that may interfere with traffic or electric service. Communication also may follow the project to promote the improved service or to explain increases (or decreases) in electric bills that occur as a result. Two-way communication that results in mutually beneficial relationships between organizations and publics happens throughout the process. In your timeline, that communication may be labeled as research in early stages and evaluation in later stages as you gather feedback.

Production of Media and Communication Materials

Print tactics require lead time for copywriting, design, printing and distribution. Audio, video and multimedia communications need time for scripting, production and editing. Interpersonal and social media channels need to be established and relationships need to be developed as part of an ongoing process of relationship building and maintenance. Program timelines should take all of this prep time into account.

Events

Some programs are planned around a single major event such as an election or a grand opening. In planning these programs, the event date becomes the focal point around which all other tasks are scheduled. How far in advance do announcements need to be made? How much time should be allotted to

Special events, like this grand opening concert for T-Mobile Arena in Las Vegas featuring The Killers, are focal points in public relations calendars and timelines.

How does an event like this support broader public relations goals?

the production and placement of those announcements? Who will live-tweet the event as it happens? How soon after the event will results of the program be evaluated?

Other programs include multiple events. Event types include holiday celebrations, speeches and panels, press conferences, celebrity appearances, carnivals, contests, building dedications and so on. Events can be geographically dispersed (broadcasts, webcasts, virtual conferences). They can be dictated by tradition or law (homecoming, the U.S. Census). They can even be participant-driven, such as **unconferences**—conferences organized for active peer-to-peer exchange of ideas and information—meet-ups and grassroots rallies. But if events are to be part of a larger public relations plan or program, their place on the calendar must be considered carefully in planning.

Unconferences
Meetings or conferences organized by their participants for active peer-to-peer exchange of ideas and information. Unconferences are less structured and more participatory (e.g., fewer one-to-many presentations) than traditional conferences.

Evaluation

Strategic communicators who write SMART objectives realize they've done themselves a favor when it's time for evaluation. If objectives are specific and measurable, it will be clear what needs to be measured (e.g., number of primary caregivers who report washing hands or pounds of recyclable material collected). If objectives are attainable, relevant and time-bound, the right time to measure results also will be readily apparent. Furthermore, if benchmark research is designed well, conducting evaluation research will largely be a matter of repeating earlier research and comparing results.

SMART objectives make it clear when, what and how evaluation should be conducted.

Planners have several options for timeline formats. Gantt charts are types of bar charts that show project timelines including the start and duration times of tasks. Looking at each task (normally presented in horizontal rows), a planner can consider how long a task will take or how often it needs to be repeated. Looking at any particular time (normally presented in vertical columns), a planner can consider which tasks will occur at the same time and which resources will be needed. Gantt charts can be relatively simple, like the sample presented in Figure 6.4 that was created with standard spreadsheet software. Planners can design more advanced interactive Gantt charts using relatively inexpensive project management software available online.

Sample Plan

Activity	Plan Start	Plan Duration
Client meeting	1	1
Agree on goals	1	1
Benchmark research	2	3
Set objectives	4	1
Client meeting	4	1
Formative research	2	7
Develop print materials	5	2
Event planning	5	2
Recruit volunteers	5	2
Print media production	5	2
Social media setup	3	2
Social media activation	4	1
Print announcements	7	2
Volunteer training	6	2
Client meeting	8	1
Event	9	1
Social media participation	4	9
Social media monitoring	4	9
Evaluation research	12	1
Debrief with client	13	1

Figure 6.4 Gantt chart for a 14-week plan with primary event in week 9.

Other options for timelines are to use a standard calendar or to develop a bulleted list that is organized based on times relative to a focal event. For example, the list may start with what should be done 6–11 months before the event, include monthly and weekly tasks leading up to the event, and end with what needs to be done in the days and weeks after the event has passed (Figure 6.5). Simple checklists of tasks with due dates also are helpful in planning.

Budgets

Achievable goals and objectives depend on the budget, and the budget depends on the resources needed to achieve the goals and objectives. In some cases, the budget is set in advance, and the planner works to develop a program within that budget. In other cases, the planner develops a proposal and then requests or negotiates a budget to carry out the plan. Either way, gaining budget approval and then achieving the goals and objectives within that budget indicate professionalism in public relations. Both processes entail reaching agreement with clients or management on the value of your work and having them invest valuable resources in getting the work done.

Three key resources to consider in any public relations budget are personnel, administrative costs and supplies, and media. These three categories overlap. For example, if you hire an influencer to use Snapchat to promote your product at a music festival, that could be considered either a personnel expense or a media expense. If you buy paper and color toner to produce posters or fliers, that could be categorized as administrative or as media in the budget. And if you hire translators for an international

6–11 months out

- Final decision on chairs/co-chairs
- Develop event committees (fund development/marketing/auction/volunteer)
- Discuss & determine event theme
- 1st meeting w/co-chairs

3–6 months out

- Select event date & book event venue
- Evaluate vendor needs & requests for proposals (RFPs) for catering, rentals, A/V, printing
- Develop, print and compile silent auction/corporate sponsorship solicitation packets
- **Media:** Send calendar listing to society "glossies" (at least 4 months out)

3 months out

- Distribute corporate marketing and program book packet to potential sponsors/advertisers
- Mail underwriter letters to identified targets
- Develop detailed budget for event and review with event stakeholders
- Create payment portal for tickets
- Draft contracts/finalize RFPs for services
- Start collecting email addresses from event stakeholders for "Save the Date"

2–3 months out

- Follow-up on all corporate sponsorship/silent auction/program ad solicitations
- Update web page event information
- **Media:** Define media/publicity strategy (coordination of advertising, PR, and social media)
- Event site visit
- Create Save the Date & e-mail
- Start collecting snail mail invitation lists from all event stakeholders

6–10 weeks out

- Start recruiting volunteers for the night of duties
- Send invite to printer
- **Media:** Distribute calendar release 8 weeks out and full press release to media targets 6 weeks out

4–6 weeks out

- Finalize event web page info
- Mail formal invitations
- Have silent auction committee develop a silent auction check-out procedure
- Identify banner/signage needs, design & send to printer
- **Media:** Follow up with media targets to secure event coverage/coordinate email/social media invites

2–3 weeks out

- Finalize budget
- Finalize silent auction and program (with ads) and design forms/programs
- Create first draft of run of show (event schedule & script) and review with chairs
- Create list of all vendors to be paid day/week of event
- Review volunteer duties
- Program book, silent auction listings to printer
- **Media:** Encourage all event stakeholders to distribute personal email invitations

Week of event

- Create vendor day-of point person list (with emails & <u>cell</u> phone numbers)
- Create a detailed load in/sound check schedule
- Create sorted guest lists (seating charts/table assignments)
- All printing (programs/silent auction forms/labels) & signage picked up
- **Media:** Send digital reminder to all contacts and those of event stakeholders

Immediate follow-up

- Close-out (All income/expenses collected and logged)
- Confirm all receivables paid

2–6 weeks after (closeout, evaluation & stewardship)

- Committee and attendee acknowledgments
- Special "thank-you's" to corporate sponsors, underwriters and silent auction donors
- Thank-you event for volunteers
- Close out receipt of income and payment of expenses and create closing financial report
- Share event results with all event stakeholders

Figure 6.5 List of tasks for a one-year plan culminating in an event at the end with follow-up.

PUBLIC RELATIONS BUDGET

HubSpot

Fill in your **projected expenses** here. (Those "$100" entries are placeholdes.)

Fill in your **actual expenses** here. (Those "$100" entries are placeholders.)

	Jan-17		Feb-17		Mar-17		Q1		Amount Left	Apr-17		May-17		June-17	
	Budget	Actual	Budget	Actual	Budget	Actual	Budget	Actual		Budget	Actual	Budget	Actual	Budget	Actual
SUBSCRIPTIONS															
Press release service (e.g. PRWeb)	100.00	100.00	100.00	100.00	100.00	100.00	300.00	300.00	0.00						
Research/contact service (e.g. Cision)	100.00	100.00	100.00	100.00	100.00	100.00	300.00	300.00	0.00						
Reputation monitoring software (e.g. Vendasta)	100.00	100.00	100.00	100.00	100.00	100.00	300.00	300.00	0.00						
CONTENT															
Press releases	100.00	100.00	100.00	100.00	100.00	100.00	300.00	300.00	0.00						
Newsletters	100.00	100.00	100.00	100.00	100.00	100.00	300.00	300.00	0.00						
Reports	100.00	100.00	100.00	100.00	100.00	100.00	300.00	300.00	0.00						
Guest posts	100.00	100.00	100.00	100.00	100.00	100.00	300.00	300.00	0.00						
EVENTS / TRADESHOWS															
Admission	100.00	100.00	100.00	100.00	100.00	100.00	300.00	300.00	0.00						
Transportation	100.00	100.00	100.00	100.00	100.00	100.00	300.00	300.00	0.00						
Accommodations	100.00	100.00	100.00	100.00	100.00	100.00	300.00	300.00	0.00						
Meals	100.00	100.00	100.00	100.00	100.00	100.00	300.00	300.00	0.00						
MEDIA RELATIONS / AWARDS															
Dinners	100.00	100.00	100.00	100.00	100.00	100.00	300.00	300.00	0.00						
Gifts	100.00	100.00	100.00	100.00	100.00	100.00	300.00	300.00	0.00						
Award entry fees	100.00	100.00	100.00	100.00	100.00	100.00	300.00	300.00	0.00						
AGENCY															
Retainer fees	100.00	100.00	100.00	100.00	100.00	100.00	300.00	300.00	0.00						
Expenses	100.00	100.00	100.00	100.00	100.00	100.00	300.00	300.00	0.00						
Other	100.00	100.00	100.00	100.00	100.00	100.00	300.00	300.00	0.00						
TOTAL	$1,700.00	$1,700.00	$1,700.00	$1,700.00	$1,700.00	$1,700.00	$5,100.00	$5,100.00	$0.00	$0.00	$0.00	$0.00	$0.00	$0.00	$0.00

Year-to-Date Summary	Budget	Actual	Amount Left
SUBSCRIPTIONS	$900.00	$900.00	$0.00
CONTENT	$1,200.00	$1,200.00	$0.00
EVENTS / TRADESHOWS	$1,200.00	$1,200.00	$0.00
MEDIA RELATIONS / AWARDS	$900.00	$900.00	$0.00
AGENCY	$900.00	$900.00	$0.00
TOTAL	$5,100.00	$5,100.00	$0.00

Your **year-to-date totals** will automatically populate here.

Public Relations Year-to-Date Summary

Legend: AGENCY, MEDIA RELATIONS / AWARDS, EVENTS / TRADESHOWS, CONTENT, SUBSCRIPTIONS

This budget template from HubSpot.com opens as an Excel file and can be customized for any public relations program.

How are the categories of personnel, administrative costs and supplies, and media included in the template?

conference, that could be considered either an administrative expense or a personnel expense. The key is to organize your budget in a way that makes sense to the person or people funding it and to make sure that you carefully think through the categories so you don't leave out any major expenses.

> Organize budgets in a way that makes sense to the people funding it.

Personnel

Even in programs with no budget, people invest time and depend on others to do so as well to achieve public relations goals. Class projects and **pro bono**

Pro bono
Public relations work conducted as a public service without fee or payment.

Billable rate

Amount that an agency or firm charges clients per hour of an employee's time.

work for nonprofit organizations often are planned and conducted with almost no financial resources, but this doesn't mean that people aren't investing. In such cases it is important to note the time required. Although the hours worked by volunteers, students or employees with salaries paid for by other sources may not show up as dollar figures, those hours should be acknowledged in the plan as required resources.

On the other end of the accounting spectrum for personnel costs, agencies often apply very specific billing formulae to account for their employee's time working on client accounts. I'll always remember the first time I saw a billing sheet. I was working in an unpaid summer internship during weekdays and operating a driving range golf ball picker on nights and weekends for $6.50 an hour. My supervisor at the internship was just a few years older than me. He asked me to review a project budget, and I just about fell out of my chair when I saw that he was getting $150 an hour for his work. I did the math and figured he must be making more than $300,000 a year! How could this be? Why wasn't he driving a Ferrari?

When agencies bill clients for their work, they often include billable hourly rates as a major part of the budget, but the amount billed is considerably larger than the amount the employee gets paid. Author, consultant and PRSA Fellow James Lukaszewski offers the following example.[12] Suppose an account supervisor at a public relations agency earns a salary of $65,000 a year. Assuming the employee is paid for 40 hours a week over the course of 52 weeks, her hourly pay comes out to $31.25. However, the agency also pays for her benefits including costs such as health insurance and retirement contributions. These fringe benefits can cost the firm up to 30 percent or more of her base pay. With 30 percent fringe added, her hourly cost to the agency is $40.63 per hour. Of course, agencies wouldn't make any money if they only charged their clients their actual costs, and they have many other expenses to cover besides those payroll costs, so they bill clients at a rate of three or even four times the cost of paying the account executive. Using a multiple of three, the **billable rate** for the account supervisor would be $121.89 per hour. Using a multiple of four, the billable rate would be $162.52 per hour, even though she is earning an annual salary of $65,000 and not $338,000. Now I understand why my internship supervisor was driving a nice Toyota but not splurging on an Italian sports car.

We can see how important it is to factor in the amount of time people will spend on particular projects when developing budgets. While an agency's HR and accounting departments may handle all the specifics of salaries, fringe and billing, planners must still provide an estimate of how many people will work on which projects and for how long. Other personnel costs to consider include hiring freelance writers and editors, photographers, artists, spokespeople, social media influencers or any type of temporary workers such as event security staff for a concert or drivers to take nurses to remote communities in an international healthcare campaign.

Administrative Costs and Supplies

In agencies or established businesses, regular and ongoing administrative costs such as electricity, paper and internet services are often considered **overhead expenses**, meaning public relations planners normally wouldn't need to account for them specifically in developing a campaign strategy or program budget (though clients pay for them indirectly with marked-up prices for services). Beyond those costs, or if you are working independently, you have to think about budgeting for any stuff that you will need for your campaign that you don't plan on having donated or paying for out of your own personal funds. These costs may include anything from specialty items like coffee mugs or T-shirts, to nametags, pizza and drinks, soap for handwashing, bins for recycling, computers and tablets—you name it. If you are organizing an event as part of a larger program, you may estimate the total cost of the event in your initial program proposal rather than getting too specific with each line item. Other major non-media expense categories include travel, facility rentals, speaker fees and research costs.

Media and Communication Expenses

Advertising and promotion are important costs to consider in most public relations programs. For traditional media, price quotes can be attained to get an accurate estimate of how much to budget for advertising. As discussed in Chapter 3, newspaper ads can range from $14 per column inch in a student newspaper to hundreds of thousands of dollars for a full-page ad in a national or international publication. As with print media, advertising sales representatives from radio and TV stations can give you quotes for media space (e.g., a 30-second spot during prime time). Someone budgeting for a national branding campaign may have to choose between, say, spending $386,000 for a full-page color ad in *The Wall Street Journal*, or $326,000 for a 30-second TV spot during a top-rated prime-time network sitcom. Of course, many factors go into such decisions, and when the stakes are high, professional media planners are part of the process. **Media planning** entails considering factors such as strategy and audience demographics to make sure that advertising budgets are spent wisely and in line with SMART objectives. **Reach** (the percentage or number of people exposed to a message) and **frequency** (the average number of times people in an audience are exposed to a particular message in a given period) are two of the most important variables. Media planning is a career path in and of itself.

Advertising in digital and interactive media has evolved into new models of buying and selling media. **Programmatic media buying**, for example, involves automated real-time bidding (RTB) that is preprogrammed by marketers and automated to buy space when certain criteria are met. In programmatic media sales, publishers use software called supply-side platforms (SSPs) and buyers use demand-side platforms (DSPs).

OK, who ordered pizza? Even smaller expenses like food and snacks for events add up when you are working independently.

Where might you find pizza in a public relations budget?

Overhead expenses
Costs of running a business that are not directly related to the product or services delivered.

Media planning
Choosing media channels to achieve strategic communication goals and objectives. Media planning drives advertising purchases.

Reach
Percentage or number of people exposed to a message at least once via a specific communication channel during a defined period of time.

Frequency
The average number of times people in an audience are exposed to a particular message in a defined period of time.

Programmatic media buying
Automated media buying that is preprogrammed so that advertising purchases are completed when certain criteria set by buyers (marketers) and sellers (media) are met. Programmatic media buying commonly occurs via computer-run, real-time auctions.

Twitter product developer and executive Ameet Ranadive explains the process with an example:

> Based on its knowledge about this user (e.g., the user recently searched for flights to Hawaii on a travel website), a DSP will bid on the right to serve an ad to this user. The RTB exchange will then run an auction for the ad impression generated by this user. The winning DSP will serve a creative—potentially a dynamic display ad with personalized content, perhaps including the recently browsed flight details, price, and image of the destination—to the user.[13]

Programmatic media buying can be used for everything from basic ads on news websites to promoted tweets to Google search returns to sponsored posts in Facebook. Again, this type of media planning requires specialized expertise, but understanding the basics will help public relations planners work with media planners in buying space in digital and interactive media.

At this point, you may be thinking, what about "free" media? You can write your own newsletter, distribute your own fliers or set up your own Twitter account, Facebook group or Tumblr blog for free, right? It's true that these communication tactics don't incur advertising costs, but you will have other costs to consider. An effective social media presence requires time and effort—in other words, personnel costs. If you are including fliers in your budget, you should include the cost of designing and printing.

> A social media presence may be "free" of advertising costs, but it still requires personnel costs.

For professionalism with just about any communication tactic, public relations planners must also consider the costs of production. The American Association of Advertising Agencies stopped tracking the costs of TV ad production in 2012, but in their last report in 2011, they calculated the average cost of production for a 30-second TV commercial at $354,000.[14] For a basic event flier, you might design it yourself or buy lunch for a talented friend to design it. Even so, you'll want to check with a local printer on printing prices if you don't have access to a good copy machine with a full supply of paper and toner. For example, to print in full color on premium paper, FedEx Office charges $29.99 for 50 copies and $579.99 for 1,000 copies. These numbers undoubtedly vary (and the FedEx quote probably won't apply any more by the time you read this), but it goes to show how important it is to think about production costs and to build them into your budget.

Social media command center war rooms like this one allow for 24/7 monitoring of client mentions and trends.

Setting up social media accounts may be free at first, but what other expenses need to be considered in budgeting for continued operation?

Voices from the Field

Brad Horn

BRAD HORN, now a doctoral student at the University of Florida, served as vice president of communications and education for the National Baseball Hall of Fame and Museum from 2002 to 2016. He oversaw all external affairs, media relations and education programs, as well as voting procedures. Horn also worked for the Texas Rangers Baseball Club, the National Hot Rod Association, the Fort Worth Fire (hockey team), the *Dallas Morning News* and the *Fort Worth Star-Telegram.* Horn was named a "Top 15 to Watch" by PRNews and a "30 Under 30" by *PRWeek.* Horn received his M.S. in communications management from Syracuse University and his B.S. in journalism from Texas Christian University.

You've supervised many interns and entry-level communicators. Do entry-level practitioners need to be concerned with strategic planning, or can they get by early in their careers by just being good with tactics?
Tactics help entry-level practitioners establish confidence and develop areas of specialty, but strategic planning is essential to becoming a successful public relations practitioner. Ultimately, understanding how timelines work, how pieces of the strategic puzzle fit together, and how outcomes are achieved through partnership and multifaceted execution determines the potential for success of public relations programs. Developing tools is critical for practitioners, but the strategic planning capabilities will determine how an individual advances within the profession.

A big part of your job with the National Baseball Hall of Fame and Museum was visitor engagement. What kinds of specific objectives did you set to meet engagement goals?
Building engagement with a small not-for-profit educational museum located in rural central New York requires creating an emotional connection for visitors and potential customers by expanding on the themes of heroism and celebration. In creating engagement, we developed implementation strategies to advance a relationship at all levels, from web user to newsletter subscriber, museum visitor to museum member, museum member to donor, and many other relationship advancing measures, each designed to create a stronger relationship with the organization. We also took measures to explain how these relationships benefit the organization, and how an individual's engagement grows the institution.

How have budgets for public relations programs and campaigns changed with the rise of social media?
For a small independent museum like the Baseball Hall of Fame, creativity and no-cost solutions in generating positive public relations outcomes are inherent and expected in the operation. Its charge is to promote positive publicity and build lifelong relationships with publics, through service, through loyalty and through unique communications and programs. Social media has enhanced its ability to reach audiences, but the same principles of conservative budget planning remain one of the most important fiduciary responsibilities.

Are there times when it makes more sense just to wing it and go with instinct?
Instinct is akin to a conscience for practitioners. Instinct is essential to execution of any public relations program or initiative. But decisions and implementations must be rooted in sound communications strategy and thinking, relying on instinct as a guide. Instinct alone leads to incomplete execution.

What's the coolest campaign outcome you've achieved?
In 2014, the Museum celebrated its 75th anniversary. From start to finish, that season's campaign to spotlight 75 resulted in countless successful outcomes, from President Obama delivering a speech in the Hall of Fame Gallery before Memorial Day Weekend to the *Today* show going live from Cooperstown before the start of Induction Weekend.

Ethics: Beware of Zombies; Enhance the Profession

When public relations strategy includes a social media platform like Instagram, a common element of SMART objectives relates to the number of followers or likes or comments the account receives. As you know if you have ever started a social media account, the first batch of friends and followers comes relatively easily.

That first batch of friends and followers may be all you need if you're keeping your account for personal reasons. Your network may grow slowly and organically from there as you discover new friends and others discover you. That's how most of us expect social media to work. So when we see that @Beyonce has 80 million followers on Instagram but follows no one, we know a different pattern of influence is in process. The communication is one-way. However, in between small interpersonal accounts and pure mass-communication-by-Instagram, there are many ways that strategic communicators build social media influence into their plans.

One way to harness influence in social media is to work long and hard to build a large and lasting base of friends and followers. Over time, working to provide content that people enjoy and find useful enough to like and share will earn you or your organization followers and clout. Consistent and regular interaction (i.e., two-way communication and relationship building) with others online is also a big part of what it takes to be successful in building online social networks.

As noted in the budget section, social media aren't really free. Success with social media requires an investment over time in providing valuable content and building relationships. The return on that investment in public relations comes when it's time to get the word out about your recycling drive, to introduce your company's new product, or to remind voters to go to the polls in support of your cause on Election Day. From tuning in to going viral, a large and well-maintained social media network can support each and every one of the steps in McGuire's model of strategic communication.

Now, what if I were to offer you a shortcut? A site called Corepillar.com offers 500 followers for $6 or 60,000 followers for $350. Another site, Foxfans.com, has similar prices—$59.90 for 10,000 followers. "Having a large follower base on Instagram will make you look more credible, reliable and obviously more popular," according to Foxfans.com.[15] It is widely acknowledged that these followers are not the same as the real people who would otherwise follow your account out of real interest in you or your organization. What these services offer are "zombie" followers. The companies operate thousands of fake accounts that exist for no other purpose than to follow other accounts. More sophisticated services offer packages that include automated "like" and commenting functions. One Dutch blogger who paid for a service told how real commenters called out an automated comment that said "Nice pic" when the actual post was a video. I think it's safe to say that zombie followers are not high on anyone's list of primary publics. This ain't *The Walking Dead*!

These services could be seen as an effective and budget-friendly tactic for eventually increasing real followers. A longer-term goal to increase communication via social media may be helped along by a shorter-term objective to get social media accounts up and running with a respectable number of followers. Is there really any harm buying followers to meet your social media objectives? A quick run through Kathy Fitzpatrick's guide for ethical decision-making (see Chapter 1) will help answer that.

Define the Specific Issue/Conflict

Buying followers is a quick, inexpensive, legal and effective way to boost quantitative results (followers, likes, comments, etc.) for social media objectives. However, the followers aren't real people. The benefit of buying followers is one of perception—accounts with more followers *appear* to be more credible, reliable and popular.

Identify Internal/External Factors

Major internal factors include program budget, goals and objectives. An important strategic question is whether or not purchased followers will actually contribute to the larger goals of a campaign. External factors include the perceptions of external publics who may be impressed with large numbers but feel deceived and lose trust if they were to learn that the account holder had paid for zombie followers. Could you report to a client with confidence and good faith that thousands of purchased followers would help you achieve a goal to get more people to buy a product, make a donation or volunteer time?

Identify Key Values

Authenticity, transparency and expertise are key values. A big part of what makes social media social is that people are motivated to engage other real people. Authenticity matters in any social context (not just online media). Touting fake friends or followers is not an authentic approach to self-presentation in any type of communication. Most people keep the practice hush-hush and would feel "busted" if the word were to get out that they had paid for followers. If you were to buy followers as part of a public relations strategy, would you want people to know? Probably not, and wanting to keep something a secret indicates a lack of transparency. Building a base of followers for an organization by creating engaging content and maintaining mutually beneficial relationships requires expertise. That expertise is what employers and clients pay public relations people for. Employers and clients might feel duped if they knew you "earned" your money with cheap shortcuts.

It's possible to pay for fake followers on social media accounts.

What are the pitfalls of buying zombie followers?

A big part of what makes social media social is that people are motivated to engage other real people.

Identify the Parties Involved

Again, one party is the employer or client. The practitioner himself or herself is another. I don't think I'd count the zombie followers as a party, but people in real publics who see the social media account and make decisions based on perceptions of that account would be another party. At the broadest level, anyone working in public relations whose reputation may be damaged by unethical practices in this area is also a party.

Select Ethical Principles

In Chapter 1, we applied deontological (duty-based) principles to decide whether ghost tweeting was ethically defensible for a public relations practitioner. In Chapter 5, we applied the principle of utilitarianism to evaluate how public relations research is presented. Utilitarianism focuses on the results of one's actions. For this case, let's consider **consequentialism**—a results-based system of ethics that holds that the best ethical decision is the one leading to the best outcomes or impacts.

What are the consequences of buying followers? A very narrow view would be that buying followers results in short-term success in meeting objectives. One might even expand this into an ethical argument by saying that buying followers is ethical if it leads to larger, more important consequences. For example, if you bought followers for an NGO account, and those followers led to more real followers, and those real followers donated money, and that money was used to fight the Zika virus spreading in El Salvador, preventing birth defects would be the result. Preventing birth defects would certainly be an end that one could use to justify the means of buying followers. But come on. You could drive a truck through the logic of that strategy. The following consequences are more likely:

1. Nothing happens. You spend part of your budget buying followers and no one even notices.

2. It kind of works. You buy followers and it somehow makes your account look more legit. A few real followers ensue, but they are deceived in the process because they assume you are producing content and communicating in a way that others have found worthwhile.

3. It backfires, and you get called out on it. This happens. Services like TwitterAudit.com and Socialbakers' fake followers app make it easy to check your own or others' social media accounts for fake followers. Your client may get mocked online for doing this because the lack of authenticity and transparency runs directly counter to the values listed earlier. This hurts your client's reputation and your own credibility as a professional. It also drags down the reputation of public relations as a profession in general.

Make a Decision and Justify It

Although buying followers may offer a quick and inexpensive way to meet short-term social media objectives, there are plenty of ways to justify the decision not to do so. In all likelihood, the consequences will not be positive or productive. Real expertise and professionalism in public relations means being willing and able to put in the time and effort required to build relationships. PRSA lists "Enhancing the Profession" as a key provision of conduct: "Professionals work constantly to strengthen the public's trust in the profession . . . to build respect and credibility with the public for the profession of public relations . . . to improve, adapt and expand professional practices."[16]

> Professionalism in public relations means being willing and able to put in the time and effort required to build relationships.

In Case You Missed It

Public relations professionals are some of the busiest people in business, but mere *busyness* is a waste of time without planning. These tips from the chapter will help you see day-to-day activities as ways to serve the broader missions of organizations in society.

- Awareness of a cause, new product or app is only one step in leading people to donate, purchase or download.

- When campaign goals include helping publics acquire relevant skills, public relations basically becomes an act of teaching.

- Avoid setting goals at one level (e.g., liking) when what you and your client really want is effectiveness at a greater level (e.g., acting).

- A good timeline determines when to spend resources (such as time and money) on what.

- Social media analytics allow communicators to monitor real-time feedback in response to any post.

- SMART objectives make it clear when, what and how evaluation should be conducted.

- Organize budgets in a way that makes sense to the people funding them.

- A social media presence may be "free" of advertising costs, but it still requires personnel costs.

- A big part of what makes social media social is that people are motivated to engage other real people.

- Professionalism in public relations means being willing and able to put in the time and effort required to build relationships.

SUMMARY

6.1 Analyze strategic communication outcomes.
Planning for public relations means considering a number of levels of outcomes. McGuire developed a hierarchy of effects model that outlines key steps in public communication campaigns: tuning in, attending, liking, comprehending, learning, agreeing, remembering, acting and proselytizing. Beyond exposure and attention/awareness, strategists must think about steps leading to behavior change and proselytizing when communication goes viral. Minding these outcomes helps planners set goals, identify appropriate objectives and tactics, and be realistic about expected outcomes.

6.2 Map public relations strategy from mission to tactics.
Strategic decision-making means that daily action and communication tactics can be tied with specific objectives, which help achieve broader goals, which serve an organization's mission. When public relations action and communication are implemented without this context, decision-making is more tactical than strategic.

6.3 Write SMART objectives.
SMART objectives are specific, measurable, attainable, relevant and time-bound. SMART objectives add accountability and enhance professionalism in public relations practice.

6.4 Distinguish between outputs, outcomes and impacts.
Outputs describe the tangible efforts of public relations practitioners—what people *do*. Outcomes describe the results of that work—what people *accomplish*. Impacts are the broadest and furthest-reaching results of public relations.

6.5 Develop basic timelines to organize tasks in a strategic public relations program.
As with SMART objectives, which are time-bound, timelines foster accountability in the management of strategic programs and campaigns. Key steps to consider include formative research, client/management meetings, implementation of tactics, production of communication materials, events and evaluation.

6.6 Identify key categories of public relations budget items.
Three key resources to consider in any public relations budget are personnel, administrative costs and supplies, and media. These three categories overlap.

6.7 Apply consequentialism to make ethical decisions about setting and achieving public relations objectives while enhancing the profession.
Consequentialism entails thinking through the outcomes of one's actions in making ethical decisions. The case of whether or not to buy followers on Twitter or Instagram raises questions about consequences such as

misspent budget or ineffective strategy. More important, ethical decision-making in this case means considering broader consequences such as deception of publics and damaging (rather than enhancing) the profession.

DISCUSSION QUESTIONS

1. When was the last time you changed your behavior as a result of an organization's strategic communication? Which of McGuire's steps did you go through?

2. Search for an organization that (a) has its mission statement posted online, and (b) has conducted a public relations tactic that you think was effective. Describe how the tactic might help achieve an objective, which helps with a goal, which supports the mission. What's the strategy?

3. Name a goal that you have for this year. Write three SMART objectives toward that goal.

4. Draw or chart a timeline that shows how the objectives mentioned in question 3 lead toward the goal over time.

5. When was the last time you saw public relations have a real impact (as impact is defined in this chapter)? What was the organization, and how did it make a difference on a broad level?

6. Suppose you are the leader of a student or community organization that is given a budget of $1,000 to compete with other similar groups to recycle the largest number of plastic bottles in your community. How would you allocate your budget between personnel, administrative costs and supplies, and media?

7. Not all fake followers on social media are bought. Almost every account is susceptible to at least a small percentage of unwanted fake followers (in the same way that we get spam via email). Should public relations people be responsible for removing these fake followers for clients? Why or why not?

KEY TERMS

Benchmarking   152
Billable rate   158
Consequentialism   164
Frequency   159
Funnel   146
Goals   148
Impacts   151
Impressions   146
Media planning   159
Mission   148
Objectives   147
Outcomes   151

Outputs   151
Overhead expenses   159
Planning   141
Pro bono   157
Programmatic media buying   159
Proselytizing   145
Reach   159
Strategic decision-making   146
Strategy   148
Tactical decision-making   146
Tactics   147
Unconferences   154

CHAPTER 7

Implementation

Before Chipotle had to deal with their food safety crises, they faced some challenges trying to stay green. How did the restaurant chain handle the heat?

KEY LEARNING OUTCOMES

7.1 Explain how organizational action is the foundation for credible communication.

7.2 Analyze cases of action and communication in the implementation of effective public relations.

7.3 Outline media options on a continuum from controlled to uncontrolled.

7.4 Differentiate among owned, paid, shared and earned media.

7.5 Describe the relationship between the values of loyalty and diversity.

7.6 Summarize the benefits of implementing diversity initiatives.

RELATED UNIVERSAL ACCREDITATION BOARD COMPETENCY AREAS

1.6 AUDIENCE IDENTIFICATION • **1.8** IMPLEMENTATION • **2.2** ETHICAL BEHAVIOR
4.2 BARRIERS TO COMMUNICATION • **6.4** MEDIA RELATIONS

After research and planning, it's time to implement programs and manage the communication that goes along with them. The third step in the RPIE (research-planning-implementation-evaluation) process is implementation, which includes a combination of organizational action and communication (Figure 7.1). As important as communication is in public relations, excellence in the public relations field is based on meaningful action.

We've all heard spokespeople use buzzwords about "maximizing potential," "taking it to the next level," "providing thought leadership" or "giving 110 percent." But what do those phrases mean, especially if they can't be tied to anything specific that the organization is actually doing? "Actions speak louder than words," the old adage goes. The same logic applies in the implementation of public relations. It's one thing to say your organization values diversity and inclusion, for example. It's another to manage the organization in a way that proves it.

Taking Action

Recall from Chapter 1 that Arthur Page said principled management of public relations means you have to "prove it with action." The American Red Cross doesn't just send thoughts and prayers when disaster strikes. They send aid workers with blankets, water and first aid.

In Chapter 2, on the history of public relations, we saw how public relations matured when organizations started taking it seriously as a management function based on action. With the counsel of Earl Newsom, Ford Motor Company didn't just talk about the importance of auto safety in the 1950s, it actually funded research on safety and changed its operations and vehicle design in the interest of its publics.

In Chapter 3, on convergence and integration, we explored the link between public relations, marketing and advertising based on the shared communication function of the three fields. We also learned that promotion is just one of the four P's, along with product, place and price. Kwikset enjoyed great publicity for its technological savvy when its "Kevo" deadbolt (which enables you to unlock doors at home using a Bluetooth-enabled smartphone) was named product of the year. But that publicity resulted only after the company did the heavy lifting of research and development to bring the new product to market.

"What have you done for me lately?" could have been the theme for Chapter 4 on relationships. Relationships with employees, investors, media and other organizations and publics are all predicated on organizations bringing something beyond talk to the relationship.

> Excellence in the field of public relations is based on meaningful action.

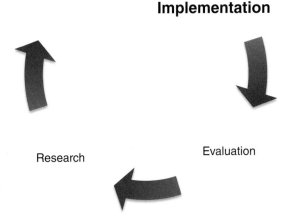

Planning

Research

Implementation

Evaluation

Figure 7.1 In the RPIE model, a well-planned, research-based public relations program will be implemented in a way that allows evaluation of outcomes.

How can action and communication both be part of implementation?

> Organizations must bring something beyond talk to their relationships with publics.

Chapters 5 and 6 on research and planning bring us to the doorstep of action. A well-planned, research-based public relations program will be implemented in line with the organization's mission and broad goals. But living up to these ideals and "walking the walk" can be tough, as Chipotle Mexican Grill can attest.

Case Study

Pulled Pork: Chipotle's Challenge to Act on Its Principles

Chipotle Mexican Grill endured one of the toughest restaurant food-safety crises in U.S. history in 2016 when multiple locations across several states were investigated as sources of *E. coli* outbreaks. Chipotle's crisis response is covered in Chapter 12, but one of the main factors in Chipotle's ability to withstand the initial shock of that massive crisis was its organizational history of building and maintaining strong relationships with its publics based on both action and communication.

Chipotle's "Food with Integrity" program outlines the company's commitment to using only quality ingredients and respecting the welfare of farmers, animals and the environment. They communicate this commitment and move beyond platitudes and into specific policy for managing their operations:

> *It means serving the very best sustainably raised food possible with an eye to great taste, great nutrition and great value. It means that we support and sustain family farmers who respect the land and the animals in their care. It means that whenever possible we use meat from animals raised without the use of antibiotics or added hormones.*[1]

For pork in particular, Chipotle works with farmers whose pigs are raised outdoors or in pens that meet specific criteria. They buy from farmers who raise pigs on a vegetarian diet without using antibiotics. "It's the way animals were raised before huge factory farms changed the industry. We believe pigs that are cared for in this way enjoy happier, healthier lives and produce the best pork we've ever tasted."[2] And Chipotle didn't just talk the talk. They walked the walk, sourcing 100 percent of their pork from farmers who abided by their strict guidelines.

Of course maintaining these standards comes at a cost, but the business model worked for Chipotle—up to a point. The chain surged in growth between 2001 when it began implementing the policy and 2014 when Chipotle shares jumped 37 percent. In 2015, analysts projected Chipotle's first-quarter profits would grow 49 percent compared to those of McDonald's, which was facing a 12 percent decline according to the same analysts.[3] Chipotle was soaring in the markets and in public relations, minding investors, customers and even pigs, all at the same time.

But that beautiful balance was knocked off-kilter in early 2015 when Chipotle discovered that one of its major pork suppliers was not complying with the humanitarian guidelines. So what did they do? They pulled the pork from about a third of their restaurants. This was a huge management decision for a burrito chain known for its *carnitas*.

In a way, Chipotle was a victim of its own success. Its eco-friendly business model became harder and harder to sustain as the chain grew. While farms that met Chipotle's standards still made up a relatively small percentage of food suppliers, Chipotle had grown into one of the nation's largest fast food chains. "Those two realities could eventually prove untenable, because . . . they simply don't add up," wrote *Washington Post* blogger Roberto Ferdman.[4] This was the public relations challenge for Chipotle.

Chipotle, however, stuck to its principles. "This is fundamentally an animal welfare decision and it's rooted in our unwillingness to compromise our standards where animal welfare is concerned," Chipotle Communications Director Chris Arnold told Ferdman. As the case continued, Chipotle management had to make tough decisions to balance their own interests with the interests of their publics. They resorted to rotating their

Yes, we have no carnitas.

How do you think pulling a major menu item affected Chipotle's reputation? How do you think it affected their sales?

restaurant menus periodically so that no one restaurant would go without carnitas for any extended period of time.

Of course, Chipotle still has its critics. The case even gave rise to the hashtag #carnitasgate, while "pork-ocalypse" trended on Twitter. Some speculated that the whole ordeal was a conspiracy to sell more of its meatless, tofu-filled "sofritas," which were introduced at about the same time.[5]

Any way you slice it, this case illustrates how much management goes into real public relations. Anyone can slap a web page up, post some tweets, or send out news releases claiming that an organization is green and sustainable, but living up to the promise while growing an organization's bottom line entails a lot of hard work (i.e., implementation).

Choosing Channels

Two-way communication and relationships are the heart of public relations. Most of what you can expect to do on a day-to-day basis in public relations is indeed communication. In between meetings, phone calls and presentations, you'll spend your time on email and social media. You'll probably chat like mad—both in person and via instant messaging. Skyping, blogging, tweeting, posting—even old-fashioned reading and writing—they're all forms of communication. In managing relationships, you have to make smart choices about when to send a text, when to "reply all" in an email, when to call someone on the phone, when to tweet, when to send a photo, and perhaps most important, when to turn off all your devices and pay attention to the people in the room with you.

Selecting the channels for communication is a big responsibility.

What factors are most important to consider before launching social media efforts?

A lot of these decisions are not unique to public relations. Most people working in modern organizations have to make these same decisions as they manage their professional interactions. What makes public relations different is that we also have to manage the communication that we plan and do on behalf of the organizations that we represent. In implementing public relations programs, we are expected to make wise and informed decisions on which channels of communication to use, when and for what purpose. When communicating to meet specific goals and objectives, we have to carefully analyze the pros and cons of various media for communications between organizations and publics.

> Make wise and informed decisions about which channels of communication to use, when and for what purpose.

Controlled and Uncontrolled Media

Traditionally, public relations practitioners have thought about media in terms of how much control they have (or how much control they give up) when using various channels and tactics for communication. Internal newsletters or television ads would be thought of as **controlled media** because communicators may write and edit, or create and produce, messages exactly how they want them. They also control where and to whom the messages are sent. If you edit your own newsletter, you choose exactly what stories you want to include, you choose the images and layout, you define the angle on the stories, and you decide whose mailboxes the newsletter lands in. If you are paying for a TV spot, you are buying control of the message. You can make creative and strategic decisions about how the message is produced (or at least you contract the people who do). You also decide where, when and how often the ad airs. Recall the concepts of reach and frequency from Chapter 6.

On the other side of the spectrum are uncontrolled media. According to the 2010 *APR Study Guide*, **uncontrolled media** include newspapers, TV and radio news, and external websites, as well as blogs and social media that are not produced internally.[6] You can spend days crafting a news release to perfectly align with your organization's goals and objectives, but the second that you attach it to an email to a journalist or blogger and hit send, you lose control. It's up to the journalist how (and if) to tell the story after that.

Of course, most communication falls somewhere in between entirely controlled or uncontrolled. Real, interactive and two-way communication doesn't allow one party or another total control. Press conferences and interviews are good examples. During a reelection campaign, Florida Governor Rick Scott found himself facing questions about a campaign appearance he made with several uniformed police officers lined up behind him. The problem was that Florida law prohibits paid public employees from participating in campaign activities while in uniform. It wasn't a major campaign crisis, but more of a "bite-sized brouhaha," as CNN's Anderson Cooper called it. Perhaps

Controlled media
Channels of communication that allow public relations practitioners to write, edit, produce and distribute messages as they see fit.

Uncontrolled media
Channels of communication that are outside of the control of public relations practitioners.

Rafael Nadal pauses during a news conference following his opening-match loss at a tennis tournament.

In what ways are press conferences controlled or uncontrolled as media events?

more damaging for Scott's campaign was the follow-up at a different press conference:

> **Reporter 1:** *Did you really think that all of those deputies were off duty?*
> **Scott:** *I'm very proud that last week the police chiefs endorsed me. I'm very proud that 40 sheriffs have endorsed me. I'm very proud of all the support from the law enforcement. We're at a 43-year low in our crime rate, so we invite them to our campaign events, and I'm very appreciative of the ones that came.*
> **Reporter 2:** *But do you think it was a problem to have on-duty law enforcement there?*
> **Scott:** *I'm very appreciative of both their support and those that come to my events.*
> **Reporter 2:** *You didn't answer that question. Should there be discipline?*
> **Scott:** *Look I'm appreciative of everybody that comes to my events, and gosh, we're at a 43-year low in our crime rate. We should be very supportive of our law enforcement.*
> **Reporter 1:** *But do you think it's OK for them to be there on duty?*
> **Scott:** *I'm very appreciative. Our police chiefs endorsed me last week . . . 40 sheriffs did. We have law enforcement come to a variety of events and others, and I'm very appreciative of anybody that comes to my events and supports my race.*[7]

For that, Governor Scott made Anderson Cooper's "Ridiculist" segment on CNN. Scott tried to control the message in an uncontrolled media environment.

So why would any strategic communicator want to mess with uncontrolled media? Well, for starters, money is a factor. You don't pay for the space for a newspaper story that runs as the result of a news release or an interview with your CEO that airs on national TV. When press events go well, organizations receive a lot of good publicity; this means that they reach publics via mass media that otherwise would be prohibitively expensive. Some also see credibility as a big advantage for uncontrolled media. When your message is vetted by a journalist or editor and told as part of a news story it may carry more credibility.

Think about the Chipotle story. What's more compelling—a statement directly from Chipotle's communications director or a story in *USA Today*? The actual effectiveness of **third-party credibility** is the subject of academic debate and very much depends on the context.

In most situations, like the Chipotle case, public perceptions of and relationships with organizations are the result of a converged mishmash of communication and experience with those organizations. A news report consists of a mix of the reporter's story and quotes from her sources. Readers will consider that story along with everything else they have heard about the organization. Of course, they also will think about any firsthand experience they have had. In implementing public relations programs, we have to consider what our organizations are doing as it affects publics (action), what we are saying (communication) and what others are saying about us (third-party communication).

Third-party credibility
Tendency of people to attribute greater trustworthiness or expertise to a source other than the original sender of a persuasive message.

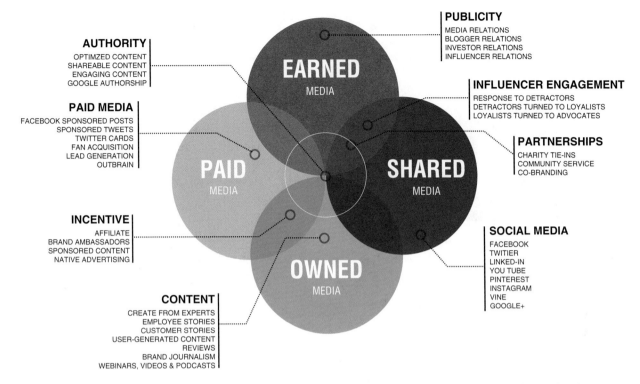

PUBLICITY
MEDIA RELATIONS
BLOGGER RELATIONS
INVESTOR RELATIONS
INFLUENCER RELATIONS

AUTHORITY
OPTIMZED CONTENT
SHAREABLE CONTENT
ENGAGING CONTENT
GOOGLE AUTHORSHIP

EARNED MEDIA

INFLUENCER ENGAGEMENT
RESPONSE TO DETRACTORS
DETRACTORS TURNED TO LOYALISTS
LOYALISTS TURNED TO ADVOCATES

PAID MEDIA
FACEBOOK SPONSORED POSTS
SPONSORED TWEETS
TWITTER CARDS
FAN ACQUISITION
LEAD GENERATION
OUTBRAIN

PAID MEDIA

SHARED MEDIA

PARTNERSHIPS
CHARITY TIE-INS
COMMUNITY SERVICE
CO-BRANDING

INCENTIVE
AFFILIATE
BRAND AMBASSADORS
SPONSORED CONTENT
NATIVE ADVERTISING

OWNED MEDIA

SOCIAL MEDIA
FACEBOOK
TWITTER
LINKED-IN
YOU TUBE
PINTEREST
INSTAGRAM
VINE
GOOGLE+

CONTENT
CREATE FROM EXPERTS
EMPLOYEE STORIES
CUSTOMER STORIES
USER-GENERATED CONTENT
REVIEWS
BRAND JOURNALISM
WEBINARS, VIDEOS & PODCASTS

In her "Spin Sucks" blog, Gini Dietrich offers this model classifying tactics that work in each media category, as well as overlaps between categories.

Can you name an organization (or organizations) using the range of tactics effectively?

Owned, Paid, Shared and Earned Media

Another way to think about the spectrum of media options is in terms of owned, paid, shared and earned. Public relations people and their organizations have always had options for all four. But new technologies have changed the way media are owned and paid for. Social media in particular have changed how we share information. And today's public relations professionals seek to earn followers, fans, likes, search engine rankings and positive reviews, in addition to earning news coverage.

Owned Media

In traditional media, owned channels include newsletters, corporate video, brochures, direct mail and even voice-mail messaging systems. Since organizations own the channels, they more or less control the message and its dissemination, as well as the opportunity for feedback or two-way communication. With the advent of the internet, owned options expanded to include intranets and web pages. While intranets allow for two-way communication on organization-owned platforms, public-facing web pages allow organizations to communicate externally.

Pardon the low resolution and snazzy fonts, but here's the very first White House home page as it appeared in 1994.

While this is a typical Web 1.0 image, do you see any evidence of movement from one-way/controlled to two-way/uncontrolled media?

Organizations can enhance the utility of owned media when they give up some control and allow for feedback and sharing.

Most early organizational web pages were designed primarily for delivering messages in a one-way fashion. Many websites still fit this description. Think Web 1.0. These websites are sometimes referred to as **brochureware** because they basically present the same information that can be delivered in traditional media like brochures. They enable organizations to disseminate information, potentially to worldwide audiences. *Potentially* is a key word here because—let's be realistic—people in Kazakhstan or Kenya probably won't search the web for a kickboxing club in Kansas. For websites to reach their potential they need to be part of a communication strategy that drives people to them. After all, websites don't get delivered to targeted publics in the same way that brochures, newsletters or in-house videos do. People have to actively search them out and find them.

Owned media include newer and emerging channels for communication as well. Podcasts, webinars, text messaging systems, blogs, apps and online video can all be owned. But like web pages in general, their utility to users is often enhanced when organizations give up some control and allow for feedback and sharing. This brings us to a more profound implication of the internet for public relations—the way it has opened new channels for two-way communication and interaction between organizations and publics.

Paid Media

Advertising is probably the first thing that comes to your mind when you think about paid media, and rightly so. As defined in Chapter 3, advertising is the stuff that fills paid media space. That space could be column inches in a newspaper, page portions of a magazine, seconds on the radio or TV, or pixels on a computer monitor or a giant high-definition LED display at a sports arena. Product and brand advertising are designed primarily to help sell products and services. **Corporate advertising** or institutional advertising is designed more to promote the organization as a whole.

Paid media also include banner ads, Google AdWords, targeted email distribution or pay-per-click services. LinkedIn, for example, sells ads that will appear on profile pages, in users' inboxes, on search results pages and in LinkedIn group pages. You can target your ads based on job titles, geography, age, gender or company size. Then you set up your account to

Brochureware
Web pages that present essentially the same material as printed materials such as brochures.

Corporate advertising
Paid media designed to promote an organization as a whole rather than sell a particular service, product or product category (also sometimes called institutional advertising).

pay per click—whereby the sponsor of an ad pays each time an ad is clicked—starting for $2 per click and going up to whatever maximum you set in a bid.[8]

Native advertising, another paid option, are ads that match the format of the primary content of the medium or channel. A sponsored column or **advertorial** in a newspaper or magazine, a promoted tweet, a sponsored Facebook post or an in-feed ad—they're all paid media. And they can get expensive! When Snapchat first offered companies the opportunity to buy one day's worth of ads to appear in users' "recent updates" feeds, they reportedly charged $750,000. Apparently it was worth it to big brands like Macy's, Samsung, McDonald's and Universal Pictures, which used the new paid service to promote the film *Dumb and Dumber To*.[9]

Bus wraps get attention.

Is this owned, paid, shared or earned media?

Whenever you see the words "Sponsored content" or "You may also like" on a web page or in an app, you're very likely looking at native advertising. A word of caution: this type of communication risks being deceptive. Stealth advertising that is designed and placed to trick people into thinking they are seeing third-party news, reviews or editorial content is a bad idea if your goal is to build and sustain trust between your organization and its publics.

Shared Media

Years ago, I was fortunate enough to take a public relations management course from the late Jack Felton. Felton was an APR, PRSA Fellow, two-time PRSA president and was honored with just about every major award in American public relations. Mark Weiner, CEO of PRIME Research, remembered Felton as "a bridge to the 'Mad Men' era of public relations" who taught us how public relations "focused on personal relationships, great ideas and service to others."[10]

One of the most important lessons I learned from Felton was the value of sharing media. Felton taught that when you see an article or story that you think a client or colleague would find interesting, you should clip it, attach a quick note, and share it. At the time, he was talking about actually using scissors to clip articles from newspapers and magazines, handwriting a note, physically attaching the note with a real paper clip, and sending it with a stamp and envelope or dropping it into a coworker's mailbox. It was good advice then, and it's good advice now. But the big difference is that you can do all this in seconds on your phone or computer with a simple click on a "share" button and a few strokes of the keyboard. Social media have made it much easier.

This ease of sharing also has big implications for organizations when they are the source or subject of stories and links being shared online. Think about your own social media use. How often do you "share" your own

Pay per click
Model of media sales in which advertisers, marketers or sponsors pay an online publisher or website owner for each time the sponsored message or advertisement is clicked.

Native advertising
Paid advertising that is presented in the form of the media content that surrounds it. Advertorials are a type of native advertising, as are promoted tweets, sponsored posts and so on. Native advertising should be labeled as "advertising," "paid content," "sponsored," etc.

Advertorial
Paid advertising that is presented in the form of editorial content.

original content, and how often do you share stories, memes, photos, videos and other content from organizations that may consider you a member of one of their publics? Organizations invest a lot of resources in developing content that they hope will be shared. When broad sharing is a goal, the biggest successes are the posts that go viral.

"Hey @Pharrell, can we have our hat back? #GRAMMYs."

When social media director Josh Martin famously tweeted these eight words and one hashtag on behalf of @Arby's during the 2014 Grammys, he instantly achieved the stuff of social media legend. Sometimes success in going viral is as much luck and timing as it is pre-planned strategy. His tweet—one of the most viral ever—took "just a few seconds" to compose and post, but by the Monday morning following the Grammys his post had been retweeted more than 70,000 times.

The tweet was a joke referring to singer-songwriter Pharrell Williams' oversized brown hat that had an uncanny resemblance to the Arby's logo. Martin posted it just as millions were watching the Grammys on TV and wondering what was up with the hat. Of those millions, a big percentage apparently also was on Twitter. "It took longer to find Pharrell's handle and make sure I spelled his name correctly" than it did to actually write and post the tweet, Martin later told *Adweek*. "It came to me organically."[11] While this was no accident—Martin was on duty that night doing "social listening" and monitoring the Grammys chatter for Arby's—no one could

Arby's Social Media Director Josh Martin scored big when his tweet about Pharrell Williams' hat at the Grammys was shared and re-shared among tens of thousands of Twitter users.

Do you think planning or luck played a bigger role?

have predicted the success. It could be said that Arby's and Martin worked to create their own luck that night.

In fact, successful efforts to share (and be shared) are often very carefully planned and implemented. GoPro's YouTube strategy is a good example. GoPro is a company that makes HD, waterproof video recording devices. With more than 4.1 million subscribers as of this writing, a big part of the company's strategy is the way it facilitates sharing among its subscribers. "Subscribers provide velocity," writes *Econsultancy* blogger Christopher Ratcliff. "YouTube loves velocity," he continues. "They'll watch it, they'll share it and your video will end up in more places."[12]

To be sure, it doesn't hurt that the nature of GoPro's product line lends itself perfectly to a social media site that is built on the concept of amazing videos. But GoPro leverages the medium particularly well by providing a forum for users to determine which videos are the best by viewing, liking, sharing, commenting and discussing. Most of the sharing is between and among the organization's publics, and GoPro representatives are careful and strategic about how they get involved. For instance, they may select and post a user video of the day, offer a few comments on popular videos, or occasionally answer product-related questions in the discussion section of their YouTube channels. However, the biggest act of sharing may be the way GoPro shares its platform by letting users provide some of the content and dominate the discussions. In communication strategy, sharing can refer to either the sharing of content such as a tweet or a video, or the sharing of a

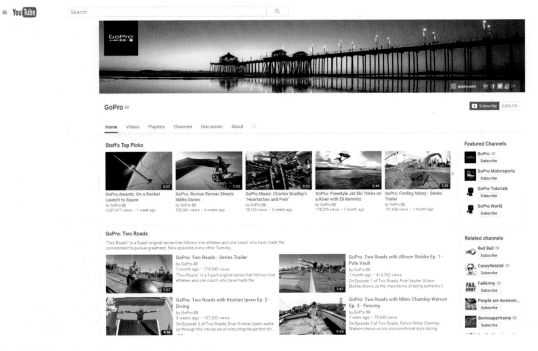

GoPro's YouTube channels have millions of subscribers.

Why is GoPro so successful in leveraging shared media?

forum or channel such as a discussion page or YouTube channel. Either way, sharing means ceding some control.

It's just as easy to find examples of organizations that have gone viral for regrettable reasons when the shared communication about them spun out of control. If you need a study break, just Google "public relations hashtag fail" for some comic relief. You'll find all kinds of examples, like when Qantas Airlines introduced #QantasLuxury asking fliers to tweet about their "dream luxury in-flight experience." The problem was that Qantas launched the effort one day after failed labor negotiations led to its fleet being grounded. Predictably, sarcastic and snarky customers had a field day on Twitter: "BREAKING NEWS: Qantas introduce #QantasLuxury class. Same as standard class, but the plane leaves the ground," tweeted a user with the handle @PuppyOnThe Radio.[13] As described in a Reuter's story, the "ill-timed public relations campaign" left the Australian airline "red faced."[14]

In the same way that public relations practitioners give up control of a news story as soon as they send a news release to journalists, they also give up control when they share information with publics on social media. Quick-witted comments and thrilling videos may generate shares and open conversations, but some of the most meaningful public relations outcomes still depend on earning the respect of influential media gatekeepers.

> Just as you give up control of a story as soon as you send a news release, you give up control of information when you share it with your publics on social media.

Earned Media

Just as advertising may be the first thing that people think of when they think of *paid* media, publicity may be the first thing that comes to mind for public relations practitioners when they think of *earned* media. The *APR Study Guide* defines publicity as "information from an outside source that is used by the media because it has news value" and "an uncontrolled method of placing messages because the source does not pay the media for placement."[15] In other words, publicity isn't bought. Publicity is earned.

A classic example is a newspaper story that is written and published as the result of a news release. If an organization has done something newsworthy, its public relations person will have a higher probability of success getting the story reported in the paper than if the news release is mostly spin and deemed by editors to have little news value. As discussed in Chapter 4 on relationships, effective public relations people understand how journalists think. They understand news value. They know when their organizations have done something that merits media coverage. When public relations people work in a management role, they help organizations perform in the public interest, and they also help organizations tell that story by garnering media coverage. They help organizations *earn* media attention.

Of course, the concept of media attention today is much broader than making news in newspapers, magazines, television and radio. In addition to traditional editors and producers, today's **media gatekeepers** are social media influencers, everyday media consumers and even computer

Media gatekeepers
People or processes that filter information by deciding which content is published, broadcasted, posted, shared or forwarded.

𝕀RS

| Filing | Payments | Refunds | Credits & Deductions | News & Events | Forms & Pubs | Help & Resources |

IRS Offers New Cash Payment Option ♥ ➕ 🖨

News Essentials

- What's Hot
- News Releases
- IRS - The Basics
- IRS Guidance
- Media Contacts
- Facts & Figures
- Around the Nation
- e-News Subscriptions

The Newsroom Topics

- Multimedia Center
- Noticias en Español
- Radio PSAs
- Tax Scams
- The Tax Gap
- Fact Sheets
- IRS Tax Tips
- Armed Forces
- **Latest News Home**

IR-2016-56, April 6, 2016

WASHINGTON — The Internal Revenue Service announced today a new payment option for individual taxpayers who need to pay their taxes with cash. In partnership with ACI Worldwide's OfficialPayments.com and the PayNearMe Company, individuals can now make a payment without the need of a bank account or credit card at over 7,000 7-Eleven stores nationwide.

"We continue to look for new ways to provide services for our taxpayers. Taxpayers have many options to pay their tax bills by direct debit, a check or a credit card, but this provides a new way for people who can only pay their taxes in cash without having to travel to an IRS Taxpayer Assistance Center," said IRS Commissioner John Koskinen.

Individuals wishing to take advantage of this payment option should visit the IRS.gov payments page, select the cash option in the other ways you can pay section and follow the instructions:

- Taxpayers will receive an email from OfficialPayments.com confirming their information.
- Once the IRS has verified the information, PayNearMe sends the taxpayer an email with a link to the payment code and instructions.

- Individuals may print the payment code provided or send it to their smart phone, along with a list of the closest 7-Eleven stores.

- The retail store provides a receipt after accepting the cash and the payment usually posts to the taxpayer's account within two business days.

- There is a $1,000 payment limit per day and a $3.99 fee per payment.

NBC News ✓   👍 Like Page
9 April · ↻

Pay taxes, buy a slurpee.

IRS Now Accepts Taxes at 7-Eleven
The IRS said payments would be accepted at more than 7,000 7-Eleven stores nationwide.
NBCNEWS.COM | BY NBC NEWS

👍 Like   💬 Comment   ➤ Share

"Pay taxes, buy a slurpee." This NBC News story posted on Facebook originated with an IRS news release.

Who are the gatekeepers determining whether the news makes its way from source (IRS) to receiver (Facebook users)? How did the IRS earn the coverage?

algorithms. Having a picture of your product pinned on a top Pinterest board, trending on Reddit ("the front page of the Internet"), getting retweeted by a celebrity, or showing up at the top of organic search results on Google are all forms of earned media.

Wikipedians define *search engine optimization (SEO)* as "the process of affecting the visibility of a website or a web page in a search engine's 'natural' or unpaid ('organic') search results."[16] While you can buy placement at the top of search results with programs like Google AdWords, effective SEO requires earning that placement by offering useful information, designing your site well and building relationships with other sites that may link to yours. On the last point, Google rewards earned links more than self-placed ones. Google treats a link from an external page as a "vote" by that page for the page to which it links. In Google's algorithms, "votes cast by pages that are themselves 'important' weigh more heavily and help to make other pages 'important.'"[17] In the same way that news operations draw a line between paid advertising and editorial content (sometimes referred to in publishing lingo as the separation of "church and state"), search engines take care to separate paid and unpaid results to protect the relevance of their search results and the credibility of their service.

> Today's media gatekeepers include social media influencers, everyday media consumers and even computer algorithms.

Mixed Media

In the universe of owned, paid, shared and earned media, communications functions and effects mix and overlap considerably. Content from an owned channel like a company blog, Pinterest board or Twitter timeline can easily be shared with a re-post, re-pin or retweet. Paid advertising, including native advertising and paid search results, can complement earned coverage in those same channels.

Case Study

The Magic Mix: Dell's Integration of Owned, Paid, Shared and Earned Media

When owned, paid, shared and earned media converge just right, it's "pure magic," according to *Mashable* contributor and public relations technology strategist Rebekah Iliff.[18] Iliff points to Dell Inc.'s annual release of the Global Technology Adoption Index (GTAI) during its Dell World event as a prime example.

Dell hosts the Dell World convention in Austin, Texas, each year for industry partners, tech media and thousands of customers. Think about the range of publics and types of public relations that are involved in such an endeavor: media relations, employee relations, investor relations, B2B relations and consumer relations to name a few.

To leverage attention and communication opportunities beyond the event itself, Dell conducts an annual study of major tech adoption trends in the areas of security, big data, cloud computing and mobility. This type of information has value to a range of Dell's publics. But rather than parsing out its communication efforts into separate tactics, Dell integrates its communication across the whole owned-paid-shared-earned spectrum.

In a sense, Dell both *owns* and *shares* the conference and its online presence, and it uses both types of tactics to promote the GTAI. Founder and CEO Michael Dell announces the GTAI at the Dell World event press conference, which is of course a push for *earned* media, and Dell *pays* for advertising space as well. Dell's vice president of global marketing Monique Bonner explains the strategy as one of integration in which the GTAI study is converted into "a variety of digital assets . . . all of which point back to specific Dell digital properties."[19] These include the following:

- An owned site at https://powermore.dell.com/2015-global-technology-adoption-index/
- Share-friendly social media platforms including Dell's LinkedIn page, Facebook account and Twitter feed (#DellGTAI)
- Promoted posts on LinkedIn and Twitter paid for by Dell
- Shareable infographics, presentation decks and online video that can also be used in earned media placements
- Pitches for earned placement in international and business media and tech sites
- Paid native advertising in the *New York Times* at http://paidpost.nytimes.com/dell/global-technology-adoption-index.html.

Dell promotes its annual Dell World event with hashtags like #DellWorld and #DellGTAI.

How does this case illustrate the interplay of owned, paid, shared and earned media?

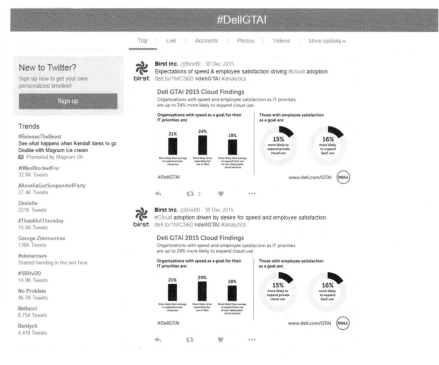

Dell publishes results of an annual study of major tech adoption trends across a variety of channels.

Which of Dell's publics would find this information valuable?

Iliff summarized the "magic" like this: "Technology enables a company to draw in the customer; then directs them to an ecosystem of content, allowing them to learn, explore, interact and ultimately make a buying decision."[20]

The ecosystem is not just comprised of content, however. The ecosystem is also made up of relationships and interaction between and among the organization and its many interrelated publics.

Ethics: Loyalty and Diversity in Communication and Action

Just as communication without action produces meaningless spin, diversity initiatives without loyalty amount to window dressing or a "misguided attempt to gain political correctness points," as media critic Eric Deggans puts it.[21] A key step in the process of ethical decision-making is identifying the diverse parties who will be affected by a decision and defining the organization's loyalty to each. **Loyalty** is a core value of public relations. It is listed in the *PRSA Code of Ethics* along with advocacy, honesty, expertise

Loyalty
A sense of obligation or support for someone or something, including both organizations and publics.

Voices from the Field

Rosanna M. Fiske

Rosanna M. Fiske, APR, is a PRSA Fellow and vice president of corporate communications at Wells Fargo. Widely known for her cross-cultural understanding and expertise, Fiske is responsible for all aspects of corporate communications including executive advocacy, social media and internal and external communications for Wells Fargo's Florida and Southeast regions, which include 1,200+ branches and more than 21,000 team members. Fiske has a proven track record developing successful, multichannel campaigns working with some of the world's leading brands such as Charles Schwab, American Airlines, GE, Google, Absolut Vodka and MTV Networks. Fiske was the first Latina CEO of PRSA, PRWeek's 2014 Diversity Champion, and named one of the Top 100 Influential Hispanics in America by Hispanic Business Magazine.

How is public relations part of the management function at your organization?
Wells Fargo is one of those companies that lives, walks and breathes its vision and values—people as a competitive advantage, ethics, doing what's right for customers, diversity and inclusion, and leadership. I have been in this profession almost 30 years and have led teams that have written visions and values for different companies, and it's just that—a writing exercise. At Wells Fargo that's not the case. You can walk into any branch and the branch manager within five minutes is going to tell you his or her favorite quote from the vision and values. We all believe in and refer back to the values to guide us in every way. We ask, "Is this something that we really should be doing?" "Is this something that would be an extension of our vision and values?"

Can you tell us about how that plays out as real action within the organization?
Each region within Wells Fargo has what we call Diversity and Inclusion Councils that serve to carry the mission of diversity and inclusion back to wherever they come from. These are not just top-down councils. Instead, they include everybody from the region presidents to team members on the frontline and line-of-business leaders. You have diversity of levels, diversity of functions, diversity of disciplines, ethnic diversity, religious diversity, gender, age, you name it. If you're a manager, whatever you learn in the council, you're going to bring it back to your team and put it to practice.

How do you make the business case for diversity?
People as a competitive advantage—one of our key values. Wells Fargo sees our diversity and inclusion councils, and really diversity and inclusion as a whole, as a great professional development and engagement opportunity. In addition, diversity and inclusion enables us to use creativity and multiple perspectives to adapt and respond to our customers' needs faster and more effectively. To be successful as a company and as team members we must be as diverse as the customers and communities we serve.

What risks and rewards do you consider when deciding to communicate with uncontrolled channels like shared social media vs. more controlled channels like owned media?
Well, I actually think most work in public relations is uncontrolled! I worked in advertising too, and in advertising you're controlling message, frequency and placement. I see social media as an extension of public relations. You have the same pull and push philosophy on social media. You can push out a lot of messaging, and it's, "is anyone listening?" You can pull a lot of messaging, if you *do* the listening.

For Wells Fargo we have owned content in a number of ways, including Wells Fargo Stories (stories.wellsfargobank.com) where we tell stories of everyday things that happen at Wells Fargo and with Wells Fargo customers. Our vision is to help customers succeed financially and you can find a lot of ways that we do that through those stories. Interestingly, if you go to one of our ATMs you'll find some of those stories—some of that owned content—showing on the screen.

continues

continued

Have you made much progress with diversity since you identified it as a core tenet for PRSA in 2011?

I was elected to the PRSA board in 2004. Right around that time we did a comprehensive member survey, and the percentage of ethnically diverse membership was in the single digits. By the time that I ended my year as CEO and chair of PRSA, we were at 13–14 percent. I was the first Latina CEO and chair, the first Latina who was national treasurer, and the second Hispanic member on the board. Since then, two more African American women, another Hispanic woman, and an Asian American have served on the board. Just in the last four or five years, the fact that we have been able to make those changes at that top level of leadership definitely shows that we're making progress.

However, you can't look at diversity and inclusion separately. You can't say, "we need a few diverse people here because we're lacking that." It really needs to be built into everything that you do. A perfect example comes from back in 2011. Whenever we provided national news from PRSA that went beyond the profession, we provided it in Spanish to Spanish-language media and to diverse media. Supplying this content in different languages and to diverse media wasn't an add-on. It was *part of* the outreach and part of the strategy.

and independence. "We are faithful to those we represent, while honoring our obligation to serve the public interest."[22]

Interestingly, **diversity** is not mentioned directly in the PRSA Code of Ethics, but it is certainly an important issue to PRSA's leadership, as it is to professional organizations worldwide. In response to a 2011 *PRWeek* Editorial titled "Agencies Must Find Answers for a Lack of Diversity,"[23] PRSA Chair and CEO Rosanna Fiske wrote that PRSA had "made increasing diversity in the profession a core tenet of our mission." Fiske noted that PRSA, along with the Arthur W. Page Society and the Council of PR Firms among others, had identified diversity as a priority to "engender not only greater diversity within our ranks, but higher value for our services."[24] So what does diversity have to do with loyalty, and what does this ethical question have to do with implementation?

In their book *Doing Ethics in Media*, ethicists Jay Black and Chris Roberts write that we expand our empathy as we grow personally and professionally. At earlier stages of moral development we tend to be loyal to ourselves and to those who have power over us such as parents, teachers and bosses. But as we mature in life and in our professional careers, we expand our worldview and our empathy with "people who are not like us—people different in race, ethnicity, physical ability, religion, sexual orientation, age, economic class, etc."[25] In public relations—a field defined as the management of relationships with all sorts of publics—empathy and loyalty go hand in hand with diversity. The more diverse decision-makers within an organization, the more effective the organization will be in relating to its various publics. Diversity initiatives that are implemented as part of an organization's mission and loyalty to both internal and external publics are more than window dressing. They are the implementation of good strategy.

The more diverse decision-makers within an organization, the more effective the organization will be in relating to various publics.

Diversity
Inclusion of different types of people and different types of views.

Doing Good by Doing Well: Kimberly-Clark's Efforts to Promote Diversity

Glass ceiling
Metaphor used to describe a present but unseen barrier to promotion for women and minorities.

When Kimberly-Clark Corp. named Sue Dodsworth to the role of vice president and chief diversity officer, they communicated all the right things. "Diversity and inclusion is critical to the success of our business," said Chairman and CEO Thomas J. Falk in the news release.[26] With global brands like Huggies, Kotex, Kleenex, Scott and Pull-Ups, it didn't take advanced analytics to understand that many of Kimberly-Clark's most important publics are women. Data available at the time showed that 85 percent of the company's customers were female.[27] While naming Dodsworth to this post sent a message, Kimberly-Clark needed more for any lasting effect. "We must build a more diverse and inclusive global organization that looks, thinks and behaves like the people that use our products," said Falk. Dodsworth had her work cut out for her.

Research and planning came first. In sharp contrast to the demographics of its customers, only 17 percent of the Kimberly-Clark's upper-level (director level or higher) employees were women. In closer analysis of HR data, Dodsworth found two **glass-ceiling** points in women's careers at Kimberly-Clark. Many women were "stuck" in the position they attained right after their first promotion, and others were stuck just below the director level.[28]

A company like Kimberly-Clark often promotes managers from areas like manufacturing or millwork that traditionally may not include many women. Dodsworth and her team analyzed hiring and promotion data and interviewed employees. They learned that women were deterred by leadership job descriptions that mentioned years of experience in these areas as desirable qualifications. As Dodsworth explained in a *Fortune* article, "When we asked why, it was, 'Because of these 10 things that I need for the role, I've only got eight.' Whereas when I talked to the men who applied, they had five and they were going for it."

Dodsworth and her team then developed and implemented a strategy that focused on career development. Dodsworth asked hiring managers writing job postings to focus more on skills that could be transferred to new positions than on

Kimberly-Clark claimed, "We're changing more than just diapers around here."

How did the company's efforts to promote diversity also promote the company's business interests?

accumulated years of past experience. Other actions included global networking forums, mentoring programs, hiring policies that were more amenable to work-life balance, and the implementation of specific business plans for recruiting and developing more women leaders. As reported in a news release announcing that Kimberly-Clark had won a 2014 Catalyst Award, the results were impressive:

- The number of women who held director-level or higher leadership positions globally increased by 71 percent.

- The number of women with racially or ethnically diverse backgrounds in "director-plus" positions at Kimberly-Clark in the United States doubled.

- Internal promotions of women to "director-plus" jobs increased from 19 percent to 44 percent.

Catalyst is a nonprofit organization dedicated to advancing business leadership opportunities for women. The Catalyst Award "annually honors innovative organizational approaches with proven, measurable results that address the recruitment, development, and advancement of all women, including diverse women."[29]

While some may see the award and the publicity it earned as "great PR," that recognition is less important to the success of the organization than the role of public relations as part of the way the organization is managed. As Dodsworth reported in the *Forbes* article, "This started as an initiative, but now it's the way we work."

In Case You Missed It

ICYMI

Communication in public relations will ring hollow without action to back it up. Here are some key points from the chapter to help you hit the right notes in implementing a successful public relations plan.

- Excellence in the field of public relations is based on meaningful action.

- Organizations must bring something beyond talk to their relationships with publics.

- Make wise and informed decisions about which channels of communication to use, when and for what purpose.

- Organizations can enhance the utility of owned media when they give up some control and allow for feedback and sharing.

- Just as you give up control of a story as soon as you send a news release, you give up control of information when you share it with your publics on social media.

- Today's media gatekeepers include social media influencers, everyday media consumers and even computer algorithms.

- The more diverse the decision-makers within an organization, the more effective the organization will be in relating to various publics.

SUMMARY

7.1 Explain how organizational action is the foundation for credible communication.

You have to walk the walk if you are going to talk the talk, and actions speak louder than words. Both of these common sayings speak to the idea that the implementation of solid public relations programs requires the management of organizational action. Communication that is not based on meaningful action is spin.

7.2 Analyze cases of action and communication in the implementation of effective public relations.

Chipotle's pork issue illustrates how an organization implemented public relations with both action and communication.

7.3 Outline media options on a continuum from controlled to uncontrolled.

Media like brochures, newsletters, intranets and advertising fall on the controlled end of the spectrum because the public relations practitioner can, to some extent, control the production and distribution of content. Social media and publicity are considered uncontrolled because public relations practitioners cede control to social media users, news editors and producers. The most uncontrolled media often provide better options for two-way communication, credibility and influence.

7.4 Differentiate among owned, paid, shared and earned media.

Owned media include organizational web pages, newsletters, intranets and other controlled media that organization employees own and operate. Paid options include advertising and other media services that require payment for placement and distribution of information. Shared options are more common in social media, where users share by re-posting, retweeting, tagging, linking and so on. Earned media include traditional publicity as well as coverage by third parties online (i.e., influencers). These channels often overlap, and integrated strategies may use all of the media types for implementing common goals, as was illustrated in the Dell GTAI case.

7.5 Describe the relationship between the values of loyalty and diversity.

At more advanced stages of professional and moral development, we expand our empathy to people who are different from us, thereby expanding our loyalty to more diverse groups.

7.6 Summarize the benefits of implementing diversity initiatives.

Understanding an organization's obligations to and relationships with diverse publics informs ethical decision-making as well as informed management of an organization. The more that diversity of public relations staff and internal publics reflects the diversity of an organization's external publics, the better suited the organization will be for building and maintaining mutually beneficial relationships, as illustrated in the Kimberly-Clark case.

DISCUSSION QUESTIONS

1. Name an organization that you believe lives up to high standards. What does the organization do to earn your respect, and how does the organization communicate about those actions?

2. Name an organization that you feel relies on spin for promotion. Give an example of why you think the organization doesn't back its communication with action.

3. Provide an example of a case when an organization benefited from something going viral, and compare that to a case in which viral communication harmed an organization. To what degree did the organizations have control of the channels in each case?

4. Pick a (non-news) organization that is often featured in both your social media feeds and in traditional media. Review its online communication to identify examples of owned, paid, shared and earned media.

5. We often think of race and gender as types of diversity. What other kinds of diversity can benefit organizations in public relations, and how?

KEY TERMS

Advertorial   177
Brochureware   176
Controlled media   173
Corporate advertising   176
Diversity   186
Glass ceiling   187

Loyalty   184
Media gatekeepers   180
Native advertising   177
Pay per click   177
Third-party credibility   174
Uncontrolled media   173

CHAPTER 8

Evaluation

What counts in public relations measurement? The Barcelona Principles (2.0!) will get you up to speed.

KEY LEARNING OUTCOMES

8.1 Explain how evaluation research can be used in public relations program development and message testing.

8.2 Describe how media monitoring services have evolved in the digital age.

8.3 Discuss how digital technology has expanded our ability to track and analyze data in evaluating public relations programs.

8.4 Evaluate public relations research practices using industry standards for research (i.e., Barcelona Principles).

8.5 Identify tools for measuring online and traditional public relations outcomes.

8.6 Analyze the relationship between independence as a core value of public relations and the ethical conduct of research, measurement and evaluation.

RELATED UNIVERSAL ACCREDITATION BOARD COMPETENCY AREAS
1.9 EVALUATION OF PROGRAMS • **2.2** ETHICAL BEHAVIOR • **5.1** BUSINESS LITERACY
5.2 RESOURCE MANAGEMENT • **5.4** PROBLEM SOLVING AND DECISION-MAKING

E valuation is the process by which we determine the value of our work. When we invest time, energy and budgets in both short- and long-term projects, we use evaluation to understand our return on investment. We also use evaluation to demonstrate to employers and clients the value they receive when they invest in us and our programs. From determining whether it's worth it to update an Instagram feed daily to pitching a million-dollar campaign proposal, evaluation is how we know—and show—the value of our work.

The "E" (evaluation) may come last in the four-step RPIE outline (Figure 8.1), but as we've discussed throughout the book, evaluation and research go together, and both are used continuously throughout strategic public relations programs. In the introduction to Chapter 5, we described research as a cyclical process. Evaluation of prior programs can be useful right at the very beginning of a new campaign or program. In Chapter 6 on planning, we discussed the concepts of formative research and benchmarking. In planning goals and objectives, it's important to understand the current state of your organization, situation and publics so that you can measure your progress against that baseline or starting point. Then in Chapter 7, we looked at how the media landscape for implementing public relations programs has changed. Digital and social media have not only expanded our options for communication, they have expanded our ability to track and analyze activity across owned, paid, shared and earned media. In this chapter, we examine what we count as successful communication and our metrics for understanding that success.

Figure 8.1 In the RPIE model, evaluation demonstrates the value of what was planned and implemented, but it also helps current and future planning and implementation.

How can evaluation of one program or campaign serve as formative research for the next?

Old and New Methods

All of the major research methods described in Chapter 5—surveys, experiments, content analysis, interviews, focus groups and direct observation—are just as useful now as they have been through the history of social science. The purposes for these methods haven't changed much. For example, surveys are still conducted to gather data that describe demographics and what people think, feel and do. In addition, as a method for evaluation, the data from surveys conducted before a campaign can be used as a baseline for comparison to data collected during and after a campaign to assess changes in cognition, attitudes and behavior.

Of course, online survey tools make it much easier to collect and analyze data than it was in the days when most surveys were conducted using paper and pencil. However, online surveys still serve much the same purpose as paper surveys. In fact, for some research with some populations, you may receive a higher response rate and a more representative sample of participants with a survey sent by snail mail or handed to respondents in person. Nielsen still mails pen-and-paper surveys, along with dollar bills as incentives, to collect data on household TV viewing behavior.

This isn't to say, however, that there hasn't been significant innovation in research methods. Nielsen and other media tracking firms also have developed **digital watermarking** technology that enables audio and video to be tracked with digital information woven into the signals that carry programming content. This helps copyright owners protect their information, and it also helps companies like Nielsen track which signals reach your TV and mobile devices. This digital research technology has the advantage of providing more accurate accounting for what content is delivered, but unlike paper surveys and diaries, the watermarking technology can't tell researchers whether you are actually paying attention.

In a laboratory setting, communication researchers might use **eye-tracking** software, or even **functional magnetic resonance imaging (fMRI)**, to observe how people pay attention to and respond to messages. Virtual reality headsets are becoming more commonly available to everyday gamers and consumers. And, with new technology for communication comes new ways to measure and evaluate the experiences. Every virtual movement can be recorded and analyzed.

Whether you use traditional or new research technology, and whether you evaluate traditional or new public relations efforts, your research decisions should be driven by the specific purpose of your evaluation. Three major areas for evaluation research are: (1) message testing, (2) media monitoring, and (3) measurement of outcomes (i.e., metrics and analytics).

Message Testing

As a way to evaluate your tactics for communication, message testing can range from informal to formal and from qualitative to quantitative. Ever type a tweet and then quickly show it to a friend before posting? That's message testing: you are doing a tiny bit of evaluation research to see how others will receive your message before you send it. Other examples of ways to test messages with more rigor include focus groups, readability tests and experiments.

Digital watermarking
Information embedded into digital audio and video signals that can be used to track when and where the content is delivered.

Eye tracking
Process of measuring eye movements to determine where people are focusing; often used in website testing.

Functional magnetic resonance imaging (fMRI)
Tests that use magnetic fields to generate images of brain activity, including responses to communication and media stimuli.

Attendees at a Facebook developer's conference try virtual-reality glasses.

How might virtual reality be evaluated as a public relations tactic?

Even informal message testing can be useful as formative evaluation in public relations.

What kind of message testing have you conducted?

Focus Groups

Focus groups have been a popular method of message testing in advertising, entertainment and public relations for decades. Focus groups can be formal. Trained moderators may lead discussions with small groups of carefully recruited participants who must respond to campaign concepts. Organizers of a health campaign may run focus groups to see what types of messages and appeals resonate most with high school students. A startup tech company getting ready to launch a new app may invite early adopters to focus groups to discuss the design of the app's icon or various display pages.

Readability Tests

Every time an editor or reviewer reads through copy and offers feedback, they are helping with message testing. This feedback is normally qualitative in the form of editorial suggestions and comments, either written or oral. But message testing also can be quantitative. For example, if you paste the text from the previous paragraph into a readability tester window on the site www.readability-score.com, the software will tell you that the paragraph has five sentences, 94 words, 156 syllables, and 484 characters, with an average of 1.7 syllables per word and 18.8 words per sentence. The software calculates that this all adds up to an average readability score for a grade level of 11.2. So if you've graduated high school, we should be OK. However, this little bit of message testing reminds me to try to keep my sentences short.

A/B testing can be used to quickly compare the effects of different digital content and messages.

Experiments

Experimental design also can be applied in message testing. Message testing experiments are known as **A/B testing** in the parlance of digital media. Let's say you want to test different news release headings as links on one of your organization's web pages. You could set up two versions of the web page—an "A" version with one news release heading and a "B" version with another heading. These are basically two conditions in a simple experiment. Your website can then be programmed to randomly display either A or B to a sample of visitors over a period of time. A/B testing programs allow you to compare the two conditions against each other to see, for instance, whether the A version or the B version generates more clicks through to the full text of the news release. The independent variable (the cause) is the type of headline, and the dependent variable (the effect) is click-through behavior. When software and computer programs are used to automatically test digital messages, marketing and advertising researchers call this **automated copy testing**.

A/B testing
Experiment in which one group of participants is randomly assigned to see one version of a message and another group is randomly assigned to see a second version. Results are then compared to test the effectiveness of message variations.

Automated copy testing
Using computer programs to automate the process of testing digital messages such as promotional copy.

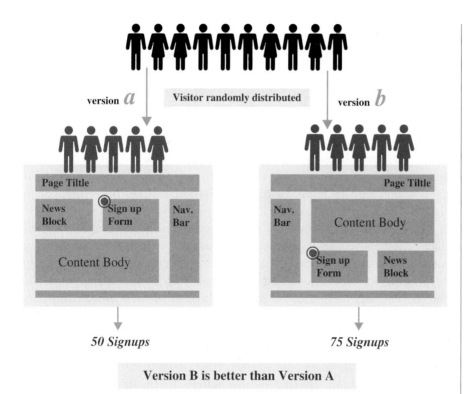

version *a* — Visitor randomly distributed — version *b*

Page Tiltle

| News Block | Sign up Form | Nav. Bar |

Content Body

Page Tiltle

| Nav. Bar | Content Body |

Sign up Form | News Block

50 Signups

75 Signups

Version B is better than Version A

Figure 8.2 This example shows how different page layouts (independent variable) can be compared to see which delivers more signups (dependent variable).

What other independent and dependent variables can be tested with A/B testing?

Media Monitoring Services

Monitoring media is another area of evaluation that has sped up considerably in the digital age. In the days before Google (and Google alerts), interns and other entry-level employees used to get paper cuts and calluses from paging through stacks of newspapers and magazines every morning looking for mentions of a client's name or product. After finding a story, they would review it to see how relevant it was and whether it was primarily positive, negative or neutral (a very basic form of content analysis). Then they would use scissors, a glue stick and a copy machine to create pages for the clip book. The clip book was a three-ring binder that included all the print media coverage they had found and categorized.

Evaluating TV coverage was another issue. In some offices, VCRs would be programmed to tape-record the morning and evening news programs whenever the public relations person expected coverage of his or her organization. Another option was to contact TV stations directly to request copies of the coverage. The cassettes or transcripts would be saved for later analysis, reporting and presentation.

Before digital tracking was easily accessible, the clip book—a binder of press clippings—was a common way to show off the results of publicity efforts.

How has computer technology changed the nature of media monitoring?

But that was for do-it-yourselfers. Bigger agencies and organizations with larger budgets subscribed to **clipping services**. Clipping services monitored print and electronic media for mentions of clients in local, national or international media. Their menu of services included monitoring coverage in different types of media, capturing related content, and conducting content analysis of news and editorial mentions. They would also calculate numbers like total number of impressions. In fact, they still do. Fortunately, **media monitoring services** have evolved with digital media and are among the most useful tools in digital public relations because of the way they support public relations professionals in the collection, analysis and reporting of media data for evaluation.

Aside from the obvious advantage of automating the process of scanning, "clipping," compiling and sorting media coverage, media monitoring services have also expanded the range of evaluation available. While legacy clipping services of the 20th century included opinion pieces and editorials, the content was limited to what was published or broadcasted, not how people responded to the content. Old clipping services measured earned media and not shared media. They offered little evidence of what publics were thinking, feeling or doing as a result of the coverage. Today's media monitoring services still measure publicity, but they also monitor online conversations and facilitate the sharing of information. Cision, cliQ, and LexisNexis Newsdesk were named finalists for the Software and Information Industry Association's 2015 CODiE awards for public relations software:

- Cision's social software "searches millions of posts and mines the data that will help you monitor the performance of key brand attributes and engagement, target emerging brand value and market drivers, and make informed business decisions easily and efficiently."[1]

- The cliQ platform monitors "millions of broadcast TV hours, online news stories, and social media mentions" and "continuously accumulates broadcast media, organizes it for lightning-fast big data analysis, and enables great content to be immediately saved and shared."[2]

- LexisNexis Newsdesk allows you to "search an unmatched, global content collection—from a single dashboard—improving your ability to monitor the buzz on companies, brands and competitors around the world."[3]

As defined in Chapter 5 on research, content analysis is the systematic analysis of any type of recorded communication. Media monitoring services enable large-scale content analysis of both traditional and social media. Social media content that is actively produced, discussed and shared by publics online can now also be monitored and analyzed, giving public relations people access to a new dimension of mediated content. That said, many of the most important goals and objectives of public relations programs—affecting what people think, feel and do—cannot be measured with only content analysis.

Media monitoring services enable the analysis of social media content that is actively produced, discussed and shared by publics online.

Metrics, Analytics and Data

Metrics and analytics are essentially synonyms for measurement and evaluation. It's not unusual for people to append the words "real-time," as in "real-time analytics," to emphasize the immediacy of digital measurement. Large media organizations with high-traffic websites can run countless A/B tests in any given day to optimize their content. These simple experiments are just the tip of the analytics iceberg. Planners and editors who have a good handle on computer programming and statistics can develop **algorithms** to test various combinations of factors (e.g., message selection, message placement, image selection, headline styles, color) leading to various outcomes (e.g., click-through rates, time spent on page, sharing behavior). This type of algorithm-building is what made BuzzFeed founder Jonah Paretti so successful in building that "viral-content machine" into one of the most powerful information sources on the internet.[4] It's what makes a site like Mashable competitive with *The New York Times* online.

While *The New York Times* employs an army of more than a thousand journalists, editors, designers and coders, Mashable gets its tens of millions of site visitors and social media followers with a team of about 60 reporters, according to Jim Roberts. Roberts had worked as an editor at *The New York Times* before joining Mashable as its executive editor and chief content officer. Mashable's front page is primarily algorithm-driven. A computer program decides which stories to promote and demote on the page based on

"What's new," "what's rising," and "what's hot" on Mashable's home page are largely determined by algorithms.

What kinds of data do you think feed the computer's decisions? How would this type of data be useful to marketers and public relations planners?

real-time analysis of which stories get the most views, shares and clicks at different times of day. "Data," he says, "is our friend—in fact it is our lifeblood at Mashable."[5]

While the term "**big data**" means many things to many different people, this is one example of what people are talking about when they use the term. *Forbes* contributing writer Lisa Arthur defines *big data* as "a collection of data from traditional and digital sources inside and outside your company that represents a source for ongoing discovery and analysis."[6] You can collect this information directly from your organization's or client's publics through **cookies** or registrations. This is known as **first-party data** because you collect the information yourself—the "first party" is you. You can also buy **third-party data** from vendors who collect and aggregate data from other sources and then sell you more data about your publics than you may even know what to do with. That's something to consider very carefully. There are so much data available that people don't really know what to do with it all.

Running a series of message-testing experiments that may have taken weeks or months to set up a few years ago can now happen almost instantly, in real time, so to speak. The problem with running 45 A/B tests in one day is that anyone doing that probably hasn't put much thought into exactly what they're testing and why. Testing messages with data from experiments is just one type of *analytics*. As defined in Chapter 5, the term refers to any analysis used to describe, predict and improve how organizations communicate with publics online. According to researcher Seth Duncan, two common applications of analytics are particularly useful in public relations: tracking visitor behavior and segmenting referring sources.[7]

Tracking Visitor Behavior

The first important use of web analytics in public relations is tracking the behavior of website visitors. When someone visits your web page, searches for a word or phrase, or clicks on an ad or other link, all that information can be recorded and analyzed. The data available from this process include number of unique visitors to a page, number of visits, number of page views, how long a user stays on a site and **bounce rate**, which is the percentage of visitors who go to your site but then leave the site instead of continuing toward other goals you may have established. Specific goals that can be tracked include downloads, registrations, completed forms, electronic petition signatures, donations or purchases.

Once you have identified your measurable goals, you can calculate a **conversion rate**, which is the number of goals reached divided by the number of unique visitors to your site. Let's say you are trying to get people to sign an online petition to make a statement to your local lawmakers. The goal is to have people sign the online petition. You track 1,000 unique visitors to your website. The data show that 700 visitors to your site leave right after seeing the first page, but 150 of them actually click through to the petition and "sign" it. Your bounce rate is 70 percent and your conversion rate is 15 percent.

Segmenting Referring Sources

A second important use of analytics outlined by researcher Seth Duncan is segmenting the referring sources for web visitors. Web analytics enable you to know whether people found your site online by directly typing in the URL (direct traffic) or as a result of organic search results or paid search results (e.g., Google Ad Words). You can also find out what keywords people used in those searches. Other referring sources that public relations people track include clicks from email campaigns, banner ads, native advertising, social media posts and coverage by news media. Notice how these could be classified as owned, paid, shared and earned, respectively (see Chapter 7).

Parsing Big Data

Again, the availability of data in digital research and evaluation is usually not the problem. It's figuring out what to do with that data. Researchers aren't the only ones facing this challenge. Those working on the creative side of public relations also can be overwhelmed by how to develop communication strategies for large-scale campaigns when such huge amounts of data are available.

Traditionally, campaign messages have been tailored for relatively general demographic profiles. A political TV ad may be created for "soccer moms" or "blue-collar workers." But with the abundance of data available now, demographic profiles easily can be segmented into hundreds, thousands or even millions of unique profiles. Think about your own social media profile. Are you a female in a relationship who shares certain Buzz-Feed content, lives in the Midwest, "likes" Hillary Clinton and posts about Lilly Pulitzer while shopping at Target? Instagram, which is owned by Facebook, knows that. Or are you a male who lives in a large city on the West Coast who tweets about the San Diego Padres, goes to a state school and travels to Mexico? Twitter probably knows that. Facebook and Twitter and all sorts of third-party companies collect, buy and sell data that can be used for targeting messages. Political campaign planners, who are at the forefront of trends in digital message strategy, have come to realize the challenges of handling all this data. "It's very easy to get overwhelmed with all the possibilities you have," said Alex Kellner in a *New York Times* article. Kellner works for a digital marketing firm and has directed digital campaigns, including one for Virginia Governor Terry McAuliffe. "More campaigns are moving in the direction of having that freak-out moment for a couple of days and saying, 'Oh my gosh. Here's all we can do. How can we get it all done?'"[8]

Thanks to some particularly foresighted public relations practitioners and researchers, we have guidelines to work with to avoid that freak-out moment, or at least to know what to do when it hits us. The Barcelona Principles provide useful instructions for keeping it real in the digital age when it comes to metrics (i.e., measurement), analytics (i.e., analysis) and evaluation.

Barcelona Principles

By 2010, public relations had matured into a field that was global, digital and relationship-focused. Social media was blowing up, and organizations worldwide had to figure out what to do about it—how to demonstrate the value of public relations in a new era of media. It was one of those opportunity-or-threat moments for the whole field. In order to earn and keep their seats at management tables, public relations executives would have to tackle the question of how to do research that would not only drive success, but also demonstrate public relations' contributions to organizational missions. That was the stage for the 2nd European Summit on Measurement in Barcelona. The group was convened by AMEC, the International Association for Measurement and Evaluation of Communication, and IPR, the Institute for Public Relations. By the end of that meeting, delegates from 33 countries had agreed to the "Barcelona Declaration of Research Principles," which was billed as the first global standard of public relations measurement.[9]

In 2015, AMEC updated the principles to "reflect the significant changes we have seen in the media landscape and the emergence of integrated communications," according to David Rockland.[10] Rockland is a partner and managing director at Ketchum and past chairman of AMEC, who led both the 2010 discussion and the international effort to update in 2015. The Barcelona Principles include seven key items. You may notice that most of these ideas resonate with other key points we've covered in prior chapters on the RPIE process.

Principle 1: Goal Setting and Measurement Are Fundamental

You may recall from Chapter 6 that good goals are supported by SMART objectives, and that the "M" in SMART stands for "measurable." *Measurable* implies *quantifiable.* For example you can count (i.e., quantify) the number of followers on Twitter, snaps on Snapchat, people who physically attend an event, real dollars donated to a cause, or downloads of applications. However, the strategic importance of those metrics depends on what they tell you about your progress toward a goal. Is 5,000 followers a good thing? It depends on your organization and its goals. For a local nonprofit that started a campaign two months ago with 25 followers, a count of 5,000 followers could be fantastic news, showing evidence of exceeding goals. For an international coffee brand or a national political candidate, 5,000 followers may be a depressingly low number. It's the combination of the number and the goal that yield actual strategic value. As stated in the original Barcelona Principles,

> *Fundamentally important, goals should be as quantitative as possible and address who, what, when and how much impact is expected from a public relations campaign. Traditional and social media should be measured as well as changes in stakeholder awareness, comprehension, attitude and behavior.*[11]

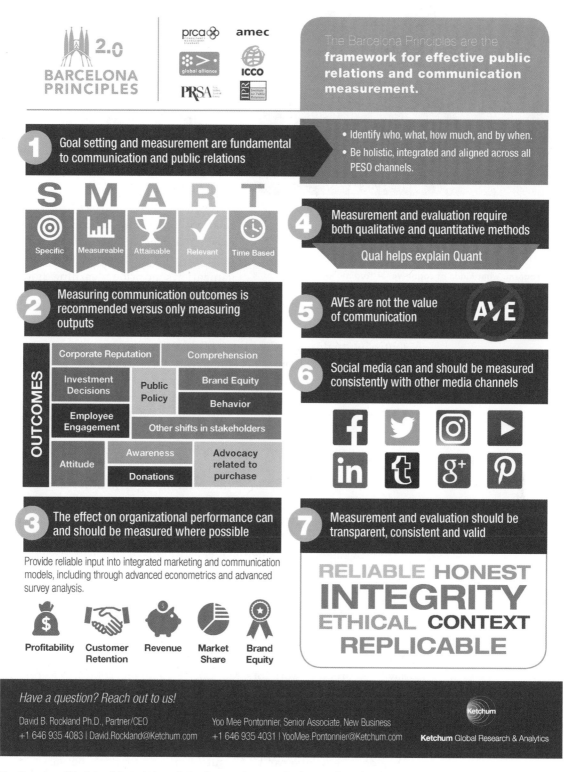

The Barcelona Principles are the framework for effective public relations and communication measurement.

1 Goal setting and measurement are fundamental to communication and public relations

- Identify who, what, how much, and by when.
- Be holistic, integrated and aligned across all PESO channels.

S M A R T

Specific | Measureable | Attainable | Relevant | Time Based

2 Measuring communication outcomes is recommended versus only measuring outputs

OUTCOMES

Corporate Reputation | Comprehension
Investment Decisions | Public Policy | Brand Equity
| | Behavior
Employee Engagement | Other shifts in stakeholders
Attitude | Awareness | Advocacy related to purchase
| Donations |

3 The effect on organizational performance can and should be measured where possible

Provide reliable input into integrated marketing and communication models, including through advanced econometrics and advanced survey analysis.

Profitability | Customer Retention | Revenue | Market Share | Brand Equity

4 Measurement and evaluation require both qualitative and quantitative methods

Qual helps explain Quant

5 AVEs are not the value of communication

6 Social media can and should be measured consistently with other media channels

7 Measurement and evaluation should be transparent, consistent and valid

RELIABLE HONEST **INTEGRITY** ETHICAL **CONTEXT** REPLICABLE

Have a question? Reach out to us!

David B. Rockland Ph.D., Partner/CEO
+1 646 935 4083 | David.Rockland@Ketchum.com

Yoo Mee Pontonnier, Senior Associate, New Business
+1 646 935 4031 | YooMee.Pontonnier@Ketchum.com

Ketchum Global Research & Analytics

The Barcelona Principles 2.0 apply broadly to all sorts of communication, media and organizations.

How will applying these principles benefit the status of public relations as a field?

Following an outbreak of rabies in Bali, Indonesia, the World Society for the Protection of Animals (WSPA) and the Bali Animal Welfare Association (BAWA) began a mass vaccination program to inoculate 350,000 of the island's dog population.

For this program, what kinds of cognitive, attitudinal and behavioral outcomes could be measured among Bali's (human!) residents?

Cognitive
Having to do with mental processes such as thinking, knowing, perceiving, learning and understanding.

Attitudinal
Having to do with affect, emotion, favor or disfavor toward an organization, brand, product, service, idea or any other attitude object.

Behavioral
Having to do with observable human action.

Likert-type items
Questionnaire items that ask people to respond to statements with a range of defined response options such as the range from "strongly disagree" to "strongly agree."

Notice that the last part doesn't focus on communication tactics or media coverage, but on what people feel, think and do as a result of public relations efforts. This leads us to a second principle . . .

Principle 2: Measuring Communication Outcomes Is Recommended

As discussed in Chapter 6, outputs are tasks that you complete, but the *outcomes* of public relations programs are changes in knowledge, attitudes and behavior. **Cognitive** outcomes may include understanding an organization's position, learning how to do something or comprehending a complex issue. **Attitudinal** outcomes may be related to advocacy, reputation, trust, commitment, satisfaction and feelings of control mutuality (see Chapter 4). The last four (trust, commitment, satisfaction and control mutuality) are key indicators of relational outcomes. If we define public relations as the management of relationships between organizations and publics, these four outcomes are as important as any. **Behavioral** outcomes include purchases, donations, healthy activities, volunteerism, public policy actions, financial investment and so on.

Measuring outcomes requires defining them specifically. Measurement forces you to think about what you are actually accomplishing with your efforts. Measurement is an antidote for ambiguity. Think about the term *engagement*, for example. There's no doubt that engagement is of huge importance in public relations. But the specific value of engagement depends on how you define it. And how you define it determines how you measure it.

Engagement can be defined as attitudinal and based on emotions—how your publics *feel* about your organization and what it is doing. This kind of outcome might be observed with qualitative interviews or measured with a quantitative questionnaire that includes **Likert-type items**, which ask respondents how much they agree or disagree with statements about the organization. For example, Charlotte-Mecklenburg Schools in North Carolina includes items in their survey of employee engagement that say "I am proud to work for CMS" and "I would feel comfortable referring a good friend to work for CMS."[12]

Engagement also can be cognitive and based on what people think, learn and know. Can people recall your hashtag? Do they understand how to register for your service? Will they remember your brand name when they do a keyword search? Cognitive engagement can be measured with questionnaires or even quizzes and tests. But cognitive engagement may also be inferred from metrics like how much time people spend reading a web page (or how far they scroll down), the number of people who watch a YouTube clip from beginning to end, or the keywords they use when searching for information.

Beyond implying cognitive activity, reading, scrolling, viewing and searching also can be considered behavioral outcomes because these activities indicate that people are *doing* something as a result of your public relations efforts. When you host a web page, curate information for a social media presence, send a news release or post a Vimeo video, those are outputs. When people scroll and download information from the web page, comment on and share your social media posts, write about your news or watch and recommend your videos, those behaviors are outcomes. The Barcelona Principles remind us about the importance of measuring outcomes, but we also need to remember that not all behavioral outcomes are equal when it comes to achieving our goals. This leads us to a third principle . . .

Principle 3: The Effect on Organizational Performance Should Be Measured

Collecting data that show that 80 percent of people who open a video watch it to the end or that people spend an average of four minutes reading your story on Medium definitely indicate levels of attention and behavior as outcomes, but these metrics don't necessarily mean success in supporting your organization's goals and mission. When goals are marketing-based, the metrics should include the steps involved in the conversion funnel discussed in Chapter 6. The funnel entails traceable steps like searching for key terms, clicking on links, browsing product offerings and making purchases.

Programs like Google's Brand Lift allow marketers to run A/B testing with video ads on YouTube. As part of this service, Google randomly selects two groups of people that fit the profile of campaign target demographics. An "A" group is served a specific video ad from the campaign, and a "B" group sees unrelated ads. In other words, A is the treatment group in the experiment and B is the control group. Then Google tracks those same users later to see which exact words they use when doing searches. Any significant differences in searches between the groups can be attributed to the campaign video. After a few days, if the "A" group searches for the specific brand name or related key words more than the "B" group, Google calls that a "lift in brand interest," and it's one of many ways the company monetizes its data by packaging it for marketers, advertisers and public relations people who use their paid services.[13]

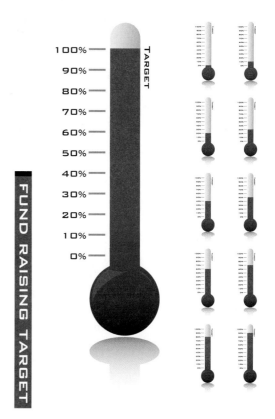

Nonprofit organizations often share progress toward fundraising goals as part of their strategy.

Which of the Barcelona Principles apply to this tactic?

Programs like Google
Analytics and Brand Lift
can help measure both
sales and non-sales-driven
organizational
performance.

Programs like Google Analytics and Brand Lift are designed specifically with marketers in mind, but there's clearly a role for public relations in the marketing mix, and the same measurement tactics can be applied on non-sales-driven organizational performance. "Our field is growing in its service to NGOs, charitable organizations, governments, the military; organizations that fall outside the business perimeter," said Ketchum's John Paluszek, who is a past chair of the Global Alliance for Public Relations and Communication Management. "We should be talking about 'organizational results' instead of only 'business results.'"[14]

Principle 4: Measurement and Evaluation Require Both Qualitative and Quantitative Methods

Among the many videos posted on the Starbucks brand channel on YouTube is a video from November 2013 titled "Hiring Veterans and Military Spouses." The caption reads,

> *As America draws down combat operations over the next few years, more than 1 million active duty members of the U.S. military will return home and transition to civilian life. As they transition, many will be looking for jobs in the private sector. So will their spouses, who currently face an unemployment rate that is more than double the national average.*

Was the video a success? That question may be answered in both quantitative and qualitative terms.

A quick look at the YouTube page revealed that in 2016, the Starbucks channel on YouTube had 93,746 subscribers and this particular video had been viewed 6,215 times.[15] It had 34 thumbs up, 2 thumbs down, and 6 comments. That's all quantitative information, but reading the first four comments gives us some qualitative insight:

1. "All lies."
2. "Ya right they may hire you but your going to make minimum wage and be treated as if you some dumb high school drop out"
3. "Pay taxes properly!!"
4. "Cool!!!"

Given the size of Starbucks as an organization and the professional production quality of the video, which includes interviews with former U.S. Secretary of Defense Robert Gates and Starbucks CEO Howard Schultz, it would be hard to say that this YouTube video on its own yielded significant return on investment. Quantitatively, 6,215 views and 34 likes probably falls well short of expectations. Qualitatively, the type of comments and the limited number of them has to be less than encouraging as well. But we should also keep in mind that Starbucks' goals for this campaign are much larger than what we can observe looking at a single YouTube video page and the publicly available analytics for it. Remember that determining the real value requires a combined understanding of both the metrics and the goal in the context of the organization's broader strategy.

In analyzing the content of comments and other forms of communication, qualitative analysis can include assessments of tone (negative, positive, neutral) and credibility of the source, channel and message. Other important dimensions identified in the Barcelona Principles are evidence of effective message delivery, inclusion of third-party spokespersons, prominence of media channels, and visual aspects.

Principle 5: Advertising Value Equivalencies Are Not the Value of Communications

When Nathan Kam, president of one of Honolulu's largest public relations agencies, guest-lectured in Amy Hennessey's public relations strategy class at the University of Hawaii, the students apparently learned an important lesson: "AVEs must die!"

AVE stands for **advertising value equivalency**, which is a calculation of the value of news or editorial coverage based on the cost of an equivalent amount of advertising space or time. If a public relations person places a story in a newspaper or magazine, she can measure the column inches and total space occupied by the story and then figure out what it would cost to

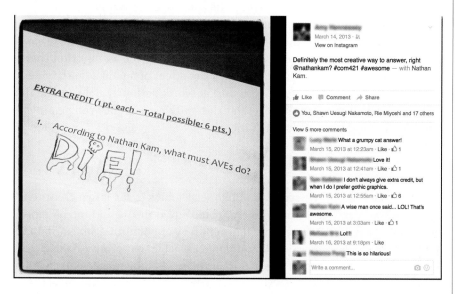

Students are being taught to avoid AVEs (advertising value equivalencies).

What was the original purpose of AVEs?

Advertising value equivalency (AVE)
A calculation of the value of news or editorial coverage based on the cost of the equivalent amount of advertising space or time.

buy an ad in the newspaper taking up the same amount of space. Likewise, if her organization is covered in a TV news story that lasts 30 seconds, she can look up the price of a 30-second advertisement during the program. Then, when she's ready to illustrate the value of her campaign, our public relations pro can compute a dollar value for all the publicity and—*voila!*—she shows success.

However, there are limits to the AVE approach of evaluating public relations programs. While Kam may have been goofing around a little in the classroom when he said that AVEs must die, he showed that he is serious about measurement and evaluation. Kam's success in running a major public relations firm depends on his ability to show clients what they are getting for their money.

The first problem with AVEs is that they falsely indicate reach based on media placement and do not measure attitudes, knowledge or behavior. Second, they use multipliers. **Multipliers** are formulae applied to circulation numbers for print media based on the assumption that more than one person on average will read each copy of a publication, or that being covered as part of a news story is more valuable than paid advertising in the same media space. So, for example, a public relations person might argue that for each copy of a magazine that goes into circulation, four people will have the opportunity to read it. They may also propose that editorial coverage in the magazine is worth twice as much as advertising because of third-party credibility. Such a practitioner would reason that since four people have an "opportunity to see" (OTS) each magazine article and that each of those four people is twice as affected by the editorial content than they would be by a normal advertisement, then the multiplier should be $4 \times 2 = 8$. If their organization, brand or cause is mentioned in a news magazine with a circulation of 100,000, they would apply the multiplier of 8 and calculate the AVE as the rate it costs to advertise for 800,000 impressions.

In addition to problems introduced in Chapter 6 with measuring campaign success based on mere exposure/impressions, the assumption that a mention in a print story has eight times the effect of a paid advertisement is at best not supported by science and at worst seriously delusional. The Barcelona group called multipliers flat-out "silly" unless they can be proven valid for a specific set of circumstances.

Principle 6: Social Media Should Be Measured Consistently with Other Media Channels

Evaluation of social media metrics should be clearly tied to defined goals and objectives.

Of course, the scope of public relations is much larger than communication on social media, but digital media and media monitoring services certainly present new opportunities to use data to improve the evaluation of public relations programs. As with the measurement of most public relations outcomes, social media metrics should be tied to clearly defined goals and objectives. Compared to other more traditional and one-way media communication, social media measurement should focus more on "conversations and communities" and less on "coverage." The Barcelona group also emphasized the importance of technology-assisted analysis.

Principle 7: Measurement and Evaluation Should Be Transparent, Consistent and Valid

The final Barcelona principle emphasizes the importance of maintaining integrity in the design, conduct and reporting of evaluation research. **Transparency** in research means that researchers are open and not secretive about their methods. If someone says that a campaign generated 100 million media impressions or that they achieved a 30 percent lift in brand interest, they should be open about how they calculated those figures. We might be suspicious of a campaign that boasts 100 million impressions if we learn that the researcher applied a multiplier of 8. On the other hand, if someone uses well-defined methods of analytics to show how keyword queries in a treatment group differed significantly from a control group in an A/B test, we would have more confidence in the researcher's results. This is especially true if we felt like we could run the same test and achieve consistent results. **Replicability** is the ability to perform a research procedure or experiment repeated times to attain comparable results. While a lot of research results in competitive business environments may be justifiably proprietary, public relations researchers should still be able to explain their methods and results clearly and transparently to those who are paying for their services.

Transparency
In research, openness in describing and explaining methods.

Replicability
The ability to perform a research procedure or experiment repeated times to attain comparable results.

Case Study

The Barcelona Principles: Somebody Had to Do It

In 2014, Andy Hopson launched "The Agency"—an integrated communications firm led by professionals and staffed by students at the University of Florida College of Journalism and Communications. Hopson, who had played key leadership roles at Ruder Finn, Burson-Marsteller, Publicis and Ogilvy before coming to Gainesville, scored quickly in recruiting an entrepreneurial and digitally dialed-in group of students for the inaugural team.

Hopson's first hire was UF junior Ryan Baum, who along with college faculty and staff led a weeklong recruitment campaign that garnered more than 270 applicants. Working all-nighters in an intensive review process, Hopson and Baum narrowed that list down to 57 star students. That highly qualified and eclectic first group came from public relations, advertising, journalism, telecommunications, psychology and economics, among other majors and academic backgrounds. Most were seniors.

The startup quickly built momentum in its first semester, signing clients including the Florida Department of Citrus, Mexican theme park Experiencias Xcaret and the American Institute of Certified Public Accountants. As Dean Diane McFarlin said in a news release midway through the first semester, "The Agency is already carving out a national niche in millennial marketing. Staffed by an ever-fresh team of UF students on a campus with 50,000 young adults, The Agency is well positioned to help guide the industry on this topic."

However, as a good portion of the startup staff began to be fitted for commencement caps and gowns, The Agency faced one of its biggest challenges and toughest clients. That challenge was recruitment, and the "client" was their own organization. With his extensive agency experience, Hopson was no stranger to quick-turnover personnel situations. But ensuring continuity in new business development and national and international client service while building a sustainable revenue model in an academic environment presented a problem/opportunity that few (if any) had ever faced before.

As discussed in Chapter 5, strategic planning involves using research to develop a situation analysis and articulate a focused problem or opportunity statement that helps define goals and objectives. When Hopson, Baum and other strategists analyzed the situation, an opportunity statement emerged: "Off to a fantastic start, The Agency must establish a strong means of maintaining ever-fresh talent by recruiting the very best available students." They decided the best way to do that was to exceed the application numbers from the initial recruiting campaign (recall that 270 had initially applied before 57 were chosen). Exceeding prior application numbers became the goal.

After further research and creative development, the students launched The Agency's new web page at http://theagency.jou.ufl.edu/ with the following notice:

> Somebody had to do it.
>
> Merging the industry with the classroom presents so many opportunities. The opportunity for students to excel alongside professionals. The opportunity to provide national brands with original insights from millennial minds. The opportunity to do what needed to be done, although nobody had.
>
> Led by professionals, staffed by students and inspired by faculty. The Agency was established to offer an immersive learning experience to public relations and advertising students and to provide them with the competitive advantage necessary to excel in the job market.
>
> Looking back, the problem was clear. But it took fresh minds to reimagine an industry . . .
>
> . . . Are you #TheSomebody we've been looking for? Only one way to find out. All it takes is a five-minute app to throw your hat into the ring.
>
> Somebody had to do it. With you, we'll do more.

As part of a recruitment campaign, agency members replaced their social media profile pictures with themed photos including hashtags.

How could the success of this social media tactic be measured?

In addition to the web page launch, tactics included a Facebook page, Twitter and Instagram hashtags, a customized BuzzFeed quiz, email announcements through departmental lists, posters and promotion events at the agency location during high-traffic periods of the class day. The face-to-face recruiting events lent themselves well to plenty of selfies and Snapchat snaps. Agency members replaced their social media profile pictures with photos specifically composed for the campaign theme.

Perhaps the most impressive parts of the campaign, however, were the results and how the students tracked them. Near the end of the campaign, Baum sent this update to the college's leadership:

Hey all,

I just wanted to check in and report on a highly successful recruitment campaign. After getting over 270 applications last time, I was afraid we peaked early, but the numbers are in and over 356 applications were submitted in only five days. I haven't yet corrected for people submitting to multiple pillars, but we easily cleared 300 unique applicants—even with a fourth of the college graduating and ineligible to apply.

Some other fun numbers:

- *#TheSomebody had 318 posts from 223 unique Twitter handles over the five-day period, with over 192,136 impressions.*

- *Our Buzzfeed quiz (shout out to Chlo) had over 1,100 views with students, faculty and family members taking it throughout the week.*
- *Our Facebook posts reached the news feeds of 6,508 people, and 655 people directly engaged with them.*
- *It took the recruitment team only five days to pull this campaign together from scratch.*

On that note, it wouldn't have happened without an incredible team [Baum acknowledges team members].

Though we are losing a great team after only a semester, their hard work has established a legacy The Agency will be feeling for quite some time.

Let me know if any of you have any questions about recruitment or hiring!

Best,
Ryan Baum
Executive Assistant, The Agency

These students managed a campaign that bodes well for the future of The Agency, but moreover, their campaign holds promise for the future of public relations research and evaluation. See how the Barcelona Principles apply?

1. **GOAL SETTING AND MEASUREMENT ARE FUNDAMENTAL TO COMMUNICATION AND PUBLIC RELATIONS.** The team set a clear and measurable goal at the outset: exceeding application numbers from the prior campaign. It's worth noting that the evaluation research of a prior campaign became benchmark research to start this program.

2. **MEASURING COMMUNICATION OUTCOMES IS RECOMMENDED VERSUS ONLY MEASURING OUTPUTS.** Baum's report goes beyond saying how many tweets the team sent, how many Facebook updates they posted, how many hours they worked at events, or how many different visual concepts they developed. Instead, the metrics focus on what their key public did as a result of these efforts: posting, sharing, tweeting, taking the BuzzFeed quiz and ultimately applying for positions in the agency.

3. **THE EFFECT ON ORGANIZATIONAL PERFORMANCE CAN AND SHOULD BE MEASURED WHERE POSSIBLE.** While this campaign did not directly serve the business goals of an external client, recruiting new talent is definitely an important result to track as part of The Agency's own organizational success.

4. **MEASUREMENT AND EVALUATION REQUIRE BOTH QUALITATIVE AND QUANTITATIVE METHODS.** One of the unique aspects of the

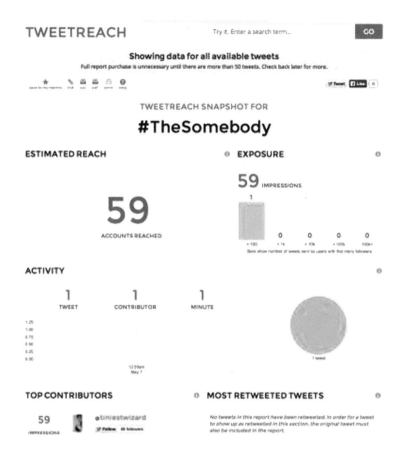

TWEETREACH   Try it. Enter a search term...   GO

Showing data for all available tweets
Full report purchase is unnecessary until there are more than 50 tweets. Check back later for more.

TWEETREACH SNAPSHOT FOR

#TheSomebody

ESTIMATED REACH   **EXPOSURE**

59   **59** IMPRESSIONS

ACCOUNTS REACHED

ACTIVITY

1   1   1
TWEET   CONTRIBUTOR   MINUTE

TOP CONTRIBUTORS   **MOST RETWEETED TWEETS**

59   @tiniestwizard   No tweets in this report have been retweeted. In order for a tweet
IMPRESSIONS   to show up as retweeted in this section, the original tweet must
                                       also be included in the report.

Tools like Tweetreach allow you to track social media activity including the use of a hashtag in a campaign.

How does this help transparency and replicability?

campaign was how applicants could "throw their hats into the ring" by tweeting with the hashtag #TheSomebody. "I am #The-Somebody who perseveres & is not afraid to roll-up their sleeves. I want to be #TheSomebody who inspires."[16] "I'm #TheSomebody who will be the first in my family to graduate college—and from the greatest in America no less."[17] Reviewing the tweetstream showed evidence of positive creativity and interest (and quite a bit of humor in the photos), and no evidence of hashtag hijacking. Likewise for the other social media tactics.

5. **AVES ARE NOT THE VALUE OF COMMUNICATIONS.** Students got an "A" on this one! Aside from mentioning reach and Twitter impressions, which looks to be explained as a calculation based on the number of followers of people who tweeted the campaign hashtag, they eschewed AVE-type metrics in favor of outcomes like viewing, posting and submitting applications.

6. **SOCIAL MEDIA CAN AND SHOULD BE MEASURED CONSISTENTLY WITH OTHER MEDIA CHANNELS.** And clearly social media were measured in this case.

7. **MEASUREMENT AND EVALUATION SHOULD BE TRANSPARENT, CONSISTENT AND VALID.** At the outset of this campaign, Baum and his team benefited from the accounting they did of results from the inaugural membership drive. Then with the new campaign, they carefully tracked and documented their success in a way that enables them to hand over the data and methods for collecting it to their successors.

Measuring the Right Outcomes

Writing for *The Public Relations Strategist*, Andre Manning and David Rockland wrote the following in early 2011:

> *If we don't use AVEs, then what are the right metrics? And, since social media is the hottest thing going on in public relations, and the Barcelona Principles specifically address its measurement, how do we make sense out of all the different approaches that the approximately 300 suppliers of social media measurement are pushing?*[18]

Measurement consultant and author Katie Delahaye Payne is widely recognized as a pioneer in social media measurement as it relates to public relations. Her answer to the question of how we can make sense of it all can be gleaned from her book *Measure What Matters*. In the book, she advocates measuring what people are saying, what people are thinking and what people are doing (Table 8.1).

In a similar approach, social change agency Fenton recommends a *see-say-feel-do* model for social media metrics (Table 8.2). Fenton represents clients ranging from the Wikimedia Foundation to the United Nations Foundation to the ACLU to Patagonia.

These approaches are not too dissimilar from the basic psychology of attitudes, cognition and behavior applied earlier in this chapter and the discussion of engagement. The outcomes also align loosely with McGuire's steps in the persuasion process covered in Chapter 6.

TABLE 8.1 KATIE PAYNE'S "MEASURE WHAT MATTERS"

OUTCOME TO BE EVALUATED	DESCRIPTION	MEASUREMENT
WHAT YOUR MARKETPLACE IS *SAYING*.	What people are saying about your organization in print, broadcast or online in social networks, blogs or communities.	Media content analysis including analysis of visibility, tone, messages, sources and conversation type.
WHAT YOUR MARKETPLACE IS *THINKING*.	People's opinions, awareness, preference, perceptions of relationship with your organization or engagement.	Facebook likes and shares, retweets, email forwards, re-blogs on Tumblr, recommends on Medium.
WHAT YOUR MARKETPLACE IS *DOING*.	Whether the behavior of your publics has changed as a result of your efforts.	Careful study of specific programs conducted by your team and systematic analysis of changes in awareness, web traffic and sales; analytics.

SOURCE: Adapted from Katie Delahaye Payne, *Measure What Matters: Online Tools for Understanding Customers, Social Media, Engagement, and Key Relationships* (Hoboken, NJ: John Wiley & Sons, 2011).

TABLE 8.2 FENTON'S "SOCIAL MEDIA METRICS THAT MATTER"

OUTCOME TO BE EVALUATED	DESCRIPTION	MEASUREMENT
SEE	Exposure to brand and messaging.	Page views and likes on Facebook, followers on Twitter, website traffic, email signups, RSS subscriptions, advertising impressions, Medium views and reads, and YouTube views.
SAY	Sharing information within and across social networks.	Facebook likes and shares, retweets, email forwards, re-blogs on Tumblr, recommends on Medium.
FEEL	When people "engage with your messages or content, internalize your messages, and add their two cents."	Facebook comments or shares with comments, retweets with personalized messages, blog comments and YouTube comments.
DO	The conversion goal: "the thing you want people to DO."	Donations, advocacy actions, event attendance, membership, volunteerism and sales.

SOURCE: Adapted from "Social Media Metrics Guide," Fenton, accessed May 14, 2015, http://www.fenton.com/new/wp-content/uploads/2013/04/social-media-metrics-guide.pdf.

Voices from the Field

Michelle Hinson

Michelle Hinson is director of public relations measurement for CyberAlert, a fully integrated media monitoring, measurement and analytics service. She is also an adjunct instructor in public relations at the University of Florida. Michelle serves as current chair and is a founding member of IPR's Measurement Commission, which develops and promotes standards and best practices for research, measurement and analytics that contribute to ethical, strategic and effective public relations. She is also CFO of the International Public Relations Research Conference, one of the top venues for presentation of new public relations research and for interaction among scholars and professionals.

How is "big data" changing the way practitioners do evaluation research? How is it making it easier? Harder?

"Big data" and technology go hand-in-hand. "Big data" exists thanks to advances in technology. As a result of this partnership, "big data" offers a myriad of opportunities for PR professionals to garner high-level insight, often in real-time, to better understand complex concepts such as impact, audience intentions and what drives behavior. That is the curse and the cure of "big data" when it comes to evaluation research—vast amounts of data available at our fingertips almost anytime we want it. While it's getting easier to collect, access, and assess data, knowing what do with it is getting harder. Professionals must be able to sift through the endless amounts of data available to get to the golden nuggets that provide true context and understanding.

What advice do you have for college students about preparing for public relations careers that will involve digital measurement?

Get comfortable with numbers. Make statistics your new BFF. Question everything. Then question again. Old-school rules still apply. Professionals must understand the research process including how to choose appropriate methodologies and interpret results. Become familiar with media monitoring and measurement tools and vendors and know the pros and cons of each. Don't be afraid to play. Think of digital measurement as a hobby to practice in your spare time. Set up Google Alerts and Google Analytics. Try a few free media monitoring trials just for fun. Compare the results and capabilities of the various vendors. Become familiar with best practice and industry standards including the Barcelona Principles and Social Media Measurement Standards.

What isn't changing in public relations evaluation as a result of new technology?

What isn't changing is the need for public relations professionals to master the basics of campaign planning and execution and to use research to inform each step of the public relations process. One of the most important factors in public relations programming is setting well-defined, measurable, SMART objectives linked to business outcomes. How can we evaluate success (or failure) if we haven't defined it? Setting measurable objectives before a campaign can also help us refine strategy if and when needed and prove value/return on investment to our colleagues in the C-Suite.

What's the coolest research result you've seen recently?

The coolest research result I have seen recently is one that has not yet been published because the study was a bust and is undergoing a second round of testing. I am delighted to be a part of it because failure is a great teacher. A task force of the IPR Measurement Commission conducted a study to test social media standards for social media coding. Coders (including myself) used the approved coder instructions to code for several factors including: message integrity communicated; no message, partial message, amplified message, etc., and the presence of visuals. What we found was there was a large variance between how coders interpreted instructions. So much so that we could not actually verify the standards. Conclusion? Training, experience and collaboration between coders are key elements in achieving consistency. Next steps are to rewrite the coding documents to be more explicit and contain more examples, identify outliers in coding early and retrain and encourage collaboration among coders to increase consistency. Hopefully, with these enhancements we will be able to actually test the standards, which was the original objective of the study.

Ethics: Independence

"There are lies, damned lies, and statistics." This quote, often attributed to Mark Twain, was the source of sociologist Joel Best's book title *Damned Lies and Statistics: Untangling Numbers from the Media, Politicians, and Activists.*[19]

> *Statistics, then, have a bad reputation. We suspect that statistics may be wrong, that people who use statistics may be "lying"—trying to manipulate us by using numbers to somehow distort the truth. Yet, at the same time, we need statistics; we depend upon them to summarize and clarify the nature of our complex society.*[20]

"That's what I want to say. See if you can find some statistics to prove it."

Ethical public relations requires balancing advocacy and loyalty with independence.

How would you respond to a request like this?

Public relations can easily be lumped in with media, politicians and activists in Best's book title. In fact, one of the most critical books on public relations is subtitled *Lies, Damn Lies, and the Public Relations Industry.*[21] Yet, at the same time, we *need* statistics in public relations; we *depend on* statistics in public relations to summarize and clarify the nature of our complex society.

As discussed in Chapter 2, advocacy is a longstanding value in the history and current practice of public relations. As stated in the PRSA Code of Ethics, "We provide a voice in the marketplace of ideas, facts, and viewpoints to aid informed public debate."[22] The ethics section at the end of Chapter 2 discussed the tension between the ideal of advocacy in ethical persuasion in public relations and the elusive ideal of objectivity in journalism. Transparency was recommended as a way to deal with this tension, particularly in media relations and communicating with external publics. But public relations people also have to avoid excess in advocacy in their roles as counselors to clients and organizational leadership. In public relations counseling, practitioners must balance advocacy and loyalty with **independence**. As defined in the PRSA Code of Ethics, independence means "we provide objective counsel to those we represent" and "we are accountable for our actions."

Summarizing and clarifying the nature of complex society and of the data that we use to interpret human attitudes, knowledge and behavior are essential parts of the internal counseling function. Remember that two-way communication means public relations people interpret the organization to publics *and* interpret publics to the organization.

Independence
In public relations ethics, the value of autonomy and accountability in providing objective counsel.

Why would a public relations practitioner or client organization pledge to support research standardization?

There are many traps that a public relations person could fall into in the interpretation and reporting of data to their clients and organizations:

- A computer program may code sarcastic comments as positive.
- **Spambots** and zombie followers (Chapter 6) could inflate numbers for comments and followers.
- Some channels could be left out and others included in analyses, making public relations results look better.
- In global and cross-cultural campaigns, some languages or keywords could be left out and others included in analyses.
- News releases could be counted as media coverage.
- And of course, AVEs and multipliers could be misused!

Spambots
Computer programs that automatically send unsolicited email or post comments in online forums.

As critics of public relations like to point out, unbridled advocacy and subjectivity in collecting and analyzing data can lead to lies—even damned lies—and these traps only make it harder for a loyal advocate to keep numbers straight. Public relations researchers and ethicists have hashed this out carefully and recommend industry-wide standards for research to help practitioners perform "in a true counseling function rather than simply as an advocate for whichever client is paying the bill."[23]

The most prominent group working to standardize research practices in public relations is the Coalition for Public Relations Research Standards. They have drafted standards for measuring social media, traditional media, the "communications lifecycle" (e.g., awareness, knowledge, interest, relationships, behavior) and financial return on investment (ROI). One example of their early efforts is a "Sources & Methods Transparency Table" that assists researchers in consistently reporting where they obtain their social media data and how they analyze it.

The coalition's charter members include the Council of Public Relations Firms, Global Alliance for Public Relations and Communication Management, Institute for Public Relations, International Association for Measurement and Evaluation of Communication, and the Public Relations Society of America. Among the first major client organizations that pledged to abide by voluntary standards were General Electric, General Motors, McDonald's USA and Southwest Airlines.

Abiding by a clearly stated set of standards in research, measurement and evaluation empowers public relations researchers to conduct research that is both transparent and replicable. It allows them to maintain their independence as counselors in presenting research with integrity.

In Case You Missed It

Digital technologies have not only expanded our options for communication, they have profoundly enhanced our ability to track and analyze social media activity. Here are a few takeaways from this chapter:

- You can use A/B testing to quickly compare the effects of different digital content and messages.

- Media monitoring services help you analyze social media content that is actively produced, discussed and shared by publics online.

- Use programs like Google Analytics and Brand Lift to measure both sales and non-sales-driven organizational performance.

- Remember that the goals for your public relations campaign are usually much larger than what can be observed from evaluating the metrics for just one tactic such as an online video or promo piece.

- Your evaluation of social media metrics should be clearly tied to defined goals and objectives.

SUMMARY

8.1 Explain how evaluation research can be used in public relations program development and message testing.
Evaluation of prior programs can be useful at the start of a new program for formative research and benchmarking to understand the current state of the organization, to assess their situation, and to set a baseline for measuring progress. Informal and formal message testing research, including focus groups, content analysis and automated copy testing, can be used for message and strategy development throughout a campaign or program.

8.2 Describe how media monitoring services have evolved in the digital age.
The process of monitoring media coverage has sped up considerably. Traditional clipping services monitored print and electronic media for mentions of clients in local, national or international media. Today's media monitoring services still measure publicity, but they also monitor online conversations and facilitate the analysis and sharing of information all day every day in real time.

8.3 Discuss how digital technology has expanded our ability to track and analyze data in evaluating public relations programs.
Data analytics are particularly useful in public relations for tracking online visitor behavior and segmenting referring sources. Media

monitoring services present new opportunities to use data to improve the evaluation of public relations programs with social media components. Compared to traditional media, social media measurement can focus more on conversations and communities and less on coverage.

8.4 Evaluate public relations research practices using industry standards for research (i.e., Barcelona Principles).

Seven principles for evaluating public relations research, measurement and evaluation provide a working template for understanding industry standards: (1) goal setting and measurement are fundamental to communication and public relations, (2) measuring communication outcomes is recommended versus only measuring outputs, (3) the effect on organizational performance can and should be measured where possible, (4) measurement and evaluation require both qualitative and quantitative methods, (5) AVEs are not the value of communications, (6) social media can and should be measured consistently with other media channels, and (7) measurement and evaluation should be transparent, consistent and valid.

8.5 Identify tools for measuring online and traditional public relations outcomes.

Tools ranging from traditional surveys and direct observation to advanced technology for content analysis and behavioral tracking can be applied in the measurement of media content, attitudes, knowledge and behavior as outcomes of public relations programs.

8.6 Analyze the relationship between independence as a core value of public relations and the ethical conduct of research, measurement and evaluation.

Public relations counselors must balance advocacy and loyalty with independence. Independence in this context means providing objective counsel and being accountable for actions including proper conduct and reporting of research. Industry standards empower public relations researchers to conduct research that is both transparent and replicable. Abiding by such standards helps practitioners maintain their independence as counselors in presenting research with integrity.

DISCUSSION QUESTIONS

1. Discuss your experience with message testing. If you haven't been part of formal message testing, how have you seen it portrayed on TV or in movies, books and so on?

2. How do media monitoring services assess *publicity* (mentions in news media)? Review online services to identify at least one quantitative and one qualitative example. Here are some possible sites to check:

   a) http://www.cision.com/us/pr-software/media-monitoring/
   b) http://www.criticalmention.com/media-monitoring/

c) https://iqmediacorp.com/media-intelligence/

d) http://www.lexisnexis.com/en-us/products/newsdesk.page

3. How do media monitoring services assess *online conversations*? Review services to identify at least one quantitative and one qualitative example. (See list in question 2 for sites.)

4. Find a public relations case study online that illustrates some or all of the Barcelona Principles and describe how each of the principles is (or is not) evident in the case. Here are some possible sites to check:

a) http://www.prnewsonline.com/category/case-studies/

b) http://prcouncil.net/resource/case-studies

c) http://www.prweek.com/us/the_work

5. Describe one tool or app for measuring attitudes or behavior online, and explain how it can be used in public relations.

6. Identify a case when an organization had to release "bad news" (perhaps a news story about an organizational crisis). Discuss what kind of research was involved and how you think the public relations person balanced advocacy and independence.

KEY TERMS

A/B testing   194

Advertising value equivalency
  (AVE)   205

Algorithm   197

Attitudinal   202

Automated copy testing   194

Behavioral   202

Big data   198

Bounce rate   198

Clipping services   196

Cognitive   202

Conversion rate   198

Cookie   198

Digital watermarking   193

Eye tracking   193

First-party data   198

Functional magnetic resonance imaging
  (fMRI)   193

Independence   215

Likert-type items   202

Media monitoring services   196

Multipliers   206

Replicability   207

Spambots   216

Third-party data   198

Transparency   207

CHAPTER 9

Writing

Telling the NCAA's stories means writing about more than just sports. How do they do it?

KEY LEARNING OUTCOMES

9.1 List five key purposes of good writing in public relations.

9.2 Analyze news and feature styles of storytelling.

9.3 Discuss the role of news media, social media and search engines as intermediaries between public relations writers and publics.

9.4 Apply writing tactics for news media, social media and search engines.

9.5 Compare and contrast styles for social media writing and business writing.

9.6 Explain how expertise in public relations writing relates to public relations ethics.

RELATED UNIVERSAL ACCREDITATION BOARD COMPETENCY AREAS

1.7 DIVERSITY • **2.2** ETHICAL BEHAVIOR • **4.2** BARRIERS TO COMMUNICATION

6.2 REPUTATION MANAGEMENT • **6.4** MEDIA RELATIONS

ove 'em or hate 'em, **listicles** are part of the online media landscape. The term listicle is a portmanteau word, combining "list" and "article." (Spork is another portmanteau, combining spoon and fork.) You've no doubt run across many listicles in your online browsing: for example, "8 Simple Things You Have Been Doing Wrong Your Whole Life,"[1] or "The 6 Most Ridiculous Things People Claimed to Legally Own,"[2] which had 1,362,519 views before I became number 1,362,520.

Critics complain that listicles are lazy writing, that they simply recycle content, and that they encourage shallow reading and thinking in an age of shrinking attention spans. If you look up *listicle* on Wikipedia, you will find the definition along with a cross-reference to **clickbait**.[3] Like popsicles—another portmanteau, come to think of it—listicles can be sweet and appealing, but not very substantive and nourishing.

But elsewhere, listicles get more love. In "Five Reasons Millennials Love Listicles," *Forbes* millennial contributor Steph Denning writes that the rise of listicles "reflects a more profound reality that we need a way to filter and process the information being thrown at us."[4]

Taking the writer's perspective, Arika Okrent describes listicles as literary form in *The University of Chicago Magazine*: "The true essence of the list form is consecutive order, taking a mass of stuff and finding a way to break it into pieces and lay it out in a line," she writes. "That also happens to be, in a way, the essence of language."[5]

The debate over listicles draws our attention to the challenges of public relations writing in a digital age. Actually, the debate over listicles draws our attention to the challenges of public relations writing in *any* age. At times, we must draw attention, but we don't want to cheaply bait readers with fluff or spin. We write to communicate important and useful information with both form and substance. As representatives of complex organizations in society, we also have a responsibility to curate important information. We are charged with filtering and processing. We have to take a "mass of stuff" and make sense of it.

Public relations practitioners use a number of writing tactics to do their jobs. From features and factual news to tweets and texts, this chapter will cover some of public relations' most common writing assignments. But why not start with a list?

Five Reasons to Write Well in Public Relations

Writing is one of the most sought-after skills that employers screen for when hiring public relations talent. Many aspects of public relations work can be taught on the job, but writing takes a lifetime of learning and improvement. You probably had to demonstrate that you could write well to

Listicle
An online article presented in the format of a numbered or bulleted list.

Clickbait
Promotional or sensational internet content designed primarily to entice users to visit another website.

The Ten Commandments may be the greatest list of all time. Imagine Moses on BuzzFeed!

Why have listicles grown in popularity as a style for online writing?

be admitted to college. If you're enrolled in a public relations program, you will have to write even better to earn your degree. The bar will be set even higher after graduation! Why is writing so important in public relations? What follows are discussions of five of the most important reasons.

Relationships

In any kind of writing, but especially in professional writing, the best writers have a good sense of who their readers are. A great news release speaks to the journalist or the editor running the story as well as to the readers of their publications. A clever tweet resonates with followers who may be inclined to retweet. A persuasive PSA (public service announcement) script convinces a teenager to second-guess risky behavior. A thoughtful thank-you note plants the seed for a donor to consider a larger gift in the future.

While writing tactics like these appear to be one-way communication, two-way communication is the essence of their larger context. Each tactic requires the writer to understand readers, listeners, watchers, fans or followers. Remember that when you write for public relations, you are writing to build and maintain relationships.

Influence and Persuasion

Simply because you engage in two-way communication doesn't mean you can't use influence and persuasion. Think about your personal relationships with friends and family. From small decisions, like where to eat lunch or what to wear, to big decisions, like where to live and whom to associate with, you and your closest friends and family influence each other. At times you may be persuaded, and at other times you are the one doing the persuading. It's the overall balance of your relationships, however, that determines whether or not they are symmetrical.

The same idea applies in public relations. The most influential "influentials" in social media engage their publics. They don't use megaphones. Instead, they interact with their readers, which helps them write in ways that earn them respect and credibility. Good research in strategic planning, as discussed in Chapters 5 and 8, is another tool that helps writers understand their publics' thoughts, feelings and behaviors, thereby making it easier for writers to influence those publics.

Goals and Objectives

It takes clear writing to articulate your goals and objectives as part of a public relations strategy. Write crisp, clean proposals and you'll get business. Write clear reports and you'll demonstrate results. Sharp technical writing convinces readers of the value of what you plan to do, the way in which you are going to do it and the success that you will have when you're done. But you also have to do the work you propose. In order to achieve those goals and objectives and to implement that brilliant strategy, you have to pull off the tactics. In public relations, that means writing well.

OK—I know what some of you may be thinking now. "Wait, what? I'm going to do most of my work in meetings and on the phone. I'm going to shoot videos and shake hands and talk to people. Where's the writing in that?" There's some truth to that. However, those meetings will lead to reports and news stories. Those phone calls will be followed up with emails. Handshakes may turn into deals that need to be formalized in writing. And those videos may need scripts and captions and written responses to the comments they generate on YouTube. Go ahead and include that little "Excuse-my-typos-I-wrote-this-with-my-phone" disclaimer on your email signature, but there's only so far you can go in achieving the communication goals and objectives for your organization without doing some good writing.

A common misperception of social media management and public relations is that anyone can do it.

What kinds of expertise are needed to write well for social media?

Reputation Management

Professor Craig Carroll defines a *corporate reputation* as "a widely circulated, oft-repeated message . . . revealing something about the organization's nature."[6] While the practice of **reputation management** includes many activities such as planning, analyzing feedback and evaluating an organization's reputation, a major component also entails writing. Think about the reputation of big brands like Apple or Toyota. Think about the reputation of your school. And think about the reputation of smaller organizations to which you belong. No doubt a big part of those reputations is based on their actions (Chapter 7), but what people write about these organizations also is important.

Carroll says that reputation management can happen "through controllable media (advertising, marketing, public relations or sponsorships) or uncontrollable media (word of mouth, news reports, commentary or social media)." As search engines have become primary portals for publics to learn about organizations, *writing* for search engine optimization (SEO) (Chapter 7) has become an important part of reputation management, too.

Impression Management

Social, mobile and multimedia venues provide us with new ways to communicate and extra latitude in our writing styles. Some contexts allow you to write less formally than others, and some contexts have new grammar that you'll know better than your professor or boss. For example, the website Urban Dictionary lists multiple definitions for "cray cray." One definition explains that the term stems from the word *crazy*, but a second

Reputation management
Acting and communicating—often in writing—to influence an organization's reputation as part of a process that includes planning, analyzing feedback and evaluating.

Impression management
Process in which people influence perceptions of themselves or their organizations by regulating and controlling information in social interactions.

definition may be more apt: "A desperate attempt to say 'crazy' made by some adult trying to be cool."

Closely related to the concept of reputation management is **impression management**. Most college students don't talk to their parents the same way they talk to their friends, which is quite different from how they may speak during a class presentation or a job interview. Psychologists will tell you that this is all part of being a well-adjusted adult. I can only imagine the response I would get if I spoke with my dean in the same way I talk trash with my surfing buddies or play around with my 7-year-old after school. The same goes for writing. The most effective writers understand the contextual difference between a text, a tweet, a cover letter, a news release, an annual report and so on. Successful public relations people also realize that how they present themselves in social media requires a mindful balance between being authentic and being professional.

Impression management involves presenting yourself in ways that help you achieve your goals and aspirations in social interactions. When you work in public relations, you are responsible for managing the impression of your organization as well as your own impression. In face-to-face interactions, this may come naturally, but it takes careful attention and deliberate practice in writing. People will look to you for expertise in writing across all the media that serve as channels of communication between your organization and its publics. In order to be hired and promoted, you'll need to demonstrate fluency and flexibility in how you write across all the different contexts.

When presenting yourself in social media, balance being authentic with being professional.

Storytelling

When you think of storytelling, you may think of sitting around a campfire, reading to a child or even open mic night at a coffeehouse, but storytelling is serious business for anyone who works in professional communications. Journalists tell stories for a living, as do advertisers, social justice advocates and international diplomats. In public relations we tell stories—nonfiction stories—that help us represent our organizations and build mutual understanding with publics. Brian Solis and Deirdre Breakenridge, authors of *Putting the Public Back in Public Relations*, describe the importance of storytelling in discussing blogger relations. They write that excellent public relations in social media contexts has less to do with the mechanics of online publishing and "more to do with storytelling, an understanding of what you represent, why it matters to certain people, and a genuine intent for cultivating relationships."[7]

Excellence in social media requires good storytelling— understanding your organization's stories and why those stories matter to your publics.

Telling the NCAA's Story—One Athlete at a Time

"Mikal McKoy was assigned two jobs when he moved in with his father in 2009: Get an education, and don't get caught in the streets."[8]

Are you wondering what this opening sentence has to do with public relations? What's the purpose? Or are you more interested in finding out who Mikal McKoy is and what happened to him? Either way, the goal is to get your attention and engage you. Telling a story is one of the best ways to do that. As writing god William Zinsser wrote, one of the best approaches to writing is to just tell a story. "It's such a simple solution, so obvious and unsophisticated, that we often forget it's available to us."[9] But success in public relations writing means telling stories with a *purpose*.

McKoy did both of those jobs that his father had assigned him. He earned a 3.7 GPA and admission into Albion College. "But by the second semester of his freshman year, the first-generation college student was back home in Muskegon, Michigan, living with his father and working at a metal factory that made automotive parts." The narrative arc continues. One of his best friends was shot and killed, and that friend was someone with whom he shared dreams of returning to school, playing college football and earning a degree.

"After those conversations, it opened my eyes," McKoy said in the story. "We made this commitment. Now, I have to do it."[10] The first-generation college student returned to Albion the next year, working two campus jobs to pay for school and earning a spot on two of the college's teams—football and track. He went on to study psychology and get involved in mentoring programs for under-represented elementary and middle school boys.

The story, as told by Rachel Stark, features emotion, direct quotes and visual details. Stark writes for NCAA *Champion* magazine. In telling McKoy's story, Stark is telling the NCAA's story. Interviewed for *Public Relations Tactics* about her job as assistant director of strategic initiatives for the NCAA, Melissa Kleinschmidt, APR, said, "My goal is to tell the stories of how college sports give student-athletes the skills they need to succeed on the playing field, in the classroom and throughout life."[11]

On Writing Well author William Zinsser reminded writers of the power of "just telling a story."

Why did the NCAA tell Mikal McKoy's story?

Writing compelling stories candidly and credibly is tricky in any context, but doing so as part of a deliberate communication strategy may be one of the toughest jobs in public relations. It's easy to fall back to the relative safety of a corporate voice to conservatively deliver your organization's key messages. But ironically, writing conservatively can also be a risky strategy. Writing trainer Ann Wylie advises public relations professionals to drop the corporate "'At XX, we . . .' construction." With tongue in cheek, she outlines three reasons:

1. It's patronizing. "At Wylie Communications, we don't believe our insurance company *really* understands us."
2. It's formulaic. "At Wylie Communications, we feel that this cliché might make us vomit."
3. It's off target. "At Wylie Communications, we prefer that you write about us instead of about your organization and its beliefs, understanding and knowledge."[12]

Wylie recommends focusing on the reader. She says you should write with more "you's" and fewer "we's." This is pretty solid advice for any kind of persuasive writing. Tell readers what's in it for them. In public relations, however, you inevitably will have to tell your organization's story (or side of a story) at times. When you have to do that, one option is to tell an interesting story. Human interest is what's in it for your readers. The NCAA wants publics to know that "nearly 20% of all student-athletes are first-generation college students" and that "their athletic ability positions them to succeed beyond their collegiate experience."[13] Telling stories like McKoy's is one way to get the job done.

Features

Feature stories like those published in NCAA's *Champion* have long been a primary tactic in public relations writing. Rather than plainly reporting facts and information, a feature story digs deeper into some angle of an event, a person's life, an organization or a place.

Among the crazy array of media I've consumed in the past 24 hours are a memoir in *The New Yorker*, "Off Diamond Head: To Be Thirteen, with a Surfboard, in Hawaii,"[14] a *BBC News* story, "Godzilla Finally Gets Citizenship in Japan,"[15] and a customer testimonial video by an audience research vendor called Instant.ly, "How Bumble Bee® Seafoods Took Concept Testing to the Next Level."[16] All are features. At first I thought it would be a stretch to call *The New Yorker* piece a public relations tactic. Then I learned the article is the first chapter of the author's forthcoming book—it's part of a promotional strategy for book sales. Godzilla and Bumble Bee are also quite strategic.

Feature story
A story that explores some angle of an event, a person's life, an organization or a place.

Case Study

Godzilla Earns Citizenship; Shinjuku Earns Publicity

The Godzilla story, as it was told on the BBC website, has an interesting start:

> *Most residents of Tokyo's pulsing Shinjuku ward, home to the busiest railway station in the world, are of the homo sapiens variety. Shinjuku has a population density of about 17,000 people per square kilometre but undeterred by this it has granted citizenship to a new resident, who only goes by one name—Godzilla.*

Notice that the "why?" of this story is missing from the first few sentences. The **delayed lead** is common in feature writing. The first sentence's job in a story like this is to make the reader want to read the second sentence. Then, every sentence should do the same, "each tugging the reader along until he is hooked," according to Zinsser. Well, I was tugged along far enough in this one to learn that Godzilla earned his honorary citizenship for his role in promoting tourism.

Although the story byline in this case goes to BBC Asia writer Heather Chen, public relations people from Japan and Shinjuku likely did much of the legwork. When you work in public relations, your role in producing feature stories often happens in the background. You may write queries to media about their interest in the story, write the supplemental materials (in this case Godzilla's citizenship certificate), or even write full drafts of the story to send to reporters to use as they wish.

The Godzilla story ended up all over the world in all kinds of media, including international wire services, national newspapers, local TV stations, newspapers and online-only media like *Gawker*, *BuzzFeed* and *Elite Daily*. There's no telling how many authors edited the story and put their own bylines on it, and the public relations team was likely thrilled about all the earned media even though their names were not mentioned. This isn't to say that you never get credit for writing feature stories in public

Delayed lead
A style of beginning a story in a way that entices readers to continue reading without summarizing the story's main points.

When Shinjuku granted Godzilla honorary citizenship in Japan, traditional and online media all over the world reported the story.

Why did this story have such broad appeal? What public relations goals did it accomplish?

When readers and users have
the opportunity to become
part of the storytelling
process, stories have a better
chance of going viral.

relations. You are more likely to put your own name in the byline when you
write for paid, owned or shared media (Chapter 7) such as native advertising, internal newsletters or your organization's social media sites.

And, yes, storytelling happens via social media too. Godzilla's story flew
across Facebook and Twitter as people added their own voices. "Japan ap-
pointing Godzilla as its official tourism ambassador fills my heart with terrible, destructive love," tweeted Marjorie Liu (@marjoriemliu) to her
more than 16,000 followers.[17] Twitter user and gaming magazine
content manager Matt Bertz (@mattbertz) added his voice to the
story too: "If Japan and Godzilla can mend fences, maybe there is
hope for the middle east after all."[18]

Transmedia storytelling is an important context for public
relations writing. When shared/social media are added to the storytelling mix, stories have more of a chance of going viral because
readers and users have the opportunity to become part of the storytelling process as well. Granting citizenship to Godzilla turned
out to be just the right kind of stunt to generate lots of media attention and
participation in platforms that thrive on user-generated content.

It is important to remember, though, that both traditional news media
and social media are uncontrolled. On the whole, the Godzilla story was
received, reported and shared in good fun. However, for every success story
like this, there are several more that get almost no attention, and a few that
backfire altogether. The best strategy for feature writers is to know readers
and publics well enough to have a sense of what will be perceived as interesting, funny or even shocking enough to draw attention and participation,
but to avoid tastelessness, insensitivity or offensiveness.

The third example of a feature story that caught my attention is an
online video feature. The one-minute, forty-four second Instant.ly video
features Bumble Bee Seafoods' director of innovation talking about how
the company has used the online research services to test brand concepts.
It's safe to assume it won't go viral. It's not funny or shocking, but it is a
feature, and it's probably the most strategic of the three examples. I watched
the video because Instant.ly sent me an email that read:

> How are major brands innovating in today's fast-paced marketplace? Kara
> Sterner, Director of Innovation at Bumble Bee Seafoods shares how using
> new tools like Instantly Concept Test™ helps the company prioritize new
> ideas and make faster, educated decisions about what consumers are most
> likely to purchase.

They sent me the email because I'm on their mailing list as someone who
has used their services recently. They know there's a fair chance I'll consider

using their services again in the future, and getting me interested in another client's success story is one way to keep me on the hook. When I clicked on the link, I'm sure they tracked that data. After watching the video online, I had the opportunity to click to "request a demo." In other words, they're moving me through their funnel, and the script for the Bumble Bee testimonial is a feature written for a specific audience with specific goals. That's what makes it strategic.

In *Writing PR: A Multimedia Approach*,[19] Meta Carstarphen and Richard Wells list the following as feature types that public relations writers may produce:

1. How-to features
2. Personal profiles
3. First-person accounts
4. Opinion and editorial
5. Humor or satire
6. Historical writing
7. Round-up stories with perspectives from multiple sources
8. Photo essays
9. Stories about products or services
10. Trend articles

What they all have in common as basic elements, according to Carstarphen and Wells, are human interest and timelessness. **Human interest** stories have a personal or emotional angle. By *timeless*, they mean that these stories maintain their relevance and value long after they have been told.[20] Of course, features can have a chronology or be tied to particular events in time, but they do not need to be timely in the same way that breaking news does.

It's difficult to nail down an exact definition of *feature story*. One approach is to define it with examples (as I've tried to do with the Godzilla and Bumble Bee Seafood features). Another is to distinguish features from the second major type of storytelling in public relations: straight news.

News

Whereas a feature writer may delay the most important points while appealing to human interest and emotion, straight news stories get right to the business of reporting the news with a **direct lead**. Even if readers never read past the first paragraph, they can get the gist of the content from direct leads. In the first sentence, reporters tell readers *who*, *what*, *when*, *where* and *why*. This news style of writing is often called the **inverted pyramid** because all of the most important information in the story is presented at the broad top of the story, and the narrower supporting details are written below as the story continues to the bottom. Figure 9.1 illustrates the structure.

Human interest
A personal or emotional storytelling angle that focuses on the human condition.

Direct lead
A style of beginning a news story that summarizes the story's main points (e.g., who, what, where, when, why, how) in the first sentence or two.

Inverted pyramid
A style of newswriting in which the most important information is presented at the broad top of a story and narrower supporting details are written below.

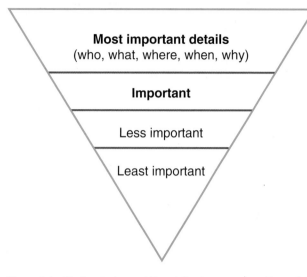

Figure 9.1 The inverted pyramid has defined a generation of journalistic style.

How has communication technology influenced the way we tell stories?

Online news feeds, blog rolls, email preview panes and search engine results favor good leads.

The inverted pyramid has played an important role in defining an era of journalism. Although the exact history of the inverted pyramid is murky, most journalism historians seem to agree that the convention grew with the rise of technologies for mass communication. One story maintains that reporters during the U.S. Civil War learned to place all of the important information in the first line or two in case telegraph lines were cut during wire transmission. The inverted pyramid also made sense as multi-page newspapers grew in size and popularity because many readers would not turn past the front page to finish reading complete stories that continued on inside pages.

In any case, traditional mass media technology encouraged the telling of succinct, fact-based stories without a lot of fluff or extraneous information, and news readers came to expect that. Concise writing became a news virtue, and if public relations people wanted to work with journalists to get their stories out through mainstream media, they needed to understand the function of a good news lead and the type of information required to support it. The same values apply today when it comes to telling stories in direct news style. Online news feeds, blog rolls, email preview panes and search engine results all favor writers who know how to write a good lead.

As with features, sometimes the public relations person's role in telling news stories resides in the background, setting up the press conference or interview, compiling the fact sheet, or even drafting the entire news story with a direct lead and supporting details. In media relations, your job is to help others tell your organization's story (or your organization's side of the story) in their outlets. To do this, you need to understand news values and the way that journalists write and organize their stories.

At other times, you will have the opportunity to tell your organization's news stories directly to your publics. The internet has increased these opportunities to serve as a direct source for news about your organization.

Writing for Intermediaries

Public relations writers can earn attention online beyond their direct networks through three main intermediaries: (1) traditional news media gatekeepers (i.e., earned media), (2) social media (i.e., shared media) and (3) search engines. The three overlap considerably, but public relations writers must use different writing strategies and tactics for success in each.

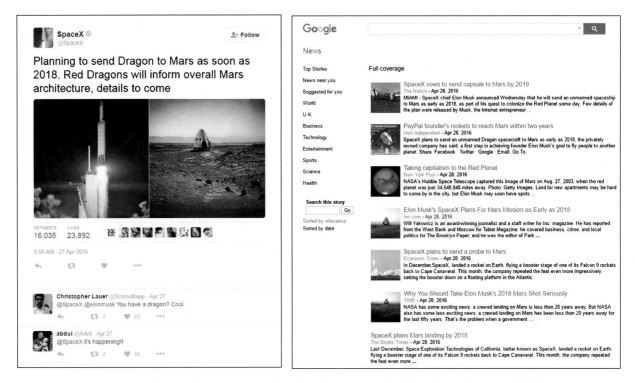

When SpaceX used Twitter and Facebook to announce its plans for a Mars mission, the information made news worldwide.

What information did news media use in their leads? Who? What? Where? When? Why?

Writing for News Media

In the gatekeeping model of media relations, publics find stories based on what editors and producers decide is newsworthy. Back when people obtained their news primarily by reading daily newspapers and watching 30-minute newscasts, publics relied on the editorial judgment of the gatekeepers in these news organizations to decide what news they should read or watch. In this model, people let others serve as the first filter of what news and information they should pay attention to.

To some extent, this gatekeeping still happens online. People still go to news websites without knowing exactly what the editors will deliver. They still count on editors to decide what's important. And that's why news releases, backgrounders and fact sheets written primarily for journalists and editors are still key public relations tactics, even as their channels for delivery have moved online. Writing for these media requires attention to traditional news values, **Associated Press (AP) style** and other conventions of news writing.

NEWS RELEASES

A **news release** is basically a news story, written in news style, by a public relations practitioner writing on behalf of an organization or client. News releases are often referred to as press releases because historically they

Social media release
A news release that applies the conventions of social media and includes content designed for social media distribution and sharing.

Video news release
A news release that provides broadcast journalists with pre-produced news packages including audio and video material.

Dateline
Text at beginning of news story that describes when and where a story occurred (e.g., "BEIJING, June 16—").

(Note: This sample general press release will help increase awareness about flu shots. Please complete and send it to local media even if you don't have a specific event.)

Contact: (Your Name)
(Telephone Number)

(Insert Date)
For Immediate Release

**The (Insert State) Diabetes Control Program
and CDC Encourage People with Diabetes to Get a Flu Shot
Despite Vaccine Delays**

Recent reports about flu vaccine delays should not discourage millions of Americans from trying to get their annual flu shot, particularly if they have a chronic illness such as diabetes, say the Centers for Disease Control and Prevention and the **(Insert State)** Diabetes Control Program.

About 16 million people in the United States have diabetes and **(Insert state data here)** in _____. Failure to get vaccinated could leave many of them at risk for life-threatening influenza and pneumonia infections.

"This year it is more important than ever for people with high-risk conditions like diabetes to get vaccinated because they are more likely to have problems associated with flu and pneumonia," said Dr. Frank Vinicor, director of CDC's Division of Diabetes Translation. "Despite reports of the vaccine delay, we are recommending that people at high risk request vaccinations from their physicians as early as possible in the flu season. Physicians with no vaccine should direct patients to places that have a supply such as public health clinics or other private sources," Dr. Vinicor added. (The CDC website for supply information is www.cdc.gov/nip.)

According to CDC, deaths among people with diabetes increase 5 to 15 percent during flu epidemics and people with diabetes are three times more likely to die with complications of the flu and pneumonia. Despite these alarming figures, only half of the people with diabetes receive an annual flu shot and two out of three have never been immunized against it.

Organizations often create templates for news releases.

What are the advantages and disadvantages of writing with templates?

were written for distribution to members of the press. With a news release, a public relations writer drafts and edits a news story, pitches it to reporters and editors, and hopes that various news media will retell the story. In other words, news releases are tools for seeking earned media (Chapter 7). **Video news releases** (VNRs) serve the same function for TV media, providing broadcast journalists with pre-produced news packages including audio and video material. **Social media releases** (SMRs) adopt the conventions of social media to include sharable online material such as useful chunks of text, quotes, photos, infographics, suggested tweets, social media handles, hashtags and embeddable multimedia elements.

With the web, releases are more likely to directly reach non-media publics who find news directly from the organization. The "press" may or may not be involved as intermediaries in the distribution of an organization's news. Therefore, in today's media environment, *news release* is probably a better term than *press release*. In any case, public relations writers should keep two key characteristics in mind when they produce news releases: format and newsworthiness.

Format is important, so that the news looks like news. In pitching a straight news story to journalists or editors in news organizations, public relations writers should do the following:

- Start with a good headline and **dateline**.

- Write using the inverted pyramid style.

- Include important factual information that the journalists would need to support the main points of the story.

For traditional print news releases, public relations writers follow certain conventions, such as including "For Immediate Release" with a date at the top. Many news release writers still include the word "-more-" at the bottom of the page if the release continues to another page, and "-###-" or "-30-" at the end of the story to let journalists know they've reached the last page. These symbols are a bit archaic, but in the right context, they signal that you understand the news business and its traditions. Check with your client or employer for templates, or work with them and news media to develop a consistent format for your news releases.

With most traditional news media, you'll want to write with AP style. If you ever have taken a newswriting or editing course in a journalism program, you know that journalistic training includes some tough lessons on editing. In some of the best J-schools, journalism students are slapped with 50-percent-off grade penalties for fact errors and harsh point reductions for AP style errors. Students who graduate from these programs are sharp writers, but they also are sharp critics of others' sloppy newswriting. Don't let your news be discarded because you overlook simple AP style editing rules. As discussed in Chapter 4, the best way to understand the needs of journalists is to develop solid working relationships with them.

The more important factor in whether your news release gets traction with third-party media is the actual newsworthiness of the information it delivers. Newsworthiness, also covered in Chapter 4, means that a story includes elements of timeliness, proximity, conflict and controversy, human interest or relevance. But there's no direct formula for calculating news value. To understand which news from your organization is newsworthy, you need to understand the perspective of journalists and their audiences.

FACT SHEETS

Fact sheets can accompany news releases or be presented on their own. They present factual information about an organization or its events, people, products or services. They may be presented as frequently asked questions (FAQs), advice sheets, infographics or even listicles. But rather than applying a news story or feature narrative style, they focus more on the delivery of useful information. With just one or two clicks or taps, a reporter—or anyone else interested in the story—can access all sorts of related facts and background information written by people working in public relations.

BACKGROUNDERS

Picture practicing public relations before the internet. If you sent a news release to a journalist, she may have needed additional information on your organization or its key people. Without Google, she could have gone to the library or to her news organization's **morgue** (storage space for archived files), but chances are she wouldn't have had that background information at her fingertips unless she

10 Things to Remember About AP STYLE

1. Spell out whole numbers less than 10 (e.g., three cats, 11 dogs). Use figures for ages, dimensions, decades, ratios and other uses.

2. Spell out the 50 U.S. state names in running text. Use state abbreviations in datelines.

3. Make sure to capitalize:
- Formal titles directly before names (e.g., Gov Jay Inslee, Vice President Biden, Pope Francis)
- Trademarked names (e.g., Mace, BandAid, Xerox)
- Internet vs. Website vs. the Web

4. Directions and regions:
- Use lowercase letters to indicate compass directions.
- Capitalize to indicate a well-known region (e.g., South Florida).

5. Format of times: Use figures (except for noon and midnight) and a.m./p.m. (e.g., 8 a.m., 11:15 p.m.).

6. No comma before "and" in a simple series.

7. Never underline or italicize. Use quotation marks with the names of magazines, newspapers, the Bible or books that are catalogs of reference materials.

8. Simplify wording:
- "In order to" should be "to"
- "Utilize" should be "use"
- "In spite of" should be "despite"

9. Spelling preferences:
- Backward, forward, toward: no "s"
- Broadcast, forecast, telecast: same form for present and past tenses (i.e., no "-ed" for past tense)
- Verb form (two words) vs. noun/ adjective form (one word): break up (verb) breakup (noun and adjective)

10. Hyphens as joiners:
- Telephone numbers: 555-555-0123
- Compound adjectives: little-known actress, full-time job (but no hyphen with -ly adverb; widely recognized style)
- After "to be" verbs: Mark is well-dressed.

THE PLANK CENTER
FOR LEADERSHIP IN PUBLIC RELATIONS

@PlankCenterPR
plankcenter.ua.edu

Knowing AP style is a big help in media relations.

AP has updated at least one of these rules. Can you identify it?

regularly covered your organization. So you would have provided it, or at least had it available upon request.

For bigger media events, public relations people developed (and still develop) **media kits** that include news releases, fact sheets and backgrounders, as well as photos, graphics, position papers and anything else that might be useful for a reporter researching and producing a story. As technology advanced, public relations people began producing electronic media kits on CD-ROMs that could include all of the above plus audio, video and interactive components. Today, all this information can be shared online with less need for printed materials and physical disks, but reporters still need background information for context. Regardless of the medium, it still makes sense to package background information in an easily accessible format for whoever is writing about your organization. Three useful tools are backgrounders, bios and profiles.

Backgrounders provide the stories behind the straight news stories. They often are written as features and give depth and context to news stories by explaining the history—or background—of an organization or one of its events. Like fact sheets, backgrounders deliver information that will be useful to anyone writing a story about the organization, but backgrounders use a narrative structure that connects the factual information in a meaningful way that explains context. For example, the National Oceanic and Atmospheric Administration (NOAA) regularly issues press releases, such as one with this lead:

> *NOAA, working with private industry partners and the U.S. Navy, has confirmed the location and condition of the USS Independence, the lead ship of its class of light aircraft carriers that were critical during the American naval offensive in the Pacific during World War II.*[21]

That's the start to the news release. The website with the news release also includes high-resolution maps and images and links to information from industry partners such as a fact sheet on Boeing's unmanned underwater vehicle called the Echo Ranger that was used in the search. But what if a reporter isn't familiar with NOAA in the first place? A NOAA backgrounder tells the story, starting with this lead:

> *October 1970. President Richard M. Nixon was on his way to the Middle East when Egyptian President Nasser died. The Pittsburgh Steelers were putting a lot of faith in their new rookie quarterback, Terry Bradshaw. The top grossing movie of the month was Tora! Tora! Tora!—and the National Oceanic and Atmospheric Administration, a new federal agency to observe, predict and protect our environment, was born.*[22]

Note that this backgrounder offers historical context for the founding of NOAA. As with the Godzilla story, the writer uses a delayed lead to generate readers' interest and then transitions into background on the NOAA

Regardless of the medium, you should package background information in an easily accessible format.

Fact sheet
Short (often one-page) document that presents factual information in concise format.

Morgue
Storage space for archived files of old stories, notes and media materials kept by news organizations.

Media kits
Packages of information assembled by public relations people for news media. Common contents include news releases, fact sheets, backgrounders, position papers, photos, graphics and so on.

Backgrounder
Writing tactic used to give depth and context as background information for news stories.

itself, which would apply to any NOAA-related story. The USS *Independence* news is presented specifically by NOAA's National Marine Sanctuaries. It's mission "to serve as the trustee for the nation's system of marine protected areas, to conserve, protect, and enhance their biodiversity, ecological integrity and cultural legacy" is posted on its "About" page, along with "information about our history, the steps taken in designating a marine protected area, and the legislation that helped to create our marine sanctuaries."[23] Background information on the USS *Independence* is also available as a resource for media.

BIOS
A biographical profile, or bio, is essentially a backgrounder for a person.

"After 64 years on the seafloor, *Independence* sits on the bottom as if ready to launch its planes," said James Delgado in the NOAA news release. Who's James Delgado? Delgado is identified in the release as the chief scientist on the *Independence* mission and maritime heritage director for the National Marine Sanctuaries, but his longer bio is also available on the NOAA website:

> *James P. Delgado, PhD, FRGS, RPA, has led or participated in shipwreck expeditions around the world. His undersea explorations include RMS Titanic, the discoveries of Carpathia, the ship that rescued Titanic's survivors, and the notorious "ghost ship" Mary Celeste, as well as surveys of USS Arizona at Pearl Harbor . . .*[24]

The bio goes on to outline Delgado's professional career and accomplishments.

Writing for Social Media
With social media, people find organizations online via links and referrals from other people. They can then read, comment, share or create their own stories related to these organizations. They can participate, and they can interact. This is the essence of social media. Public relations writers must observe carefully before diving in. You wouldn't just walk into a room at a party and try to lead a discussion without first getting to know who was in that room, what they are talking about and how they are communicating. The same goes for online communication. You must work to understand both the social and technological contexts first. Then, you can join the conversation. "The most important lesson in social media," write Solis and Breakenridge, "is that, before engaging anyone, you must first observe and understand the cultures, behavior, and immersion necessary to genuinely participate in the communities where you don't already reside."[25]

> Before jumping into an online conversation, first you need to know how people are talking and what people are talking about.

BLOGS AND LONGER FORM
Blogs were among the first social media writing forms adopted on a wide scale by public relations practitioners. They remain primary vehicles for

Blog
Online post (or web log) with reflections, comments and often links provided by the writer.

The Whole Foods "Whole Story" blog features posts from various individual bloggers.

How do corporate blogs help "humanize" a company?

longer-form writing in social media. Blogs are sort of the old-timers of social media, but in 2004, they were a hot new thing. *Blog* was the most sought-after new word in Merriam-Webster's online dictionary that year.

Webster's 2004 Word of the Year was defined as "a Web site that contains an online personal journal with reflections, comments, and often hyperlinks provided by the writer."[26] Compared to other forms of published writing, blogs were easy to update. The reverse-chronological order of most blogs made it easy for writers to regularly add new posts and accumulate serial content. Linking enabled blogs to be more social, too. Public relations writers quickly recognized the potential utility of blogs for communicating with stakeholders and publics. However, to realize that potential would require some adaptation of traditional corporate writing. Dave Winer, who developed much of the software that enabled blogging to catch on in the 1990s, suggested that the only real requirement in identifying a blog was that the "personalities of the writers come through."[27]

Writing with personality was—and still is—a big part of blogging well. It is also still a tough challenge for many businesses and other types of organizations. Technology journalist Erica Swallow has outlined 10 tips for successful corporate blogging:[28]

1. *Establish a content theme and editorial guidelines.* While you can write about anything you want on your own personal blog, readers of an organization's blog should know what to expect, and the

general theme should be closely related to what your organization does. Guidelines will help different writers from within the organization work together to support this theme.

2. *Choose a blogging team and process.* This team does not have to all come from the communications department. You want good writers, but you also want authentic voices that represent different parts of your organization.

3. *Humanize your company.* As Dave Winer advised, let the personalities of writers come through. Let your team tell their stories (and their co-worker's stories) as they relate to the theme of the blog. Use the blog and its comments section to have real conversations.

4. *Avoid PR and marketing.* Um, yeah, about this one, it depends on how "PR" is defined. Swallow equates PR with salesmanship. You do want to avoid that on blogs. It's a different story altogether, however, if you define public relations as building and maintaining relationships.

5. *Welcome criticism.* Criticism is part of human communication, and it's also a great opportunity to respond to constructive feedback.

6. *Outline a comments policy.* Of course, not all criticism is constructive. Guidelines for handling comments will make it transparent to both bloggers and readers which comments will be deleted and why.

7. *Get social.* Take advantage of social media affordances to connect your blog to your organization's other social media activities and to encourage sharing among your publics.

8. *Promote your blog.* Even if your blog has great content, you'll still need to drive people to it via other channels. Post new blog headlines to your other feeds with links back to the blog. Promote the URL in your email signature. Remind employees about it when you see them face-to-face.

9. *Monitor mentions and feedback.* Comments and feedback on your blog are not limited to the comments section of the blog. People will also comment on their own blogs and other forums. Google alerts and other search services can be set to monitor for specific terms and links, and notify you when your blogs get mentioned.

10. *Track everything.* In other words, use analytics. While number 9 on Swallow's list refers mainly to qualitative feedback, this last item reminds us to set up systems for tracking quantitative data. "At the minimum, make sure you're tracking site traffic, where referrals are coming from, and traffic-wise which posts are doing best," advises Swallow.

Most, if not all, of this advice applies to **microblogs** as well.

Microblog
A shorter blog post limited by space or size constraints of the delivery platform.

MICROBLOGS AND SHORTER FORM

Microblogging, according to Merriam-Webster, is simply "blogging done with severe space or size constraints." Wikipedia editors define microblogging as "the practice of posting small pieces of digital content—which could be text, pictures, links, short videos, or other media—on the Internet." Under that definition, you can count Instagram, Facebook, Twitter, Tumblr, Snapchat, Yik Yak and China's Sina Weibo, which claimed 130 million active users ahead of its initial public offering in 2014, as microblogging platforms. But before you dive in to reach all those users, you'll want to think about your public relations strategy and the technology and culture of each.

For example, let's compare Twitter to China's Sina Weibo. Like Twitter, Weibo users are limited to 140 characters per post. Also like Twitter, Weibo's active user base is considerably smaller than its total population. According to one study, the number of users actually posting original content on Weibo was about 5 percent.[29] Re-posting is a common activity on both platforms. Like Twitter, Weibo also includes hashtag functions and shortened URLs.

However, since Chinese characters convey so much more information than Roman characters, that 140-character limit may be less of a constraint on Weibo than Twitter. And perhaps the most obvious difference between Weibo and Twitter is that most Twitter users log in from countries like the United States, Brazil and Japan, while most Weibo users are in China. But before you hire a translator to expand your social media reach into China, consider some of the cultural differences.

In comparing the two social media platforms, Edelman Digital's Cathy Yue noted that Weibo and Twitter present content differently, follow different business models, and attract different demographics (users are generally younger on Weibo than Twitter). Censorship is also a big factor. You would want to do a lot of research and work with people who really understand both the technology and the context of a platform like Weibo before representing your organization there. Yue concludes, "In order to successfully engage on Sina Weibo as a brand, it's important to keep in mind a classic Chinese saying, 'Precise knowledge of self and precise knowledge of the threat leads to victory.'"[30]

The 140-character limit on Twitter and Weibo allow for very different styles of writing.

What cultural differences would you research before starting a Weibo account?

Writing for Search Engines

Sometimes, we have to write for robots.

As public relations writers, we must understand newsworthiness and the conventions for newswriting, if we plan to get our stories out via news media. We must understand the cultures and contexts of social media, if we plan to write for social. And, if we want publics to find our organizations and stories when they do internet searches, we must understand how to write for search engines. Whereas journalists act as gatekeepers in news media, and everyday internet users serve as influencers in social media, *computers* are the intermediaries when we write to reach publics via search technology.

Search engine optimization (SEO) was defined in Chapter 7 as "the process of affecting the visibility of a website or a web page in a search engine's 'natural' or unpaid ('organic') search results."[31] In the same way that people rely on news media to select the most newsworthy information in the day's news or friends in their social networks to provide feeds of interesting information, they count on search engines to filter for the content that is most relevant to their search queries. So what do these robots look for?

Although all search engines operate differently, with different rules (i.e., algorithms) for how search results are produced, some common elements that factor into most searches are: keywords (of course!), headlines, meta tags, links and URLs.

KEYWORDS

If you want your page to be found when people search for keywords, include those words on your page. It sounds obvious, but it takes planning to integrate keywords with your writing. If your company sells beach umbrellas, your decision would be fairly straightforward. You would want to make sure you mention "beach umbrellas" on your page. On second or third references, you would want to write "beach umbrella" instead of "our product." Research on other words that people use also will help. Maybe "shade" and "sun protection" make sense as keywords too. But don't go overboard to the point of ridiculous repetition. If you mention beach umbrellas 15 times in two paragraphs, you'll come across as annoying to human readers, and the computers will figure out your trick too. There's a point of diminishing returns—search engine algorithms actually punish excessive repetition. Google calls it "keyword stuffing," and warns against filling your pages with duplicate words because it "results in a negative user experience, and can harm your site's ranking."[32]

HEADLINES, PAGE TITLES AND DESCRIPTIONS

In print media, headlines capture attention and make the difference between whether someone reads a story or not. The same applies online, except potential readers have to go through the extra step of clicking or tapping on your headline from all the other ones that are going to be really similar in search results. Experts recommend aiming for 8–12 words.[33] For example, eBay's beach umbrella headline is simply "Beach Umbrella | eBay," and the page description reads, "Find great deals on eBay for Beach Umbrella in Outdoor Umbrellas and Stands." Rio Brands' headline reads, "Sun

Keep your web page headlines short—eight to 12 words; you need them to stand out from among the multitude of similar search results.

Protection and SPF Umbrellas | Rio Brands," and the page description says, "Rio Brands' line of SPF beach umbrellas and multi-position sun shades offer sun protection up to 99.8% of UVA and UVB rays." Notice that the Rio Brands title and description have more words, but that they also add some important keywords including "sun protection," "SPF," "UVA" and "UVB."

The headline also helps you distinguish your page from others with similar keywords but different purposes. The Skin Cancer Foundation hosts a page that is highly ranked on Google with the title "How to Hit the Beach Safely." The descriptive text reads, "Before a day at the beach, you need strategies to keep from returning browned or burned by solar ultraviolet rays (UVR). Here's our five-step plan to make sure your next beach trip isn't just fun, but also sun-safe."

META TAGS AND URLS

Meta tags are the snippets of text that you use to describe a web page to search engines. When you post a web page you should enter the page title and description as meta tags. Your webmaster or IT people can help if you are not the one who actually uploads the web pages, but you will want to work with them to make sure they include the right words. For titles, avoid default tags like "Untitled" or "New Page 1." The page description and specific keywords should also be entered as meta tags. Google recommends using different titles and descriptions for each page.

Another recommendation is to include keywords in the URL. Remember that the URL also shows up in search results pages, and many people decide whether to click based on the URL structure. There's a lot of information about the broader website's content with a URL. Think about how much information there is in comparing the two web pages in Table 9.1.

LINKS

Like public relations itself, linking is a two-way street. Search engines reward pages that have good relationships with other pages. When you link to other pages, avoid generic **anchor text** like "click here." Instead, choose the words carefully that you use to link to other pages (including other pages on your own website).

On the other side of the street are inbound links, or **backlinks**, which are links on others' pages that direct people to your pages. Search engines count these kinds of links as votes for your page, and the more you have, the higher your pages will rank in search results. That said, search engines are designed to sift out "unnatural links," which are "placed there specifically to make your site look more popular to search engines."[34] Earning **natural links** means nurturing relationships with other sites by offering information that the writers and designers of those sites will find valuable. This brings us back to the core of good writing: useful and original information and good storytelling. Even in writing for robots, we have to think about the humans who will take interest and see value in what we write.

To earn natural links, nurture relationships with other sites by offering information they will find valuable.

TABLE 9.1 **META TAGS FOR TWO RELATED WEB PAGES**

TITLE	"How to Hit the Beach Safely," SkinCancer.org	"Golf: You've Got Skin in the Game," SkinCancer.org
URL	http://www.skincancer.org/healthy-lifestyle/outdoor-activities/how-to-hit-the-beach-the-sun-safe-way	http://www.skincancer.org/healthy-lifestyle/outdoor-activities/sun-safety-tips-for-sports-enthusiasts
KEYWORDS	sunburn, sun protection, skin cancer prevention, UVA, UVB, sun protective clothing, UV-blocking sunglasses, sun hats	sun protection, sports enthusiasts, sunscreen, sun protective clothing, sun hats, UV-blocking, sunglasses
DESCRIPTION	Before a day on the beach, you need strategies to keep from returning browned or burned by harmful solar ultraviolet rays (UVR). Here's our five-step plan to make sure your next beach trip isn't just fun, but also sun-safe.	How do you play it safe in the sun? The Skin Cancer Foundation asked several athletes who are uniquely qualified to advise readers—they're also dermatologists! As skin experts, all of them take certain general precautions and recommend you do the same: Avoid outdoor athletics between the peak sun hours of 10 AM and 4 PM; wear protective clothing, hats and UV-blocking sunglasses.

Business Writing

While not unique to public relations, emails, memos, proposals and old-fashioned letters on letterhead are a major part of the writing you will do in public relations. Every time you write something as an employee of your organization, you are managing your own impression as well as that of your employer or client. Business writing often calls for more formal structure and style. As with any of the types of writing mentioned in this chapter, you'll want to observe the norms. Train yourself with practice, peer feedback and adaptation.

Being able to **code-switch** from the syntax of text messaging and Instagram to the formalities of an interoffice email or a client status report is a critical career skill. If you have a vacation planned that is going to delay a client project, you probably don't want to LOL about it or include #SorryNot Sorry in the email to your boss or client. *And u r smart 2 not get too cute w txt punctuation*

Code-switching
Alternating between two or more languages or cultural styles.

We present ourselves differently in different contexts.

What are the major contexts for which you write in an average day, and how do you adjust your style for each?

and emojis!!! ☺ With careful observation and practice, you may notice other more subtle conventions that apply, depending on the context. A few examples are contractions ("we will" or "we'll"?), salutations ("Hi Tom," or "Dear Dr. Kelleher:"?), formal titles ("Ole Miss" or "University of Mississippi"?), and punctuation ("." or "!!"?). When in doubt, *The AP Stylebook* is an excellent fallback, but many organizations also publish their own style guides for consistency in organizational communication. In fact, public relations writers are often tasked with developing these style guides for in-house use.

Just because you are writing formally does not mean you have to sacrifice your voice. As Zinsser reminds us, "It's what stockholders want from their corporation, what customers want from their bank, what the widow wants from the agency handling her social security. There is a deep yearning for human contact and a resentment of bombast." Write for clarity. Be concise. Remember your reader.

Voices from the Field

Cornelius Foote

Cornelius Foote has worked at *The Miami Herald, The Washington Post, The Dallas Morning News* and the *Tom Joyner Morning Show.* In addition to being a newspaper reporter, Foote has led advertising sales teams, helped develop strategy and launch websites, and developed and managed public relations for Tom Joyner and his media company. President of Foote Communications LLC, a Dallas media consulting firm, Foote is also chairman of the National Kidney Foundation Serving North Texas, president of the National Black Public Relations Society Inc., past chairman of the National Association of Minority Media Executives and a longstanding member of the National Association of Black Journalists.

Has public relations writing become easier with the rise of social media or harder?
Public relations writing has gotten harder. You must now learn how to tell your clients' stories in multiple

ways. You've got to learn as many facets of the story to develop pitches that will resonate in print, in broadcast, on the internet and in social. You now need to think through headlines, sub heads, leads and keywords to hook readers—and to cater to search engines. In addition to being a strong writer, a public relations professional today must know how to take that 600-word press release and convert it into a Facebook and Twitter campaign. Good PR professionals suggest ideas for posts, tweets and hashtags rather than relying on the social media team.

What role does writing play in social media success?
There's an expectation that any "younger person"— 21–28 years old—already knows social media and can pick up this kind of writing on the fly. That's really not the case. Good, short writing tied to a social media campaign is not random. It requires

skill. It also requires the ability to understand the analytics, measuring and tracking which posts and tweets are resonating most with the customers. Quite often, I'll get requests in my PR consulting business from clients who want my help to launch their social media efforts. Often, they want an instant viral campaign instead of a consistent, sustainable campaign that requires a well thought out editorial calendar tied to themes and involving various levels of engagement from the customer. While I'm always eager to gain new business, I've ended up talking clients out of pursuing this strategy when they're not ready.

Are there any forms of public relations writing that have become obsolete in recent years?

Two to three page press releases. I know publicly traded companies are required to have certain language and boilerplates. The problem is too many other releases are written in such a cumbersome, wordy style that is a throwback to the old days. As a former newspaper reporter, I used those kinds of press releases to generate story ideas, and then I did all my original reporting, fact gathering and interviews to gather quotes. The only benefit companies get from these traditional, lengthy press releases is coverage, because many news websites publish feeds from PRNewsWire or BusinessWire. But these sorts of releases don't guarantee quality stories about companies' new products or services.

How is new technology helping or hurting the quality of writing you see from new graduates and young practitioners?

What I've found is that it's hard for many students to think critically and write long articles or essays because they're so used to writing for the moment. The lack of critical thinking has stunted curiosity for many who are only thinking about what's in front of them—literally—their smartphones! In other ways, technology is enabling these new graduates and young practitioners to use their devices to help their clients—and co-workers—understand the importance of creating and producing content that's mobile-friendly.

What's your favorite new convention in public relations writing? What annoys you most?

There's no single "new convention" that's my favorite. What is exciting is that now we can tell a client's story without solely relying on a straightforward press release. What annoys me the most is when companies and agencies try to adapt to the new world order of social media by creating a series of hashtags that are too long and not relevant.

Overall, one of the most important characteristics of good public relations writing today—as it was yesterday—is the ability to tell a good story. If anything, public relations professionals must work that much harder to get their clients to realize that their story has to stand out above the rest.

Ethics: Expertise and Writing for Mutual Understanding

The most effective writers know their readers. Public relations writing, in particular, depends on expertise in fostering mutual understanding. By definition, public relations is building and maintaining mutually beneficial relationships between organizations and publics. But this expertise is not just a matter of effectiveness; it's also a matter of ethics. Along with advocacy, honesty, independence and loyalty, the PRSA Code of Ethics lists *expertise* as a core value of the profession:

> *EXPERTISE*
> *We acquire and responsibly use specialized knowledge and experience. We advance the profession through continued professional development,*

Golden rule
Ethic of reciprocity—treat others as you would,like to be treated yourself.

research, and education. We build mutual understanding, credibility, and relationships among a wide array of institutions and audiences.[35]

Media ethics scholars Jay Black and Chris Roberts note that almost every major world religion, political culture and philosophical system includes some version of the ethic of reciprocity, or the **golden rule**.[36] In Christianity, "Do unto others as you would have them do to you." In Confucianism, "Do not do to others what you would not like yourself." In Islam, "Hurt no one so that no one may hurt you." In Judaism, "Love your neighbor as yourself."

We all know the golden rule, and we learn it very early in life: "How would you feel if someone did that to *you*?" It's an important lesson on the kindergarten playground, and just as important in the business of managing relationships between organizations and their publics. In public relations, you have an ethical responsibility to work hard to understand publics.

Case Study

Words Matter: A Strange Choice for an Agency Name

sarah jeong @sarahjeong · 6 Dec 2014
Hmmm @StrangeFruitPR

♻ 1   ♥ 7   ...

sarah jeong
@sarahjeong

👤 Follow

wait

you're a PR firm

you are

experts

in PR

lol

@StrangeFruitPR

RETWEETS 7   LIKES 36

10:01 PM - 6 Dec 2014

This Twitter user mocked @StrangeFruitPR for lack of expertise in public relations.

What does expertise have to do with public relations ethics?

As one Texas-based public relations firm learned, reciprocity takes research and planning, and getting one important turn of phrase wrong can spell disaster, especially if you make that turn of phrase the name of your firm.

Southern trees bear strange fruit,
Blood on the leaves and blood at the root,
Black bodies swinging in the southern breeze,
Strange fruit hanging from the poplar trees.[37]

These haunting lyrics from a 1937 poem by Abel Meeropol about racism and lynching in the U.S. South entered the American psyche on the voice of jazz legend Billie Holiday, who recorded the song *Strange Fruit* in 1939. Throughout the century that has followed, *Strange Fruit* has served as a painfully important cultural reminder of one of the nation's ugliest memories. In 2012, two public relations practitioners starting a firm in Austin, Texas, "thought the name would be perfect for a hospitality PR firm that specializes in food and drink."[38]

Sorry, that page doesn't exist!

Thanks for noticing—we're going to fix it up and have things back to normal soon.

@ StrangeFruitPR   Search

Bahasa Indonesia Bahasa Melayu Deutsch English Español Filipino Français Italiano Nederlands
Portugués Türkçe Русский हिन्दी 日本語 简体中文 繁體中文 한국어

© 2013 Twitter About Help Status

The @StrangeFruitPR account on Twitter was removed, as were the firm's website and Facebook page.

In what ways does removing the accounts help rectify the problem? In what ways is damage from an incident like this irreversible online?

It's hard to imagine a scenario in which "strange fruit" would be an appropriate name for anything outside of serious racial dialogue. Of course, not everyone is familiar with the reference and history, and it would be understandable if someone used the term in everyday conversation without awareness of its deeper cultural significance. But if you are naming a new business, that is not everyday conversation. That single word or phrase should be as carefully conceived as any you ever write.

Strange Fruit Public Relations founders claimed they Googled the term when they thought of the name and found the Billie Holiday song, but figured it was not at all related to their firm and that "it wouldn't be top of mind in the public consciousness." For a period of time after they named the firm in 2012 that reasoning appeared to hold up. But then in early December 2014 @StrangeFruitPR became a thing on Twitter.[39] As Twitter user @BlackGirlDanger, put it: "You named your hospitality PR firm after a song about black people hanging from trees, @StrangeFruitPR? Really?"

The firm first tried to explain on Twitter: "Our passion is telling the stories of hospitality professionals. We chose our name bc these incredibly talented artists stand out in a crowd." They also tried to ingratiate on Twitter: "We believe in hospitality. Including all. No exclusion. The author & its famous singer hoped for a world where that would be a possibility." Ultimately, however, the company's principals shut down the @StrangeFruitPR Twitter account along with the company's website and Facebook page.

They eventually emailed a longer statement to the *Austin American-Statesman*: "We were wrong. . . . We extend our deepest and sincerest apologies for the offense caused by the name of our public relations firm. . . . We now know we were naïve to think that, and should have known better."[40]

Words matter.

In Case You Missed It

While principles of good writing apply across all media, writing for social media requires understanding both technology and culture. Here are a few takeaways from this chapter:

- When presenting yourself in social media, balance being authentic with being professional.

- Excellence in social media requires good storytelling—understanding your organization's stories and why those stories matter to your publics.

- When readers and users have the opportunity to become part of the storytelling process, stories have a better chance of going viral.

- Online news feeds, blog rolls, email preview panes and search engine results favor good leads.

- Regardless of the medium, you should package background information in an easily accessible format.

- Before jumping into an online conversation, first you need to know how people are talking and what people are talking about.

- Keep your web page headlines short—8–12 words; you need them to stand out from among the multitude of similar search results.

- To earn natural links, nurture relationships with other sites by offering information they will find valuable.

SUMMARY

9.1 List five key purposes of good writing in public relations.
Five of the most important reasons to write well in public relations are: (1) to build and maintain relationships, (2) to influence and persuade, (3) to strategize (to both identify and achieve goals and objectives), (4) to manage your organization's reputation, and (5) to make your own impression as you build your professional identity.

9.2 Analyze news and feature styles of storytelling.
In straight news writing, writers report on the facts of a story (who, what, where, when, why, how), usually in inverted-pyramid style with the most important information in the lead and the narrower supporting details later in the story. Feature writers dig deeper into some angle of an event, a person's life, an organization or a place. Feature stories are more likely to be told with a delayed lead.

9.3 Discuss the role of news media, social media and search engines as intermediaries between public relations writers and publics.

In news media relations, publics find an organization's stories based on what editors and producers decide is newsworthy. In social media, people find organizations online via links and referrals from peers or others in their social networks. With respect to searches, they count on search engines to filter for the content that is most relevant to their queries. The three overlap considerably, but different writing strategies and tactics are necessary for success in each.

9.4 Apply writing tactics for news media, social media and search engines.

Tactics for news media include news releases, fact sheets, back-grounders, bios and so on. Examples of each are easy to locate online. One way to think about tactics for social media writing is to consider longer-form blogs and shorter-form microblogs that are common on platforms like Twitter, Instagram, Snapchat and Tumblr. Writing for SEO requires thinking about keywords, headlines, titles, meta tags and links, as well as original content that others will find valuable.

9.5 Compare and contrast styles for social media writing and business writing.

Although writing for social media requires understanding many conventions (hashtags, re-posts, etc.), writing for social media is generally less formal than business writing. Both benefit from clarity, conciseness and authenticity.

9.6 Explain how expertise in public relations writing relates to public relations ethics.

As a core ethical value of public relations, expertise means being able to "build mutual understanding, credibility, and relationships among a wide array of institutions and audiences." Practicing moral reciprocity (i.e., the golden rule) at the level of organization-public relations requires writing for mutual understanding. Working to understand diverse publics is part of that expertise.

DISCUSSION QUESTIONS

1. How would it help or hurt your job prospects if a potential employer reviewed all your social media profiles online right now?

2. Find a feature story that you think a public relations person had a role in writing. What kinds of strategy, goals and objectives does it serve?

3. Imagine you are announcing your own graduation and getting hired at your dream job. Write (a) a text to your best friend, (b) a microblog

post for your own personal account, (c) the headline for a blog entry on LinkedIn or another job-focused site and (d) the headline for a news release to send to your hometown newspaper. How are the four similar and different?

4. Do you feel like you are sacrificing authenticity when you change your voice for different contexts (e.g., texting, blogging, business writing)? Why or why not?

5. Will AP style be important to you in your career? Will you write in inverted pyramid style? Why or why not?

6. What's the worst public relations mistake you've seen written online? (You can search for one if none come to mind.) Was information removed from the web, and did that help? What might the writer have done differently to avoid the mistake?

KEY TERMS

CHAPTER 10
Multimedia and Mobile

Can Snapchat work for more than selfies? See which major sports league was early to the game in giving it a shot.

KEY LEARNING OUTCOMES

10.1 Identify sources for multimedia elements such as writing, images, audio and video.

10.2 Analyze how different components of multimedia are integrated for effective communication in public relations.

10.3 Assess the strategic value of mobile tactics.

10.4 Discuss how publics' uses and gratifications of mobile media may help drive public relations strategy.

10.5 Apply privacy as an ethical value to consider in handling data gleaned from mobile media.

RELATED UNIVERSAL ACCREDITATION BOARD COMPETENCY AREAS

1.8 IMPLEMENTATION • **2.2** ETHICAL BEHAVIOR • **2.4** PRIVACY ISSUES
2.5 OTHER LEGAL ISSUES • **6.5** NETWORKS

Selective attention
Process of filtering information by focusing on some stimuli in the envrionment while ignoring others.

Multimedia
The combination of any two or more forms of media such as text, graphics, moving images and sounds.

Even in the days when most news was printed on paper, when tweets were sung by birds, when a snap meant something broke, and when chatting was something you did with the person in front of you, your average human couldn't pay attention to all of these stimuli at the same time. The internet hasn't helped matters.

In the digital age, it may appear that people focus intently as they stare into their smartphones but, actually, as they swipe and tap on their devices, they must rapidly make decisions about what to pay attention to and what to ignore. They must also decide *whom* to communicate with and whom to ignore. This is **selective attention**, and every time you scroll and stop on a news feed, click on a link in a tweet, or view a snap on Snapchat, you select what to pay attention to in the virtual world.

So how do public relations professionals get and keep people's attention in this environment? How do we maintain relationships and engage in interactive communication without being annoying? As discussed in Chapter 9, telling a compelling story is one way. Elegant use of technology is another. But knowing what will make a story compelling and what will make technology elegant from the user's perspective hinges on understanding publics and their use of media.

No doubt you already have experience creating and communicating with mobile and multimedia. You've more than likely written captions for photos on Instagram, dropped a music track to a video clip or slideshow, or showed off your creativity with friends using Snapchat. Experience using social media creatively is certainly a plus for anyone entering the field, but to manage effective public relations, that firsthand experience must be combined with professional knowledge.

As illustrated in Figure 10.1, some of the most in-demand communicators in public relations are those who understand current and emerging communication technologies but who also have a firm grasp on research, strategy and relationship building. Chapter 9 covered writing, based on the idea that the best writers understand both their strategy and their readers. Whereas excellent writers demonstrate a command of words and sentences, excellent multimedia and mobile communicators master the various elements of sight, sound and motion in digital media.

Multimedia

The ability to combine media elements in meaningful ways is one of the most powerful aspects that drove early growth of the intenet and the web.[1] Today, in societies in which mobile communication technology is widely available, multimedia is changing the very nature of interpersonal communication as well as communication between organizations and publics.

Technically speaking, **multimedia** is simply the combination of any two or more forms of media such as text, graphics, moving images and sounds. A slideshow with music is multimedia because it combines images

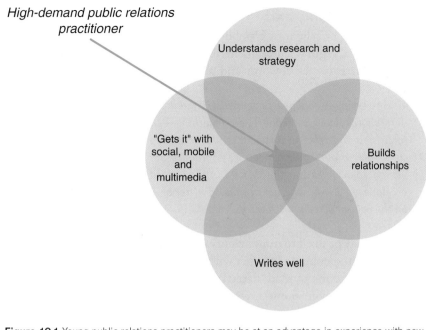

High-demand public relations practitioner

Understands research and strategy

"Gets it" with social, mobile and multimedia

Builds relationships

Writes well

Figure 10.1 Young public relations practitioners may be at an advantage in experience with new media, but that's only part of the recipe for career success.

How can you improve in other areas?

and sound. A web page with video clips is also multimedia if it combines text and video. Regular old television is multimedia because it combines audio and video. However, advances in computer technology—particularly mobile devices—have made the production and playback of all sorts of multimedia far more accessible and widespread. Anyone with a smartphone can capture audio, photos and video just about anywhere that their devices will function. And mobile allows us to consume multimedia just about anywhere. The key to creating good multimedia is understanding text, graphics, audio and video and how they work together to enhance users' experiences.

To create good multimedia, you must first understand how text, graphics, audio and video work together to enhance users' experiences.

Text

Text may be the last thing we think of when we think of multimedia, but writing is a media element just like images, audio or video. We write words in emails, tweets, posts and pitches to introduce other media content. We write words in infographics. We write words to serve as captions and subtitles for images and videos. We write copy for advertising and PSAs, bullet points in presentation decks, and reviews and descriptions of music and movies. Even our long-form writing is more likely to integrate media, as more materials are digitally produced, delivered and consumed.

Texting, Tweeting and Pitching

Robert Wynne, principal of a public relations firm in Manhattan Beach, California, and regular *Forbes* contributor on public relations topics, explained the importance of words and text in multimedia:

> *You are trying to convince the media, the public, your employees, your vendors, shareholders, someone, to do something—change their opinion, reinforce their attitudes, write about or film your client, vote for your issue or candidate, or purchase your service or product. Sometimes this is done in person, sometimes over the phone. But the majority of communications are done via words, whether in email, Twitter or online media. It all starts on the page or screen. With words.*[2]

Words may be used to draw attention, as when a public relations person tweets to invite people to interact with multimedia. The art of the pitch—persuading someone to read, listen or watch further—is still very much a word-based endeavor. Sometimes you write words to explain other elements of multimedia. Other times words are foremost, and sounds, images, video and animation play the supporting role for the text. Social media news releases, for example, are built mainly around text with the accompanying multimedia elements to help tell the story. *Who*, *what*, *where*, *when* and *why* are still at the heart of news releases, even if abbreviated to a brief lead sentence or a bulleted list of key points.

Infographics

Infographics, which include a mix of words, images and numbers, can further the central message of a press release or other public relations tactic and highlight components that bring text to life.[3] One of the main benefits of infographics is they enable writers to deliver critical information with concise text, while adding color, context and detail with other media. A downside to infographics is that they often don't display well on mobile devices. Although infographics are a relatively static form of multimedia, **user-centered design**—design deliberately focused on the end-user experience—is a key concern.

Captions and Subtitles

When you post a picture on social media, the words you use to describe that image enhance the context and the meaning. As *Wall Street Journal*'s Elizabeth Holmes put it, "A picture may be worth a thousand words, but on social media you need a caption."[4] Part of the beauty of mobile photo-sharing apps like Facebook and Instagram is that they allow users to tag people and indicate locations without using the caption for that basic descriptive purpose. However, this has "put creative pressure on photo sharers" to tell stories and add meaning, says Holmes. Your goal for captioned pictures should be for the image and the writing to complement each other. Your viewers will probably look first at the image. (Think of how you scan images as you scroll

---

Infographics
Visual presentations designed to communicate information simply and quickly with combinations of images, charts, tables or text.

User-centered design
Process by which media, messages and other products and services are developed with continuous and deliberate attention to how end users will experience them.

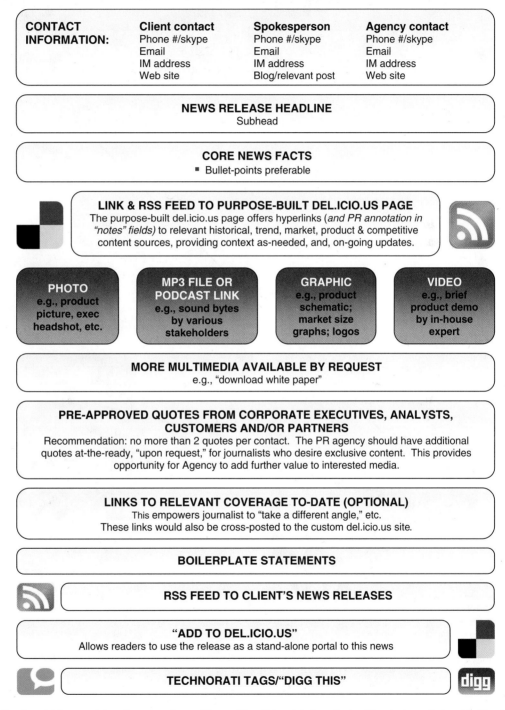

SHIFT Communications' model for a social media news release offers a different template from the traditional release featured in Chapter 9.

What are the advantages and disadvantages of this social media news release compared to traditional releases?

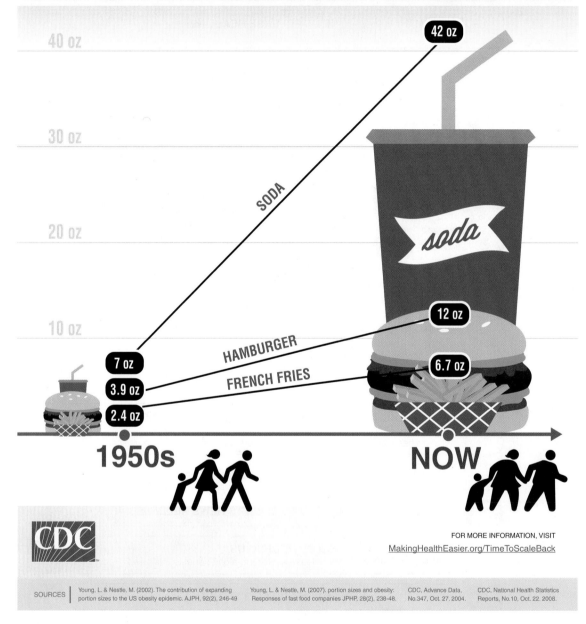

THE NEW (AB) NORMAL

Portion sizes have been growing. So have we. The average restaurant meal today is more than four times larger than in the 1950s. And adults are, on average, 26 pounds heavier. If we want to eat healthy, there are things we can do for ourselves and our community: Order the smaller meals on the menu, split a meal with a friend, or, eat half and take the rest home. We can also ask the managers at our favorite restaurants to offer smaller meals.

40 oz

42 oz

30 oz

SODA

20 oz

10 oz

7 oz

HAMBURGER

12 oz

FRENCH FRIES

3.9 oz

6.7 oz

2.4 oz

1950s

NOW

Infographics support key messages by bringing text and data to life.

What is the relationship between text, data and images in this infographic?

through your social media feeds.) If the image gets their attention, they will look to the caption for more information. If the caption is written well, they will look again at the image, perhaps from a different perspective with new focus on a particular part of the image or a new understanding of what they see. A good caption encourages this loop of engagement.

In addition to captions presented below or alongside images and video, the growth of digital and social media has led to an increase in captions placed on top of images and video. Snapchat and other apps make it easier than ever to add words and drawings to images. Closed captioning (text that presents spoken words on screen during a video) has always been recommended for accessibility for hearing-impaired viewers. However, as more people view video on mobile devices in noisy or public places, subtitles become crucial for helping viewers understand what they're watching. Captioning is also useful for **autoplay** videos. Have you ever experienced that moment of panic when a **NSFW** (not safe/suitable for work) web ad or social video starts playing automatically on your device in an office, library or classroom? Mute buttons get a lot of use these days, and descriptive text and subtitles become that much more important.

This image was posted on the American Express Instagram account. What meaning does the photo convey to you? Now consider that the image was posted on Father's Day with the caption "Hats off to you, Dad."

What public relations purpose does the combination of picture and words serve?

Images

"Uh oh, we're being challenged again," wrote Allen Mireles in an article for Cision. Cision is a public relations and social media software company. Mireles is described on the website as a wordsmith, and her words convey the anxiety that some writers may feel as they face the growth of image-based social media. "That's right, PR is being nudged away from the familiar comfort of text-based communications to more visual forms of communications, especially in our digital campaigns."[5] Photo-based platforms of social media have been built, adopted and grown into central channels for many public relations efforts. Snapchat, Instagram and Pinterest wouldn't exist without images. And the vast majority of the images shared via these platforms wouldn't exist without mobile devices.

This isn't to say that working with images and photos is something new to public relations. In their 1984 text *Managing Public Relations*, Grunig and Hunt noted that photos and illustrations "represent a basic form of visual communication used in each of the four public relations models."[6] (The four models are defined in Chapter 2.) What's changed significantly is the technology.

Autoplay
Feature that enables automatic playing of videos or other multimedia elements on users' devices.

NSFW
Shorthand for "not safe/suitable for work."

The NBA Gets in the Snapchat Game Early

With new ways of posting and sharing photos, come new ways of telling stories. The NBA was an early adopter of Snapchat. For example, to help tell the story of Kevin Durant's 2014 Most Valuable Player award sponsored by Kia Motors Corp., the NBA made use of the Snapchat's "Stories" feature. With a series of three photos posted to the app, they encouraged fans on Snapchat to also watch on NBATV.com and NBA.com as Durant accepted the award.[7] The first snap showed the lectern where the MVP would soon stand, with the words "4:30 pm/et on NBATV & NBA.com. KD!" running across the image. The second snap showed Durant sitting for an interview with NBA legend Grant Hill and the words "The 2014 #KiaMVP & Grant Hill!" The final snap featured Durant at the lectern with the trophy on a pedestal in the foreground, and "Kevin Durant, the 2013-14 #KiaMVP!"

It's not unusual for early-adopter organizations to get lots of attention when they use emerging platforms like Snapchat was in 2014, but that success can be fleeting if the attention doesn't lead to longer-term relationships. Amid the fast growth of Snapchat's popularity in 2014, one research firm reported that 77 percent of college students were using the app at least once a day. The researchers also asked college students what they were using it for, and "creativity" was the most common answer, chosen by 37 percent of the respondents. (You may be interested to know that only 2 percent reported using Snapchat primarily for "sexting.") More important for public relations practitioners, though, were the findings in the same study that 73 percent of college students said they would open a snap from a brand they knew and almost half said they would open a snap from an organization even if they'd never heard of the brand.[8]

At the same time that the then-new Snapchat was wooing brands, the effectiveness of Instagram and Pinterest advertising was dropping fast, as demonstrated by a 2015 Forrester Research study. By the Forrester metrics, interactions created from brands on Instagram dropped from 4.2 percent in 2014 to 2.2 percent in 2015. On Pinterest, the rate dropped from 0.1 percent to 0.04 percent in that same period of time.[9] As discussed in Chapter 6, there's a big difference between 73 percent of students saying they would open a snap on a novel platform and .04 percent of users actually interacting with brands on an older platform (like Pinterest was in 2015). Timing, context and content are all important factors in using mobile and multimedia to engage publics, and it takes careful strategy to convert short-term attention to long-term relationships.

The NBA benefited from being one of the first organizations to use Snapchat.

What new apps are novel right now as ways for organizations to communicate with publics?

When using photographs or images as public relations tactics, you have three options for obtaining them: (1) create them yourself, (2) hire a professional to take photos or create original images, or (3) buy images or obtain permission to use others' material.

Creating Your Own Images

Advances in digital camera technology have increased the accessibility of do-it-yourself photography. Your average smartphone camera can generate image quality that used to be reserved for only those willing to invest heavily in expensive digital cameras. But just because the camera phone in your pocket *can* capture amazing images at very high resolution doesn't mean your photos are automatically high enough quality for your organization's communication needs. Factors to consider in taking photos include lighting, composition, angles, background and props. Yes, social media have widened our latitude for what we accept and expect in shared imagery. Hastily snapped selfies, for example, have found a place in our digital culture. But just as expectations for writing styles vary from one context to another, it is important to carefully consider the appropriate image style depending on the purpose and public.

Each social media platform has its own written and unwritten rules and unique cultural and technological dimensions. Some of the main differences are technical, including how long the images last, who gets to see them, what type of editing is available, and so on. For example, images sent via Snapchat will last from just 1 to 10 seconds before they disappear, while images uploaded to Instagram will last until you delete them. Other big differences are social and cultural. Just look at the different profile pictures people post on Twitter, Facebook and LinkedIn. In discussing LinkedIn profile pictures, Entrepreneur.com's Kim Lachance Sandrow writes, "Here's a friendly reminder, particularly for the 39 million students and recent college grads lurking on LinkedIn: It's not for Man Crush Monday, not for swiping right and not for stalking your 8th grade crush."[10]

Hiring Photographers and Using Others' Images

For LinkedIn, you may want to consider hiring a professional photographer or at least working with a friend or colleague capable of taking a photo that you feel is high enough quality to represent you on your profile as you wish to be seen by potential employers. The same logic applies to photos that will represent your organization to potential publics.

Very often, the best image for your public relations needs already exists, but just because that .JPG, .PNG or .GIF file is only a right-click away doesn't mean you can grab it and paste it into your blog post or newsletter without permission. Chapter 11 will discuss common copyright issues in more detail, but the good news is that there is an abundance of great imagery available online that can be used legally and with good karma, if you pay attention to copyright and permission requirements.

This stock photo, "Girl playing soccer with grandfather in wheelchair as goal keeper," made BuzzFeed's list of "50 Completely Unexplainable Stock Photos No One Will Ever Use."

When might it be appropriate to use stock images in public relations?

Public domain images are "free" images, including images produced by government entities (e.g., an image of a fish from the U.S. Fish and Wildlife Service), those that are so old that the copyrights have expired (e.g., the *Mona Lisa*), or those that the original creators have explicitly released for public use. Be careful, however, in making unchecked assumptions. Use of government logos or seals such as the logo for the Fish and Wildlife Service, a photograph or modified version of the *Mona Lisa* as it is presented in a copyrighted book, or certain types of **Creative Commons** licenses are restricted.

Many images are available for sharing as long as you obtain permission, properly attribute the image to its source and, in some cases, link back to that source. Even Getty Images, one of the world's largest for-profit **stock image** providers, permits free use of its images online, as long as the images are embedded with the proper HTML code:

> *Embedded images will include photographer attribution and, when clicked, will link back to www.gettyimages.com where the image can be licensed for commercial use. This will provide people with a simple and legal way to utilize content that respects creators' rights, including the opportunity to generate licensing revenue.*[11]

Audio

Audio is often underappreciated in the world of social media. When you think of the most sharable and influential content online, you probably remember certain images you have seen, stories you have read, or videos you have watched. Of course you can find and listen to your favorite music online, but audio's role in the business of strategic communication and storytelling in public relations is often a rather quiet one.

Two big factors working against audio in social media are simply structural. First, audio lends itself well to background tasking but not so much to sharing. You can listen to the radio or an e-book or podcast while you walk or drive because you don't have to look at anything. You can just hit the play button and get on with whatever you are doing. But that advantage becomes a disadvantage when it comes to sharing. "When you're driving a car, you're not going to share anything," said public radio show host and podcaster Jesse Thorn, when interviewed by Stan Alcorn for an article

Public domain
Works of intellectual property for which the copyright has expired, the creator has forfeited rights, or copyright laws do not apply, making the works freely available for public use.

Creative Commons
Nonprofit organization that encourages fair and legal sharing of content by helping content creators make their work available with clear terms and conditions.

Stock images
Images that are professionally produced for selling or sharing, commonly available in searchable databases.

asking the question, "Why doesn't audio go viral?"[12] The second issue Alcorn identified was skimming—or rather the fact that audio can't be skimmed like text and video. Your news feed or search results are made up of chunks of text, still images and videos. The intenet hasn't offered the equivalent sampling of audio. But while audio isn't as sharable as its counterparts in multimedia (text, photos and video), it's still critical in public relations.

Radio Is Still Huge

In 2014, radio ranked behind only TV and computers as a source for Americans' news, according to the American Press Institute.[13] In an analysis of Nielsen Media Research data, the Pew Research Center reported that 91 percent of Americans who were 12 or older had listened to traditional AM/FM radio in the week before a 2014 survey.[14] The Pew fact sheet also cited a 2015 study by Edison Research indicating that the percentage of Americans 12 years or older who reported listening to online radio such as Pandora or Spotify in the past month rose from 27 percent in 2010 to 53 percent in 2015. Radio must still be considered as an option in any public relations strategy that involves mass media.

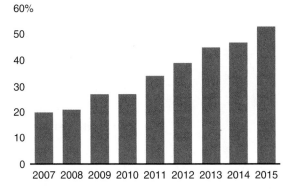

% of Americans ages 12 or older who have listened to online radio in the past month

Online radio listening more than doubled between 2007 and 2015.

Will online radio continue its rise? Why or why not?

Can Audio Go Viral?

In June 2013 when Stan Alcorn reviewed the top 100 most-shared news articles on Facebook, he found that although three were NPR stories, none of the three included audio. Only two of the 100 were YouTube videos with audio. "Because audio doesn't go viral," Alcorn almost concluded. "Except that sometimes it does."[15]

One notable example is the podcast *Serial*, which was produced in collaboration with WBEZ Chicago as a spinoff of the public radio program *This American Life*. It debuted on iTunes in October 2014. The first 12 episodes featured host Sarah Koenig exploring the nonfiction story of the 1999 Baltimore murder case of 18-year-old victim Hae Min Lee and the trials of her possibly wrongfully convicted boyfriend Adnan Syed. By February 2015 the podcast had been downloaded 68 million times, and Syed had been granted an appeal. Koenig's powerful storytelling and investigation cast doubt on the original case, and many speculated that the podcast and the publicity it generated were at least part of the reason an appeal was granted after *Serial* put this case so prominently in the public eye (or should we say public ear?).[16] Widely described as "addictive," the weekly installments of the podcast weren't exactly public relations tactics, but they did illustrate the power of audio as a medium for storytelling. "If produced and distributed properly, podcasts can achieve extraordinary market reach and message depth," writes CyberAlert's William Comcowich.[17]

If you add a decent external microphone to your smartphone or camera, you can noticeably improve the quality of audio that you capture.

Audio in the Multimedia Mix

Professional producers of multimedia have always had an appreciation for the power of audio when combining multimedia elements. You can really get a sense of the importance of sound when you see **mashups** of video clips with incongruent audio, often with really funny results. Many who work in public relations think of the recording, mixing and reproduction of sound as something best left to the professionals. That may be changing, however, with more user-friendly multimedia software. While you still want to hire skilled producers for higher-stakes, bigger-budget productions that need to command a tone of professionalism, much of an organization's more conversational multimedia can be produced in-house. Adding a decent external microphone to your smartphone or camera can noticeably improve the quality of audio you capture. Using basic consumer-grade software to add audio to your visual media can also enhance effectiveness. Have you ever noticed how much greater impact a slideshow has when the right music or narration is added? In the same way that a picture may convey very different meaning depending on the words used to describe it, the meaning of a video clip or slideshow can vary dramatically depending on the audio. With a little practice and training, and some affordable hardware and software, you can up your multimedia game.

Video

If audio is an underappreciated member in the ensemble of multimedia production, video is still the star of the show. As Cutlip and Center pointed out in their classic text *Effective Public Relations*, television was "*the* communications phenomenon of the 20th century," unrivaled in its capacity as a publicity medium to "provide a window on the world,"[18] and recent data show that TV is still a top source for people to get their news. While it's fair to say the internet has supplanted TV as *the* communications "phenom" so far in the 21st century, excitement about video keeps cranking.

The growth of services like YouTube and Vimeo that made it easy for users to convert, upload, share and watch video online was obviously part of the movement. By the end of the first decade of the millennium, billions of video streams were being watched by hundreds of millions of unique users each month, and the largest video service by far was YouTube. In 2015, the service claimed more than 1 billion users and that "the number of hours people are watching on YouTube each month is up 50% year over year."[19]

In the same way that the culture of consumer-generated media has made amateur photography acceptable in many contexts of organization-public communication, publics are often more accepting of video produced and uploaded by everyday smartphone users, if the content is meaningful or entertaining enough.

In 2016, Snapchat reported that more than a third of its users were using the "Stories" feature to broadcast photos and videos, and that the number of video views had exceeded 10 billion a day in April, up from 8 billion daily video views in February of that year.[20] An Interactive Advertising Bureau (IAB) survey of more than 1,000 U.S. viewers in 2014 found that **original digital video** was perceived as more mobile, edgy and unique than TV. Original digital video was nearly on par with prime-time TV and preferred more than daytime TV genres, sports and news.[21] In public relations, publics may prefer nonprofessionally produced video, if it means that they are getting real perspectives from real people within an organization and if the video is a part of a larger strategy of two-way communication. On the other hand, a professional producer can create powerful messages using techniques of filmmaking and video production that cannot be matched by your average public relations person who pulls out a smartphone and shoots a quick clip for upload to Instagram, Facebook, Pinterest, Vine or even LinkedIn. As with still images and photos, you have the option of shooting and editing videos yourself or hiring a professional to produce them.

Original digital video
Video that is recorded, produced and uploaded digitally for sharing online, as opposed to video originally produced for other channels like television or theaters.

Explainer video
Video produced to demonstrate a product, service or process.

Publics may prefer nonprofessionally produced video, if it means they get to hear from real people and the video is part of a larger strategy of two-way communication.

Producing Videos Yourself

If you have a quality video camera and multimedia editing software and know how to use them, that will be your best bet for making videos. But it also means you probably don't need video tips from an introductory public relations text! For the rest of us, here's some basic advice from a few experts.[22]

- **THE BEST CAMERA IS THE ONE YOU HAVE WITH YOU.** When asking a tech-savvy neighbor about the benefits of his iPhone 3GS in 2009, he said the best new feature was the video camera—not because of the superiority of the video quality but because it meant always having access to the camera for impromptu recording and capturing unexpected events. "Whether shooting video of my kids taking their very first bike rides, or recording quick interviews with guest speakers for students in other classes, having quick access to a camera was crucial."

A public relations person may shoot quick video to respond to questions from online publics, to demonstrate a product or process—sometimes called an **explainer video**, to showcase employees doing their jobs behind the scenes or to interact with communities at music festivals.

U.S. Representative Jesse Jackson Jr. used his phone to shoot video of a demonstration in front of the U.S. Capitol.

Under what circumstances do you think it is acceptable for high-profile communicators to use mobile video in lieu of professionally produced video?

- **CONSIDER UPGRADING YOUR RIG.** Even if your main camera is on your mobile device, you can upgrade the quality of your video considerably with accessories. As mentioned previously, an external microphone will allow you to capture clearer audio and eliminate background noise, which is especially important when shooting videos outside or at crowded events. "People will forgive bad video, but they won't forgive bad audio," said Paolo Tosolini, director of emerging media at RUN Studios, a video creative agency in Seattle, Washington, in an interview with Ragan.com.[23] Investing in a tripod designed to work with your device will eliminate shaking. And mounting a light on your phone or using a portable light will help if you think you'll be shooting in a darker location or room with bad lighting.

- **PUT SOME THOUGHT INTO COMPOSITION.** Try to find interesting backgrounds that aren't too distracting. Putting an interviewee in front of a blank white wall will only provide viewers with a dreadfully boring talking head. Also avoid shooting video of people in front of windows—you want to make sure natural light works in your favor and not to obscure your interviewee into a mere silhouette. "Unimaginative visuals are the hallmark of bad corporate video," wrote Martin Jones, CEO of March Communications.[24] Consider interviewing people outside, or inside with an interesting background that will give viewers a sense of place without distracting them from the subject. Test a few different angles, if necessary, until you find one that works well for your purpose, which—by the way—should be consistent with your broader communication strategy. Are you using the video to contribute to a conversation, make transparent some inner working of your organization or invite new members to join your organization? You can imagine how the video set for a fundraising message from your CEO would be composed differently from, say, a demonstration of how to install a replacement part that your company shipped to consumers following a safety recall.

- **TRY TO MATCH CONTENT TO CHANNELS.** In sharing videos on Pinterest, for example, content strategist Jamie Wallace suggests pinning video infographics, humor videos and how-to's. "People share content (including pins) for the same reasons they decorate the inside of their school lockers, hang art in their homes, and decorate their offices with postcards, funny sayings, and family photos. These things provide a visual representation of the person, her ideas, and her ideals," says Wallace.[25] Matching video content to channels also means considering technical aspects. Vine videos are limited to about six seconds. Snapchat was designed to allow only 10-second videos (though users soon discovered a hack to extend that time). Even the age-old advice to always shoot video in a **landscape orientation** for best viewing on TV and computer screens for YouTube and Vimeo has changed. It used to be that **vertical video** (video framed in a tall, portrait orientation) was seen "as the mark of an amateur," according to the *New York Times'* Farhad Manjoo.[26] But that all began to change with vertically oriented smartphones, tablets and the video apps that became popular with them. Differences in opinion about the aesthetics will probably never be resolved. However, in 2015, Snapchat reported that vertical performed "up to nine times better" than landscape on many of its engagement metrics. In that same time frame, YouTube tweaked its mobile apps to allow for vertical and Facebook began allowing full-screen playback of vertical videos.[27]

- **THINK BEYOND BASIC RECORDED VIDEO.** If you're feeling creative and are comfortable with the software, you might consider creating animations or video infographics. Another option is live-streaming video, which allows online viewers to watch whatever you point your camera at live. Live video streaming has been available since the turn of the millennium, but its everyday usability has improved as bandwidth and connection speeds have increased. Since the mid-2000s, services like Ustream, Twitch, Bambuser and Google Hangouts made it possible for organizations to offer live video feeds to online users, but the rise of mobile-friendly services like Twitter's Periscope and Facebook Live led to renewed interest among public relations practitioners in adding live-streaming to their quiver of online communication tactics.[28] So what are some uses for apps like Periscope and Facebook Live in public relations? Public relations practitioners use live-streaming services to host press conferences, open corporate events to outside audiences, launch new products and engage in live public forums. These direct-to-public channels for communication do afford organizations more control, but in comparison to traditional coverage by third-party media, reach and credibility may be issues, as discussed in Chapter 7.

This "PSA" against shooting vertical video went viral with more than 7 million YouTube hits. Puppets Mario and Fafa of *Glove and Boots* made a humorous and compelling appeal for mobile users to stop shooting vertical videos.

When might this advice not hold?

Mobile video services like Periscope and Facebook Live enable you to live-stream events and thereby open your organization to more publics.

Hiring Experts

Depending on your budget and needs, you may choose to farm out video production work. With a quick keyword search, you can find companies that specialize in explainer videos, PSAs, television commercials and the integration of video into digital multimedia presentations. **Freelancers** for video production can be paid by the hour or hired by the project. Services include scripting, basic video production, 2D and 3D animations, talent, video editing and **post production**.[29] On sites like Elance.com you

Freelancers
People who work on a project-by-project basis instead of working more permanently for a single employer (e.g., freelance writers, photographers, video producers).

Post production
Process in media production that occurs after raw audio, video or images have been recorded—includes editing, combining media elements, transitions and special effects.

can find video contractors who have produced videos for as little as $11 all the way up to international companies that handle multimillion-dollar projects. The world's largest media companies are now investing in the production of videos for social media. Disney's Maker Studios, for example, describes itself as follows:

> Entertainment is changing. Millennials are living a mobile, social, on-demand life. Maker is the global leader in short-form video reaching this diverse, tech-savvy group. . . . With 55,000 independent creator partners from more than 100 countries, Maker is home to top digital stars, channels, and content. With growing scale driven by a robust technology platform and direct-to-consumer distribution, Maker is dedicated to developing talent, creating premium programming, and building lasting brands with engaged audiences.[30]

Maker is an interesting case of convergence in every sense of the word as discussed in Chapter 3: technological, cultural, economic and professional. The very same media (e.g., YouTube) that seemed to challenge mass media (e.g., TV) based on a model of user-generated content and social sharing are now integral parts of the business plans of the most mainstream of mainstream media companies like Disney. Video was the essence of TV as *the* communication development of the 20th century. Now it's in everyone's hands.

Mobile

In delivering a keynote address to an annual online video conference in 2015, YouTube CFO Susan Wojcicki revealed the media giant's three top priorities: "mobile, mobile, and mobile." There was perhaps no greater illustration of the importance of mobile to multimedia (and vice versa) than the revelation that the company that revolutionized the process of both uploading and downloading video via social media changed its whole operating model to accommodate mobile trends. Wojcicki noted that a majority of video views were coming from mobile devices and that YouTube's revenue from mobile was growing at a rate of 100 percent from year to year.

While the business models of online media companies have shifted to accommodate the profound increase in communication via mobile devices, the very grammar of online communication has changed too. Public relations practitioners have had to learn new techniques for composing images, producing live video, delivering audio and writing short messages.

Will you use Periscope or Facebook Live? How long should your podcast segments last, and how many should you include in a series? How can you condense that 140-character tweet down to an even shorter Snapchat caption? When should you apply that Instagram filter? Depending on your experience with social and mobile media, you may be a step ahead of some of your more senior public relations colleagues when it comes to answering these types of questions.

However, there is so much more to effective public relations than personal experience with emerging platforms and technology. Multimedia and mobile are tactics. In the bigger picture of effective public relations, tactics are driven by strategy, and strategy is designed to achieve goals and objectives that are developed from research (see Chapters 5 and 6). Without proper management and strategy, pumping out explainer videos, live streams and mobile app notifications is no more indicative of effectiveness or relationship quality than faxing press releases or placing flyers on car windshields. Implementing mobile tactics means weighing their advantages in light of strategy. Key dimensions to consider include the extent to which mobile tactics are social, personal, local and—to some degree—snackable.

Social

The combination of mobile and social media use hit a tipping point in the United States in 2014 when the average number of minutes that consumers spent with digital media on mobile devices began to exceed the amount of time they spent on desktop machines. And Facebook was the number one app by far that they used on mobile.[31] Add to that the growth of mobile usage of Instagram, Twitter, Snapchat and YouTube, and you can see how it would be difficult to develop a mobile strategy that doesn't build on social uses of the technology.

Communication via social media means considering not just how you will reach your organization's followers, fans and subscribers but also how they will reach back to your organization and how they will share multimedia content with one another. Think about how your organization can become part of the social conversation. What kinds of mobile content will people respond to and share, and why? How will your organization respond to that shared content? Social means interactive, and interactive means that individuals in your organization have the opportunity to communicate with individuals in your publics. That back-and-forth is very likely to happen via mobile media, so make sure any tactics you plan make sense for the devices on which the communication will happen.

Personal

Mobile media also allow for a tremendous amount of personalization. Marketers were among the first to mine user data to figure out new ways to personalize communication as they sought to sharpen their sales pitches. They learned to use individual data that are available from apps, registrations and browsing histories

In planning for social, consider how you will reach followers, fans and subscribers but also how they will reach back and how they will share content with one another.

The Starbucks app recalls customers' previous orders in recommending future orders.

How might this type of personalization be used to support public relations goals besides sales and marketing?

Geolocation
Function of communication devices that identifies the specific geographic location of the device.

Geofilter
Feature of social media (particularly Snapchat) that encourages communication among users within a specified geographic area by allowing users to post images with location-specific overlays.

to reach mobile consumers with messages tailored to their individual profiles.

When you use your mobile device to shop for plane tickets, download an audiobook, or put in a coffee order for pickup, there's a good chance that the app you use will present you with options based on your prior purchases and browsing history. Public relations practitioners can work with app developers and marketers who have developed loyalty programs to obtain a better understanding of their publics' uses of mobile and to coordinate on communication strategy. Of course, public relations people can also "personalize" the old-fashioned way by engaging individuals with one-to-one conversation or by facilitating forums for the interaction of individuals within organizations and publics using mobile media.

Local

Localization is basically the geographic version of personalization. Unless you deliberately disable **geolocation** functions in your mobile apps, many apps you use will track your location and apply that to your communication preferences. Geolocation makes apps like Uber or Yelp much more convenient as you try to arrange a ride across town or find a local restaurant when traveling. The ads that you hear on Pandora or Spotify also can be localized, allowing both national and local marketers to reach you based on your registered location.

In developing public relations strategies, you should know *where* you plan to reach your publics and communicate with them. Mobile media offer you the opportunity to engage publics almost anywhere they go, provided they opt in to communication that they feel is worthwhile. Snapchat's **geofilter** service allows individuals and organizations to send messages and promote events to other Snapchat users in a specific geographic location.[32] For example, if you were planning a grand re-opening of a newly renovated community garden, you could set up a geofilter for everyone using Snapchat in that area at that time. This would enable you to communicate with them, and them to communicate with one another. The service is free for public places such as parks and landmarks and can be purchased for businesses and brands.

Snackable

What do you do with that little bit of extra time you have waiting in line, sitting in a doctor's office or passing time during a break between classes? Maybe you check Facebook real quick or swipe through some Snapchat stories? Can you ignore the little notification alert button telling you there's something you haven't seen? Like tasty snacks, these little morsels of content—text updates, photos, GIFs, videos, live streams and so on—are hard to resist. While information snacking is not unique to mobile media, trends in mobile media use have resulted in increased consumption of

Snapchat's geofilters allow users to share place-themed messages and promote events in specific geographic locations.

What kinds of organizations can benefit from the combination of social and local mobile content?

snackable content. Snackable content refers to those easy-to-consume pieces of content that are available on the go. On the one hand, mobile media have led to a *decrease* in our attention spans as we squeeze more and more communication tasks into the rest of our daily lives. On the other hand, carrying our devices with us also means we *increase* the total hours of the day that we pay attention to media.

Case Study

Snack Attack: An Iconic American Brand Faces Fallout for Going Digital

Snackable content may have a place in public relations strategy, but planners should be attentive to how digital tactics serve objectives and goals. To extend the snack metaphor, we want to do more than deliver empty calories. Interestingly, one of the best examples comes from a real snack brand.

Frito Lay's Cracker Jack brand has been known for more than a century as an iconic American snack of caramel-coated popcorn and peanuts. It's featured in the lyrics to *Take Me Out to the Ballgame* ("Buy me some peanuts and Cracker Jack . . ."), and it has become part of the American lexicon as an adjective describing exceptionally positive qualities (e.g., "That crackerjack public relations grad can get a job in any city she wants!"). But perhaps most important of all to generations of snackers, Cracker Jack's unique selling proposition has been "A Prize in Every Box." Millions of kids and adults have puzzled over how the little decoder ring, temporary tattoo or plastic figurine always seems to end up at the very bottom of the box. There's even a Cracker Jack Collectors Association (http://www.crackerjackcollectors .com) "dedicated to the collecting of Cracker Jack prizes and related items." So when Cracker Jack decided to leap into the business of digital snacking by replacing its toy surprises with QR codes, many of its most loyal publics went nuts.

As announced in a Frito Lay news release, the company decided to "contemporize" its logo and packaging, and as part of that move began offering digital prizes instead of physical ones. "The new Prize Inside allows families to enjoy their favorite baseball moments through a new one-of-a-kind mobile experience, leveraging digital technology to bring the iconic Prize Inside to life," said senior director of marketing Haston Lewis.[33]

"Totally disappointed," one commenter said on Facebook.[34]

"Huge baseball fan, huge computer guy, but this? Nope," commented another.[35]

Within days a Facebook community emerged, called "Put the PRIZE back in Cracker Jack," and garnered the attention of mainstream media such as NPR and *PCWorld*. The *Chicago Tribune* ran an editorial with the

Some Cracker Jack fans were disappointed when in-box surprises were replaced with digital apps for mobile.

Did the brand take digital tactics too far, or might the tactic make sense in light of broader public relations strategy?

sarcastic heading, "Cracker Jack Prizes Go Digital: More Staring at a Screen? What a Treat!"[36]

The downloadable apps included one called "Dot Dash" and another called "Dance Cam" that enabled users to simulate experiences baseball fans know from ballpark video boards. Another one, "Get Carded," allowed users to create their own autographed trading cards, in digital format of course.

In fairness, the apps sounded pretty cool, but do you think they made sense as part of a larger strategy to maintain relationships between the organization and its publics? As with all public relations tactics, the evaluation of digital apps requires assessing how well they achieve objectives and goals as part of strategies to advance the organization's mission and its relationships with key publics.

Uses and Gratifications of Media

In media research, when communication scientists want to understand *what people do with media*, as opposed to *what media do to people*, they have applied an approach called **uses and gratifications**.[37] The user-oriented approach of uses and gratifications is particularly well suited to the study of new communication technologies.

Public relations researcher Ruth Avidar and her colleagues explored how and why 21- to 31-year-old Israelis were using smartphones.[38] The results imply that some major reasons people choose mobile media are for instrumental purposes (uses) and for pleasure (gratifications): relationships, information, diversion and amusement and participation.

Avidar et al. found that uses and gratifications such as staying in touch with friends and family, sending personal messages, and acknowledging others were most important. In other words, *relationships* were the top reason these young Israelis used smartphones. *Information* was the second-highest rated reason found in this study and included obtaining news updates, seeking information and managing information. Information was followed by *amusement* and *diversion*, which included gaming, relaxation, passing time and fighting boredom. Interestingly, *participation* was rated lowest in this study of how and why millennials use mobile media.

Think about your own use of mobile devices. What kinds of apps do you use for maintaining relationships, obtaining information, amusing yourself, seeking diversion and participating in online activities? And what role do organizations practicing public relations have in those experiences? Are they the subjects of those news feeds? Do they provide the news? Do they provide the apps? How do you communicate directly with them via mobile?

In developing strategy for mobile media, consider asking what people are doing with mobile media instead of what mobile media will do to people.

Uses and gratifications
Approach to studying communication that focuses on how people use media and the gratifications they seek from media, as opposed to studying the effects of media on people as passive audiences.

While thinking about your own experiences with organizations is a good exercise to help you develop questions to drive your planning, it's not normally a good idea to think of yourself as representing your organization's publics. It takes research to understand your publics from their perspectives.

Ethics: Privacy and Safeguarding Confidences

It seems like anywhere people wait, mobile media are being used.

How do you use mobile media when you're waiting in line? What kinds of organizations attempt to communicate with you in that time?

It's not just our tablets and phones on which we communicate. We also communicate more than we realize on the **Internet of Things (IoT)**. Although experts haven't yet agreed on a single definition, the basic idea of IoT is that more and more objects in our environment are connected to each other in a way that enables them to communicate via a network, and by extension the internet at large.

"The premise behind the IoT," according to eMarketer, "is that any object, whether natural or manufactured, can gain the ability to transmit data over a network."[39] Cars with built-in GPS are on the IoT. Home security systems that can be activated remotely and that report activity are on the IoT. My running watch can transmit data about my workout over the internet, and I can share that with other users including running groups and organizations that may want to advertise running-related products and services to the group and me. Even my dog has a small microchip, which was implanted at the same time he received immunizations as a puppy. If he gets lost, he can be scanned for a unique ID number from the chip, which can be reported to a pet-finding service to match his number to my contact information in a database.

As members of publics, we often communicate without even trying. When was the last time you checked your privacy settings for location services on all your apps? Do you actually read the **end-user license agreements (EULA)** you agree to when you register for new apps? Most of us skim those EULA screens and trust that the organizations won't do anything evil with our data. From a public relations standpoint this trust may indicate a healthy relationship between the end user and the organization using the data. But it also raises the stakes for the organization we entrust.

Safeguarding confidences is a key provision in the PRSA Code of Ethics. The provision is commonly read to mean keeping client information confidential, but the larger intent also applies to publics: "To protect

Internet of things (IoT)
Global network of physical objects that are connected to one another in a way that enables them to communicate with one another and the intenet at large.

End-user license agreements (EULA)
Legal agreement between a software provider and the person using the software.

Voices from the Field

Shane Santiago

SHANE SANTIAGO is vice president and digital director at St. John & Partners. Santiago honed his craft at various agencies—including Ogilvy Interactive and GMMB, a FleishmanHillard agency—developing interactive campaigns for a wide range of clients before founding SBS Studios in 2006. SBS Studios cultivated relationships with brands such as Marriott International, Discovery, the NBA, Disney, the Ad Council, ADCOLOR, Comcast, Axe and Sony Pictures. St. John & Partners acquired SBS Studios in 2013. Santiago serves as an ADCOLOR advisory board member and was named an ADCOLOR Innovator in 2012.

Are you seeing more do-it-yourself multimedia tactics in public relations now? Why would you recommend or not recommend public relations people produce more of their own multimedia?

I think we're seeing it more in terms of a blur of traditional public relations and social channels. As such, many tactics come across as more authentic if it feels as if it's coming straight from a brand/source/advertiser. I do recommend a general knowledge base or capability for public relations practitioners to produce their own multimedia—they're already likely great writers, so creating content today should just be an extension of that. Especially with all the access afforded to technology to produce high-quality content, it's easier/more accessible than ever.

How is the technology of multimedia and mobile media helping or hurting diversity in public relations?

Diversity is an issue regardless of technology when it comes to public relations, advertising and media. I think in terms of many communities of color, access to technology is actually not an issue that hurts diversity since those communities typically index highly with mobile and social use. It's more of access to public relations as a practice in those communities

as a viable career path that is the issue. If anything, technology would better prepare diverse communities if they did have more awareness of public relations as a job option.

How is mobile media changing the way practitioners develop strategy? How is it making it easier? Harder?

It makes things more accessible. Mobile puts everything at your fingertips. Research. Participants. Social channels. The list goes on. Mobile is the cost-of-entry as a tool for job performance today and it's expected of colleagues and clients for you to be accessible by mobile device.

What advice do you have for college students about leveraging their familiarity with digital and mobile media for public relations career success?

Embrace technology. Students are digital natives, yet just because you are active on digital/mobile/social channels doesn't make you an expert. Use it as a differentiator when job seeking. Learn to code, learn how it works, learn how/why your peers are sought on these channels and use the technology to address behavioral tendencies.

Internet of Things (IoT)—cool or creepy? What does all this connectedness mean for public relations?

IoT is typically an opt-in experience, so definitely cool. It empowers a relationship with technology to provide experience AND utility and does so in a way that makes it relevant to an individual. Connectedness means public relations practitioners need to understand all the various use-cases and experiences in which they can reach their publics, and that goes so much deeper today than before. Truly understanding "a day in the life" of their publics and all the relevant cross sections of experience and technology is vital to success.

the privacy rights of clients, organizations, and individuals by safeguarding confidential information."[40]

Apple Computer Inc. is as big of a player as any in the global arena of mobile, multimedia, big data and the Internet of Things. That company knows more about its customers than their customers know about themselves. Think of all the data it holds from people running apps, using Apple Pay, making purchases with their Apple IDs, and working on their desktops, laptops, iPads and iPhones. Think carefully about the pitch for its first-generation Apple Watch:

These apps offer a lot of information, entertainment and convenience, but they require trusting organizations with private information.

Which organizations do you trust with your private data and why?

> *To wear it is to love it.*
> *Receive and respond to notifications in an instant. Track your daily activity. Control your music using only your voice. Pay for groceries just like that. With Apple Watch, important information and essential features are always just a raise of the wrist away.*[41]

Media ethicists Jay Black and Chris Roberts frame privacy issues as questions of competing values. We weigh the value of privacy with the values of information, entertainment and convenience. "The bottom line," they write, "is that while a great deal of information about millions of us is conveniently and centrally available for a multitude of uses, do we want corporations and government to know this much about us?"[42] Your answer may depend on how much you trust the organizations.

Apple CEO Tim Cook was quite focused on this issue in a speech he gave at the Electronic Privacy Information Center (EPIC) in 2015: "Like many of you, we at Apple reject the idea that our customers should have to make tradeoffs between privacy and security," Cook opened. He criticized tech companies that lull "their customers into complacency about their personal information."[43] He went on to discuss ways that Apple lets its consumers control their information, as well as the company's efforts to keep the information private using encryption.

As publics, we make decisions every day about which organizations we trust with our personal information. Organizations have to earn that trust—not just with speeches, but with everyday management. When ethical public relations is part of an organization's management function, organizations must take safeguarding confidences and protecting the privacy of their publics seriously.

In Case You Missed It

ICYMI

Social media platforms are increasingly designed for mobile use and multimedia content. Multimedia and mobile communication are changing the very nature of interpersonal communication as well as communication between organizations and publics on social media. Here are a few takeaways from this chapter:

- To create good multimedia, you must first understand how text, graphics, audio and video work together to enhance users' experiences.

- If you add a decent external microphone to your smartphone or camera, you can noticeably improve the quality of audio that you capture.

- Publics may prefer nonprofessionally produced video, if it means they get to hear from real people and the video is part of a larger strategy of two-way communication.

- Mobile video services like Periscope and Facebook Live enable you to open your organization to more publics via social media by live-streaming events like press conferences and live public forums.

- In planning for social, consider how you will reach followers, fans and subscribers but also how they will reach back and how they will share content with one another.

- In developing strategy for mobile media, consider asking what people are doing with mobile media instead of what mobile media will do to people.

SUMMARY

10.1 Identify sources for multimedia elements such as writing, images, audio and video.

Advances in computer technology—particularly mobile devices—have made the production and playback of all sorts of multimedia far more accessible and widespread. Content for multimedia can be attained in three major ways: (1) create it yourself, (2) hire a professional or (3) purchase or otherwise obtain permission to use others' material.

10.2 Analyze how different components of multimedia are integrated for effective communication in public relations.

The key to good multimedia is understanding the various elements and how they work together to enhance users' experiences. Images, audio and video can be presented with or without text. Text can be written to invite, explain or otherwise support other elements of multimedia. At other times, words are foremost, and sounds, images, video and animation play the supporting role for the text. One of the main benefits of multimedia is that they allow an efficiency of communication, as producers can artfully combine elements for the best user experiences across a wide variety of social and mobile contexts.

10.3 Assess the strategic value of mobile tactics.
The evaluation of mobile tactics requires examining how well the tactics achieve objectives and goals as part of strategies to advance the organization's mission and its relationships with key publics. Key dimensions to consider include the degree to which mobile tactics are social, personal, local and snackable.

10.4 Discuss how publics' uses and gratifications of mobile media may help drive public relations strategy.
Major uses and gratifications of mobile media include relationships, information, diversion and amusement, and participation. Mobile media also offer excellent opportunities to obtain feedback from publics. Research should be conducted to understand publics from their perspectives.

10.5 Apply privacy as an ethical value to consider in handling data gleaned from mobile media.
In exchange for information, entertainment and convenience, mobile media users entrust organizations with tremendous amounts of private information. Safeguarding confidences and protecting privacy are key ethical values that public relations professionals and their organizations must honor, if they are going to maintain public trust.

DISCUSSION QUESTIONS

1. Think about the best paper or essay you have ever written. Now suppose you were asked to publish it online. What kind of images or other multimedia elements would you add? Identify at least two elements, and explain how you would produce them or get permission to do so, if someone else produced them.

2. Identify a news story posted online by a reputable news organization, and track that story to one of its public relations sources that supplied original multimedia elements (e.g., images, video, audio, animations). What characteristics of multimedia elements helped the story get selected for publication by the news organization?

3. How have you used mobile media to communicate with an organization? What were your "uses and gratifications"? What were the organization's objectives? Why was (or wasn't) their strategy effective?

4. Thinking more about your experience interacting with an organization via mobile, what specific information do they now have about you? What makes you confident (or not confident) they will handle it properly?

KEY TERMS

CHAPTER 11

Legal

We all know Amazon as a major player in the global marketplace for books, movies and even selfie sticks, but what's its role in the marketplace of ideas, and what free-speech laws apply?

KEY LEARNING OUTCOMES

11.1 Discuss the importance of understanding national laws in international contexts.

11.2 Describe limits to free speech, including libel and slander.

11.3 Identify common types of intellectual property and how they are protected.

11.4 Summarize the role of public relations professionals in providing public information.

11.5 Identify federal agencies that influence and regulate the business of public relations.

11.6 Analyze legal and ethical concerns related to privacy and handling of confidential information in public relations.

RELATED UNIVERSAL ACCREDITATION BOARD COMPETENCY AREAS

2.2 ETHICAL BEHAVIOR • **2.3** FIRST AMENDMENT ISSUES • **2.4** PRIVACY ISSUES

2.5 OTHER LEGAL ISSUES • **5.3** ORGANIZATIONAL STRUCTURE AND RESOURCES

Where did you get this textbook? If you're a student at a U.S. college or university, you probably purchased it from your campus bookstore or directly from the publisher. Or perhaps you borrowed it from a library or from a friend. In any case, the price of the "first sale" book printed and sold in the United States is based on the idea that written materials can be sold by those who hold the U.S. copyright. If you are studying in Thailand and purchase a textbook at a local bookstore or from the publisher's global website, you may pay considerably less than students in the United States pay for the same text, depending on a range of global economic factors.

But what if someone buys textbooks that were printed and first sold in Thailand at a much lower cost and then ships the books to a relative in the United States or puts them on eBay to sell to students in the United States at a higher price? When Supap Kirtsaeng moved from Thailand to the United States to study mathematics at Cornell University, he realized the textbooks he purchased were much more expensive in the United States than the same books in Thailand. So, he asked family and friends to purchase copies in Thailand. He then sold those books in the United States at a higher rate. After reimbursing his friends and family, he kept the profit. Is that legal?

According to a 2013 U.S. Supreme Court decision, yes, it is legal. John Wiley & Sons Inc., the book's publisher, sued Kirtsaeng, but Supreme Court Justice Stephen Breyer wrote in *Kirtsaeng v. John Wiley & Sons, Inc.* that "the 'first sale' doctrine applies to copies of a copyrighted work lawfully made abroad."[1] The first sale doctrine holds that if you purchase a copy of a work from a copyright holder, you can do what you want with your copy, including selling it to someone else.[2]

As Justice Breyer observed in his 2015 book *The Court and the World: American Law and the New Global Realities*, the Kirtsaeng case indicates a new reality that has implications for public relations. "At a moment when ordinary citizens may engage in direct transactions internationally for services available only locally before," Breyer wrote, "it has become clear that, even in ordinary matters, judicial awareness can no longer stop at the border."[3] At the heart of *Kirtsaeng* is the idea of **intellectual property**— who *owns* the ideas in books, websites, videos, poems, blogs, photos, graphics, software and so on. Intellectual property is any product of the human mind that is protected by law from unauthorized use by others. Also central to the case is the question of the reach of U.S. laws in determining how this property is bought, sold, copied and shared across borders. The Wiley textbooks were hard copies of printed materials, but think of the implications for everyday public relations when all it takes for international distribution is a couple of keystrokes to copy and paste and the tap of an icon to upload digital property for global distribution.

Intellectual property is just one of many legal concepts that communications professionals run across in day-to-day public relations. Those

Intellectual property
Any product of the human mind that is protected by law from unauthorized use by others.

working in public relations also need "judicial awareness"—as Justice Breyer put it—to determine what's legal. For instance, consider the following:

- *Defamation:* Can you sue when someone from another country tweets something mean and nasty about you or someone else in your organization?

- *Sunshine laws:* If you work for the government, do you have to share the results of that survey you ran with anyone who asks?

- *Business regulations:* Can you tell your buddies that the value of your company stock options is about to double?

- *Appropriation:* Can you use that picture of Rihanna on your Facebook event page?

- *Privacy:* Can you write about your colleague's baby shower on your company blog?

These questions provide just a small sample. While you will not become a legal expert as a result of reading this chapter, you will gain an awareness of some common legal issues that apply to your work in public relations. Many legal issues are based on laws written by local, state and federal governments and interpreted in court cases. Others are regulations enforced by federal agencies. If you work in public relations, you may even play a role in communicating legal information, such as when you write social media policies or handle media inquiries related to your organization's legal disputes. Even though this chapter focuses largely on law and policy in the United States, this awareness must extend across international borders.

The First Amendment

Congress shall make no law respecting an establishment of religion, or prohibiting the free exercise thereof; or abridging the freedom of speech, or of the press; or the right of the people peaceably to assemble, and to petition the Government for a redress of grievances.

At its core, the practice of public relations in democratic societies is a communication function, dependent on free speech. Sometimes that speech is primarily political, as when practitioners engage publics about ideas, policy and laws that involve their organizations (e.g., public affairs, political campaigning). Other times that speech is primarily commercial, as when practitioners communicate strategically in support of their organizations' financial goals (e.g., integrated marketing communication, investor relations). Over the years, U.S. courts have ruled that the Constitution protects political speech more than commercial speech. For

It's easier than ever to buy, sell, reproduce and share intellectual property across international borders.

Why would public relations professionals be concerned with laws related to intellectual property?

The First Amendment protects free speech, but courts have ruled that some forms of speech are more protected than others.

Which of these signs gets the least legal protection and why?

example, courts are more likely to uphold laws and regulations that prohibit false advertising for products and services than laws that restrict political campaigning.

As introduced in Chapter 2, the PRSA Code of Ethics identifies advocacy as one of its core values: "We serve the public interest by acting as responsible advocates for those we represent. We provide a voice in the marketplace of ideas, facts, and viewpoints to aid informed public debate."[4] The First Amendment generally guarantees the right to exercise such advocacy, but the right to free speech has its limits.

In a classic 1919 Supreme Court opinion, Justice Oliver Wendell Holmes wrote that you cannot falsely yell "Fire!" in a crowded theater and cause a panic. Some circumstances present enough of a possibility of harmful outcomes that they justify limits on First Amendment freedoms—this is sometimes called the **clear and present danger** doctrine. Let's hope you never find yourself in a situation in which your work in public relations puts you at risk of causing such danger, but you may well face situations in which you need legal counsel to understand your rights (and the limits on those rights) as a professional communicator. Working with the press and communicating on behalf of an organization requires understanding your role in the marketplace for ideas that the First Amendment serves to protect.

amazon Case Study

Amazon v. NYT: A Case in the Court of Public Opinion

If you've ever shopped online for a book or movie or even a selfie stick or Halloween costume, you're probably well aware that Amazon is one of the world's largest marketplaces for physical goods and digital products. Its founder Jeff Bezos is widely heralded as an entrepreneur extraordinaire and a visionary in marketplace innovation. The company has redefined how people buy, sell and recommend books. It has even changed how people *read* books (think Kindle).

Along with its enormity in the world's marketplace of physical and digital products, Amazon also has grown into a formidable voice in the marketplace of ideas. As such, the company invested heavily in its public relations firepower when it hired former White House press secretary Jay Carney as senior vice president for corporate affairs in early 2015.

Less than six months after Carney's hire, David Streitfeld and Jodi Kantor published a lengthy *New York Times* article calling Amazon a "bruising workplace," based on dozens of anecdotes about the harsh working conditions. One of the most damning stories was a vivid vignette from an interview with former Amazon employee Bo Olson. "You walk out of a conference room and you'll see a grown man covering his face," Olson was quoted. "Nearly every person I worked with, I saw cry at their desk."[5] Several other former employees relayed tales of hostile peer evaluation systems, 85-hour workweeks and pressure to work through holidays and vacations.

At this point in the case, we can already see the First Amendment in action. As journalists, Kantor and Streitfeld exercised their right to free speech, as did many of the sources cited in their article. Though the story would certainly offend Amazon management, expose some of its executives to public criticism, and possibly even hurt its recruiting and profits, the article was protected speech under the Constitution's First Amendment.

Amazon spokesman Jay Carney checks his phone during his prior job as White House press secretary.

Why would high-power communicators take to a self-publishing platform like Medium to air their differences?

Of course, Amazon and Carney also have the right to respond. And respond they did. In a roughly 1,300-word retort posted on his page (@JayCarney) on the self-publishing platform Medium.com titled "What *The New York Times* Didn't Tell You," Carney disputed many of the claims.[6] Carney wrote that Olson's "brief tenure at Amazon ended after an investigation revealed he had attempted to defraud vendors and conceal it by falsifying business records," and that Olson had admitted this and resigned immediately after being confronted with the evidence.

Again, we see the First Amendment in action in that Carney is allowed to publish his opinions and advocate strongly on behalf of his employer. Another First Amendment question emerges—what gives Carney the right to discuss the terms of a former employee's resignation? It seems likely that Carney would have cleared his Medium piece with Amazon's legal department before publishing, and this illustrates the importance of public relations people working well with attorneys.

Daniel Pearson of *Seattle Weekly* offered an interesting conclusion more about the court of public opinion than the court of law: "Let this be a lesson for all you Amazonians: Jeff Bezos and his team want to hear your complaints, but if you go public with them, expect to have any dirty laundry the company has on you to get hung up in the wind."[7]

The battle in the court of public opinion raged on. Later in the very same day that Carney published his piece on Medium, *New York Times*

Obtain permission (or seek legal counsel) before publicly discussing private information about any current or past employee.

Executive Editor Dean Baquet responded with his own Medium piece. Carney responded again. It may never end.

Who wins in this battle? You do, concluded *Fortune*'s Matthew Ingram. He wrote that both sides in the Amazon-NYT case are guilty of some degree of spin, "but at least we can see it happening and judge for ourselves whom to believe."[8] That's what the marketplace of ideas is, and always has been, all about. Social media and platforms for self-publishing like Medium help the process. It's remarkable that some of the most privileged voices in the world are now using platforms like Medium to exercise their free speech. You can too.

Limitations on free speech kick in when your right to free speech infringes on others' rights. In public relations, you may run into situations in which your right to free speech infringes on someone else's reputation, intellectual property, financial interests or privacy.

Defamation

One of the ways that someone can hit the legal limits for free speech is to infringe on someone else's reputation. **Defamation** is a statement that injures someone's reputation. Slander and libel are both forms of defamation. **Slander** refers to spoken communication, while **libel** refers to written or recorded communication that can be reproduced and shared repeatedly. This means that Facebook posts, Instagram posts, and tweets are subject to libel laws. In fact, there's even an informal term for Twitter libel.

The word "twibel" rose in public consciousness after fashion designer Dawn Simorangkir sued punk rocker and actress Courtney Love Cobain for libelous Twitter statements. Following a dispute over payments for wardrobe items, and according to the libel complaint filed by Simorangkir in 2009, Love Cobain tweeted to her tens of thousands of followers that Simorangkir was a "nasty lying hosebag thief," and that police should "haul her desperate cokes [*sic*] out ass to jail" because "she has a history of dealing cocaine, lost all custody of her child, assault and burglary."[9] The parties later settled out of court for $430,000. Had Love Cobain spoken these statements in person instead of tweeting them, the defamation case would have been one of slander instead of libel.

Before you sue the first person who writes something mean and nasty about you or about someone else in your organization, however, keep in mind that courts are rather strict on what counts as defamation.[10]

1. *The statement must actually be false and hurt someone's reputation.* Truth is a fantastic defense in libel cases. And even false statements have to do more than just hurt someone's feelings. They

Defamation
False communication that injures someone's reputation.

Slander
Oral communication that is false and injures someone's reputation.

Libel
Written or otherwise recorded false communication that injures someone's reputation.

have to actually cause damage to the person's reputation in a way that can be proven.

2. *The statement must be published or spoken to at least one other person besides the person who is the subject of the statement.* Other people must also be able to identify the subject of the statement. For example, a private text probably would not count, but a tweet mentioning someone's recognized Twitter handle would.

3. *The false statement has to be factual.* Name-calling and hyperbole can't really be proven true or false and, therefore, cannot be the basis of a defamation suit. Courtney Love Cobain might have been able to get away with calling Simorangkir desperate, or even a hosebag, but she would have had to prove the allegations about drug dealing, burglary and assault, if she fought the case.

4. *The statement must be made with fault.* This concept of fault means that the defendant was either careless and negligent in making the statement or the defendant actually knew the statement was false and hurtful and made it anyway. If the subject (plaintiff) is just a private citizen in the context of the case, he or she would need to show only that the defendant was negligent and acted carelessly. If the plaintiff is a public figure, he or she has to prove the defendant knowingly made a false statement.

Courtney Love Cobain became the first celebrity sued for defamation on Twitter ("twibel") in 2009. In this photo, she arrives at court for an unrelated case.

Why do you think she settled out of court in the twibel case?

The fourth point is an important one for this book because public relations people often represent **public figures** in their work. Public figures may include celebrities, politicians and business leaders. Although the exact definition of who counts as a public figure depends on the legal context and decisions of courts, the general idea is summarized well in the landmark Supreme Court case of *Gertz v. Robert Welch, Inc.* in 1973. The Court held the following:

> *Because private individuals characteristically have less effective opportunities for rebuttal than do public officials and public figures, they are more vulnerable to injury from defamation. Because they have not voluntarily exposed themselves to increased risk of injury from defamatory*

Public figure
Someone "of general fame or notoriety in the community" who is subject to less protection in libel cases than a private individual.

falsehoods, they are also more deserving of recovery. The state interest in compensating injury to the reputation of private individuals is therefore greater than for public officials and public figures.

Basically, if you work for a politician, a celebrity, a CEO or any other famous person, you may have to deal with quite a bit more flak before you can sue for libel than you would if you were representing a private citizen.[11] The courts have said that public figures just have to deal with libelous comments unless they can prove **actual malice**. According to the Supreme Court in *New York Times Co. v. Sullivan*, another landmark First Amendment case, actual malice means "that the statement was made with knowledge of its falsity or with reckless disregard of whether it was true or false."[12]

Intellectual Property

When you communicate on behalf of an organization, you often must ask who owns the information being exchanged and whether you, or someone else, have the rights to the words, images, music or multimedia being exchanged. As discussed in Chapter 10 on multimedia and mobile, digital convergence has made it much easier to acquire, mix, mash, share and re-share content online. In many cases, re-pinning on Pinterest, re-blogging on Tumblr or re-tweeting on Twitter are great ways to build social capital. Often, the people who created the content might even be excited that you are helping them go viral and obtain more exposure. But not always. When you share someone else's intellectual property without permission or proper attribution, you run the risk of legal trouble.

Copyright, Trademarks and Patents

Three major types of intellectual property that can be claimed are copyright, trademarks and patents. **Copyright** is a claim to authorship of an original work, including the rights to reproduce, distribute, perform, display or license the work. These "works" include literature, music, drama, choreography, pictures, graphics, sculptures, music and even architecture. Copyrighted works are often indicated with the symbol ©, but the symbol is not necessarily required for the owner to claim copyright.

Trademarks are any words, names, phrases, symbols or designs used to distinguish a product or service from others in the competitive marketplace. Registered trademarks are indicated with the symbol ®.

Patents cover inventions. With patents, the United States grants patent holders "the exclusive right to exclude others from making, using, importing, and selling the patented innovation for a limited period of time."[13]

Actual malice
When a defamatory statement is made with knowledge of its falsity and reckless disregard for the truth.

Copyright
Claim to intellectual property rights of an original work of authorship including rights to reproduce, distribute, perform, display, license and so on.

Trademark
Word, name, phrase, symbol or design used to distinguish a product or service from others in the competitive marketplace.

Patent
Claim to intellectual property rights of an invention.

The U.S. Patent and Trademark Office (USPTO) authorizes both trademarks and patents. Trademarks and patents are particularly important to startups as they are used to develop organizational identity (e.g., trademarking logos) and to innovate with new products and services (e.g., patenting inventions).

Plagiarism

As a student, you've learned the importance of proper attribution. If you present someone else's specific ideas or words as your own, that's **plagiarism**. Digital media have made it much easier to "borrow" someone else's words, but that same technology makes it easier to identify plagiarism. Just put quotes around a sentence or excerpt of text and run a web search for that quoted material, and if the words have been plagiarized, there's a good chance you'll uncover an earlier source. Services like Turnitin, which boasts the ability to search more than 45 billion web pages, 337 million student papers and 130 million academic articles, offer automatic checking for possible plagiarism.[14] However, building on the contributions of others is essential to good scholarship. The key to avoiding plagiarism, then, is proper attribution. When words or specific ideas are not your own, you must let your instructors and anyone else reading your work know where those words and ideas come from. Give credit where credit is due!

Plagiarism is an issue outside of the classroom too. When an executive or organizational leader uses someone else's words without attribution in public communication, plagiarism can become a public relations problem. You may have read about high-profile politicians or commencement speakers who have been called out for lifting major parts of their speeches from other sources without attribution. When this happens, an opportunity for public honor turns into a case of public shame.

Easy sharing and reposting of others' ideas, words, images and works of art are essential parts of what makes social media work, but that spirit of sharing and free-flowing information doesn't excuse plagiarism. Skye Grove, a rising "celebrity Instagrammer" in South Africa who had reached more than 40,000 followers on her Instagram account, was featured on national TV and successfully began selling her photography online. That all came to a stop when another Instagram user contacted the internationally popular technology news website Memeburn to report suspicions that Grove had plagiarized many of her images, including some that she sold.[15] Memeburn investigated and found evidence of several suspected instances of plagiarism.

A week later, Grove's Instagram and Twitter accounts had disappeared, although it is unclear whether she deleted them voluntarily or whether they were removed for violating terms of service. Grove also was suspended without pay from her job as a communication manager for the NGO Cape

Plagiarism
Presenting someone else's words or ideas as one's own.

The key to avoiding plagiarism is proper attribution. Give credit where credit is due!

This photo by Stephen Ball was downloaded from Flickr and published here with the express written consent of its owner.

Do you like it when people repost your content on social media? When is it OK, and when would you consider it to be plagiarism?

Town Partnership.[16] Before deleting her Instagram account, Grove explained:

> For a long time I didn't believe my work was good enough. I wanted to impress people with my photography but didn't believe I was good enough. So, from time to time, I posted photos that didn't belong to me but that I claimed as my own. The more I honed my skill, the more I became compelled to be true to myself. . . .[17]

In an email to Memeburn, Cape Town Partnership CEO Bulelwa Makalima-Ngewana explained that she had no reason to believe that Grove's mistakes were made as part of her official duties at the organization, but she also noted, "Personal and professional reputations are intertwined in the current social media climate."[18] With that hard lesson learned, Grove returned to both social media and her job later in the same year.

While attribution of words or ideas to a specific source is often enough to avoid plagiarizing, plagiarism is different from **copyright infringement**. If you want to include the full lyrics to a Maya Angelou poem on your for-profit Etsy page, use a Jack Johnson song as the soundtrack to a surf video you will distribute via paid downloads, or take an image from ESPN .com to put on T-shirts to sell at homecoming, attribution is not enough. Even if you make that attribution clear on the web page or video or T-shirt, you need permission to use the copyrighted material, because that material is someone else's intellectual property. Profiting from someone else's work or taking it out of context without permission can be treated as a form of stealing. You can get in trouble for copyright infringement even if you've cleared yourself of plagiarism.

Fair Use

If you're essentially selling someone else's property for a profit, chances are they are going to want a cut. But, you may ask, doesn't the First Amendment protect our free speech? And what if we're not trying to make a profit? How can we participate in the marketplace of ideas if the only way to work with someone else's ideas is to obtain their permission and pay for the right? The concept of **fair use** helps answer some of these questions. According to the U.S. Copyright Office, the following four factors are often taken into consideration in determining whether use of copyrighted material without permission qualifies as fair use:[19]

1. *The purpose and character of the use.* Is it transformative? Have you transformed the original work in some way to give it new meaning? Or have you added something to the work that serves the public interest? Parody, exaggerating or humorously imitating the work or style of another, may be considered fair use. In a way, ridiculing a work actually makes it more likely to be considered fair use. Using material with significant commentary or

criticism for the purposes of education or research also may qualify as fair use.

2. *The nature of the copyrighted work.* Published works and works that primarily consist of factual material are more likely to qualify for fair use. Repeating facts and spreading knowledge serves a public benefit. But to encourage original imaginative and creative works, courts are more protective of original creative expression—for example, a screenplay or a song would be more protected than a news item in a financial report or traffic update.

3. *The amount and substantiality of the portion taken in relation to the copyrighted work as a whole.* Quoting a few lines from a 500-page book or sampling a few notes from a symphony might be more likely to be seen as fair use than quoting four lines from a six-line poem or playing the entire chorus from a pop song.

4. *Effect of the use upon the potential market for or value of the copyrighted work.* According to the copyright office, courts "consider whether the use is hurting the current market for the original work (for example, by displacing sales of the original) and/or whether the use could cause substantial harm if it were to become widespread."

Sports leagues are notoriously zealous about protecting copyrights. If you watch sports on TV often, you are probably quite familiar with the disclaimers. For baseball, it's "Any rebroadcast, retransmission, or account of this game, without the express written consent of Major League Baseball, is prohibited." For football, it's "This telecast is copyrighted by the NFL for the private use of our audience. Any other use of this telecast or of any pictures, descriptions, or accounts of the game without the NFL's consent, is prohibited."

Therefore, when sports websites Deadspin and SBNation used Twitter accounts (@Deadspin and @SBNationGIF) to post short GIF clips of key plays in NFL games, the NFL did not see that as fair use. Rather than trying to take Deadspin and SBNation to court, however, the NFL and other sports organizations like the Ultimate Fighting Championship (UFC) went straight to Twitter with a takedown notice. They demanded that Twitter "immediately disable access to

SBNation posts animated GIFs of NFL games and other sporting events on its Twitter account.

What fair-use questions come into play here? Bonus question: How many trademarks can you identify in this picture?

the individual who has uploaded the copyright infringing content" and to "terminate any and all accounts this individual has through you."[20] The UFC further demanded that Twitter take down the two accounts within 10 minutes of receiving the email!

We can't be sure how the courts would have ruled on the posting of animated GIFs of sporting plays on Twitter, because Twitter complied with the takedown notice. While both @Deadspin and @SBNationGIF went back online within a few days, and they both continue to post GIFs, they clearly had to work out legal issues with both Twitter and the original copyright holders to continue the practice. Publishing content is an important part of public relations. So is maintaining relationships with other content providers. This case illustrates how legal issues may come into play in both functions.

Digital Age Intellectual Property Issues

The @Deadspin and @SBNationGIF case raises another interesting point about intellectual property in the digital age. In addition to the NFL's and UFC's claim to original copyright on one side and arguments that could be made for fair use on the other side, we must also consider the role of Twitter and other social media platforms. Now—as you're thinking about legal issues—may be a good time to review the terms of service for your Instagram, Facebook, Snapchat and Tumblr accounts. Take Twitter, for example. Here's what you've agreed to if you have a Twitter account:

- By tweeting anything at all to your account, you grant Twitter "a worldwide, non-exclusive, royalty-free license (with the right to sublicense) to use, copy, reproduce, process, adapt, modify, publish, transmit, display and distribute" the content.

- At the same time, everything tweeted "is the sole responsibility of the person who originated such Content."[21]

So, basically you need to assume that anything you post on Twitter can be used against you or your organization if something goes wrong, but that Twitter also has all the rights to anything you post when things are going well. In an age of participatory media, user-generated content and global memes, we have to balance enthusiastic participation in a culture of sharing with respect for intellectual property. Use caution when posting anything that may be seen as offensive or illegal.

> Balance participation with respect for intellectual property; use caution when posting anything that may be seen as offensive or illegal.

CREATIVE COMMONS

Sometimes intellectual property holders want to put their content out there for everyone to use, share, mash up and redistribute. Other times they want to claim their content and protect it like a financial asset. In public relations, you (or your organization) may face these issues as the owner of intellectual property in some cases and as the party who wants to use someone else's intellectual property in other cases. The nonprofit organization **Creative Commons** serves to assist both sides.

Creative Commons offers free legal tools at http://creativecommons.org/ that make it easy for content creators (i.e., licensors) to designate the permissions that they want to allow. For example, by answering a series of questions, a licensor may determine that he would like to offer an "Attribution-NonCommercial-ShareAlike" license. This license gives others permission to share and adapt the work, as long as they give appropriate credit (attribution), don't use the material to make money (noncommercial), and distribute any remix or transformation of the original with the same license as the original (ShareAlike). Once the licensor has agreed to the terms, the Creative Commons tool generates a nifty little graphic and link, which will clearly indicate the permissions that the licensor can use to post on a web page.

Kaiser Health News, a national health policy news service that is part of the nonpartisan Henry J. Kaiser Family Foundation, invites other organizations to republish their content for free. "We don't require much," the site says about sharing its content. "We make it available under the Creative Commons CC BY 4.0 license."[22]

LINKING

Hyperlinks are what originally distinguished the web from other media. A link makes a connection to other content. While that other content may be copyrighted, linking to content is generally not considered copyright

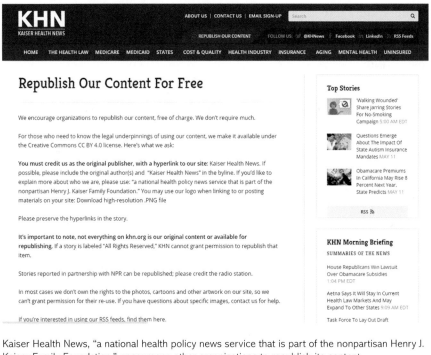

Kaiser Health News, "a national health policy news service that is part of the nonpartisan Henry J. Kaiser Family Foundation," encourages other organizations to republish its content.

How does the organization benefit from the Creative Commons license?

Boing Boing editor, blogger, journalist and science fiction writer Cory Doctorow was an early adopter of Creative Commons licenses.

What kinds of permissions are indicated in this photo? How do they benefit him as an author and benefit those who want to share his work as fans?

Deep link
Hyperlink that bypasses an organization's home page and takes users directly to resources deeper in an organization's website structure.

Framing
When clickable material in a link is actual content from the site to which it links.

When in doubt about your ownership rights of social media content, check the provider's terms of service.

infringement. That said, some organizations have tried out policies requiring users to obtain permission before posting **deep links**, which are links that bypass an organization's home page and take users directly to otherwise copyrighted material. In 2002, National Public Radio (NPR) tried to make users obtain permission to link to stories with a policy stating, "Linking to or framing of any material on this site without the prior written consent of NPR is prohibited." It did not go over well. Author and *Boing Boing* editor Cory Doctorow called the policy "brutally stupid" in that an organization dedicated to public discourse would obstruct users from accessing content that would otherwise be freely available.[23]

Framing refers to clickable material in a link that is actual content from the site to which it links. For example, when a web page includes a clickable photo, graphic, or chunk of text from another page, this is considered framing. At least one court has found framing to be copyright infringement when the "framed link duplicates or recasts" material from the original page.[24]

REPOSTING

Linking and framing issues are *so* Web 1.0. At least back then, in order to publish a link or frame, a user would have to consult the original source, copy the URL, and paste it as a hyperlink. Now all we have to do is click a button or two to retweet, re-blog, re-pin, or otherwise rebroadcast someone else's work. Along with technologies that facilitate commenting and conversation, the easy creation, sharing and re-sharing of information on social media are hallmarks of Web 2.0 communication. But this easy sharing and re-sharing leads to questions about who owns what content and who is responsible for inappropriate or unauthorized content.

If you post original content on Twitter, Pinterest, Facebook or Tumblr, you can't really be too upset if someone else shares that material. The facility for sharing is part of the deal of social media, and the rules are laid out in the terms of service you agree to when you sign up for an account. On the other hand, if you are challenged for reposting someone else's intellectual property without permission, don't count on getting much help from your social media service provider in your defense. The same idea applies if you were to repost libelous or obscene material. Remember, the terms of service are primarily written to protect the service provider. Practice common sense and conservative decision-making about attribution and permission on social media. If for some reason you think you need to push the limits, first check the terms of service you've agreed to. If you are still uncertain, consult a legal expert.

Public Information and the Freedom of Information Act

Intellectual property laws apply to information and ideas that can be claimed as privately owned by people and organizations. As discussed in Chapter 9, some works have entered the public domain, meaning that copyrights have expired, been forfeited by the owner, or otherwise do not apply. If you work in public relations for a publicly funded or government organization, you may find that laws that determine what you *must* communicate are much more a part of your day-to-day work than laws about what kinds of information you can claim and protect. Although there are some exceptions, most information that the government collects and uses in the United States is treated as public information.

The **Freedom of Information Act** (FOIA) is a U.S. federal law that went into effect in 1967 to ensure that the government makes its information accessible to citizens. With a few exceptions (nine categories to be exact—ranging from national defense secrets to personnel records to information about oil and gas wells), FOIA requires government agencies to make information public. According to the U.S. Department of Justice, about 100 agencies are subject to FOIA, and several hundred offices are tasked with responding to requests for government information. Beyond just responding to requests as they come in, government agencies are also expected (and in some cases required) to proactively make government information available in a useful form. Many of these agencies are working to develop and improve online interfaces for delivering and presenting data for public consumption. For example, www.usaspending.gov enables users to enter custom information to generate a report and graph illustrating how government money is spent.

States also have specific freedom of information laws called **sunshine laws** that stipulate which documents and records must be open to the public and also which meetings and events must be open. These state laws echo the sentiment of Supreme Court Justice Louis Brandeis, who wrote in a 1913 *Harpers Weekly* article that government in the open serves well the public interest: "Publicity is justly commended as a remedy for social and industrial diseases. Sunlight is said to be the best of disinfectants; electric light the most efficient policeman."[25]

Freedom of Information Act (FOIA)
U.S. federal law passed to ensure that the government makes its information accessible to citizens.

Sunshine law
State law that stipulates which documents and records must be open to the public and which meetings and events must be open.

This user-friendly website allows anyone to track various types of government spending.

Why does the U.S. government invest in making this information available?

Protecting Publics

In addition to information that must be made available to citizens in the marketplace of ideas in democratic societies, laws and regulations also stipulate which information should be made available to consumers in the marketplace for goods and services. Depending on the area of public relations that you work in, you will need to become familiar with various government agencies that are responsible for protecting your key publics. Do you work with food and drug consumers? There's an agency for that: the Food and Drug Administration (FDA). Does your organization advertise and promote consumer goods and services in the United States? If so, you'll need to know the Federal Trade Commission (FTC). Do you work with stockholders and financial publics? There's an agency for that too: the Securities Exchange Commission (SEC). In fact, hundreds of government agencies enforce regulations related to all sorts of organizations and their public relations efforts.

Safety and Accuracy

You've no doubt seen drug ads featuring peaceful landscapes or serene elderly couples happily arranging flowers or riding bicycles under blue skies with laughing grandkids. Have you noticed that the voiceover in those ads often shifts—almost imperceptibly—from the benefits of the drug to an unsettling list of disclaimers that tell you about possible side effects like dizziness, dry mouth, frequent urination, diarrhea, hallucinations, coma or even death![26] That's because pharmaceutical advertising in the United States is regulated by the **Food and Drug Administration (FDA).** The FDA requires that product claim advertisements include the following:[27]

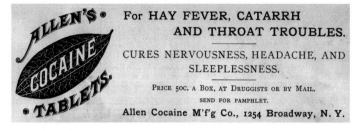

For HAY FEVER, CATARRH AND THROAT TROUBLES.

CURES NERVOUSNESS, HEADACHE, AND SLEEPLESSNESS.

PRICE 50C. A BOX, AT DRUGGISTS OR BY MAIL.
SEND FOR PAMPHLET.

Allen Cocaine M'f'g Co., 1254 Broadway, N. Y.

The pharmaceutical industry is regulated quite a bit more than it used to be.

How do regulatory agencies try to protect publics when it comes to advertising and marketing?

- The name of the drug (brand and generic)

- At least one FDA-approved use for the drug

- The most significant risks of the drug

That said, the FDA's regulatory authority extends well beyond drug ads. At www.fda.gov, the agency includes information for a range of organizations and publics including consumers, patients, health professionals, scientists, researchers and industry. In addition to food and drugs, the agency regulates the business of (and communication related to) medical products, animal and veterinary products, cosmetics and tobacco products. If you work in public relations in any organization that deals with these types of products and services, you'll definitely need to become familiar with the FDA. The FDA's regulations are likely to affect how your organization communicates with its publics.

Of course, food and drug companies are not the only organizations regulated by government. The **Federal Trade Commission (FTC)** serves a mission to protect consumers of all types of products and services and "to enhance informed consumer choice and public understanding of the competitive process."[28] The FTC acts as a watchdog over truth in advertising and promotion. If you promote your products or services as environmentally friendly, make health claims or state that your products are "made in the USA," the FTC requires that you can back up those claims with evidence. The FTC is also concerned with how products and services are marketed to children, any type of online advertising and marketing, and the practice of telemarketing. In fact, the agency runs the National Do Not Call Registry for telemarketers. Unfortunately—if your inbox looks anything like mine—they haven't had tremendous success fighting the growth of email spam.

Financial Information

As discussed in Chapter 4, investor relations (maintaining relationships and communicating with financial publics such as current stockholders, potential investors and financial analysts) is an important sector of public relations. The **Securities and Exchange Commission (SEC)** regulates communication activities with investors, including **initial public offerings (IPOs)**. IPOs are highly choreographed financial events in which

Food and Drug Administration (FDA)
U.S. federal agency responsible for regulating food, drugs and health-related products and services including the promotion of these products and services.

Federal Trade Commission (FTC)
U.S. federal agency responsible for regulating all types of consumer products and services, including the promotion of these products and services.

Securities and Exchange Commission (SEC)
U.S. federal agency responsible for regulating financial activities and investing.

Initial public offering (IPO)
Financial event in which a private company offers sale of stocks to public investors for the first time.

Material information
Any information that could influence the market value of a company or its products.

Insider trading
When a company's employees or executives buy and sell stock in their own organization or share information with others who buy or sell before the information has been made public.

private companies first offer sale of stocks to public investors. As they would in any new corporate initiative or offering, public relations people play a role in the successful launch of IPOs. For example, before Fitbit, the company that makes fitness tracking bracelets, went public in 2015, it hired two major public relations agencies, FleishmanHillard and Burson-Marsteller, to help it gear up to sell more than 22 million shares of stock.[29] By the end of Fitbit's opening day of trading on Wall Street, shares were up to $29.68, and the company was valued at $4.1 billion.[30]

The SEC also regulates financial reports. As professional communicators, public relations professionals often write, edit and present annual reports and other financial documents (see Chapter 9). The stakes for accuracy in these required reports are extremely high, and enthusiasm and optimism must be carefully balanced with attention to accuracy.

If you work in public relations and are involved with IPOs or the creation or dissemination of financial reports, you will undoubtedly have access to **material information**, which is any information that could influence the market value of a company or its products. As a result, public relations executives must be especially careful not to illegally take advantage of inside information for their own financial gain. Known as **insider trading**, this may include tipping off friends, family or associates so that they benefit illegally from information that has not yet been made public. The SEC carefully monitors for cases of illegal insider trading. As an example, the SEC's web page cites a 2012 case of a public relations executive charged with insider trading on information she gained while representing a bank in California:

> The SEC alleges that Renee White Fraser and her firm Fraser Communications were contacted by Pasadena-based East West Bancorp (EWBC) for marketing and public relations support during its acquisition of San Francisco-based United Commercial Bank. The very next day after agreeing to take on EWBC as a client, Fraser bought 10,000 shares of EWBC stock. She sold all of her shares after EWBC's stock price jumped 55 percent after the public announcement of the acquisition.[31]

Fraser paid $91,530 as a penalty, which was more than twice the amount she profited from the alleged insider trading.

Privacy

As your level of responsibility grows in an organization, so does your access to information about internal and external publics. Depending on the type of organization you work for, you may have access to employee performance evaluations, student academic records, volunteer contact information and even photos of your colleagues with their families from their Instagram accounts. In addition to the obvious legal and ethical issues that may arise if you release negative information about someone, you must be careful even when your intentions are positive. If you write a biography of an employee or student who is receiving an award, you should check with that person to make sure it is accurate and that the person consents to the information being released. Likewise, if you pull a photo of someone from a social media account, you'll want to obtain permission before using that photo on your company web page.

Externally, **customer relationship management (CRM)** describes the process of tracking and forecasting customers' interactions with an organization. Ridiculous amounts of data can be collected and analyzed to better serve customers with personalized experiences that are customized to their browsing history and preferences. These relationships—facilitated by data and technology—can be mutually beneficial. Customers gain customized experiences and convenient service. Organizations obtain lots of data to use to support their business decisions. Think about the organizations that offer you the most convenient and customized services. Maybe Google? Facebook? Amazon? Netflix? How about your online news sources or favorite retailers for shopping? Your school? Your bank? Your hospital? You as a customer (or student or patient, etc.) put an enormous amount of trust in these organizations. Public relations people have to be very careful with that trust.

In many cases, the right decisions about privacy of both internal and external publics can be made with good business sense and careful ethics, but you must also be aware of the legal rights and responsibilities of people inside and outside your organization. According to Cornell University Law School's Legal Information Institute, there are a "bundle of torts" to watch out for in privacy cases.[32] These torts (acts that can lead to lawsuits) include intrusion into seclusion, appropriation of likeness or identity, public disclosure of private facts and portrayal in a false light.

Intrusion into Seclusion

Intrusion into seclusion is what most people think of when they hear "invasion of privacy." It includes trespassing into someone's private space such as a home or car, but it also includes electronic surveillance to access online activity that someone could reasonably expect to be private. Since intrusion into seclusion must be highly "offensive to a reasonable person" and cause "mental anguish or suffering," public relations people are unlikely to encounter this type of invasion of privacy in the context of their daily professional communication.[33]

Appropriation of Likeness or Identity

Appropriation of likeness or identity applies in cases in which a person's name, picture, or other personal attribute (signature, voice, portrait, etc.) is used without permission. When the subject is a celebrity, that person can claim a right to publicity, meaning that you cannot use the person's likeness for commercial purposes. For example, when Old Navy made a

Customer relationship management (CRM)
Process of tracking and forecasting customers' interactions with an organization, often leveraging data for sales support.

YouTube video titled "Super C-U-T-E," featuring a model who looked a lot like Kim Kardashian, the video registered more than 2 million views. Kardashian sued. According to *USA Today*, the suit was filed in a Los Angeles court for an unspecified amount of damages, claiming Kardashian had "invested substantial time, energy, finances and entrepreneurial effort in developing her considerable professional and commercial achievements and success," and had earned "popularity, fame, and prominence in the public eye."[34] Apparently, the resemblance between the model and Kardashian was enough for Kardashian to consider it an appropriation of her likeness. The video has long since been removed from YouTube.

Public Disclosure of Private Facts

You can find yourself in legal trouble for publishing information that has not previously been released, if that information is personal and not deemed to be of legitimate public interest. Examples of private facts include a person's health status, sexual orientation or financial situation. In public relations, you may want to celebrate your organization's diversity, publicly

Will the real Kim Kardashian please step forward? One of these is Kim Kardashian. The other is a model named Melissa Molinaro.

How could using a celebrity look-alike in promotional materials be considered a privacy issue?

congratulate an employee on expecting twins or encourage retirement savings by highlighting the financial success of one of your organization's retirees. However, even with the best intentions, you must be careful to obtain consent before publicizing anyone's private facts. Any of these situations could be seen as public disclosure of private information.

Even with the best intentions, obtain consent before publicizing anyone on social media.

Portrayal in a False Light

Portrayal in a false light occurs when someone spreads wrong information about a person that reasonably can be considered offensive or objectionable. False light overlaps with defamation, but a key difference is that plaintiffs claiming false light can seek damages for emotional harm caused.[35] A Southwest Airlines gate agent sued a customer for social media complaints that the agent felt cast her in a false light. The customer, Natalie Grant-Herms, ranted heartily on Twitter and Facebook when not allowed to board a flight at the same time as her young children:

> Nashville. Gate A25. Flight to Denver. Her name is Jennifer. She said "get over it. Follow the rules. Or don't fly."

> She has done this to me before. She has the WORST customer service . . .

Southwest's customer service staff apparently defused the situation as indicated in later tweets by Grant-Herms:

> Well, we've caused quite a stir, tweeps. @southwestair just called me. I appreciate their concern & prompt attention 2 the problem.

> I've got wifi on my flight. I'm impressed with how quickly @southwestair responded to my complaint. I'll keep u posted as to what they do.[36]

However, the gate agent, Jennifer Patterson, was not appeased, and she sued Grant-Herms. Patterson lost her case in a lower court but appealed. While the appeals court agreed with the lower court that Patterson did not have a case for defamation, it concluded that Patterson did have a case for false light invasion of privacy:

> We believe that a reasonable person could find, under the entire circumstances of the incident, that Ms. Grant-Herms' posting of selective facts placed Ms. Patterson in a false light by implying that Ms. Patterson was rude and a bad service agent, one who was more concerned with adherence to the airline rules and procedures than the welfare of the child, and that these implications caused injury to her.[37]

Voices from the Field

Cayce Myers

CAYCE MYERS is an assistant professor in the Department of Communication at Virginia Tech where he teaches public relations. His research focuses on laws and regulations affecting public relations practice. Dr. Myers holds a Ph.D. in mass communication from the University of Georgia, Henry W. Grady College of Journalism and Mass Communication, an LL.M. from the University of Georgia School of Law, and a J.D. from Mercer University Walter F. George School of Law. He is also the legal research editor for the Institute for Public Relations.

Justice Stephen Breyer has written about how new "global realities" are changing the way we approach law and that our "judicial awareness" must extend beyond borders more than ever before. What does that mean for public relations?

Public relations practice is increasingly international, and large companies and PR firms usually have offices spanning the globe. Because of this, practitioners need to be aware that their work may be subject to other countries' laws. In the United States there are specific protections given to corporate speech, commercial speech, intellectual property and privacy that are not found outside the United States. Given the diversity of laws that affect public relations it is important for practitioners to think globally when they produce content of any kind.

What's one of the most common legal mistakes new public relations practitioners tend to make?

We live in a society where social media and mobile technology are everywhere. New public relations practitioners may not realize that sharing, posting and messaging can have legal consequences. For example, using intellectual property of another for promotional purposes without permission can lead to expensive and unnecessary lawsuits. In addition, because tweets, posts and sharing can be done in a matter of seconds, there is a misperception that this content is not really important. However, words, no matter how few or seemingly unimportant, can be the basis for a lawsuit.

How about senior public relations professionals—what legal pitfalls should they watch out for?

The biggest issue for senior practitioners is keeping current on new laws affecting public relations. Well-established legal doctrines, such as defamation, copyright, trademark and trade secrets, are now being applied to new media. While this does not necessarily represent a change in core legal tenets, new applications of the law may not be obvious to seasoned practitioners. There are also major changes in agency regulations of new media. These changes represent only the beginning of what is sure to become a major recalibration of older laws and regulations to fit the contours of new media.

The rise of social media has led to a big increase in sharing others' information. It also has provided more space for public relations people to communicate less formally with publics. Will legal concerns eventually put a damper on these trends?

There is recognition that social media platforms have power, and some entities have attempted to restrict access and use. However, as recent decisions by the National Labor Relations Board show, organizations will have a difficult time restricting use of social media by employees, though content regulation has increased for promotional material. In effect, these new laws mandate greater amounts of authenticity, transparency and honesty—all of which should be embraced by PR practitioners.

In writing social media policies, can organizations really limit what employees say or require them to obtain approval before posting?

Like many things in law the answer to this depends on the circumstances. If a social media account is owned by the organization then limits can be set on what can be posted. However, regulation of private accounts of employees is very restrained. The National Labor Relations Board has struck down social media policies that require employees to get pre-approval from managers before posting about workplace grievances. However, straightforward, well-written policies can survive legal scrutiny. For instance, employers can prohibit employees from engaging in harassment, disclosure of trade secrets, or posting their intellectual property. The bottom line is organizations can regulate social media speech in limited circumstances, but employees do not forfeit their speech rights because they work for a specific organization.

Public relations people and lawyers—at times they've had a rocky relationship. How are they doing these days? Are they getting along any better (or worse) than they used to?

There will probably always be some level of disagreement between lawyers and public relations people because each profession has a different perspective. Lawyers are trained to be risk adverse and sometimes have to deny allegations or risk further legal exposure. Communication of any kind, even if it is good PR, can also become evidence that is used against an organization at trial. Conversely, public relations practitioners are communicators. They value transparency, honesty and fostering relationships with key publics. Practitioners recognize that winning in the court of public opinion can be as important, if not more important, than winning in a court of law. Because of these perspectives there is a natural tension between lawyers and PR practitioners. However, some of the best PR and legal strategy comes when practitioners and lawyers work together. The truth is that PR practitioners and lawyers need each other to best serve the needs of their clients.

Ethics: Safeguarding Confidences— Who Owns Your Social Networks?

At this point in your life, you have probably heard the saying that just because something is legal doesn't make it ethical. As a public relations professional, privacy is one area in which you may need more than a legal interpretation to make ethical decisions. Safeguarding confidences is a core principle in the PRSA Code of Ethics, which states, "Client trust requires appropriate protection of confidential and private information."[38] The principle applies not just to clients, but also to the privacy rights of other individuals internal to and external to your organization.

In business law, a **trade secret** is information that is not generally known to others and not readily available to others who could profit from its disclosure or use.[39] As much as public relations ethics focus on disclosure and public information, these values of openness must be balanced with other values including competition and privacy. Trade secrets may include recipes, business processes, research methods, or the formula for a product like WD-40 (named for its "water displacement" function discovered by researchers on their 40th try[40]). How about your social network on Facebook or LinkedIn? Would you ever consider that a trade secret? And if so, do you think that information could be owned by anyone besides you?

According to some courts, yes, social media accounts can be considered trade secrets when those accounts contain client lists or valuable information about customers. Professor Cayce Myers serves as research editor for

Trade secret
Business information that is not generally known to the public and not readily available to others who could profit from its disclosure or use.

A LinkedIn network could be considered one of an organization's "trade secrets."

How can public relations professionals ethically balance personal and professional uses of social networks?

the Institute for Public Relations (IPR) in the area of public relations law. Myers believes that because some accounts on social media contain abundant information about clients and customers, they could conceivably be considered "trade secrets." Myers writes, "If an employee can take these connections with them to a new job or startup they have a competitive advantage to steal valuable clients from their old employer."[41] Myers advises that public relations people keep personal and professional social media accounts separate as much as possible.

So, legally, organizations can claim ownership of an employee's social media accounts in certain circumstances. But many organizations encourage employees to use their own voices and networks in opening and maintaining dialogue with publics, including clients and customers. The first chapter of this book cited Arthur Page's principles of public relations management to advocate for allowing employees to speak with their own authentic voices and to follow Page's principle that a "company's true character is expressed by its people."[42] Is it ethical for organizations to encourage employees to work their networks on social media but then to turn around and claim corporate ownership of those networks and relationships? Is it right to treat someone's social interactions as "trade secrets" in the name of safeguarding confidences?

Myers offers advice that makes sense from both a legal and ethical standpoint: Make sure to clarify expectations. If organizations offer employees reasonable social media policies including details of who owns what accounts, misunderstandings can be avoided. Employees will know which social media interactions are "private" as in personally private and which are "private" as in organizationally owned "trade secrets."

In Case You Missed It

Social media have been called the Wild West of the internet, a place where participants make up the rules as they go. While it is true that technology often advances faster than the law, these legal principles still apply.

- Obtain permission (or seek legal counsel) before publicly discussing private information about any current or past employee.

- If you work for a public figure, the standard for claiming libel is much higher than if you represent a private citizen.

- When you share someone else's intellectual property without permission or proper attribution, you may run the risk of legal trouble.

- The key to avoiding plagiarism is proper attribution. Give credit where credit is due!

- Balance enthusiastic participation with respect for intellectual property; use caution when posting anything that may be seen as offensive or illegal.

- When in doubt about your ownership rights of social media content, check the provider's terms of service.

- Even with the best intentions, obtain consent before publicizing anyone on social media.

SUMMARY

11.1 Discuss the importance of understanding national laws in international contexts.

The internet has opened borders for online marketplaces to offer goods, services and ideas more than ever before. Trends in globalization have led to a great deal more international exchange, and this means that the laws of any one country such as the United States must be interpreted in a more global context. As Justice Stephen Breyer put it, "Judicial awareness can no longer stop at the border."

11.2 Describe limits to free speech, including libel and slander.

Rights to free speech may be limited when they infringe on others' rights or someone else's reputation, intellectual property, financial interests or privacy. Slander and libel are both forms of defamation, which is any statement that injures someone's reputation. Slander refers to spoken communication, while libel refers to written or recorded communication that can be reproduced and shared repeatedly.

11.3 Describe common types of intellectual property and how they are protected.

Intellectual property includes writing, inventions, logos, images or designs, and all sorts of combinations thereof. These forms of intellectual property can be claimed and protected with copyrights, registered trademarks and patents. Creative Commons licenses allow content creators to designate the specific types of permissions they wish to allow.

11.4 Summarize the role of public relations professionals in providing public information.
Public relations people who work for publicly funded or government organizations in the United States are responsible for making information available to citizens under the Freedom of Information Act and various open-records laws (i.e., sunshine laws). Although there are some exceptions, most information that the government collects and uses in the United States is treated as public information and must either be offered when requested or proactively made available in a useful format. Interactive online technologies have facilitated the latter.

11.5 Identify federal agencies that influence and regulate the business of public relations.
Depending on your area of public relations, you will need to become familiar with various government agencies that are responsible for protecting your key publics. The FTC regulates all types of consumer products and services including the promotion of these products and services. The FDA regulates food and health-related industries. The SEC regulates financial information.

11.6 Analyze legal and ethical concerns related to privacy and handling confidential information in public relations.
Safeguarding confidences is a core principle in the PRSA Code of Ethics. The principle applies not just to organizations and clients, but also to the privacy rights of individuals internal to and external to an organization. Competing values in privacy cases mean that public relations people have to consider both law and ethics. Clarifying expectations about what information is considered proprietary to an organization and what information is private to individuals will help avoid both ethical and legal problems.

DISCUSSION QUESTIONS

1. Describe the last time you entered an exchange (a purchase or exchange of goods, services or ideas) with someone from a different country. What laws applied?

2. Years ago Edward Bernays wanted public relations people in the United States to be licensed like doctors, lawyers and architects. Some opponents of the idea argued that the First Amendment would prohibit such licensure. Why?

3. Identify a piece of your own intellectual property that you would consider publishing online (perhaps a photo, term paper, blog entry, infographic, song or artwork). Select a specific type of Creative Commons license you would apply (see http://creativecommons.org/choose/) and explain why you chose that particular type of license.

4. Would you support a tax increase to hire more public affairs people and develop better technology to make government information more available than it currently is? Why or why not?

5. What's your dream job in public relations? Assume you get the job. Name at least one regulatory agency you would need to know more about and why. (If your answer is "none," explain why your work would not be regulated by any agency.)

6. Again, assume you've landed your dream job in public relations. But your new employer requires you to sign an agreement that any social media accounts you use for any tasks related to your job may be accessed by the company. How would you handle the situation?

KEY TERMS

Actual malice   282
Clear and present danger   278
Copyright   282
Copyright infringement   284
Creative Commons   287
Customer relationship
  management (CRM)   293
Deep link   288
Defamation   280
Fair use   284
Federal Trade Commission (FTC)   291
Food and Drug Administration
  (FDA)   291
Framing   288
Freedom of Information Act (FOIA)   289

Hyperlink   287
Initial public offering (IPO)   291
Insider trading   292
Intellectual property   276
Libel   280
Material information   292
Patent   282
Plagiarism   283
Public figure   281
Securities and Exchange
  Commission (SEC)   291
Slander   280
Sunshine law   289
Trade secret   297
Trademark   282

CHAPTER 12

Issues and Crises

How was one of the most iconic brands in the automobile industry brought to its knees?

KEY LEARNING OUTCOMES

12.1 Analyze responses ranging from advocacy to accommodation in public relations conflict cases.

12.2 Identify stages in the issues life cycle.

12.3 Describe how issues management can prevent or lessen the impact of crises.

12.4 Discuss how traditional media, social media and offline word of mouth interact in the spread of crisis information.

12.5 Assess competing values in ethical conflicts of interest in the context of public relations issues and crises.

RELATED UNIVERSAL ACCREDITATION BOARD COMPETENCY AREAS

2.2 ETHICAL BEHAVIOR • **3.1** ISSUES AND RISK MANAGEMENT • **3.2** CRISIS MANAGEMENT
3.3 COUNSEL TO MANAGEMENT • **5.4** PROBLEM SOLVING AND DECISION MAKING

M uch of this book so far has been about how to conduct public relations as part of a management function that helps organizations meet goals and avert crises. However, even the very best public relations professionals working for the most responsible organizations face issues and crises. Some crises, such as natural disasters, are unavoidable, while other crises are not. One of the toughest jobs in public relations is being called on to help organizations navigate crises they created themselves. Before delving into ways organizations respond to crises, this chapter covers how issues evolve and how issues may be identified and managed proactively to minimize the need for crisis management.

Managing Conflict

"My god they're throwing guitars out there!" Though not quite as legendary as Paul Revere's "The redcoats are coming!" this exclamation from a passenger in the window seat of a United Airlines airplane started a bit of a revolution. Baggage handlers at Chicago's O'Hare International Airport had picked the wrong guy's guitar to toss around. The result was a flashpoint case illustrating the power of individuals to confront large powerful organizations on social media.

After hearing the startling observation from the back of a plane, Dave Carroll and fellow band members of *Sons of Maxwell* looked out to see that, indeed, their instruments were being heaved carelessly by United Airlines luggage handlers. Concerned about his $3,500 Taylor guitar, Carroll immediately brought the issue to the attention of a flight attendant. The flight attendant referred him to a "lead agent" in the terminal who said he needed to talk to another lead agent and dismissed his request before she disappeared into a crowd. Carroll then spoke to a third employee, who referred him to a fourth at his next airport.[1] This all-too-familiar story line of poor customer service goes on and on. Carroll's guitar was smashed, and for nine months he tried and failed to reach an acceptable resolution with the airline.

The narrative was so ridiculous it was almost funny, and so Carroll decided to tap into that sentiment with the YouTube music video "United Breaks Guitars." The video featured a catchy tune and clever lyrics describing the whole experience, and it struck a chord with millions of frustrated passengers. In fact, the video went viral during the summer of 2009. Fifteen million views later, Carroll's bio not only describes him as a singer-songwriter, but also a master storyteller, professional speaker, and social media innovator.

On the other side of the story, United Airlines saw its market value drop $180 million in the four days after Carroll's video was uploaded to YouTube. While a claim that Carroll's social media attack was the main reason for the financial loss would be hard to prove, the damage to the airline's reputation was "undeniable" according to a Huffington Post business report.[2]

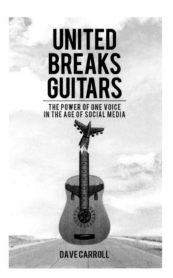

Musician Dave Carroll became famous for launching a musical protest on social media with his YouTube hit "United Breaks Guitars."

How do social media change the way organizations and customer publics interact in conflict?

Tweet

@HVSVN

Don't fly @BritishAirways. Their customer service is horrendous.

⬆ Promoted by

9/2/13, 7:57 PM

Hasan Syed drew international media attention when he paid to reach 50,000 people with this tweet complaining about British Airways, largely because he was the first customer widely known to have used this tactic.

Would you ever pay for a promoted tweet (or Facebook post or Snapchat story, etc.) to complain about an organization? What would make it worth/not worth the cost?

United Airlines wasn't the first airline to feel the impact of social media in managing issues, conflicts and crises. And it certainly wouldn't be the last. In 2013, Twitter user Hasan Syed slammed British Airways for losing his luggage. His tweets reached a mere 400 followers, which in most cases would have been the end of the story. However, then Syed paid $1,000 for another 50,000 users to see the tweets as part of Twitter's promoted tweets advertising service. In doing so, he demonstrated the power of paid advertising as a social media tactic available to individuals.[3] Although Syed paid for the promoted tweets, his investment went much further than the 50,000 exposures delivered by Twitter when international media such as *Time*, *The Guardian*, *BBC*, *Mashable*, *The Australian* and *NBC News* picked up the story.

Beyond airlines, any organization with publics online has had to come to terms with a shift of communication power when issues arise. Brandon Stanton, a photographer known for his Humans of New York photography project, declined an offer of $50 per photo from New-York-based fashion powerhouse DKNY to display his work in their stores. When Stanton found out that DKNY had gone ahead and displayed his photos in a store window in Bangkok without his permission, he posted the following on his Facebook page: "I don't want any money. But please REBLOG this post if you think that DKNY should donate $100,000 on my behalf to the YMCA in Bedford-Stuyvesant, Brooklyn."[4]

Recognizing that it was facing both a legal and a public relations issue, DKNY responded with the following statement: "DKNY has always supported the arts and we deeply regret this mistake. Accordingly, we are making a charitable donation of $25,000 to the YMCA in Bedford-Stuyvesant Brooklyn in Mr. Stanton's name."

Stanton accepted the apology: "We are going to take them at their word that it was a mistake, and be happy that this one had a happy ending." Even legal issues can be raised—and settled—on social media.

Respond quickly and appropriately to challenges on social media to prevent issues from becoming crises.

Dave Carroll versus United Airlines. Hasan Syed versus British Airways. Brandon Stanton versus DKNY. Each case presents a conflict that played out on social media and, therefore, played out in the public eye. Managing conflict, especially public conflict, is a major function of public relations. Public relations scholars have studied how public relations people in all sorts of organizations (not just big corporations like airlines and fashion companies) make decisions on how to communicate with publics when two-way relationships become contentious.

To help understand this decision process, University of Missouri Professor Glen Cameron and his colleagues developed a contingency theory of conflict in public relations.[5] A **contingency theory** suggests that the best course of action in any situation depends on the specifics of the situation. In conflict, the action or communication tactic that a public relations person chooses depends on factors internal and external to the organization. Internal factors may include an organization's size, structure and culture, as well as the autonomy of a public relations department within an organization and the level of practitioner experience. External factors may include the threat of litigation, business competition, political support, and the size and power of publics. Contingency theory also describes response

Contingency theory
A theory that proposes that the best course of action in any situation depends on the specifics of the situation.

DKNY displayed a New York photographer's work in this storefront window in Bangkok without his permission. The photographer called DKNY out on Facebook.

Did DKNY handle the situation well by apologizing and donating $25,000 to a charity? Why or why not?

options ranging from **pure advocacy** (firmly pleading the organization's case without compromise) on one side to **pure accommodation** (completely conceding to a public's demands) on the other side. In many cases, social media have given publics greater power relative to organizations. But that doesn't mean public relations people have to always accommodate publics, nor do they always have to go to battle and advocate hard on one side of an issue.

United Airlines and DKNY had to consider very different contingencies. If you have ever actually read all the fine print in an airline passenger contract, you'd probably *not* be surprised to learn that United Airlines did *not* have to reimburse Carroll. In contrast, DKNY faced a legitimate legal challenge based on Stanton's claim to intellectual property. United Airlines customer service agents had no reason to believe that Carroll would find an audience of millions for his complaint (especially on YouTube in 2009). DKNY likely realized that Stanton already had quite a following on Facebook and other social media.

The two organizations also offered very different levels of accommodation. United Airlines pretty much refused to accommodate Dave Carroll, while DKNY accommodated Brandon Stanton by apologizing and offering a $25,000 charity donation. Although the case had a happier ending for DKNY than it did for United Airlines, this doesn't mean that more accommodation is always better. In fact, that's the point of contingency theory. Sometimes you should advocate, and other times it makes more sense to accommodate.

> Sometimes it's better to advocate rather than to accommodate.

Continuum of options for managing issues and conflict, according to contingency theory.

Case Study

Is the Customer Always Right? . . . A Big Win for Little Italy

Contingency theory reminds us that firm edicts, such as "The customer is always right," are sometimes just too simple. When an angry customer called Little Italy Restaurante in Anchorage, Alaska, to complain about a delivery driver, owner P.J. Gialopsos advocated for her employee rather than accommodating the customer.[6]

The driver, who has a speech impediment and autism, delivered the wrong order, leading the customer to complain irately, use foul language and accuse the driver of being on drugs. When the driver returned to the restaurant, he was visibly upset and reported that the customer had called him names and belittled him. Instead of apologizing and accommodating the customer, Gialopsos opted to "fire" the customer. She told her staff to refuse calls and to not deliver to the customer's address.

Gialopsos said later in an interview that this wasn't the first time a customer had called about the driver, but that normally when she explained the situation, customers were understanding. Acknowledging the driver's disability, she described him as a hard worker and successful university student with a good sense of humor. "So (the driver) is a little awkward socially—gee whiz—that doesn't give you a right to call him a foul name and make his day miserable," said Gialopsos. A few days after the incident, she posted about it on Facebook. The post went viral. Within two days, the post had 14,000 likes and more than 15,000 comments. Gialopsos, the driver and the driver's family were delighted with the overwhelmingly positive feedback. For example, a Facebook post from Judy Berry read:

> So proud of Anchorage's own Little Italy Restaurante & its owner P.J. Gialopsos for standing up for her employee. How refreshing to see her stance that perhaps "the customer isn't always right" when they berate an employee with development disabilities. Thank you also to Little Italy for shining a spotlight on Autism & for hiring people whom others may not![7]

Interestingly, Gialopsos said she did not notice any substantial increase in business immediately following the incident.[8] Was the Facebook love enough to consider this case a public relations "win"? Was advocacy the right strategy here given the circumstances? In deciding to advocate for her employee instead of accommodating the customer, many internal and external

Remember, the customer may not always be right.

Little Italy Restaurante owner P.J. Gialopsos chose to advocate for her employee instead of accommodating an unhappy customer.

What contingencies (i.e., internal and external factors) made her approach to the conflict right or wrong?

contingencies were at play. How do the contingencies in this case compare to what the public relations staff of large, complex organizations like United Airlines or British Airways face when they receive a customer complaint?

You will probably never see a YouTube video of an airline passenger singing about his luggage that arrived undamaged or a viral Facebook campaign celebrating a company for attaining proper permissions for artwork. Most small business owners won't get 15,000 hits and national media attention for sticking up for their employees. In fact, the vast majority of issues will not rise to the level of a major public issue or crisis. It's also important to remember that customers are only one type of public with which we maintain relationships. Perhaps the best public relations "crises" are the ones that never happen, meaning that full-blown crises are averted with effective communication and issues management—not just with customers, but with all publics.

Managing Issues

Organizations face all sorts of issues that can develop into crises, if they are not managed appropriately. **Issues management** is an area of public relations that focuses on proactive monitoring and management to prevent crises from happening.[9]

Issues Life Cycle

In order to manage issues, you must first be able to identify them. The earlier you uncover an issue, the more options you will likely have for dealing with a situation. Issues management scholars have outlined several stages in the issue life cycle:

1. *Early/potential:* when a few people begin to become aware of possible problems
2. *Emerging:* when more people begin to notice and express concern
3. *Current/crisis:* when the negative impact on an organization becomes public and pressure on the organization builds
4. *Dormant:* when the organization has no choice but to accept the long-term consequences

The longer an issue exists without being addressed, the more entrenched publics become in their opposition and the fewer options for strategic response are available to organizations.[10]

Monitor social media to uncover issues sooner and give you more options for dealing with a situation.

Issues management
Systematic process whereby organizations work to identify and resolve issues before they become crises.

Case Study

The Issue Life Cycle of Volkswagen's Dieselgate

Volkswagen's diesel emissions scandal, dubbed "dieselgate" by some and "the diesel dupe" by others, provides an example of how an issue can grow into a full-blown crisis with major consequences.

EARLY/POTENTIAL

At the earliest stages, issues are often identified first by experts or specialists who pay close attention to small changes in the internal or external environments of organizations. When these experts or specialists perceive a potential problem and people within an organization begin planning to respond in some way, the issue has entered the *early/potential* stage.

In 2012, Arvind Thiruvengadam, an assistant professor at West Virginia University, and a few of his colleagues won a grant from the International Council on Clean Transportation (ICCT) to test the environmental friendliness and fuel efficiency of diesel cars. As part of their research, Thiruvengadam and his team ran emissions tests on a 2012 Volkswagen Jetta and a 2013 VW Passat. In the decade prior, Volkswagen's marketing message had emphasized "clean diesel."[11] Therefore, Thiruvengadam and his team expected to find that these two VW models, which were designed for sale in the United States would run cleaner than cars sold in other countries with more lax emission standards. Instead, the researchers were surprised to find that the two VWs emitted significantly higher levels of pollutants.

In May 2014, the ICCT alerted the Environmental Protection Agency (EPA) and the California Air Resources board about the unexpected findings. At this point, Volkswagen had a *potential* issue. In fact, it was later revealed that people inside the company had known about the emission problem since 2005, so the early/potential stage for this issue lasted nearly ten years. Corporate culture likely played a big role in the case. In exploring the role of Volkswagen's management in the circumstances leading to the crisis, *The New York Times* described the company's corporate culture as "confident, cutthroat and insular."[12]

EMERGING

In the emerging stage, groups begin to form and take sides on an issue. In their book *Risk Issues and Crisis Management in Public Relations*, Michael Regester and Judy Larkin describe the emerging phase as a time when industry insiders, specialist media, professional interest groups, activist organizations or any other publics with direct interest, begin to notice and to voice concerns or opinions.[13] Media attention may be sporadic in this stage, but if public relations people are monitoring the media, including specialty media like blogs and trade publications, they still may have an opportunity to intervene and begin to formulate plans for action. As mentioned previously, the more an issue develops, the fewer options there are available for proactive management both internally and externally.

There was very little media attention for several months after the fuel efficiency researchers published their results. Volkswagen denied there was a problem and offered other explanations for why results from the road tests did not meet the expected standards.[14] Meanwhile, regulators continued to investigate. The issue was *emerging*.

CURRENT/CRISIS

In the current/crisis stage, the issue matures, and pressure builds as the impact of the issue on the organization becomes clear. Public relations people have very little control of the situation at this stage. Strategy options become mainly reactive. According to Regester and Larkin, issues become enduring and pervasive in the current stage. They increase in intensity. In September 2015, the EPA publicly accused VW of using "defeat devices" hidden in its diesel cars that manipulated the results of emissions tests. Basically, the devices were software designed to detect when cars were undergoing an emissions test and then improve performance accordingly.[15] Volkswagen had been caught cheating.

On September 21, 2015, Volkswagen Group of America's chief executive Michael Horn had to use what should have been an occasion to celebrate—the company's launch event for its 2016 Passat—to issue an apology instead. "Our company was dishonest, with the EPA and the California Air Resources board, and with all of you, and in my German words, we have totally screwed up," Horn told the Brooklyn, New York, audience. "We have to make things right, with the government, the public, our customers, our employees and also very important, our dealers." Volkswagen was amidst a crisis that had spun well beyond its control.

Consider for a moment how you would feel if you owned one of the approximately 10,000 affected cars in the United States sold by Volkswagen (e.g., VWs, Audis or Porsches). You've chosen to invest in what you believe to be smart, environmentally friendly technology, only to learn that your now highly devalued car emits "up to nine times the legal limit of smog-produced nitrogen oxide pollutants."[16] Is it safe to say you'd be, um, peeved?

Now think of how dealers and employees felt, not to mention the governments and regulators who were deliberately deceived. When an organization has damaged relationships like this with so many key publics, it is clearly in *crisis* mode. In Volkswagen's case, all they could do at this point was react to a series of painful consequences as they unfolded:

"We have totally screwed up," announced Volkswagen Group of America's chief executive Michael Horn in September 2015.

If you were an owner of one of the cars (or maybe you are) affected in "diesel dupe," what could Volkswagen do "to make things right"?

- The company admitted that 11 million of its diesel cars had been "rigged to fool emissions tests," going back to 2005 when it began focusing major marketing efforts on selling diesel cars in the United States.[17]

- Volkswagen chief executive Martin Winterkorn resigned on September 23, 2015.

- By September 25, 2015, Volkswagen stock had plummeted more than 50 percent below its 52-week high in March 2015.[18]

- The value of used VW and Audi diesels fell more than 13 percent in the month following the EPA announcement.[19]

- By late October 2015, more than 350 U.S. lawsuits against Volkswagen had been filed, and legal experts expected many of those suits to be consolidated into mass class action suits. Volkswagen reportedly had set aside $7.3 billion to prepare for the fallout from the crisis, no doubt including the millions of vehicle recalls.[20]

Following its diesel crisis, Volkswagen became the target of the brandalism movement (e.g., www.brandalism.org.uk) as part of a protest campaign tied to international climate change talks.

How could Volkswagen have responded (if at all)?

- The company faced the likelihood of regulatory action following investigation from governments across the globe, including Germany, France, Australia, India, China, the European Union, South Korea and Sweden—just about any country where the diesel cars were sold.

- At the end of 2015, Hans-Dieter Pötsch, chairman of Volkswagen's supervisory board, said in a press conference that an organizational climate of poor ethical standards was partly to blame, and "there was a tolerance for breaking the rules."[21]

DORMANT

According to Regester and Larkin, an issue reaches the *dormant* stage when an organization comes to terms with the consequences.[22] This does not mean, however, that the issue is over and gone. Rather, this means that the organization has had to accept, and live with, the consequences of its actions (or inaction). In June 2016 the company agreed to pay up to $14.7 billion to settle claims with U.S. regulators and individual owners in a class action lawsuit.[23] (Final approval of the settlement was still pending as of this writing, as Volkswagen continued to struggle with international fallout.)

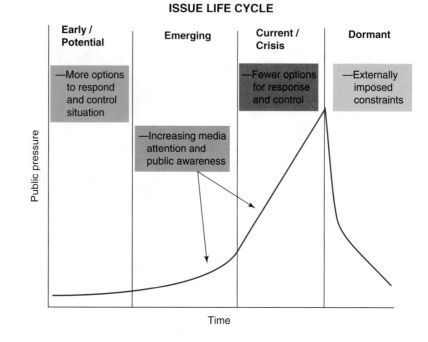

ISSUE LIFE CYCLE

This illustration of the issue life cycle shows how public pressure builds over time as an issue moves from potential to emerging to current/crisis.

Is the Volkswagen dieselgate issue "dormant" now? What role did media coverage play?

Proactive Issues Management

Now that we've seen how organizations can get into trouble, let's look at how they can work to prevent issues from turning into crises. Regester and Larkin have outlined a seven-step process for proactive issues management: (1) monitoring, (2) identification, (3) prioritization, (4) analysis, (5) strategic planning, (6) implementation and (7) evaluation.[24] Notice how these seven steps run parallel to the four-step RPIE process presented earlier in this text (Table 12.1).

TABLE 12.1 OVERLAP BETWEEN RPIE AND PROACTIVE ISSUES MANAGEMENT

FOUR-STEP PROCESS FOR PUBLIC RELATIONS (RPIE)	SEVEN-STEP PROCESS FOR PROACTIVE ISSUES MANAGEMENT
RESEARCH	Monitoring Identification
PLANNING	Prioritization Analysis Strategic Planning
IMPLEMENTATION	Implementation
EVALUATION	Evaluation

1. Monitoring

The first step to avoiding crises is to continuously monitor your organization's internal and external operating environments. What is being said about your organization offline, on social media and in traditional media? Listen carefully at meetings and events, systematically pay attention to internal and external communications, formally and informally analyze media content (including social media) and keep lines of communication open with opinion leaders. Remember that it is just as important to listen to your organization's detractors as it is to listen to supporters. The methods for research outlined in Chapter 5— primary and secondary, quantitative and qualitative, formal and informal—are all ways to monitor the environment. Your goal is to find any early, potential or emerging issues and turn them into opportunities instead of crises.

> It's just as important to listen to detractors as it is to listen to supporters.

One example of systematic monitoring is the practice of **responsible supply chain management**, which occurs when organizations carefully monitor all stages of production and distribution to ensure that working conditions are safe, wages are fair and that generally high ethical standards of social and environmental responsibility are maintained. This helps organizations avoid public relations crises of the type Nike and Gap faced in the 1990s and 2000s when news broke that their supply chains included child labor and sweatshops.[25]

2. Identification

Once you notice an issue, you'll need to be able to describe it and determine if it is something significant or just a random blip on the radar. Think about financial data. Company stock values rise and fall every day, but that does not mean that every time a company's stock value falls that the organization faces a crisis. Instead, analysts watch data over time and in a broader context to identify trends. Is the daily dip in stock prices part of a larger pattern? Are there other factors in the environment such as legal challenges, competitor activity, potential boycotts or broader political and economic changes that suggest a trend that needs further attention?

Identifying issues works the same way. Even in a small organization, you have to assess the environment and look for patterns. In a student organization, you might pay close attention to meeting attendance numbers or data on new applications to identify issues with membership. A nonprofit might compare year-end or holiday donations from year to year in the context of trends in competition. The website www.yourmembership .com notes that increased competition is becoming a more common issue for established nonprofits as smaller nonprofits use social media to compete with established organizations for both funds and volunteers.[26]

3. Prioritization

Most organizations have issues. A big part of the *management* in *issues management* is deciding which issues require resources and when.

Responsible supply chain management
Careful monitoring of product production and distribution to ensure that generally high ethical standards of social and environmental responsibility are maintained.

producebunny
@producebunny

#Chipotle should pay more attention to food safety than hyping anti-GMOs. Foodborne pathogens are deadlier than GMOs

A FAREWELL TO GMOs

When it comes to our food, genetically modified ingredients don't make the cut.

CHIPOTLE.COM/GMO

4:37 PM - 10 Nov 2015

↰ ⇄ ♥ ...

This Twitter user faulted Chipotle for not prioritizing its issues well.

How should Chipotle balance its attention to the two issues of GMOs and food-borne illnesses?

Prioritizing issues means weighing the potential scope and impact of each. When investigating an active E. coli outbreak in the United States, the Centers for Disease Control and Prevention (CDC) released a report that linked 53 illnesses in nine states with 47 people who said they had eaten at a Chipotle restaurant. Twenty people were hospitalized.[27] Chipotle was then criticized by some for paying more attention to GMO issues (see Chapter 7) than the more immediate issue of restaurant food-safety procedures.

4. Analysis

Once issues have been identified and prioritized, they need to be analyzed to determine how they might affect the organization and its publics. Chipotle expected that same-store sales would fall 8–11 percent in the quarter following the E. coli outbreak.[28] Volkswagen's sales dropped 24.7 percent after its diesel crisis. Volkswagen sold 23,882 cars in November 2015 compared to 31,725 cars in November 2014.[29] Of course, issues management, and public relations in general, is about much more than sales. Analysis should include all sorts of publics besides customers. How, specifically, will employees be affected? Will they have to work longer hours? Earn less pay? Will they face public criticism? If you work for a nonprofit organization, you may analyze an issue's impact on volunteers and donors. In a college or university, you would consider students, faculty, staff and alumni. Each public will have its own specific concerns related to the issue.

5. Strategic Planning

After research and analysis, including the identification of key publics and how the issue will affect them, you can begin developing communication and relationship management strategies for each. If your role in public relations gives you a voice in the management of the organization (let's hope so!), you can work on both the strategic action response to the issue and the messages that will be communicated in conjunction with that response. For example, on the same day that the CDC released one of its key reports about the E. coli outbreak, Chipotle announced new food-safety procedures that it had developed, including improved programs for training employees for safer food handling.[30] Strategy at this stage means considering the specific actions that should be taken as well as whom should take these actions, when and with what resources. Even if the management plan is developed outside of the public relations department (Chipotle worked with an outside consulting group to develop its new safety procedures), your communication plan must be coordinated with those management operations. Such strategy involves goals, objectives, timelines and budgets, as outlined in Chapter 6 on planning.

Ensure your communication plan matches the crisis response action plan, even if the response plan was developed outside of the public relations department.

6. Implementation

Implementation includes both action and communication. This is where policies and programs are put into action, and you activate owned, paid, shared and earned media (Chapter 7). In issues management, the underlying purpose of implementation is to prevent negative outcomes and encourage beneficial ones. In response to sweatshop and child labor problems that arose in the 1990s and persisted well into the 2000s, both Nike and Gap began funneling considerable resources into preventing further supply chain issues. Nike and Gap now tout their efforts on websites that they host to draw attention to their corporate social responsibility efforts. Nike's site (www.nikeresponsibility .com) includes detailed reports, interactive maps of factory locations, and infographics listing performance goals and progress toward reaching those targets.

Socially responsible management also can be leveraged by organizations of any size to recruit and retain top talent. Millennials regularly report that engaging in socially responsible work is a big draw for employment.[31]

7. Evaluation

In the evaluation stage, you assess the results, just as you would with any other public relations strategy (Chapter 8). If you're working with clearly articulated goals and objectives from your strategy, you will be able to measure the beneficial outcomes. However, many of the most important results of issues management stem from the crises *prevented*, or negative outcomes averted. These kinds of outcomes can be harder to measure with certainty because they are based on speculation about what might have occurred had the issue not been managed properly. Think of all the car companies that have not cheated (and been caught) on emissions tests. Think of all the restaurants that have *not* had E. coli outbreaks, or the student groups that maintained membership despite changes in leadership, or the nonprofits that rode out bad slumps in the economy, and so on. In some cases, alternate models can be used to illustrate what would have happened if a crisis occurred and had been managed poorly. And this is a happy outcome! Managers, experts and others with deep knowledge of an organization and its day-to-day and year-to-year options will appreciate knowing they avoided a boycott, illness outbreak, bankruptcy, product recall, lawsuit, embarrassing media scandal or any

Nike monitors its global business practices and promotes its corporate social responsibility by reporting details on an extensive website.

Is Nike reacting to past crises, practicing proactive issues management, or some combination of the two? What benefits does this bring to the organization?

other potential crisis. What's more important—and this may be the result of either an issue averted or a crisis that played out all the way—is that evaluation allows you to learn lessons from experience and develop strategies for the future. Evaluation of how one issue was managed informs the first efforts of monitoring for the next one.

Crisis Types

Not all crises are preventable, and how organizations respond to crises should depend on the degree to which people attribute responsibility for the crisis to the organization. Public relations scholars Tim Coombs and Sherry Holladay have developed one of the most well-researched and practical theories for crisis management called **situational crisis communication theory (SCCT)**. SCCT is a contingency theory because it suggests that how organizations should respond to crises depends on the situation. Coombs defines an **organizational crisis** as "a significant threat to organizational operations or reputations that can have negative consequences for stakeholders and/or the organization if not handled properly."[32] When people think that an organization is responsible for a crisis (e.g., Volkswagen), its reputation suffers, and the crisis leads to more anger, less purchase intent and greater likelihood of negative word of mouth about the organization. While issues management focuses on how to prevent organizational crises, crisis management deals with how to repair damage and rebuild reputation.[33]

Situational crisis communication theory (SCCT)
Theory that proposes effective crisis communication entails choosing and applying appropriate response strategies depending on how much responsibility for the crisis is attributed to the organization by key publics.

Organizational crisis
A major threat to an organization's operations or reputation.

Who's to blame? That is the question at the heart of initial crisis assessment. Researchers have identified three main groups of crisis types: (1) victim crises, (2) accident crises and (3) preventable crises.

Victim Crises

When publics see the organization as a victim, they assign minimal responsibility for the crisis to the organization. Natural disasters such as hurricanes, tsunamis and earthquakes are prime examples. People outside of an organization can cause victim crises too, such as cases of sabotage, terrorism or product tampering.

One of the most famous examples of crisis management in the history of public relations stemmed from a victim crisis that arose because of product tampering by someone from outside an organization. In 1982, news broke that six adults and one 12-year-old girl in the Chicago area had died from cyanide poisoning after taking capsules of Extra-Strength Tylenol.[34] Since the tampered-with bottles of Tylenol capsules had come from different production facilities but were all purchased in the Chicago area, investigators ruled out sabotage or foul play at Tylenol factories. Police suspected that someone had purchased the bottles from local stores, poisoned the capsules, and then returned the products to store shelves. The murderer was never caught.

Tylenol's parent company Johnson & Johnson cooperated extensively with news media in expressing sympathy and sharing accurate information about both the crimes and the organization's response. At a cost of more than $100 million Johnson & Johnson quickly pulled more than 30 million bottles of Tylenol from store shelves. They did not return the product to market until months later after developing now-standard tamper-resistant packaging.[35] The combination of quick, ethical action and communication earned the Tylenol case a place in history as an example of "how a major business ought to handle a disaster."[36]

Rumors are another category of victim crises. Social media have accelerated the pace that false, damaging information can be spread. For example, when *The Sacramento Bee* and *Los Angeles Times* reported that the city of Glendale, California, was issuing fines to residents for having brown lawns during a severe drought, the city received loads of angry emails and calls. The original story contained a factual error that sparked the rumor when it identified Glendale—instead of Glendora, California—as the town with the "lawn maintenance" ordinances.[37]

Rumors abound online. Just check the rumor-busting website Snopes.com for daily examples. For example, the NFL did not fine Cam Newton $253,552 for giving away footballs, Pope Francis did not post a selfie to Instagram and UPS isn't using its planes to smuggle illegal immigrants into the United States. Oh, and Oprah Winfrey is not pregnant.

A sample of Extra-Strength Tylenol is presented side-by-side with a sample of cyanide-laced medicine in a medical examiner's office in October of 1982.

Why is this classified as a "victim crisis"? Would Tylenol's response have been different if it were an accident or preventable crisis?

Every time Cam Newton gives a child in the stands a ball he is fined $5,512. To date he has a fine total of $253,552

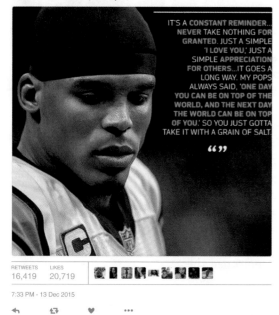

IT'S A CONSTANT REMINDER... NEVER TAKE NOTHING FOR GRANTED. JUST A SIMPLE 'I LOVE YOU,' JUST A SIMPLE APPRECIATION FOR OTHERS...IT GOES A LONG WAY. MY POPS ALWAYS SAID, 'ONE DAY YOU CAN BE ON TOP OF THE WORLD, AND THE NEXT DAY THE WORLD CAN BE ON TOP OF YOU.' SO YOU JUST GOTTA TAKE IT WITH A GRAIN OF SALT.

" "

RETWEETS	LIKES
16,419	20,719

7:33 PM - 13 Dec 2015

Fact-checking site Snopes.com found this Facebook post/tweet to be false—the NFL did not fine Cam Newton $253,552 for giving footballs to children. Notice how many "likes" the post received.

Should the NFL respond? Why or why not?

Accident Crises

Accidents happen. Industrial accidents, mechanical failures or IT crashes could all be considered accidents. In situations like these, an organization may not get a full pass as it would in a victim crisis, because publics still might question the organization's operations. In an industrial accident, were the appropriate safety procedures in place? In a mechanical failure, was the equipment maintained properly? In an information systems crash, were the data backed up in a timely manner? In any of these situations, if people label the source of a crisis as an accident, the amount of responsibility that they attribute to an organization is still relatively low compared to the next category, preventable crises.

Preventable Crises

Consider an airline crash. If investigators determine that an act of terrorism took place, the airline would likely be considered a victim. If, instead, they determine that a mechanical failure was to blame, this could be seen as an accident. If, however, the mechanical failure was due to improper maintenance by the ground crew or a skipped preflight inspection by a pilot, publics would see the crisis as preventable.

Preventable crises caused by mismanagement, illegal activity or unethical action are the worst kind for organizations, and they may be intensified when the organization already has a reputation for breaking rules or a history of similar crises. Urban Outfitters faced outrage from African American community leaders and clergy when it started selling a board game called "Ghettopoly" in its clothing stores in 2003. It included characters with intentionally misspelled names like "Malcum X" and "Martin Luthor King Jr." One game card read, "You got yo whole neighborhood addicted to crack. Collect $50."[38] The store stopped selling the game, but continued to offend people with other poor product choices. More than 10 years later, the store offered a "vintage" Kent State sweatshirt for sale online at $129. The sweatshirt was stained blood red, hauntingly reminiscent of (and insensitive to) the 1970 massacre on campus in which four Kent State students were shot and killed by members of the Ohio National Guard. The *Washington Post* noted, "It seems like every few weeks, Urban Outfitters is in the news for some new controversy."[39] Urban Outfitters issued the following apology, which many find difficult to accept given the company's history: "Urban Outfitters sincerely apologizes for any offense our Vintage Kent State Sweatshirt may have caused. It was never our intention to allude to the tragic events that took place at Kent State in 1970 and we are extremely saddened that this item was perceived as such. . . ."

Crisis Response Strategies

In addition to classifying the most common types of organizational crises, Coombs and Holladay offer an outline of crisis response strategies: deny, diminish, rebuild and reinforce. SCCT recommends selecting a response strategy appropriate to the situation.

Deny Strategies

Organizations applying deny strategies aim to absolve themselves of responsibility. They may claim there is no crisis at all or blame another organization or person for the crisis. They may also confront the accuser directly. **Scapegoating** or attacking the accuser is generally not received well by publics. For example, when Chipotle co-CEO Monty Moran appeared to blame the CDC for the intensity of its E. coli crisis by saying that it was "fueled by the sort of unusual and even unorthodox way the CDC has chosen to announce cases related to the original outbreak," *Fortune* Senior Editor Geoff Colvin characterized the response as "how crisis leadership is *not* done."[40]

In other cases, deny strategies might make more sense. The City of Glendale denied newspaper reports that it was issuing tickets to local residents for having brown lawns during a drought. The reports were indeed false, and Glendale officials called out the factual error in reporting on its own "Facts Versus Rumors" web page:[41]

> *The Sacramento Bee incorrectly named the City of Glendale as involved with a Code Enforcement case regarding a browning lawn. The newspaper has since updated the article with the correct name of the city in question. Glendale is not currently issuing citations to residents who have browning lawns but will instead use this time to educate residents and business on how to further conserve water.*

Within an hour of the newspaper's correction, Glendale staff also reposted the corrected article to the city's social media accounts to head off further rumor spreading.

Diminish Strategies

Diminish strategies acknowledge the existence of a crisis, but they minimize the organization's responsibility for the crisis or any bad intentions. The organization may also try to reframe the situation. For example, when state school systems receive media attention for low scores on national standardized tests, they may use a diminish strategy that questions the validity of the tests, claims that the school system is under-resourced compared to other states, or focuses on how hard teachers are working with so little compensation.

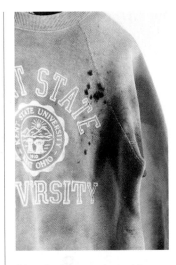

Urban Outfitters apologized for selling this sweatshirt, saying it was not their "intention to allude to the tragic events that took place at Kent State."

Do you believe the apology? Why or why not?

Use your social media accounts to correct rumors and repost corrections made by others.

Scapegoating
Blaming an outside person or organization for a crisis.

Following BP's tragic Gulf of Mexico oil spill, CEO Tony Hayward became the subject of ridicule for saying, "I'd like my life back."

Why might people have responded so negatively to his initial apology?

Rebuild Strategies

Crises test relationships. If the heart of public relations is relationship management, then there is perhaps no greater role for public relations in a crisis than rebuilding relationships. If an organization is responsible for a crisis, one of the most important communications it must issue is a public acceptance of that responsibility. If you realize you've screwed up in an interpersonal relationship and you want to repair the damage, you apologize. The same goes for organization-public relationships.

Apology, accepting responsibility and asking for forgiveness or understanding, is key to your rebuild strategy. That said, we all know that forced apologies come across as fake and insincere. One kid trips another on the playground and laughs. No remorse whatsoever. But then the teacher steps in and forces an apology. The words "I'm sorry" are muttered, but the relationship between the two kids doesn't improve. Adults have the same issues—even CEOs of major companies. When, in 2010, British Petroleum's CEO Tony Hayward stepped in front of a microphone following the largest U.S. marine oil spill ever, he appeared at first to apologize to local communities and families. "I'm sorry. We're sorry for the massive disruption it's caused their lives." But then Hayward delivered one of the most infamous lines in the history of corporate crisis management. "There's no one who wants this over more than I do. I'd like my life back." Hayward later had to issue a statement that apologized for his apology![42]

An apology that doesn't play well can have a **boomerang effect**, causing more damage than it repairs. Domino's faced a crisis when a video of Domino's employees "tampering" with pizzas went viral. The video, which showed a prankster employee in uniform at a Domino's store sticking cheese up his nose and then putting it on a sandwich, received almost 1 million views before it was taken down. AdAge.com dubbed it "Boogergate."[43] Fighting fire with fire, Domino's CEO Patrick Doyle then posted his own YouTube video: a formal apology stating, "We sincerely apologize for this incident."[44] The apology received mixed reviews based on its delivery.[45]

Apology
Act of taking responsibility for an issue or crisis and seeking forgiveness or understanding.

Boomerang effect
Unintended consequence of an apology or other attempt to create positive response results instead in a negative response.

Dear Target Guest,

As you have likely heard by now, Target experienced unauthorized access to payment card data from U.S. Target stores. We take this crime seriously. It was a crime against Target, our team members and most importantly you–our valued guest.

We understand that a situation like this creates stress and anxiety about the safety of your payment card data at Target. Our brand has been built on a 50-year foundation of trust with our guests, and we want to assure you that the cause of this issue has been addressed and you can shop with confidence at Target.

We want you to know a few important things:

- The unauthorized access took place in U.S. Target stores between Nov. 27 and Dec. 15, 2013. Canadian stores and target.com were not affected.
- Even if you shopped at Target during this time frame, it doesn't mean you are a victim of fraud. In fact, in other similar situations, there are typically low levels of actual fraud.
- There is no indication that PIN numbers have been compromised on affected bank issued PIN debit cards or Target debit cards. Someone cannot visit an ATM with a fraudulent debit card and withdraw cash.
- You will not be responsible for fraudulent charges–either your bank or Target have that responsibility.
- We're working as fast as we can to get you the information you need. Our guests are always the first priority.
- For extra assurance, we will offer free credit monitoring services for everyone impacted. We'll be in touch with you soon on how and where to access the service.

Please read the full notice below. And over the coming days and weeks we will be relying on corporate.target.com and our various social channels to answer questions and keep you up to date.

Thank you for your patience, understanding and loyalty to Target!

Gregg Steinhafel

Target sent this letter to customers after experiencing a credit and debit card data breach.

Would you categorize this as an apology?

Relationship management, as discussed throughout this text, is about both communication and action. Apologies go a lot further when they are backed up with behavior. Doyle's YouTube apology continued, "We thank members of the online community who quickly alerted us and allowed us to take immediate action. Although the individuals in question claim it's a hoax, we are taking this incredibly seriously."[46] Domino's shut down the store where the incident happened, opened a Twitter account for consumer

Compensation
Crisis response strategy of offering products, services or money to help make amends with publics.

Bolstering
Attempting to offset reputational damage to an organization during a crisis by emphasizing the good work that the organization has done in the past.

inquiries, and worked openly with bloggers and reporters. Social media expert Brian Solis suggested that these rebuild strategies helped keep the crisis for Domino's from becoming even worse.[47]

Compensation is another classic rebuild strategy. Organizations may offer products, services or money to help make amends with publics. When Target experienced a credit card breach, they wrote to the owners of about 40 million credit and debit card accounts to explain the situation and to offer a year of free credit monitoring service.[48] Interestingly, Target did not actually apologize, but they did offer compensation. In thanking customers for their patience, understanding and loyalty, they clearly were pursuing a rebuild strategy.

Reinforce Strategies

Another common response to crises is to reinforce relationships. Reminding people of all the good things your organization has done in the past is one way to reinforce a relationship during or following a crisis. This is called **bolstering**.

Case Study

Bolstering to #Staystrong in the Fight Against Cancer

When world famous cyclist Lance Armstrong was diagnosed with testicular cancer in 1997 at age 25, he started the Lance Armstrong Foundation to raise money to fight cancer. The organization grew fast and became one of the world's most recognizable philanthropic organizations, aided by a partnership with Nike, which honored Armstrong and the foundation with its iconic yellow Livestrong bracelets. Armstrong won seven Tour de France races between 1999 and 2005, and the foundation grew to more than 100 employees with thousands of volunteers. But then crisis hit when Armstrong fell from grace in 2012.

The United States Anti-Doping Agency (USADA) released a report showing a "systemic, sustained and professionalized doping conspiracy" by Armstrong and his cycling team.[49] Armstrong was forced to vacate his cycling titles, and he resigned as chairman of the foundation, which formally changed its name from the Lance Armstrong Foundation to Livestrong. The foundation had some serious bolstering to do. It launched a campaign around the theme "Stillstrong," which was "intended to remind people that the charity is still operational and providing key services to cancer patients."[50] The charity still operates today, constantly reinforcing its mission and story:

LIVESTRONG has served millions of people affected by cancer through collaborative programs and direct support services that fill critical financial, emotional, physical and practical gaps in care. Though Lance is no longer involved with LIVESTRONG, he remains the foundation's single biggest donor. The progress he helped generate within the field of cancer survivorship stands as a lasting legacy.[51]

Ingratiation is another reinforcing strategy. In a crisis, many of an organization's most important relationships are with the people who help to solve the crisis or aid its victims. Thanking first responders, praising volunteers and expressing appreciation to authorities who are involved in the crisis cleanup are ways organizations work to curry favor with key publics. However, as with apology strategies, ingratiation strategies risk backfiring if they are seen as insincere.

Be careful of issuing apologies or applying ingratiation strategies on social media unless they are clearly sincere and authentic.

Social Media and Crises

One of the biggest challenges in managing crises is handling the rapid spread of information and the constant demand for that information. Prior to the rise of social media, crisis managers talked about the importance of the "golden hours"—the first few hours after a surprise crisis breaks—when an organization has its best opportunity to try to get out ahead of crisis communication with accurate information. With social media, those hours are reduced to minutes or even seconds. Social media have increased both the volume and speed of communication in crisis situations and opened new channels for both organizations and publics to communicate. Crisis managers may see social media as a blessing (for communicating quickly and directly with publics) and a curse (for fueling the uncontrolled spread of misinformation and rumors). Recognizing the importance of social media in particular in the ecology of crisis situations, public relations scholars Yan Jin, Brooke Fisher Liu, Julia Daisy Fraustino and their colleagues have developed a **social media crisis communication model (SMCC)** that highlights the interaction among social media, traditional media and word-of-mouth communication in crisis situations. Think for a minute about a recent organizational crisis that you've heard about. How did you receive the information? There's a good chance that all three sources came into play. You may have heard about the crisis in a conversation with friends or family (word of mouth), seen it on TV or read about it in the newspaper (traditional media), and seen it on Twitter, Facebook and so on (social media). SMCC emphasizes

Ingratiation
A type of reinforcing crisis response strategy in which stakeholders are praised or thanked to win their good favor.

Social media crisis communication model (SMCC)
Model describing the role of social media influencers, followers and inactives in spreading information in crisis situations.

Social media creators
Influential social media users who are among the first to identify and post about crises online.

Social media followers
Social media users who receive crisis information from social media creators.

Social media inactives
People who receive crisis information indirectly from social media via traditional media and offline word of mouth.

that these sources are not mutually exclusive. If you learned about a crisis from a friend who used Facebook to repost and comment on a CNN.com article, this is an example of how word of mouth, traditional media and social media sources are all integrated in the crisis communication process.

The SMCC identifies three types of social media users for public relations practitioners to pay attention to during a crisis:

1. Influential **social media creators** are among the first to identify crises online and then post about them.

2. **Social media followers** receive their information from the influential creators.

3. **Social media inactives** receive information from traditional media and offline word of mouth. This does not mean that social media are not involved. Instead, what social media inactives learn offline may be informed by what their sources have learned from social media.

By understanding the relationship among these three sources, public relations professionals can think strategically about how an organization communicates during a crisis.

In most cases, it is good practice for the crisis team to centralize the flow of information. For example, a FEMA training manual instructs, "The need to control information released to the media and public requires that the crisis plan clearly designate the person or persons responsible for this function."[52] Historically, these sources would operate with tactics such as periodic press conferences or conference calls that enabled the organization to communicate consistently and accurately with the news media. This is still common practice. Today, however, those news media then report breaking news via print, radio and television, as well as via social media platforms. SMCC describes one process whereby news media act as influential social media creators who share breaking news with followers on social media in addition to reaching social media inactives with traditional outlets like radio, TV and newspapers.

SMCC also outlines another process for the spread of information in which the organization itself acts as a social media creator, as when companies set up new Twitter accounts for crisis-specific updates and inquiries. While it's difficult to think of anything either controlled or "centralized" about the wildly crowd-fueled nature of how major crises break on social media, this doesn't mean public relations people can't play an important role in the process. As representatives with inside knowledge of the latest news related to the crisis, public relations people have the option of becoming influential social media creators. In that role they can work to communicate accurate and useful information directly with followers and indirectly with inactives.

Make yourself and your organization "influential social media creators," by setting up and maintaining crisis-specific social media accounts.

Voices from the Field

Barry Finkelstein

BARRY FINKELSTEIN is senior vice president and associate director of public relations for Luquire George Andrews, a leading advertising, PR and digital marketing firm based in Charlotte, North Carolina. A frequent speaker on such topics as crisis communication, social media and integrated communications planning, Barry has served on the boards of the Georgia and South Carolina Chapters of the Public Relations Society of America. He also chaired the Client PR Committee for the American Association of Advertising Agencies (4A's).

What's the biggest crisis you've ever had to manage? What was the most important thing you learned from it, and what would you do differently if you had another chance?
The one that sticks out to me is the Atlanta school bus drivers' strike in the early '90s, because it impacted thousands of families who were depending on buses to get their kids safely to school. We spent the first few days on defense, doing press briefings a few times each day to let parents know when the buses would be running, or if they'd even be running at all. Around the third day we devised a strategy to use PR to turn the situation in our favor by inviting the news media to cover the hundreds of people who were lining up to apply for positions as replacement bus drivers. The strike literally ended the next day, and that was my big takeaway: I wish we had been more proactive from the outset in using PR to not just manage the crisis, but to try to resolve it.

How do you go about monitoring for emerging issues for clients?
It varies by client. Some are in crisis-prone industries like utility companies or quick-service restaurants, so we have well-defined systems to alert us to internal events like robberies or fires, while also relying on traditional and social media monitoring to stay aware of any negative stories that are breaking. And for all of our clients, we stay abreast of trends and issues in their respective industries by monitoring traditional and social media for keywords tied to potential issues.

How are social media changing the way practitioners manage issues and crises? How is it easier with social media? Harder?
Social media have transformed the nature of crisis communications. News—and misinformation, in particular—now travels at the speed of light. Through social media, organizations are able to communicate with their most important publics in real time and without the editorial filter of the news media, which can be very advantageous in the event of a crisis. However, this also means organizations have a responsibility to be accurate and transparent in communications. Perhaps even more important, organizations have an opportunity to use social media to *listen* to audiences and publics in a time of crisis, which may help an organization determine what steps and messages will resolve the matter with the least damage to the organization's reputation. But again, organizations must be careful not to squelch social media posts that may be negative toward their brand. It's OK to correct misinformation—and even to manage social media content that is offensive or intentionally misleading—but one of the keys to social media success is to allow publics to feel like their voices are being heard and valued.

What's the biggest crisis you've ever averted? And what did you do to avoid it?
Years ago I worked with a behavioral health system that was under investigation by "60 Minutes" for practices that were alleged to be a threat to patient safety. They were reluctant to participate in the story, but we knew if they did not participate, the story would be one-sided and almost certainly lead to more media and regulatory scrutiny. Ultimately, we persuaded the CEO to be interviewed after intensive media training, and the resulting story was more balanced and greatly minimized any follow-up coverage.

How does someone become a crisis communication expert?
Crisis communications is one of those areas where experience truly is the best teacher. I've been

continues

continued

doing it for more than 20 years, and each episode teaches me something that will allow me to better counsel the next client. There are certainly some basic principles that can be picked up by reading articles and books or attending seminars. But the most important lesson in crisis communications is probably one you learned from your parents: Do unto others as you would have them do unto you. Put yourself in the shoes of the publics who will be most affected by the situation, and chances are you will instinctively know the right things to do and say.

Ethics: Conflicts of Interest

Public relations people are often faced with the challenge of balancing conflicting loyalties among various publics. If conflicts aren't managed well, they can become crises. Some of the most difficult ethical dilemmas that you may face in public relations, however, arise when *you yourself* are one of the parties in a conflict of values involving your organization.

The PRSA Code of Ethics includes the following principle: "Avoiding real, potential or perceived conflicts of interest builds the trust of clients, employers, and the publics."[53] One example of a conflict of interest provided in the code is failing to disclose that you have a major financial interest in a competitor of your organization or client. For example, if you work for Coca Cola, you wouldn't want to own stock in PepsiCo. However, sometimes conflicts of interest are unavoidable. In *Doing Ethics in Media*, Jay Black and Chris Roberts present a particularly sticky example that they developed as a hypothetical case study from real-world, firsthand experiences.[54]

In the scenario, you work as a public relations officer for a big mill operation in a small town that is facing tough economic times. The company has been good to you. They were very generous and supportive when your spouse (also a company employee) died in an accident at the plant a few years back. They've also rewarded your hard work with a series of promotions. You feel a strong sense of loyalty. But that loyalty is seriously tested when, in a meeting with upper management, you learn that the company's long-term plans include major layoffs at your plant. Thousands will lose jobs. You are upset, but the reasons for layoffs are understandable. Environmental problems and economic forces have made the plant's continued operation unsustainable. You're asked to keep the information confidential so the company will not lose its last major contract and set of work orders.

To make matters worse, you have family members who will be impacted in major ways. Your sister works in real estate and is planning to close some big deals on local homes in the area, and you now know the local real estate market is about to tank because of your company, taking those deals down with it. Your brother-in-law works at the company too, as a shift foreman. What do you do?

What makes this decision so difficult? It's the conflict of interest. On one hand you are a loyal employee and representative of the organization and you have accepted the responsibility of safeguarding confidences to lessen the impact of a crisis. On the other hand, you are very close to your sister and her husband, and your close family ties make it even more difficult to ignore the interests and values of the local community as a public with which you are deeply connected.

One tenet of crisis management that may help both the organizational and personal crisis is "Tell it all and tell it fast." Ralph Barney, a founding editor of *Journal of Mass Media Ethics*, offered this in response to an earlier version of this case when it was first published: "A principled response would be to make public the plans the company has for the plant, thereby demonstrating a willingness to serve larger society."[55] In a case like this, "larger society" includes your family and friends in the community. While you may serve as an advocate for your organization, traditional news media and social media influentials will no doubt serve to advocate for the interests of larger society. If these sources get wind of the story before your company is ready to release it (a common occurrence for organizations that try to keep a crisis secret for too long), your organization will be behind the eight ball.

Social media crisis communication theory suggests that your organization can serve as a primary source of information to publics during a crisis if you act fast enough. Crisis communication researchers have applied the term **stealing thunder** to describe this strategy. In law, attorneys are known to "steal thunder" when they expose weaknesses in their own cases and address those weaknesses before their opponents have the opportunity to do so.[56]

Negative information spreads extremely fast in the communication ecosystem of traditional media, social media and word of mouth. But if you work with traditional media and/or act as a social media creator for crisis-related information, it is possible to get ahead of the story and save some people from harm. One possible solution is for the public relations practitioner to apply both crisis communication theory and a deep understanding of the affected publics to make a case to upper management that "telling it all and telling it fast" is a better strategy than prolonged secrecy.

Stealing thunder
Crisis response strategy in which an organization exposes its own problems (and works to address those problems) before opponents have the opportunity to do so.

In Case You Missed It

While classic principles of conflict management, issues management and crisis management still hold, social media have increased options for detection, prevention, response and communication. Social media must be used with a clear understanding of their role in the communication process.

- Respond quickly and appropriately to challenges on social media to prevent issues from becoming crises.

- Sometimes it's better to advocate rather than to accommodate.

- Remember that the customer may not always be right.

- Monitor social media to uncover issues sooner and give you more options for dealing with a situation.

- It's just as important to listen to detractors as it is to listen to supporters.

- Ensure your communication plan matches the crisis response action plan, even if the response plan was developed outside of the public relations department.

- Use your social media accounts to correct rumors and repost corrections made by others.

- Be careful of issuing apologies or applying ingratiation strategies on social media unless they are clearly sincere and authentic.

- Make yourself and your organization "influential social media creators" by setting up and maintaining crisis-specific social media accounts.

SUMMARY

12.1 Analyze responses ranging from advocacy to accommodation in public relations conflict cases.

In conflict, the action or communication tactic that you choose depends on the specifics of the situation. Contingency theory holds that response options range on a continuum from pure advocacy on one side to pure accommodation on the other.

12.2 Identify stages in the issues life cycle.

Stages in the issue life cycle include (1) early/potential, (2) emerging, (3) current/crisis and (4) dormant. As issues grow, publics become more active and an organization's options for proactive management become more limited.

12.3 Describe how issues management can prevent or lessen the impact of crises.

The seven-step process for proactive issues management—
(1) monitoring, (2) identification, (3) prioritization, (4) analysis,

(5) strategic planning, (6) implementation and (7) evaluation—runs parallel to the four-step RPIE process. Actively monitoring the environment with research increases the likelihood of identifying issues early enough to allow for proactive, strategic public relations rather than reactive, constrained damage control.

12.4 Discuss how traditional media, social media and offline word of mouth interact in the spread of crisis information.

Traditional news media are still an important source of information in crises, and—as has always been the case—offline word of mouth interacts with news media as people discuss what they learn from news media and as news media report on issues that people discuss. Social media offer greater opportunities for people to discuss and share information interpersonally (online word of mouth) and new channels for traditional media to reach publics. During a crisis, it is useful to identify (1) influential social media creators, who are among the first to identify and post about crises online, (2) social media followers, who receive their information from the influential creators, and (3) social media inactives, who receive information from traditional media and offline word of mouth. Both traditional media and offline word of mouth may be informed by social media activity.

12.5 Assess competing values in ethical conflicts of interest in the context of public relations issues and crises.

Public relations professionals face difficult ethical dilemmas when they have a deep personal connection with one of their organization's publics in a conflict or crisis situation. A classic dilemma involves a plant closing that will negatively affect the practitioner's close family and friends. One possible solution is for the practitioner to apply both crisis communication theory and deep understanding of the affected publics to make a case to upper management that "telling it all and telling it fast" is a better strategy than prolonged secrecy.

DISCUSSION QUESTIONS

1. Describe a time that you thought an organization was right to advocate instead of accommodate a key public during a publicly disputed issue. What contingencies of the situation made advocacy a better strategy than accommodation?

2. Select an organization to which you belong (could be a club, school, place of employment, etc.), and then identify one early/potential issue for the organization.

3. Following up on number 2, briefly outline recommendations for how the organization can handle the seven-step process as it relates to that issue.

4. What is the biggest organizational crisis you've seen in the past month? Were you a social media creator, a social media follower or a social media inactive in the case? How so? What role did the organization play in communicating to you about the crisis?

5. Suppose you find extremely biased information on the Wikipedia page for your organization. This information makes your organization look bad. Technically, anyone can edit Wikipedia entries, but why would it be a conflict of interest for you to do so? (You can find hints at https://en.wikipedia.org/wiki/Wikipedia:Conflict_of_interest and http://www.instituteforpr.org/wp-content/uploads/Beutler_WikiPrimer.pdf.)

KEY TERMS

CHAPTER 13

Global

one laptop per child

With a billion dollars of investment and the inspiration of one of the information age's best visionaries, did the One Laptop per Child program work?

KEY LEARNING OUTCOMES

13.1 Explain why issues of public access and usage of digital communication technology are critical in planning for global public relations.

13.2 Analyze cases of international public relations involving intercultural communication.

13.3 Compare high-context and low-context communication.

13.4 Apply cultural dimensions (e.g., uncertainty avoidance, masculinity-femininity) to public relations strategy and practice.

13.5 Explain the relationship between intercultural public relations, international public relations and public diplomacy.

13.6 Discuss the ethics of balanced dialogue in global public relations.

RELATED UNIVERSAL ACCREDITATION BOARD COMPETENCY AREAS

1.6 AUDIENCE IDENTIFICATION • **1.7** DIVERSITY • **2.2** ETHICAL BEHAVIOR
4.2 BARRIERS TO COMMUNICATION • **6.5** NETWORKS

Do you like potstickers? How about gyoza? Maybe you're a fan of ravioli, khinkali, mandoo, momos, pelmeni, kreplach, pieroji or empanadas. Whether you're in the mood for Chinese, Japanese, Italian, Georgian, Korean, Nepalese, Russian, Jewish, Polish or Argentine food, respectively, there's a good chance that some form of dumpling will be an option.

The dumpling was *not* an option, however, as an emoji in 2016. We had a pizza emoji, a hamburger emoji, and a taco emoji, but no dumpling emoji. And many people were not happy about it. Enter the Dumpling Emoji Project, which was a campaign "designed to bring together like-minded emoji enthusiasts" to influence a group called the Unicode Consortium to adopt the dumpling emoji![1] The Unicode Consortium is a group of corporations, government organizations, research institutions and various other tech-savvy associations and individuals that defines universal standards for computer languages. These standards allow people using all sorts of software and operating systems all over the world to communicate with one another. The consortium includes a committee that decides which emojis become available on your smartphone, tablet or any other device that uses Unicode text. Voting members include Apple, IBM, Oracle, Microsoft, Adobe, Google, Yahoo, Facebook, SAP, the Chinese telecom company Huawei and the Government of Oman.

Emoji-less dumplings found advocates in Jennifer 8. Lee, a former *New York Times* tech reporter and co-founder of the digital publishing company Plympton, and designer Yiying Lu. Lee and Lu organized the Dumpling Emoji Project (http://www.dumplingemoji.org) and launched a Kickstarter campaign that raised more than $12,000 for the cause. They used the money in 2016 to fund international coordination and travel to make their case in person at a meeting of the Unicode Technical Committee in California. The campaign was a success, according to an entry on the group's Kickstarter blog:

> By the end of the gathering, the powers that be had heard our voices loud and clear, passing not one, but four emoji as candidates: the DUMPLING, FORTUNE COOKIE, CHOPSTICKS, and the TAKEOUT BOX. Starting in 2017, all four of these emoji are expected be available on billions [of] keyboards worldwide as part of Unicode 10.[2]

On one hand, the emoji project demonstrates a rather straightforward campaign with a clear goal, well-chosen tactics, a rather small budget and easily observed outcomes. On the other hand, the emoji project illustrates the interplay of many important facets of global public relations that will be defined and discussed in this chapter, including international communication, intercultural communication and even perhaps some international diplomacy.

Anyone thinking about a public relations career needs to be ready to embrace the globalization of the field, which happens whenever public relations efforts spread across national, geographic or cultural borders. Fluency in intercultural and international interactions has become a key ingredient in boosting prospects for career success. In this chapter, we approach the topic of global public relations by considering factors that influence communication between people from different cultures and different nations as well as communication between people from different cultures within the same countries.

The Dumpling Emoji Project raised more than $12,000 in a campaign to include the dumpling emoji as part of Unicode text.

Why do you think anyone would care so much about the universal availability of a dumpling emoji?

Digital Divides—At Home and Abroad

"Let's make Fremont Fiber Optic!"[3] The person who started this discussion thread in the Reddit online social media community was seeking support from neighbors in Fremont, California. The "redditor" asked others to e-mail the mayor of Fremont and request that the city join the "Next Century Cities" movement, a group of community leaders seeking faster, cheaper access to the internet nationwide.

You may wonder if this is a case of #FirstWorldProblems. The "first world problems" meme grew in popularity on social media in the 2000s as a way of mocking complaints about inconveniences like slow internet speeds in wealthy nations when citizens of poorer, underdeveloped "third world" countries face more pressing concerns like widespread hunger, disease and political oppression. Indeed, half the world doesn't even have access to the internet.[4] But the Next Century Cities website argues that affordable, reliable high-speed internet access is not just a luxury or a convenience.[5] According to the group, accessible broadband connections are part of a "necessary infrastructure" in today's world for residents to participate in their communities, for students to learn, for businesses to successfully engage in commerce and for everyone to share knowledge.[6] In other words, the internet is necessary to make democracies work.

The term **digital divide** refers to a gap in access to digital information and communication technologies between the "haves" and "have-nots." The digital divide concept is a relative one—meaning that it could be used to describe the difference between populations that are completely wired with the

Digital divide
Gap between those people with relatively little access and use of information and communication technologies and those people with greater access and usage.

Don't assume that your publics are online simply because you are.

Globally, Internet Access Varies Widely

Do you access the internet at least occasionally? Or do you own a smartphone?

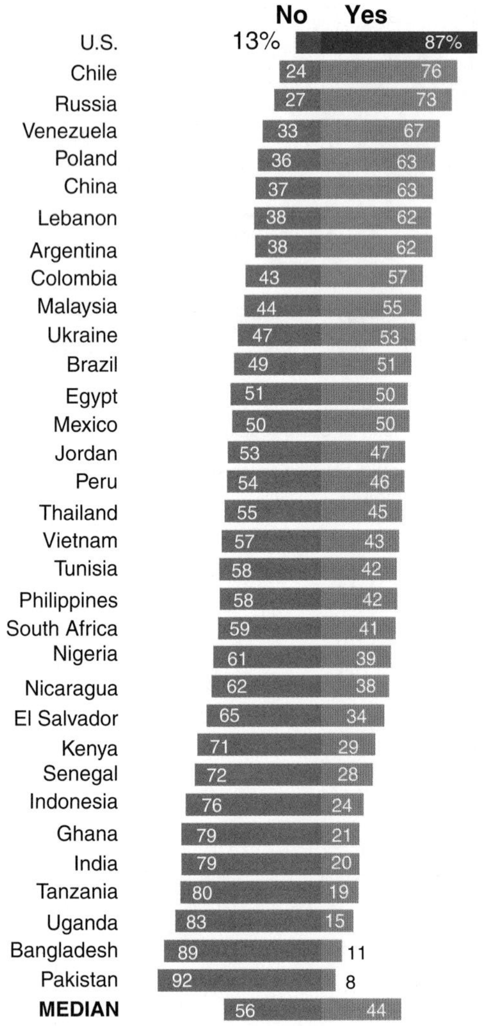

Country	No	Yes
U.S.	13%	87%
Chile	24	76
Russia	27	73
Venezuela	33	67
Poland	36	63
China	37	63
Lebanon	38	62
Argentina	38	62
Colombia	43	57
Malaysia	44	55
Ukraine	47	53
Brazil	49	51
Egypt	51	50
Mexico	50	50
Jordan	53	47
Peru	54	46
Thailand	55	45
Vietnam	57	43
Tunisia	58	42
Philippines	58	42
South Africa	59	41
Nigeria	61	39
Nicaragua	62	38
El Salvador	65	34
Kenya	71	29
Senegal	72	28
Indonesia	76	24
Ghana	79	21
India	79	20
Tanzania	80	19
Uganda	83	15
Bangladesh	89	11
Pakistan	92	8
MEDIAN	56	44

Note: U.S. data comes from a January 2014 Pew Research Center survey. Median percentage excludes the U.S.
Source: Spring 2014 Global Attitudes survey. Q67 & Q69.

Figure 13.1 Data from the Pew Research Center show that internet access varies widely in different countries.

How might practicing public relations in Bangladesh be different from practicing public relations in the United States?

Access divide
Gap between people with access to digital technology and those without access.

latest fiber optic connections and those that have slower access to the internet via older technologies, such as dial-up; or, it could be used to describe the relative difference between parts of the globe with internet access and parts of the globe without any access at all. Either way, we have to be careful not to assume that all of our publics are online simply because we ourselves are feeling fully immersed in digital communication. Furthermore, even if our publics have access to the same communication technologies we use, that doesn't mean they are using them to engage us, our organizations or society at large.

In the 2000s, social scientists started to pay attention to a second type of digital divide. They labeled the first digital divide the **access divide** (the gap between people with access to digital technology and those without access) and identified the second divide based on usage. The **usage divide (or second digital divide)**, focuses on differences in how people from different groups (or publics in the case of public relations) actually use the technologies to which they have access. What if every school in a community has computers, but kids aren't using them to learn? What if every household has a high-speed internet connection, but people are connecting only for games and entertainment?

In planning programs for global public relations, it is essential to consider differences in digital access and usage. If you live in the United States, most of the world would think of you as fairly privileged when it comes to communication technology. Recent data support that assumption, showing that the vast majority of Americans own a smartphone or access the internet at least occasionally. Of course, the data look very different in other nations. A majority of people in countries like Bangladesh, Uganda, India and Pakistan *did not* own a smartphone or access the internet "at least occasionally" in 2014 (Figure 13.1).[7]

International differences in technology access and usage are not black and white. They are better thought of as dynamic and relative. Consider the different stories that statistics tell about India. India was listed near the bottom of some lists for the percentage of its population that regularly accesses the internet or owns smartphones—Pew Research data from a 2014 survey showed that only 20 percent of Indians in one poll reported accessing the internet regularly or owning a smartphone.

On the other hand, World Bank data from the same year showed that India was second only to China in the number of mobile cellular telephone subscriptions. The number of mobile subscriptions in India exceeded the billion mark in 2015. That's more than three times the entire population of the United States! So how can India have one of the lowest internet access rates at the same time that it has more than a billion mobile phone subscribers? One reason for the discrepancy is the dynamic nature of technology adoption. Most of India's mobile users first subscribed for telephone service and not internet access, and we can't assume that most mobile subscribers have smartphones with internet access. However, Amresh Nandan, research director at global technology consulting company Gartner Inc., said that will likely change. The next wave of adoption in India is "exploding growth in data usage and internet access through the mobile, which will get millions of Indians conducting business, getting social and participating in governance through their phones."[8]

Another important indicator of technology access and use is the speed of internet connections. To think about internet access as a simple question of who has it and who doesn't misses the point that communication technology is continuously advancing, and people will always have different levels of access. Even in Silicon Valley, a world hub of internet innovation, citizens of the Fremont, California, community are constantly reaching for more, faster and cheaper. This reminds me of lyrics from a Ben Folds song: "No matter what you might do; there's always someone out there cooler than you."[9] The United States barely cracks into the top 20 list of countries for average connection speeds. In mid-2015, we averaged 11.7 mbps (megabytes per second). Nineteen other countries were faster, topped by South Korea with speeds twice as fast at 23.1 mbps (Table 13-1).

While the internet makes it easy for us to reach publics in our communities and all over the world, access and usage vary greatly from community to community and from nation to nation. Any careful thinking about public relations requires attention to how people access and use communication technology (if they have access at all). Whether communication is wired, wireless or altogether offline, effective global communication also requires an understanding of cultural contexts.

Usage divide (or second digital divide)
Gap between people who use information and communication technologies for education, self betterment, civic engagement, etc. and those who use the technologies for less constructive reasons.

Think carefully about how your publics are accessing and using communication technology in other parts of the world.

Technology merges with tradition in India as sisters and brides from the Rabari Samaj community take a selfie on a mobile phone before participating in a mass marriage.

How could India have one of the highest rates of mobile subscriptions and one of the lowest rates of internet access at the same time? What would that mean for practicing public relations in India?

TABLE 13.1 **NATIONAL RANKINGS FOR INTERNET CONNECTION SPEEDS**		
GLOBAL RANK FOR CONNECTION SPEED	**COUNTRY**	**AVERAGE MBPS (MEGABYTES PER SECOND)**
1	South Korea	23.1
2	Hong Kong	17.0
3	Japan	16.4
4	Sweden	16.1
5	Switzerland	15.6
6	Netherlands	15.2
7	Norway	14.3
8	Latvia	14.2
9	Finland	14.0
10	Czech Republic	13.9
20	United States	11.7

Data from Akamai's 2015 State of the Internet Report show the United States ranked 20th in the world for average connection speeds.

How might practicing public relations in South Korea be different from practicing public relations in the United States?

one laptop per child

Case Study

One Laptop per Child

In 2005, Nicholas Negroponte founded the non-profit One Laptop per Child (OLPC) organization. The organization leveraged $1 billion of investment and partnerships with individuals, U.N. agencies and organizations like eBay, Red Hat, Google and News Corporation to pursue a broad goal of providing a "rugged, low-cost, low-power, connected laptop" computer for each primary-school child in developing nations.[10] Negroponte, who delivered the very first TED talk in 1984 and co-founded the MIT Media Lab in 1985, envisioned a program that would bridge both the access and usage divides. In a 2006 TED talk, he shared a personal anecdote from a remote village in Cambodia:

> *I was recently in . . . a village that has no electricity, no water, no television, no telephone, but has broadband internet now. And these kids, their first English word is "Google" and they only know Skype. They've never heard of telephony. They just use Skype. And they go home at night—they've got a broadband connection in a hut that doesn't have electricity. The parents love it, because when they open up the laptops, it's the brightest light source in the house.[11]*

The nonprofit One Laptop per Child organization aimed to provide every child in developing nations with a laptop, but even with a billion dollars of investment and an inspiring vision the initiative struggled.

What lessons does this case provide for public relations?

Unfortunately, even with an inspirational vision, the program was not as successful as investors, educators, scholars, policymakers and designers had hoped. The technological difficulty of producing and distributing extremely low-cost laptops was part of the problem. The program originally aimed to produce the OLPC XO model at a price of $100 per laptop, but manufacturers often had to price them at $200 or more. The laptops also were criticized for lacking connection ports for classroom projectors, having limited access to troubleshooting assistance for software issues, requiring expensive replacement parts for hardware and being made with environmentally hazardous materials.

Cultural issues also presented significant challenges.[12] In Uruguay, for example, a national evaluation of the program after it launched revealed that only 21.5 percent of teachers reported using the laptops in class daily or near-daily, and 25 percent of the teachers reported using them less than once a week.[13] The program also was deployed in parts of the United States, but results there were equally discouraging. In Birmingham, Alabama, the city invested more than $4 million to provide more than 1,700 fourth- and fifth-graders with laptops. In a survey, however, 80 percent of the students said they used the laptops either seldom or never.[14]

So what went wrong? In reviewing the data and reports, UC-Irvine Professor Mark Warschauer and Stanford Ph.D. Candidate Morgan Ames found the results to illustrate how important it is to adapt to local cultures. The OLPC programs struggled, they said, "because they ignored local contexts and discounted the importance of curriculum and ongoing social, as well as technical, support and training."[15]

No one faults the program for its intent and ambition. Even the program's critics also acknowledge that the OLPC program spurred innovation in low-cost computers with more durable, low-power hardware, and collaborative software designed to improve access, use and education. Nonetheless, analyzing the OLPC's shortfalls yields valuable lessons for designing programs that involve strategic communication across cultures.

As *Business Week*'s Bruce Nussbaum wrote, the program broke a cardinal rule of program design by not focusing first on the end users of the laptops. Nussbaum suggested that OLPC would have been more successful if it had involved its primary publics earlier in the planning. "It would have been far better to begin in the villages, spend time there and build from the bottom up."[16] Had teachers, parents and students been consulted more in the research and planning stages before implementation, OLPC strategists may have been in a better position to tailor the program to needs at the local level. Public relations professionals should apply this type of design thinking that focuses on end users (i.e., key publics) in any kind of planning. Access to technology is perhaps the first concern, but any effective communication strategy also requires careful attention to social and cultural contexts.

Public Relations and Culture

Every public has its own cultural dimensions. Naturally, Chinese groups will have different cultural characteristics from German, Pakistani or American groups. A public comprised of mostly Latinos will differ culturally from African Americans, Caucasian Europeans, Eskimos or Pacific Islanders. Of course, the concept of culture applies to any group, not just groups defined by race, ethnicity or nationality. As more and more families are becoming multiracial, categorizing people as "White," Hispanic," "Asian," "African American," and so on will become a less relevant way to understand publics, and shared interests and affinity will become more important.[17]

Intercultural Public Relations

The Peace Corps, an organization that sends thousands of young people abroad into different cultures every year, defines **culture** as "a system of beliefs, values, and assumptions about life that guide behavior and are shared by a group of people."[18] If we define a *public* as a group of people with shared interests (as we did in Chapter 1), then we see how the concept of *culture* applies to just about any public—residents of a town, students in a school, volunteers of a nonprofit, a company's top management or opponents of a political action. While we may think we understand different cultures, when we reach out to people or publics, we have to check our assumptions carefully. **Intercultural public relations** involves the interaction of an organization and publics across cultures.

Culture
A shared system of beliefs, values, customs and so on that guides behavior of a particular group or public.

Intercultural public relations
Management of relationships between organizations and publics of different cultures.

Case Study

Intercultural Communication and Potty Talk

Intercultural scholar Gary Fontaine has called it "one of the world's most persistent intercultural challenges." Archaeologists study it as a cultural artifact. You would likely approach it carefully when traveling abroad. What is it? It's a toilet. That's right, a potty. And although its function is universal, its design and use can differ significantly from one culture to another.

Now, imagine you work for a company that manufactures and sells toilets, and your job is to promote a new model in a different culture. That's what Swiss manufacturer Geberit asked Danish public relations firm Kragelund Kommunikation to do when it wanted to introduce its AquaClean shower toilet to Denmark. In case you're wondering what a shower toilet is, here's how the AquaClean website explains it: "A shower toilet combines the functionality of a toilet and the cleaning properties of a bidet . . . : at the touch of a button, the concealed spray arm extends and washes you clean with a jet of pleasantly warm water."[19]

In developing strategy, the agency studied Danish and international toilet habits. (Don't ask me how they did this.) They identified some important market challenges, including the high price of the product at €4,500 and lack of consumer knowledge—less than 5 percent of Danes had a bidet and 0 percent owned a shower toilet at the time. These challenges were compounded by the fact that Danish consumers tended to think of the toilet as a plumbing item and not a "lifestyle product." In other words, one of the biggest obstacles for Geberit and its public relations agency was cultural. Shower toilets and bidets were "considered oddities and taboos in Scandinavia."[20]

The campaign, which the International Public Relations Network (IPRN) recognized as the overall winner of its business-to-consumer project of the year award, focused on middle-to-high-income Danes aged 35 and up. The communication strategy relied on both information and emotion by emphasizing hygienic benefits and promoting cleanliness and well-being.

Kragelund Kommunikation set up opportunities for journalists from newspapers and high-end design magazines to "try the product themselves in exclusive surroundings," including a press trip to Paris. They also partnered with the ritzy Hotel D'Angleterre in Copenhagen, which installed the shower toilets in all of its rooms. Story angles included humor ("The toilet is our armchair"), cleanliness ("We feel unclean despite strong personal hygiene"), business ("Large Swiss corporation aims for Denmark") and technology ("High tech toilets with fancy features").[21]

The press trip was a success, and the story angles were effective with Danish media. Prominent bloggers also wrote about the product. While most metrics focused on media coverage and impressions, the image of Danish TV host Søren Jensen reporting "with his trousers round his ankles and sitting on an AquaClean toilet in the studio" indicates that a cultural barrier had been breached. The client later extended the campaign to other regions.

Introducing an expensive high-tech toilet to a new culture is one kind of challenge. Another is introducing a low-tech product like the Squatty Potty. Basically a step that slides against the side of a toilet, Squatty Potty allows people to do their business more like people did before modern toilets were commonplace.

Despite the cultural awkwardness of the topic, Squatty Potty's creator Robert Edwards managed to win the opportunity to pitch his idea on ABC's *Shark Tank*, where he and his mother persuaded Lori Greiner to invest $350,000 in the business. The show's producers were reluctant to feature a bathroom-related product on the show, but Edwards persisted by emphasizing a health angle. "In our second [audition] tape we really nailed down that Squatty Potty is a health tool," Edwards said in an interview.[22] The Squatty Potty also has been featured on health shows, including *The Doctors* and *The Dr. Oz Show*, and has its own Facebook page and Twitter and Instagram accounts, as well as a YouTube video with more than 15 million views. It even has a major YouTube hit with a video of a unicorn and rainbow-colored soft-serve ice cream to illustrate "the effects of improper toilet posture and how it can affect your health."[23]

Publicly discussing bathroom habits presents a number of intercultural challenges, but companies that make bathroom-related products still seek to reach international markets.

What communication strategies cleared these obstacles?

Low-Context Versus High-Context Communication

In his classic book *Beyond Culture,* anthropologist Edward Hall distinguished between **low-context communication**—in which most of the meaning of a message is stated explicitly in the message itself and requires little understanding of context and **high-context communication**—in which most of the meaning of a message is based on context or something internal to the communicators rather than being directly stated in the message.[24] Restaurant menus, brochures, web pages and even course syllabi include very detailed descriptions and instructions and are tools of lower-context communication, while tweeting and text messaging, which are limited to a very few words and characters, illustrate well the concept of high-context communication. Like so many other concepts in social science and public relations, however, high- and low-context communication are best thought of as ends on a spectrum rather than two completely separate ideas.[25]

Think about the shortest text message you have ever sent or received. For many this will be a one-letter message: "K." In the context of a chemistry lab, "K" stands for potassium. In baseball, "K" represents a strikeout. But in text messaging, the single character K—the explicit transmitted message—is often used as an abbreviation for "OK." To understand the actual meaning you have to understand the context. When it works, it may be the most efficient communication tactic ever, bringing a successful communication exchange to a satisfying conclusion with a single keystroke. But according to BuzzFeed's Katie Heaney, "K" is "the one thing you should never text anyone ever." In her eyes it "means you're too lazy to type out just one extra letter," "makes you seem mad," and sends a message that you're on a power trip.[26] The true meaning of "K" totally depends on the context, including the relationship between the sender and receiver.

When organizations develop branding campaigns, they have to be especially sensitive to high-context communication. Branding efforts rely on simple images, icons, logos, words and brief taglines to communicate enormous amounts of meaning about the organization or its products and services. The meaning depends on context. Branding magic happens when communication strategists successfully align an organization's actions, communication and culture with the cultural contexts of key publics.

A major part of the inspiration for Nike's successful "Just Do It" campaign (launched in the late 1980s) was a sensitivity to cultural trends in the United States, where obesity and procrastination were becoming

Low-context communication
Exchanges in which most of the meaning of messages is stated explicitly in the messages and requires little understanding of context.

High-context communication
Exchanges in which most of the meaning conveyed between people lies in the context of the communication or is internal to the communicators.

Story of my life

This internet meme captures some of the frustration (and humor) that occurs when cultural contexts clash.

How does this image illustrate high-context and low-context communication styles?

NOTHING SUCKS LIKE AN ELECTROLUX

The most powerful vacs you can buy are in the new 2000 series.

Electrolux is a Swedish company. This ad for British audiences was designed by British ad agency Cogent Elliot.

Do you see it as a cultural gaffe or a clever play on words?

more problematic for a large part of the population. According to Nike's former director of marketing insights and planning Jerome Conlon, the campaign developed by Nike's ad agency Wieden+Kennedy needed to reach people beyond highly motivated athletes. The campaign had to appeal to "the actual role that fitness plays in peoples lives, the actual experience of really working out, doing aerobics, going on a bike ride, etc.," wrote Conlon.[27] The power of "Just Do It" lies not in the eight letters of text. It emanates from the contextual meaning assigned to it by millions of Nike fans.

The internet is full of examples of spectacular failures of branding and strategic communication across national and cultural borders. You may have heard about the words "Coca-Cola" translating to "Bite the wax tadpole" in China, or how the Scandinavian vacuum company Electrolux ran a campaign in the United States that "Nothing sucks like an Electrolux." Another classic is that General Motors stumbled in marketing its Chevrolet Nova in Spanish-speaking countries because "no va" translates to "does not go" in Spanish. Ironically, all three of these legends of miscommunication have been taken out of context to some degree over the years.

Coca-Cola did have some difficulty translating its brand name as it sounds ("ko-ka-ko-la") into Chinese characters after entering Hong Kong and Shanghai markets in the 1920s. But when Coca-Cola officially registered its trademark in China in 1928, the series of characters approximated "something palatable from which one receives pleasure."[28] The Electrolux ad was designed by British ad agency Cogent Elliot for British—not American—consumers and included an intentional pun, with the words on a poster accompanying a picture of the leaning tower of Pisa apparently being sucked toward a vacuum cleaner.[29] On YouTube, you can also find a humorous Electrolux ad, apparently from the 1970s, that includes the tagline at the end.[30] Finally, while "no va" may translate literally to "doesn't go," apparently few Spanish speakers in GM's markets for the car in Mexico and Venezuela were put off by the single word "Nova." Snopes.com claims that sales even exceeded expectations.[31]

Logos, taglines and advertising copy are essential to marketing, but public relations also entails a great deal of longer-form communication in the management of relationships between organizations and publics. Public relations professionals are often in charge of "spelling out" an organization's goals, policies, position statements, news and responses to inquiries. This type of elaboration requires low-context communication.

You will likely deal with both high-context tactics like texts and tweets and low-context communication that spells out your organization's goals, policies and positions.

The distinction between high-context and low-context communication can be useful to people studying and practicing international communication. For example, people from western cultures such as those from America, Switzerland, Germany and Scandinavia *tend to* use more low-context communication. In low-context cultures, web users are more likely to use search features and links to seek specific information and facts about an organization. On the other hand, people from high-context cultures, such as those from Asia, Africa, the Middle East and Latin America, *tend to* rely more on interpersonal exchanges and social recommendations online.[32] One major caution in comparing people using these descriptions (high-context and low-context cultures) is that they are broad generalizations that do not apply to every individual or group within a geographic region. This is why we are careful to emphasize "tend to," as in, "Europeans *tend to* use more low-context communication than Asians."

Cultural Dimensions

To avoid stereotyping, public relations professionals (and anyone else communicating across cultural boundaries), should work to understand the various dimensions of any group's culture. Geert Hofstede is a Dutch social psychologist and professor who worked for years as a management trainer at IBM. In that role, he traveled around the world and systematically studied how IBMers operated and communicated differently in different cultures. Hofstede identified five major cultural dimensions that have been useful to understand and improve how people of different cultures communicate: **power-distance, individualism-collectivism**, **uncertainty avoidance, masculinity-femininity** and **long-term orientation** (Figure 13.2).[33]

Individuals in high uncertainty avoidance cultures, for example, are less comfortable with ambiguity. They prefer stricter sets of rules and procedures and seek to define future outcomes as specifically as possible. In low uncertainty avoidance cultures, individuals are more tolerant of not knowing how things will turn out, but it is important to still include them in conversations about the future. An organization opening a new plant in a high uncertainty avoidance culture may be required to present a detailed environmental impact statement showing exactly how they expect social, natural and economic environments to be affected.[34] Lower uncertainty avoidance cultures are more likely to seek an open-ended dialogue about the organization's plans for a new plant, and so town hall meetings or online forums for public discussion may be more effective ways to communicate plans and discuss options with low uncertainty avoidance publics.

Another example is the dimension of masculinity-femininity. Masculine cultures tend to value assertiveness, competition, achievement and material success, while feminine cultures tend to value care, collaboration, modesty and quality of

Power-distance
Cultural dimension describing the difference between cultures that value hierarchy and authority more and those that value equal distribution of power more.

Individualism-collectivism
Cultural dimension describing the difference between cultures that value loyalty to self and immediate family more and those that value loyalty to larger groups and society more.

Uncertainty avoidance
Cultural dimension describing the difference between cultures that are less comfortable with ambiguity (high uncertainty avoidance) and those that are more at ease with ambiguity.

Masculinity-femininity
Cultural dimension describing the difference between cultures that value competition, achievement and material success more and those that value care, collaboration and modesty more.

Long-term orientation
Cultural dimension describing the difference between cultures that value long-held traditions more and cultures that value entrepreneurship and innovation more.

In high uncertainty avoidance cultures, it may be wiser to focus on specific outcomes of communication rather than dialogue as an end in itself.

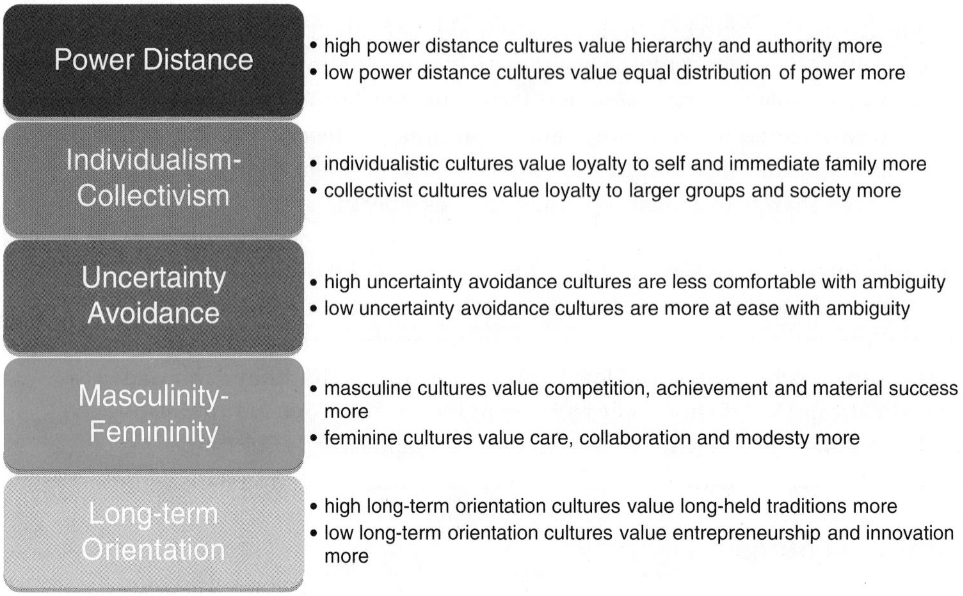

Figure 13.2 Hofstede found these cultural dimensions to be helpful in understanding differences in communication styles.

With which cultural dimensions do you identify most? Which would be the hardest for you to adapt to in intercultural public relations?

life. Consider how masculinity-femininity may play out in **gamification**, which is a strategy of applying rules and rewards of game playing (points, scoring, competition, collaboration, etc.) to other areas of behavior. Gamification is becoming more and more common in public relations.

Companies use games and apps to build customer loyalty. Starbucks stars, airline miles and Yelp badges are all little incentives that keep people coming back for more from these companies. Nonprofits and NGOs also use games as tactics toward larger goals of social impact. Games for Change (gamesforchange.org) features games like *Never Alone* and *Start the Talk*. *Never Alone* (Kisima Ingitchuna) is a game that allows players to unlock "cultural insights" in the form of short video clips about Iñupiat Native Alaskan people, if the players overcome in-game obstacles and solve puzzles related to Native Alaskan folklore and culture.[35] *Start the Talk* is a role-playing game developed as part of a Substance Abuse and Mental Health Services Administration (SAMHSA) campaign called "Talk. They Hear You." The game is designed to help players learn how to talk to kids about underage drinking.[36]

Gamification strategies that focus on points and competitions may play better as tactics in public relations efforts in masculine cultures, while games that focus on communication, care and collaboration may appeal more in feminine cultures. However, according to An Coppens, a game

Gamification
Strategy of applying rules and rewards of game playing (points, scoring, competition, collaboration, etc.) to other areas of behavior such as desired public relations outcomes.

designer at Gamification Nation Ltd., games also can be designed with both genders in mind. "For example," she writes, "measure performance based on completion, yet also allow and encourage social support which appeals to empathy and requires mutual respect."[37]

Cultural Intelligence

Cultural intelligence
Ability to adapt, communicate and interact effectively across cultures by learning and applying cognitive, emotional and behavioral skills.

Unfortunately, merely studying and understanding cultural dimensions is not quite enough to ensure successful intercultural communication. Successful communication takes **cultural intelligence**. London Business School Professor Christopher Earley and University of Colorado Professor Elaine Mosakowski define *cultural intelligence* as someone's ability to interpret the cultural nuances of others' communications, even as an outsider. "A person with high cultural intelligence can somehow tease out of a person's or group's behavior those features that would be true of all people and all groups, those peculiar to this person or this group, and those that are neither universal nor idiosyncratic."[38]

Earley and Mosakowski identify three sources of cultural intelligence: head (cognitive), body (physical) and heart (emotional/motivational). Fluency in intercultural public relations comes from a combination of head, body and heart. As professional communicators and managers, public relations professionals succeed with different combinations of the three strengths.

Build fluency in intercultural public relations with a combination of head (cognition), body (behavior) and heart (emotion/motivation).

HEAD (COGNITIVE)

Learning about high-context and low-context communication through reading is mostly a cognitive endeavor. You can study foreign languages and learn facts about cultures without ever really interacting with others from those cultures. And, while websites and corporate training programs also offer a wealth of knowledge, this type of knowledge is not sufficient to prepare you for all the situations you might encounter.[39] Before setting up a global webinar, international press conference or site visit to a location where you will be interacting with those from another culture, you'll definitely want to study up. The most valuable learning, however, will come from careful observation and awareness of your surroundings during your actual foray. Earley and Mosakowski recommend developing strategies for this immersive type of cognitive learning:

- Think about what you hope to achieve,

- learn from your experiences when you encounter something new in a different culture,

- use those experiences to inform future actions and communication, and

- plan ahead for introductions to new people.

BODY (PHYSICAL)

Physical actions such as body motions, eye contact and gestures are a huge part of intercultural communication. When do you shake someone's hand? How firmly? Do you ever hug someone in a professional setting? Who sits where at a conference table? How should you dress for an in-person press conference? What about a Skype interview? These are all questions of how you present yourself and interact in a physical sense.

For example, while organizing an event at the Japanese Cultural Center of Hawaii featuring the late Senator Daniel K. Inouye as the keynote speaker, the two most important things I had to know in planning for his introduction were physical. First, Inouye, who was a Congressional Medal of Honor winner and the highest ranking Asian-American government official in U.S. history, had lost his right arm in combat during World War II. Second, Inouye was allergic to pollen. Because we were aware of these physical issues, we made sure that when we presented Inouye with a lei as a symbol of aloha that we gave him a *maile* lei (a lei made with dark green ti leaves without flowers), and in greeting him, we were careful not to extend our right hands expecting righthanded handshakes.

HEART (EMOTIONAL/MOTIVATIONAL)

The more experience we have in intercultural interaction, the more confidence we build in our ability to learn and adapt. Social psychologists call this **self-efficacy**, which is our belief that we can perform certain behaviors to achieve certain outcomes. Prior experiences and successes help us build self-efficacy, which motivates us to persist in difficult situations and learn new strategies, which leads to more success, which leads to more self-efficacy, and so on. It's a virtuous cycle if you can maintain it. Stanford psychologist Albert Bandura identified self-efficacy as a key to social learning, and social learning is what cultural intelligence is all about. People with high emotional or motivational cultural intelligence are confident they can work with others from different cultures and find it relatively easy to adapt to different cultures and unfamiliar cultural situations.

International Public Relations

International public relations involves the interaction of an organization and publics across national boundaries. As discussed in Chapter 3, globalization and global connectivity have facilitated more opportunities for intercultural communication and *cultural convergence*, which is when diverse cultures are imported, exported, exchanged and mixed. *Economic convergence* is also a hallmark of globalization. Economic convergence is evident when multinational advertising, marketing and communication conglomerates like Omnicom, Publicis or Burson-Marsteller (WPP) conduct their business via subsidiaries operating across the globe.

Self-efficacy
One's belief that he or she can perform certain behaviors to achieve certain outcomes.

International public relations
Management of relationships between organizations and publics of different nations.

For organizations practicing international public relations, the benefits of globalization include increasing the scope of operations, making more money in new markets and opportunities for achieving greater social and environmental impact with more diverse publics. But globalization also carries with it greater risks for unintended consequences, negative social and environmental impacts, miscommunication and faux pas.

Royal Dutch Airlines partners with a dozen other organizations globally including Nike and Accenture as part of a biofuel program that "aims to reduce CO_2 emissions by 20% in 2020 (compared to 2011)."[40] This is an example of an international public relations program designed to help the environment and strengthen the organization's relationships with governments, regulatory bodies and other international companies over the course of several years. In other cases, however, international public relations issues can arise in a matter of seconds with just a few ill-advised words. When the Netherlands defeated Mexico in World Cup play, Royal Dutch Airlines (@KLM) tweeted "Adios Amigos! #NEDMEX," and accompanied the post with an image of an airport "departures" sign featuring a caricature of a man with a large mustache, sombrero and bandana.[41] That tweet created an international public relations problem because publics in Mexico were offended by what the Dutch organization had communicated.[42] One Twitter user responded, "@KLM your brilliant social media experts just lost you the 2nd largest market in Latin America in one tweet, they must feel really clever."[43]

As discussed in Chapter 3, global conglomerates are advancing the internationalization of public relations with both economic and cultural convergence. However, you don't have to work for an international company like Nike, Accenture or KLM, or for a global agency like Ketchum (Omnicom) or WPP, to work in international public relations. Even small organizations communicate regularly across national borders.[44]

Royal Dutch Airlines (@KLM) was criticized for this tweet after the Netherlands defeated Mexico in World Cup soccer.

Do you think the tweet caused long-term damage to KLM's business in Mexico? Why or why not?

Public Diplomacy

Public diplomacy is an important subset of international public relations that deals with communication designed to promote national interests. In most cases, this means that the organization, a key public, or

Public diplomacy
Subset of international public relations that focuses on promoting national interests.

Nations Unies
Conférence sur les Changements Climatiques 2015
COP21/CMP11
Paris, France

National diplomats celebrated the Paris Agreement on climate change.

What other organizations besides governments participated in the diplomatic efforts as a form of international public relations?

Mediated public diplomacy
A nation's strategic use of media to promote its agenda abroad to foreign publics.

Relational public diplomacy
Engagement between a nation and its foreign publics in cultural exchange and two-way communication with the goal of achieving mutual benefits.

Use media to gain favorable exposure that helps set the stage for more interactive relationship building.

both, are nations, but in certain cases diplomatic actors may include non-state organizations such as NGOs or corporations. If you work in communications for a government organization like the U.S. Department of State or for a U.S. Embassy or Consulate, or if you work for one of these departments' counterparts in another nation, your job will likely entail public diplomacy with the broadest mission of promoting national interests abroad. You may also be involved in public diplomacy working for an NGO or corporation.

Consider the Paris Agreement, which 195 nations adopted to reduce global greenhouse gas emissions at the United Nations Convention on Climate Change in 2015. NGOs such as Greenpeace, World Wildlife Fund and the Union of Concerned Scientists were not pleased with the agreement, which they felt did not go far enough in limiting the use of fossil fuels.[45] On the other hand, the climate change conference itself was sponsored by corporations such as Michelin, Google, Ikea, SkyPower Global (a solar energy company) and Renault-Nissan (an alliance of French and Japanese automakers).[46] To the degree that these NGOs and corporations worked to influence the nations participating in the negotiations, they were practicing public diplomacy as a form of international public relations.

In discussing public diplomacy as a form of public relations, Professor Guy Golan defines two key perspectives. First is **mediated public diplomacy**, which is a nation's strategic use of media to promote its agenda and "impact opinions held by targeted foreign audiences."[47] The second approach is **relational public diplomacy**, which is engagement between a nation and its foreign publics in cultural exchange and two-way communication with the goal of achieving mutual benefits. Mediated public diplomacy aligns well with the public information and asymmetrical models of public relations that were outlined in Chapter 2. Relational public diplomacy fits better with two-way models and the symmetrical ideal. Golan recommends integrating the two approaches, using media to gain favorable international coverage that helps set the stage for more interactive relationship building.

Voices from the Field

Guy Golan

GUY GOLAN is an associate professor of public relations and public diplomacy at the S.I. Newhouse School of Public Communications at Syracuse University. As a public affairs professional, he has worked on several international political campaigns. He researches the role that paid, earned, shared and owned media play in mediating the relationship between governments and foreign publics. He has focused on perceptions of Jihadist online recruitment and propaganda, its perceived influence, and the consequent government policy implications. Golan founded thepublicdiplomat.com, a student-run site that produces podcasts available on the website and via iTunes.

What's the most challenging intercultural communication situation you've observed in public relations?

I was once involved in public relations research that focused on publics from the former Soviet Union. We tried to conduct focus groups but faced real challenges in getting responses from participants who were suspicious of our motives and could not understand why we insisted on video/audio taping the focus group sessions.

What can students do to prepare for international and intercultural public relations assignments in advance? What kinds of things can they only learn from experience?

While higher education in public relations can teach you much regarding the fundamentals of international public relations, only extensive international travel can provide students with the nuanced understanding of global cultures and perspectives.

What do you see as the greatest opportunity for public relations as a field arising from trends in globalization?

In many parts of the world, public relations as an industry is focused on tactics rather than a strategic approach to relationship management. Students who will understand the role of research and evaluation along with the RPIE approach to campaigns can play significant roles in the global development of the field.

One scholar cited in this chapter questions whether there is even such a thing as domestic public relations anymore because organizations of all sizes are now communicating across borders. Do you agree that domestic public relations is becoming a thing of the past?

The answer as always is, it depends. There are many local clients whose stakeholder communities are limited to the city, county or region where the organization operates. For example, a local mayoral race would not likely have a global dimension.

Given changes in demographics and technology, how are new public relations practitioners entering the field more prepared? Less prepared?

Those new practitioners who take the time to study the fundamentals and who view public relations as a strategic management function rather than focusing on tactics alone will do very well.

Ethics: Dialogic Ethics

In his 1923 book *I and Thou*, Austrian-born philosopher Martin Buber developed the concept of dialogue to explain how people come to understand their own existence through their interactions and relationships with others. **Dialogic communication** happens when people enter into an exchange with an understanding of their own views and backgrounds but also with complete openness to seeing the world as others do. The growth of the web and social media as tools for public relations has led a number of public relations scholars to focus on the concept of dialogue as an ethical guidepost.

The opposite of dialogic communication is **monologic communication**, in which communicators strive to impose their view on others. Ethicists hold that the day-to-day practice of public relations leans too much toward monologic and not enough toward dialogic. They consider monologic public relations to be less ethical because it treats publics as less important than the powerful organizations conducting public relations. Dialogic public relations facilitates a fairer balance of power.

It's easy to see how dialogue and relational diplomacy can be praised as ethical public relations, but what about monologic, mediated diplomacy when a cause is perceived to be just? As part of its counter-terrorism efforts, the U.S. Department of State ran a social media campaign against ISIS in 2014. The State Department's strategy included a YouTube video that parodied ISIS recruitment efforts. The video mocked ISIS in graphic detail, juxtaposing disturbing images of prisoner crucifixions, mosque bombings and severed heads with ISIS claims that joining the organization will lead to some kind of promised land. The video concludes with a sarcastic note, "Travel is inexpensive, because you won't need a return ticket!"[48]

The counter-terrorism strategy, which also included anti-ISIS Facebook, Twitter and Tumblr accounts, was anything but dialogic in its approach to ISIS. Given the circumstances, is this monologic approach ethical?

The decision between monologic and dialogic public relations parallels questions of one-way versus two-way communication (Chapter 2), asymmetrical versus symmetrical public relations (Chapter 2) and advocacy versus accommodation (Chapter 12). Reasonable moral arguments can be made for both sides depending on the circumstances.

In using social media to counter ISIS recruitment efforts, the U.S. Department of State produced a graphic video mocking the terrorist group, showing disturbing images of extreme violence from the terrorist's own videos.

Did the State Department go too far? Can this type of persuasive tactic be justified ethically? If so, how? If not, why not?

In global public relations, reaching across cultural and geographical boundaries to get to know one another better takes extra work, but it is a must. Whether you are advocating for a new emoji, delivering educational technology, marketing bathroom goods or fighting terrorism, successful and ethical public relations requires an understanding that not everyone shares your background and culture. It's crucial that you take the time to learn about what matters most to your publics.

In Case You Missed It

Almost everyone with an internet connection can practice some form of international communication. This means navigating intercultural challenges is part of everyday public relations work. Of course cultural intelligence also comes into play practicing public relations offline. Here's some advice culled from the chapter:

- Don't assume that your publics are online simply because you are.

- Think carefully about how your publics are accessing and using communication technology in diverse cultural contexts.

- You will likely deal with both high-context tactics like texts and tweets and low-context communication that spells out your organization's goals, policies and positions.

- In high uncertainty avoidance cultures, it may be wiser to focus on specific outcomes of communication rather than dialogue as an end in itself.

- Build fluency in intercultural public relations with a combination of head (cognition), body (behavior) and heart (emotion/motivation).

- Use media to gain favorable exposure that helps set the stage for more interactive relationship building in public diplomacy.

ICYMI

SUMMARY

13.1 Explain why issues of public access and usage of digital communication technology are critical in planning for global public relations.

Internet access and usage vary from community to community and from nation to nation. Even when publics have access to communication technologies, that doesn't mean they are inclined to use them to engage organizations. Cultural factors and offline communication must be considered in planning.

13.2 Analyze cases of international public relations involving intercultural communication.

Any time public relations practitioners communicate across national borders, they are likely communicating across cultures too, and they should plan for intercultural communication challenges. In cases of public relations supporting efforts to market bathroom-related products internationally, successful strategies included focusing on culturally important values in the new markets (e.g., cleanliness and health) and persuading key influencers in other cultures (e.g., TV show hosts, doctors, investors) to publicly endorse the concept.

13.3 Compare high-context and low-context communication.

In high-context communication, most of the meaning conveyed between people lies in the context of the communication or is internal to the communicators. Taglines, tweets, brand logos and text messages are examples of high-context communication because success in this type of messaging depends so heavily on the context and the meaning assigned by the people involved. In low-context communication, most of the meaning lies in the message itself. Low-context communication requires greater elaboration and detail in composing messages. Public relations practitioners need to be able to do both and to properly adapt communication styles to publics in context.

13.4 Apply cultural dimensions (e.g., uncertainty avoidance, masculinity-femininity) to public relations strategy and practice.

Understanding cultural dimensions such as power distance, individualism-collectivism, uncertainty avoidance, masculinity-femininity and long-term orientation is an important part of cultural intelligence that involves cognitive skill in designing public relations strategy. But gaining experience and confidence (emotional skill) and learning how to actually behave appropriately (physical skill) in different cultural contexts are also keys to successful practice. Head (cognitive), heart (emotional) and body (physical) are all necessary for excellence in the practice of intercultural public relations.

13.5 Explain the relationship between intercultural public relations, international public relations and public diplomacy.

Most international public relations involves intercultural communication because different nations have different cultures, but not all intercultural public relations is international because cultures vary widely within national boundaries. Public diplomacy is a subset of international public relations that deals with communication intended to promote national interests.

13.6 Discuss the ethics of balanced dialogue in global public relations.

Dialogic approaches to public relations are commonly held to be more ethical than monologic approaches because dialogue fosters equality and may lead to an understanding of truth that arises from multiple perspectives. Equality and mutual understanding are particularly noble aspirations for international and intercultural communication. Some may argue, however, that monologic public relations that uses public relations tactics primarily for persuasion are more effective and ethical when the cause is just, such as in diplomatic efforts against terrorism.

DISCUSSION QUESTIONS

1. Do you think digital divides are getting wider or narrower in today's world? Explain with examples or data (possible sources include http://www.pewglobal.org or https://www.stateoftheinternet.com).

2. Have you ever surprised yourself by adopting a product or service that you didn't expect to like from another country or completely different culture? How were you persuaded to give it a try? Were public relations tactics involved?

3. Identify an organization that is really good at high-context communications and compare that organization to one that is really strong in low-context communications. Which would you rather work for and why?

4. How would you describe your own cultural preferences, according to Hofstede's model? (You may want to try this resource: http://geert-hofstede.com/cultural-survey.html.) Which of the dimensions would be hardest for you to adapt in practicing intercultural public relations?

5. Explore the web presence of an international embassy (sites like http://embassy.goabroad.com may be helpful). Explain how the embassy's diplomatic approach is more *mediated* or *relational*, or if it is better described as a mix of the two.

6. In the fight against ISIS, the U.S. federal government launched an initiative to counter violent extremism that includes enlisting college students to develop online campaigns and social media strategies against ISIS propaganda. See http://www.pbs.org/newshour/bb/recruiting-college-students-to-fight-extremists-online/. If recruited, would you join? Why or why not? What would be your biggest ethical considerations?

KEY TERMS

CHAPTER 14

Careers

Could griping about your job on social media ever be a smart career move? Find out what happened when an entry-level employee gave Yelp a less-than-stellar review.

KEY LEARNING OUTCOMES

14.1 Identify different types of employers for public relations jobs.

14.2 Assess how different areas of specialization in public relations match your interests and consider the knowledge and skills that jobs in those areas require.

14.3 Plan for your own continuing education in public relations including core competencies and evolving skills for a changing media environment.

14.4 Map a public relations career trajectory from entry level to executive.

14.5 Discuss ethical dilemmas related to the professional values of competition and loyalty.

RELATED UNIVERSAL ACCREDITATION BOARD COMPETENCY AREAS

2.1 INTEGRITY • **2.2** ETHICAL BEHAVIOR • **3.3** COUNSEL TO MANAGEMENT

5.3 ORGANIZATIONAL STRUCTURE AND RESOURCES • **5.5** LEADERSHIP SKILLS

When you close your eyes and picture yourself working in public relations, what do you see? Do you picture yourself in a chic urban agency or a tech startup, surrounded by hipsters and creative geniuses? Are you dressed more formally, working with laser focus on business strategy in a corporate high-rise? Perhaps you're walking the halls of a children's hospital with a therapy dog and a group of reporters? Do you see yourself working quietly, uploading data to a government web page behind the scenes? Or are you leading an environmental protest with a bullhorn and a smartphone, hashtagging the energy of a movement? Jobs in public relations allow you to make a difference in people's lives in a lot of different ways. While no two careers in public relations are alike, and career options are always changing, this chapter offers a look at major types of employers, lists sample jobs from some major areas of specialization, and describes typical responsibilities of practitioners as they move from entry level to the top of the field.

Employers

One of your first major considerations in thinking about a career in public relations is what type of employer you want to work for. Discussed throughout this book are cases and examples of public relations conducted by global agencies, for-profit companies, nonprofit organizations, international NGOs and government agencies. During the course of your career, you may work for organizations as big as the U.S. Department of Defense, Wal-Mart or Indian Railways, or as small as a two-person business. Or maybe you will start your own firm and become your own boss. As you launch your career, all options are on the table.

Gotham magazine described Quinn PR's penthouse office as one of New York's "swankiest" workspaces.

How do you picture your workplace in public relations?

Agencies

For many aspiring public relations professionals, an agency job is the first position that comes to mind when they think about starting in the business, and agencies are certainly great places to launch and build careers. Agencies provide corporate clients with specialized services including research, campaign planning and implementation, speechwriting, crisis management, special events and so on, but most large companies also include in-house public relations departments.

Agencies range in size from two- to three-person shops to the biggest public relations firms in the world like Edelman, Weber Shandwick, FleishmanHillard and Ketchum. The biggest agencies have tens of thousands of employees spread across offices all over the world. Agencies serve multiple clients, very often in different businesses. This means that if you work for an agency, you'll likely have an opportunity to work on multiple projects for multiple organizations.

In mid-size to large agencies, client work is assigned to account teams. Each client has an account with the agency, and agency employees work on multiple accounts simultaneously. From entry level to executive leadership, traditional jobs in agencies include the following:

- Account assistant
- Account coordinator
- Account executive
- Senior account executive
- Account supervisor
- Director
- Vice president

The salary for an entry-level account coordinator in an agency ranges from the high $20,000s to the high $40,000s with a median of about $36,000, according to PayScale.com data in 2016.[1]

Of course, different agencies offer different salaries and different job titles. Convergence and integration have led many firms to rethink how they organize teams and name positions. The work can be nonstop and involve ridiculous amounts of multitasking as employees jump between account projects and urgent client demands, but those who succeed gain experience in a hurry. This combination of jam-packed workdays (and nights), steep learning curves and fast-growing professional networks also means that there is quite a bit of turnover. It's not uncommon for rising stars to move up through two or three positions in their first few years on the job, and often these job changes include lateral moves from one agency to another.

Many young professionals find that agency work just isn't for them. Some will move to other careers altogether. Others will go to work doing public relations for other types of organizations, often finding their new positions with the help of contacts they made in agencies.

Corporations

Working in house as a full-time employee of one company means that your responsibility in managing organization-public relationships is primarily to a single organization. A corporate job on the client side may look like a posh gig—you have only one "client" to serve, the schedule may be more predictable, and pay

Agencies provide great learning experiences.

What appeals to you least and most about working in an agency?

If you start at an agency, be prepared to move through multiple positions in your first few years.

Workers at a Procter & Gamble social media command center manage the company's #EverydayEffect campaign to highlight its brands' positive effects on consumers.

What other publics besides consumers are important in corporate public relations?

is often higher. For example, compared to the median salary of $36,000 for account coordinators, the median salary for communication specialists working in-house at a corporation is $47,500.[2] Keep in mind, however, that the person making $48k working in-house very likely has more years of experience than the entry-level account coordinator at an agency.

In addition, while you may have only one client to serve working in-house, you will still be responsible to many publics. Corporate jobs focus on customers (marketing communications), investors (financial relations), government agencies (public affairs), employees (internal relations) and the publics who live wherever companies operate (community relations). Large corporations may employ separate departments for each of these publics and may also hire public relations agencies for help with various functions, but the departments must still work together.

As discussed in Chapter 4, corporate social responsibility programs (CSR) have become more common in response to negative public sentiment about corporations and their impact on society and the environment. CSR efforts are a prime example of the importance of balancing the interests of various stakeholders, even if you work only for a single organization.

Nonprofits and NGOs

By definition, nonprofit organizations exist to do something other than make money for shareholders. Nonprofit work may appeal to people who work hard to support the missions of those organizations, such as health, education and environmental causes. While nonprofits often benefit from the service of volunteers, as strategic organizations they operate with business models that require full-time paid staff.

Public relations jobs in nonprofits are just as demanding and require just as much accountability as corporate jobs.

Public relations jobs in nonprofits are often just as demanding and require just as much accountability as corporate jobs. In addition, in many ways the stakes are higher at nonprofits because public health, education, social justice and the environment depend on them.

In general, public relations management in nonprofits involves similar strategies and skills as for-profits (media relations and publicity, branding, community relations, public affairs, etc.). However, a major difference between nonprofits and corporations are the key publics of donors and volunteers. Fundraising and volunteer management are critical to public relations success at nonprofits.

Similar to agencies, pay at nonprofits can start low—below $30,000 for entry-level program assistants,[3] but salaries for public relations managers at U.S. nonprofits range from the $30,000s to nearly $100,000 with a median of $52,000, according to 2014 data.[4]

Nongovernment organizations (NGOs) are one type of nonprofit. NGOs are organized at local, national or international levels and advocate fiercely for humanitarian and environmental causes. Many NGOs work closely with the United Nations, and their relationships with corporations and governments range from contentious to cooperative.

Government

According to the World Economic Forum, the U.S. Department of Defense is the largest employer in the world, with 3.2 million people, followed by the People's Liberation Army of China (2.3 million). Other top-10 employers are also government-related, including the U.K. National Health Service (1.7 million) and Indian Railways (1.4 million) (Table 14.1).

The U.S. Department of Defense (DOD) employs thousands of people—civilian and military—in public relations-related positions, and DOD is

TABLE 14.1 THE WORLD'S LARGEST EMPLOYERS

EMPLOYER	PEOPLE
US Department of Defense	3.2 million
People's Liberation Army, China	2.3 million
Walmart	2.1 million
McDonald's*	1.9 million
UK National Health Service	1.7 million
China National Petroleum Corporation	1.6 million
State Grid Corporation of China	1.5 million
Indian Railways	1.4 million
Indian Armed Forces	1.3 million
Hon Hai Precision Factory (Foxconn)	1.2 million

SOURCE: US Department of Defense, International Institute for Strategic Studies, Walmart, McDonald's NHS Information Services, China National Petroleum Corporation, State Grid Corporation of China, Indian Railways, Indian Armed Forces, Foxconn
* Including franchise (420,000 excluding franchises)

Governments and large corporations are the world's largest employers.

What appeals to you least and most about working for a large government organization?

Ahsha Tribble, deputy regional administrator for the Federal Emergency Management Agency's (FEMA) Region IX Office, and Scott Carpenter, weather specialist from the National Weather Service, brief the media on El Niño weather and public preparedness.

What kinds of public relations skills would be important in public affairs jobs focused on disaster management?

▼ Salary	?
☑ $0–$24,999	(6)
☑ $25,000–$49,999	(17)
☑ $50,000–$74,999	(29)
☑ $75,000–$99,999	(25)
☑ $100,000–$124,999	(15)
☑ $125,000–$149,999	(7)
☑ $150,000–$174,999	(6)
☑ $175,000–$199,999	(3)
☑ $200,000+	(1)

This graphic shows the number of jobs returned in a keyword search on USAJOBS.gov for "public affairs," by salary range.

How much would you expect to earn in an entry-level government job?

only one sector of government jobs that include local, state and federal positions. Despite the fact that government public relations jobs are labeled with titles like public affairs coordinator and public information officer, the U.S. government is said to be the world's largest employer of public relations people in the world.[5] A quick search on USAJOBS.gov for the exact words "public affairs" returned 109 open positions. The results included jobs with the Department of the Army, Department of the Interior, the Department of Agriculture and the Department of Health and Human Services. Six of the jobs pay less than $25,000, and these are volunteer, intern and trainee positions. The majority pay between $25,000 and $100,000, with the most common job title for positions in the $25,000–$50,000 range being "public affairs specialist."

In case you're wondering, the job that pays $200,000+ is "director of the Asian Pacific American Center at the Smithsonian Institution." Interesting trivia: This position, which was open at the end of President Obama's second term, was formerly held by President Obama's brother-in-law Konrad Ng.

Historically, government jobs have been known for stability and good benefits. One of the downsides, however, is that large government agencies are often burdened with bureaucratic inefficiencies, which can be frustrating to employees as well as their primary publics—namely, taxpayers. Whereas businesses rely on clients and customers for revenue, and nonprofits rely more on donors, government agencies are funded by taxpayers. As a taxpayer yourself, you've probably been frustrated at times with local, state or federal government operations. That said, these same agencies provide essential public services, and their communication functions are critical to democratic societies.

As noted throughout this book, open communication and access to information about government operations is a foundation of democracies. The "information age" in many ways has opened government information to easier access than ever before (the USAJOBS.org site is a good example), and public relations jobs play a key role in how our societies continue to evolve.

Self-Employment and Small Business

On the opposite end of the spectrum from jobs with enormous government organizations are small businesses—millions of them worldwide. In the United States, about half of the eligible workforce is employed by a small business, and these small firms accounted for 63 percent of new jobs created from

1993 to 2013.[6] These statistics from the Small Business Administration refer to organizations with fewer than 500 employees, but you may plan to open your own business, work with a partner or two, or work in a business comprised of just a few people. More than 10 million Americans work for companies with fewer than 10 employees.[7] Most of these organizations do not have a full-time position or department labeled "public relations," but all of them will require managing relationships with publics.

Small business owners, startups and self-employed public relations practitioners often work in home offices or "'coworking" spaces such as Cove locations in Washington, D.C.

What do you see as the advantages and disadvantages of this type of work environment?

Whether you are writing code, renting sailboats or wrapping burritos, you'll need to be much more of a generalist in small businesses compared to large companies, nonprofits or government organizations. Instead of specializing in only the communication function, you will likely be involved in core operations in addition to building and maintaining relationships with customers, vendors, regulators, banks and investors, and media. If your budget for promotions is small, you may rely more on social media and word of mouth. But good media relations can still lead to big hits in influential channels, if you know how to tell and pitch your stories well (Chapters 4 and 9).

> If you work for a small business, you'll need to be much more of a generalist.

As an owner, operator, partner or employee of a small business you will be directly responsible to your organization for key management decisions. You will also be directly accountable to publics for the outcomes and effects of those decisions. In this sense, working in a small organization can be seen as one of the purest forms of public relations as a management function. Also, many public relations agencies are small businesses themselves and offer opportunities for internships and entry-level jobs that expose you to all facets of client service work from top to bottom.

Areas of Specialization

You'll find as many different areas of specialization in public relations as there are different missions of organizations. That said, some of the major categories are healthcare, sports and entertainment, political and public affairs, financial and entrepreneurial, consumer and international public relations. Within each category are countless types of public relations jobs.

This section briefly outlines some major areas of specialization and offers an example job description from each. The job ads all were found online during a brief period of time, and the openings listed are either entry level or appropriate for someone just a few years out of school. Their purpose is to get you thinking about the experiences you should seek now as you consider your future career options in these areas of specialization.

Public Relations Specialist

Healthcare may be seen as a specialty area in public relations, but public relations is considered a specialty in healthcare. Here's what a public relations specialist job entails at BioClinica, a Pennsylvania company that runs clinical trials to test new medical therapies.

JOB TITLE

Public Relations/Social Media Specialist

JOB DESCRIPTION

Responsible for expanding participation and optimizing engagement in online communities including Facebook, Twitter, YouTube, Google+ and Pinterest "while operating within the strict regulatory guidelines of IRBs [institutional review boards], sponsor companies and FDA." The public relations specialist also is responsible for media relations and special event support to drive enrollment in clinical studies.

SAMPLE DUTIES AND RESPONSIBILITIES

- Development of social media strategies for online patient communities
- Community branding
- Demographic research on existing and new communities
- Search engine optimization (SEO)
- Participation in online conversations
- Relationship development with influential bloggers
- Pitching stories to local and national media

QUALIFICATIONS

- Five years of professional experience in social media/public relations, healthcare agency experience preferred
- Ability to translate technical information into clear, everyday language (writing samples required)
- In-depth understanding of social media platforms, preferably familiar with blogs related to clinical trials and healthcare
- Knowledge of principles of search engine optimization (SEO)
- In-depth knowledge of media relations

LISTING LOCATIONS

Found on Indeed.com under "Healthcare PR jobs," with full description on company page at https://bioclinicacareers.silkroad.com/.

DISCUSSION QUESTIONS

Like many public relations jobs, the ideal candidate for this job will need proven communication skills but also a working knowledge of the organization's operations. How could you demonstrate knowledge of social media in an application or interview? How could you prepare to demonstrate knowledge of healthcare and clinical trials?

Health

The goals of healthcare are as universal as the human race. From family planning to end-of-life hospice care, governments, NGOs, hospitals (for-profit and nonprofit), private physicians, pharmaceutical companies, educational and research institutions, and medical device manufacturers are only some of the organizations that have a stake in fighting disease, caring for the ill and keeping healthy people healthy.

Sports and Entertainment

Sports and entertainment may be one of the hardest areas to break into right after college because so many people would love to work for the athletes and celebrities they already enjoy following. Most are also willing to work very, very hard to get one of those jobs. Moving from fan to employee can be a rewarding transition, but also humbling and exhausting. It takes a lot more than just pastime levels of enthusiasm to keep up with the business side of the 24/7 ups and downs of sports and entertainment.

Sports information directors, for example, are responsible for documenting and promoting the accomplishments of the athletes, teams and leagues they represent. They provide updated—often real-time—statistics for use by the media. This requires deep knowledge of sports, teams and athletes. Sports information directors must have strong organizational and analytic skills and a solid understanding of how sports media operate in order to effectively serve a media relations function. Sports and entertainment jobs also include issues and crisis management, marketing and branding, and community relations.

Piotr Trochowski of the German national football team participates in a photo shoot for the German Football Association (DFB).

What appeals to you least and most about working for a sports organization?

Political and Public Affairs

Strategic campaigns are a core function of public relations, and when people hear the word *campaign* many will think of political campaigns. Political campaigning done well is the epitome of a public communication process that builds strategy from research to achieve measurable outcomes. Some jobs in political public relations last only as long as a candidate is running for office or a referendum is being considered on a ballot. Others are tied to politicians and organizations that require continuous public relations efforts from term to term and from political initiative to political initiative. Many candidates and organizations hire agencies that specialize in political communication. If you're fired up about a candidate or a political cause, or if you think of yourself as a policy wonk and want to make a difference in the technical details of how government operates, political public relations may be for you.

> It takes more than enthusiasm to keep up with the 24/7 ups and downs of public relations jobs in sports and entertainment.

Students participating in the Massachusetts Summer Legislative Intern Program learn about career opportunities in politics.

What kinds of political and public affairs jobs appeal to you most and least?

Financial and Entrepreneurial

Financial public relations deals with investor relations, financial media relations and disclosures of financial information, as discussed in Chapter 4 on relationship management.

Community Affairs Manager

For a die-hard Detroit Tigers fan, this may seem like a dream job, but it would be a tough one to land and maybe even tougher to succeed. Would you be ready for it? Batter up!

JOB TITLE

Community Affairs Manager

JOB DESCRIPTION

Described as a "multi-functional position with a focus on customer service and community engagement," this job entails managing community partnerships, planning and implementing special events, and maintaining correspondence with an array of publics.

SAMPLE DUTIES AND RESPONSIBILITIES

- Running in-park events including pregame ceremonies like first pitches and National Anthem performances
- Planning military and veterans-related programs and events
- Handling requests for donations (fan packs, autographed items, certificates, etc.)
- Writing articles summarizing special events
- Cooperating with marketing department to keep website and social media content current
- Planning Tigers front office holiday giving program and volunteer opportunities

QUALIFICATIONS

- Bachelor's degree in sports management, communications, marketing or business
- Previous experience in event planning, outreach projects and public speaking
- Excellent interpersonal skills, creative writing and oral communication skills
- Experience writing media materials such as press releases and media advisories
- Basic knowledge of accounting and budgeting
- Ability to work with individuals of all ages and capacities, including those with developmental and physical disabilities

LISTING LOCATIONS

Found on http://www.prcrossing.com under "PR Sports Jobs" and on LinkedIn.com.

DISCUSSION QUESTIONS

How would relationship management be important to success in this community affairs position? Which specific publics would you work with as part of the job?

Grassroots campaign
A bottom-up campaign that focuses strategy on mass participation of citizens or political constituents in an effort to influence policy or legislation.

Grasstops campaign
A campaign that focuses strategy on directly influencing opinion leaders and well-connected individuals such as donors or political party leaders.

Employers range from the world's biggest publicly held companies like Bank of China, Berkshire Hathaway, General Electric, Samsung Electronics and Apple to small startup businesses raising capital for entrepreneurial endeavors. Agencies also specialize in serving clients with financial public relations needs. If you've got a good mind for business and finance, you can put your communication skills to work in financial public relations.

Consumer

Consumer public relations is one of the most visible segments of public relations, perhaps because it is so closely tied with the advertising and

Associate, Communications & Public Affairs

Grassroots campaigns focus strategy on activating citizens and political constituents to influence policy or legislation. **"Grasstops" campaigns** are designed to directly influence opinion leaders and well-connected individuals, such as donors or political party leaders. Global Strategy Group is a public affairs agency with headquarters in New York that does both. Do you have a green thumb for this kind of work?

JOB TITLE

Associate, Communications & Public Affairs Practice

JOB DESCRIPTION

The public affairs team at Global Strategy Group plans and implements grassroots, grasstops and coalition building campaigns for clients such as Google, Rockefeller Foundation and Major League Soccer. This associate position in New York reports to the vice president of public affairs and works on advocacy, corporate and nonprofit accounts.

SAMPLE DUTIES AND RESPONSIBILITIES

- Researching and writing briefing materials for senior staff such as memos, presentations and talking points
- Researching and writing fact sheets
- Developing new business proposals and presentations for prospective clients
- Assisting with development of campaign plans including grassroots and field operations as well as digital engagements
- Identifying potential coalition partners and conducting outreach to those organizations
- Managing activities of subcontractors and vendors
- Participating in internal planning and brainstorming sessions

QUALIFICATIONS

- Bachelor's degree plus two to four years' experience in grassroots campaigns and advocacy in an agency, government, political or nonprofit organization
- Experience with community organizing, field organizing, political campaigns and issue advocacy
- Demonstrated project management and multitasking skills
- Strong writing, editing and internet research skills
- Ability to build and maintain strong working relationships with colleagues, clients and publics
- Strong interest in a wide variety of policy issues
- Familiarity with digital communications and social media platforms
- Bilingual in Spanish and English highly valued

LISTING LOCATIONS

Found on Indeed.com under "Government Affairs Jobs," with full description on agency page at http://www.globalstrategygroup.com/careers.

DISCUSSION QUESTIONS

What kind of research would you do before applying for this job? What kinds of clients would you be most excited about working with? Would you still apply if some of the clients have significantly different political views from you? Why or why not?

marketing of brands we all know well and products we consume every day. When the key publics of public relations are consumers, opportunities for convergence and integration abound.

The growth of digital, social and mobile media that reach consumers in so many ways has further blurred the lines between public relations, advertising and marketing. These media afford us more feedback and information from consumer publics than we've ever had before. This convergence has resulted in entirely new career possibilities for those who "get it" when

Investor Relations Coordinator

Investor relations involves communicating about money. CORE Realty Holdings of Newport Beach, California, owns and manages commercial and multi-family real estate across the United States for private investors. Are you ready to answer the call when investors say, "show me the money!"?

JOB TITLE

Investor Relations Coordinator

JOB DESCRIPTION

The investor relations coordinator reports to the investor relations department manager and vice president of investor relations. The job requires excellent writing, proper handling of confidential financial information and time-sensitive communication with investors.

SAMPLE DUTIES AND RESPONSIBILITIES

- Writing for communication with vendors, investors, attorneys and third parties
- Discussing investments on phone with investors and their registered representatives
- Organizing and attending investor conference calls
- Preparing and distributing meeting announcements, time sensitive documents and ballots to investors
- Processing and disseminating of investor tax documents, assisting with annual compliance filings and quarterly reports

QUALIFICATIONS

- Five years of general office experience, including two or more years of investor relations experience
- Excellent written and verbal communication skills
- Proficiency with Microsoft Word, Outlook and Excel
- Detail oriented and highly organized with ability to follow projects through to completion
- Ability to multi-task and plan ahead for future projects

LISTING LOCATIONS

Found on CareerBuilder.com under "Investor Relations."

DISCUSSION QUESTION

Investor relations jobs often pay quite well, as discussed in Chapter 4. What else besides money might motivate you to pursue this career option?

it comes to communicating in these new contexts. If you're into messaging with the right voice, reading feedback well, turning raw data into useful information, and carrying on conversational communication to build relationships with consumers on a large scale, then you might just be perfect for consumer public relations.

Social Media Communications Specialist

Mars is one of the biggest food manufacturers in the world, with six business segments including brands like M&M's®, Snickers®, Uncle Ben's®, Pedigree® and CocoaVia®.

JOB TITLE

Social Media Communications Specialist

JOB DESCRIPTION

The communications specialist monitors social media platforms, identifies escalating consumer comments or complaints, and responds appropriately to consumers. The position serves as a key consumer contact across multiple brands and supports e-commerce. He or she is "responsible for understanding and properly responding with the approved brand voice in all areas of communication including ratings & reviews."

SAMPLE DUTIES AND RESPONSIBILITIES

- Reading and responding to customers on Facebook and Twitter for multiple brands
- Working with marketing communications director to execute brand strategy
- Collaborating with e-commerce, sales, corporate affairs, R&D, marketing and legal departments to ensure appropriate brand responses

- Tracking and monitoring for rapid response
- Creating daily messaging
- Writing and editing for external audiences
- Managing confidential reports and other sensitive information
- Supporting brand launches
- Building consumer advocacy for brands
- Evaluating and making recommendations for proactive opportunities

QUALIFICATIONS

- Three years' experience in related work such as consumer relations
- High school diploma or GED required, bachelor's degree preferred (in public relations, marketing, business or a science/technology)
- Experience managing consumer social media
- Experience in problem solving and critical thinking

LISTING LOCATIONS

Found on disABLEDperson.com under "Management" and at https://jobs.mars.com.

DISCUSSION QUESTION

Speaking with an authentic voice is an important skill in social media. What personal traits and communication styles would help or hinder your success in serving as a voice for these brands?

Communications and Campaign Manager

Save the Children is an international NGO working on behalf of children's interests worldwide. This position is located in Burma (Myanmar). Do you think you could make a difference in a faraway corner of the world?

JOB TITLE

Communications and Campaigns Manager

JOB DESCRIPTION

This is a two-year contract position to lead a communication and campaign team in implementing advocacy, media engagement and digital/social media strategies to raise visibility and support the goals of Save the Children's various programs and brand rollout in Burma.

SAMPLE DUTIES AND RESPONSIBILITIES

- Managing communications team
- Working closely with the Country Director to ensure common messaging
- Promoting campaigns and global advocacy partnerships including international consortiums and fund management teams such as Global Fund, Scaling Up Nutrition Civil Society Alliance (SUN CSA), Tat Lan and Leveraging Essential Nutrition Actions to Reduce Malnutrition (LEARN)
- Developing innovative ways to communicate to target audiences
- Leading communications in emergency situations
- Branding "Save the Children"
- Producing fundraising materials for donors and public supporters

QUALIFICATIONS

- Bachelor's degree in communications, arts or any related field, with overseas study experience preferred
- Seven years' experience in public relations, advertising, communications, media management, event management or related field
- Experience of implementing strategic campaigns or advocacy work, preferably overseas
- Excellent communications skills, with Myanmar language skills "a definite asset"
- Ability to speak confidently and deliver key messages to the media and donors
- Understanding of social media engagement, brand management and an eye for layout and design
- Proven ability to create an environment that motivates teamwork across various geographical areas and willingness to travel to field sites

LISTING LOCATIONS

Found on DevJ.org (search engine for international development jobs) under "Public Relations" and at https://www.savethechildren.net/jobs/.

DISCUSSION QUESTIONS

Of all the jobs supplied in this chapter, this one requires the most global and intercultural experience. What kind of career path do you think the successful applicant will have taken from college to this position? How is the commitment and lifestyle different from the other jobs described in this chapter?

International

All of the previously discussed areas of specialization can involve international work. Healthcare, sports, entertainment, political, financial, and consumer product organizations and publics are spread all over the world, and as discussed in Chapter 13, the relationships between them cross national borders more than ever before. Many organizations distinctly identify themselves as global or international and specifically seek employees with a strong desire to work and communicate across countries and cultures.

Actor Tony Hale shoots videos to announce a campaign for M&Ms in which consumers were invited to try three new peanut flavors and vote for their favorite on the M&Ms website and Facebook pages.

What specific role do you think a social media specialist would play in this type of campaign?

Education and Continued Learning

You're probably reading this text for one of three reasons: (1) you are taking public relations as a required course for your major in college, (2) you are taking a public relations course as an elective for a related degree plan, or (3) you are interested in public relations work and educating yourself independently. These three reasons represent three common tracks into the field. Practicing public relations does not necessarily require a specific college major, but public-relations-specific degree programs offer a series of courses designed to prepare students for entry into the field.

A typical course sequence for the public relations major includes an introductory course, public relations research, public relations writing, an internship and a campaigns course. Other common courses in public relations majors focus on public relations case studies, law, ethics, planning and management.[8]

If you're working on a college degree, however, keep in mind that your broader education is just as important as your public-relations-specific courses. In fact, the Commission on Public Relations Education recommends that 60–75 percent of an appropriate degree plan comprise courses in liberal arts, social sciences, business and language courses.[9] This makes sense, given the importance of relationship building, culture, persuasion, management, law, ethics, societal trends and research to public relations practice.

If you're reading this book independently—or taking advantage of any other professional development resources for that matter—that's a really good sign for your future. Adaptability is

> Your broader education is just as important as your public-relations-specific courses.

> Adaptability is a survival strategy for 21st century learning—be ready to learn, unlearn and relearn.

a survival strategy for 21st century learners, according to *Future Shock* author Alvin Toffler.[10] We all must be ready to learn, unlearn and relearn, and that's what will serve us well as the field continues to change. As Ketchum President and CEO Rob Flaherty put it in a keynote presentation to a 2015 industry-educator summit, "Half of everything needed now didn't exist ten years ago."[11]

In thinking about your education, it may be useful to identify core competencies and then to identify the other "half" of what you need to continually adapt to and learn—the half that "didn't exist 10 years ago" and that may change drastically in the next 10 years.

The knowledge, skills and abilities tested on the accreditation exam offered by the Universal Accreditation Board (UAB), and which are mapped to each chapter of this text, are lasting foundations for public relations education (see Appendix A for full descriptions). The Accreditation in Public Relations (APR) credential serves to certify professionalism and ethical standards of practitioners who have five or more years of experience in the field. Recent graduates and college seniors enrolled in a public relations or related program who are members of a UAB-affiliated student organization may apply for the Certificate in Principles of Public Relations Principles (see http://www.praccreditation.org/apply/certificate/). The six pillars of the APR exam are:

1. Research, planning, implementation and evaluation (RPIE)
2. Applied ethics and law
3. Issues and crisis management and communications
4. Communication, models, theories and history
5. Leadership in the public relations function
6. Relationship management

In 2012, public relations blogger and consultant Arik Hanson went out on a limb to suggest "10 Skills the PR Pro of 2022 Must Have."[12] In 2016, he took to his blog to revise the list. No doubt he'll revise his thinking again a few more times before 2022 arrives.[13] Learn, unlearn, relearn. Credit Hanson for his adaptability. What follows is a condensed list (from 10 items down to five) of what Hanson identifies as key skills for the future. Most of the core competencies are not new, but the contexts for practicing them have changed.

1. *Ability to write for both internal and external publics.* You must be able to write clearly for internal communication with employees, volunteers and so on as well as for owned, paid, shared and earned media that reach external publics (Chapters 7 and 9). According to Hanson, "PR folks are asked to manage social ad

campaigns all the time," and this requires knowledge of paid media services for platforms like Twitter, LinkedIn, Facebook and Instagram.

2. *Multimedia production skills.* Online video may be the first format that comes to mind, but audio shouldn't be overlooked, either as content in its own right or as part of a multimedia mix (Chapter 10). An eye for the visual appeal of still photography and logo design also is important. Hanson notes that many firms and brands have creative departments specifically tasked with developing a compelling and consistent visual style, but that practitioners with a good feel for positioning brands visually are in demand to "fill in the gaps," especially in organizations that aren't big enough to employ entire departments for this function.

3. *Ability to manage social media content.* Managing social media content systems means knowing how to tag, organize and sometimes repurpose content for different contexts and platforms. Content should be both "searchable and findable." Managing social media also requires a thorough understanding of analytics (Chapter 8). Facebook Insights and Google Analytics are examples of easily accessible sources of large amounts of customizable data, and people who can take that data and translate it into actionable ideas are in high demand.

4. *Analyzing and presenting data that make sense to management and clients.* Digital and social media can be treasure troves of data on publics and how they engage organizations, but making sense of that data in a way that informs strategy is critical (Chapter 6). Public relations practitioners who can report data with "context, actionable intelligence and clearly articulated next steps" will shine in modern organizations. Hanson acknowledges that analysis and reporting always have been essential in public relations, but the availability of ridiculously large amounts of data elevates the importance of being able to convert raw data into useful knowledge.

5. *Collaborating online.* Be prepared to work with geographically dispersed teams within your organization to complete projects and tasks (Chapter 13). If you've ever worked on a challenging group project for an online class, you know that managing workflow, deadlines, communication tools and cultural expectations can be frustrating. Take heart that much of what you learned from the process will be helpful to you when you work with dispersed teams in your career ahead. Digital collaboration also will be key to your communication with external publics, particularly in building online communities and collaborating with influential individuals across social media platforms. Hanson calls it "influencer

outreach" and notes that building and maintaining these relationships with external publics requires an ability to identify the right people and a sensitivity to the culture of online communities and their leaders—"knowing how to approach them—without offending them."

Career Tracks and Roles

You may notice that the list at the end of the previous section starts with a more tactical focus on writing and producing and then moves into more strategic aspects of research and analysis and ends with relationship management. Long before the rise of social media, research suggested that public relations practitioners could be broadly described as fulfilling either a **technician role** or a **management role**.[14] Public relations technicians of the 20th century primarily focused on producing and disseminating communication tactics such as brochures, news releases, speeches and photographs. While these tactics have evolved into more digital formats, the idea endures that technicians focus more on production and dissemination, and managers organize strategy and make decisions. Those in management roles are held more accountable for program outcomes.

As you move through a career in public relations, you'll be involved with both roles, but as an intern or entry-level employee you will most likely start as a technician. That is, your main responsibilities will likely be assigned based on strategy and decisions made by others. While some highly talented practitioners will make a career out of their expertise in the technical side of public relations (e.g., web design, app development, writing, multimedia, analytics), most eventually move into jobs that involve a greater degree of management.

The line between technicians and managers is a blurry one. When San Diego State University professor and public relations management expert David Dozier developed the concept, he was careful to explain that the terms do not describe completely separate categories, but rather, *predominant* roles. Some people predominantly perform technical functions and others predominantly practice management functions.

In the early 1990s, the PRSA Foundation published a career guide that outlined five levels of professional growth: technician, supervisor, manager, director and executive (Figure 14.1).[15] In the past quarter century, the media environment has changed drastically, and the lines between manager and technician roles have continued to blur, but the general order of responsibilities still applies remarkably well.

Technicians still focus on writing, editing and producing. Supervisors build on those craft skills as they become more involved in planning, budgeting for and scheduling their own efforts as well as the work of technicians.

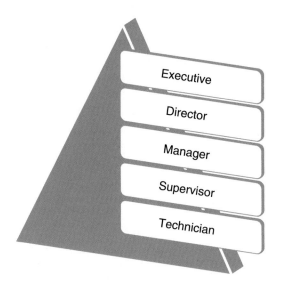

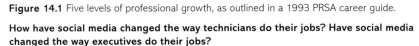

Figure 14.1 Five levels of professional growth, as outlined in a 1993 PRSA career guide.

How have social media changed the way technicians do their jobs? Have social media changed the way executives do their jobs?

Managers take on more planning and organizing responsibilities as they move into leadership positions that require them to evaluate outcomes, solve problems and consult others on decisions that affect the organization and its publics. Directors are in charge of larger staffs and entire organizational management functions defined by the organization's main constituencies (e.g., VP of internal communications, director of public affairs or VP of university relations). Top executives in public relations agencies may hold the title of CEO or president. Top corporate and nonprofit public relations positions may be called executive vice president or senior vice president or executive director. These executives are responsible for the overall mission and vision of an organization and accountable for the organization meeting its annual goals.

Case Study

CEO Versus New Hire: Who Wins?

After completing a degree in English literature from Cal State Long Beach, Talia Jane headed north to the San Francisco Bay area to pursue a career in media. Jane's job seemed promising at first. Even though her prior experience was primarily tutoring and freelancing as a writer, Jane landed an

Lady Murderface
@itsa_talia

[Follow]

An Open Letter To My CEO:

An Open Letter To My CEO
Dear Jeremy,
medium.com

RETWEETS 1,722   LIKES 1,813

3:04 PM - 19 Feb 2016

Yelp entry-level employee Talia Jane went public on Medium to get her CEO's attention about her low pay. It worked. And she was fired.

Do you admire what she did? Why or why not?

interview with Yelp/Eat24 and was hired on the same day that she interviewed.[16] (Eat24 is a food delivery app purchased by Yelp.)

Although her goal was to work in a media job at Yelp and "be able to make memes and twitter jokes about food," Jane took the entry-level job in customer service to get started. But the pay was low. So low, she wrote in a letter to Yelp CEO Jeremy Stoppelman, that she could afford to eat only free food at work and from a 10-pound bag of rice at home. Her salary, which she calculated to be $8.15 per hour after taxes, was not enough to make ends meet: "Because 80 percent of my income goes to paying my rent. Isn't that ironic? Your employee for your food delivery app that you spent $300 million to buy can't afford to buy food."[17]

Within a few hours of posting her letter on Medium, Jane was fired. Stoppelman later tweeted that Jane's firing was not related to the Medium post, but Jane said in a BuzzFeed News interview that her manager and HR representative had told her that her post violated the company's code of conduct.[18]

Meanwhile, Jane's case caught lots of attention on social media. Thousands of people took her side by commenting on her Medium post, supporting her on Twitter, or donating to PayPal and Square Cash accounts that she posted at the end of her letter. One supporter set up a GoFundMe account, "Help A YELP/EAT24 Employee EAT/LIVE," and raised $2,755 in 28 days from 80 donors.[19]

Others were not as sympathetic. Internet users found Jane's Instagram and Tumblr accounts and commented wryly on her ability to make (and post pictures of) prosciutto brie garlic biscuits and margarita-, mint-julep-, and piña-colada-flavored cupcakes. The pictures she posted of a bottle of Bulleit Bourbon that had been delivered to her didn't help her case in the court of public opinion either.

In a blog on the website Ranker titled "Pictures From Talia's Instagram That Aren't Rice," Ranker user Ariel Kana re-posted 26 of Jane's photos. "It was a simple dream, really: To work in media, live in her own apartment, and be able to afford to eat a variety of foods," wrote Kana in the sarcastic post. But "armed only with a degree in English literature, a supportive father, and a coveted job in San Francisco at one of the internet's most visited websites, that dream could never become a reality."[20]

Jane defended her position, claiming that her posts on Instagram were designed to make it seem like she was thriving when the reality was otherwise, so people wouldn't worry about her.[21] In weighing the case, tech industry career consultant Gayle Laakmann McDowell wrote for Forbes .com that Jane's post was "Maybe unwise for her future career, but somewhat admirable that she was willing to do it anyway."[22] Do you admire what Jane did? Do you think she should have been fired? What would you do differently, if you had been in her position?

Voices from the Field

Krislyn Hashimoto

KRISLYN M. HASHIMOTO is vice president at Stryker, Weiner & Yokota in Honolulu, where she oversees the agency's travel division. Over the course of her career, Hashimoto has launched several resorts and restaurants, re-branded newly renovated properties, served as an on-property public relations consultant, and assisted with destination marketing campaigns and initiatives. She has worked as an account director with Cinch PR & Branding Group in San Francisco and in the communications department at the Office of the Governor, State of Hawaii. Her clients have included Oahu Visitors Bureau, Four Seasons Hotels and Resorts, Hyatt Hotels and Resorts, Starwood Hotels & Resorts, Hilton Hotels & Resorts, Mystic Hotel by Charlie Palmer, North Block in Napa Valley, Carmel Boutique Inns and Ghirardelli Square.

What was your first job in public relations?
My first paying job was working in the communications department for the Office of the Governor, State of Hawai'i. Prior to that, I interned in the PR department at Starwood Hawai'i.

How is the job for entry-level public relations positions changing?
When I started in PR, we were still faxing news releases both locally here in Hawai'i and to national

media, and a ton of my time was spent at the copy machine putting together clip books. In addition, co-ordinators used to be behind the scenes managing a lot of clerical work—clipping articles, formatting press releases, mailing press invitations, calling all news outlets and looking through Bacon's media books for updated contacts, etc.

The entry level position at an agency has changed quite a bit since then. With most business being handled over email today, coordinators often have direct contact with clients and are often contacted by media directly with inquiries. A successful coordinator in this digital age, in addition to managing traditional clerical needs, is expected to correspond professionally, manage social media accounts, monitor the news for relevant client issues and be a master at multitasking.

In what ways is the job not changing?
From an agency perspective—client service is still key. Also credibility and building strong relationships with everyone from clients to media.

What's the biggest misperception of public relations jobs you've come across from people outside of public relations?
In travel PR, some people think we are party planners and always out-and-about wining and dining

continues

continued

with media. I'd say that's about five percent of the job. The other 95 percent is spent writing, researching and strategizing—a lot behind a computer.

What is the best part of your job?
Storytelling. Helping our clients tell their stories in ways that set them apart from their competitors. And seeing the direct impact of our work positively impact our clients' businesses.

Ethics: Competition, Loyalty and Job Changes

As you climb the public relations pyramid from entry level into management, you'll switch jobs and employers. A lot. Most people entering the workforce don't expect to stay in any one job for much longer than three years. Mid-career employees also recognize that switching jobs is often the key to raising earnings and moving up in management. An average annual raise within a company is about 3 percent,[23] while employees switching jobs expect a 10–20 percent increase in salary.[24]

There was a time when changing jobs every two or three years was seen as suspicious, indicating a flighty work ethic, difficulty getting along with colleagues, or a lack of loyalty. "That stigma is fast becoming antiquated," according to *Fast Company's* Vivian Giang, "especially as millennials rise in the workplace with expectations to continuously learn, develop, and advance in their careers."[25] Some have even argued that frequent job hoppers are *more* loyal because they are willing to work harder for their current colleagues to make a stronger positive impression during the relatively short time that they work with an organization.[26]

All that job hopping, however, creates ethical challenges. While it is healthy and competitive to shift your loyalty to your new organization when you get a new job, what does that mean for your loyalty to your prior employer and coworkers?

Competition is a key provision in the PRSA Code of Ethics, which lists it as a "core principle promoting healthy and fair competition among professionals" that "preserves an ethical climate while fostering a robust business environment."[27] Ethical dilemmas arise when loyalty (also a key value in the PRSA code) conflicts with competition.

As a legal matter, many employees sign employment contracts that include **non-compete clauses** that prohibit them from working for competitors or sharing competitive information such as trade secrets. However, with so much personnel movement between and among

Non-compete clause
Part of an employment contract that restricts employees from working for competitors or sharing competitive information such as trade secrets even after they no longer work for the organization.

agencies and clients, ethical dilemmas are hard to avoid, even when the legal issues are clear.

For example, suppose you work for an agency and then leave that agency to work for one of the agency's clients. That's a common job change that normally would not raise many ethical issues. But what if a year later your organization—the client— decides to consider bids from other agencies? Do you help your former agency colleagues by giving them a heads-up on what they should do to keep the account? If so, do you give that same information to other agencies bidding for the work? The PRSA code suggests that you should either not offer the information at all or make sure that you give the same information to everyone in order to promote fair competition and respect among professionals.

Competition is also an important principle to honor in recruiting talent for an organization. It may be tempting to hire employees away from other organizations as a way to gain a competitive advantage, but the PRSA code discourages any hiring that could be seen as "deliberately undermining a competitor."[28]

Earlier in your career your ethical dilemmas may revolve mostly around your own role and personal and professional values as they relate to those with whom you work and compete most closely. As you move into management and become more responsible for others in your organization, your ethical responsibility expands. When you begin to approach executive levels, you must grow the scope of your ethical attention along with your career responsibilities. This ethical growth includes careful consideration about how your decisions drive your entire organization and affect your publics. Done right, ethical public relations management benefits individuals, groups, organizations and even entire societies. Done right, ethical public relations elevates the practice to a profession.

Non-competition or non-compete agreements define expectations in legal terms for employees who change jobs.

Beyond legal obligations, what kinds of ethical dilemmas might you face as you change from one employer to another in public relations?

In Case You Missed It

No two career trajectories will be the same in public relations, but that doesn't mean you can't prepare for the journey. Here are some general tips to consider as you weigh your career options.

- If you start at an agency, be prepared to move through multiple positions in your first few years.

- Public relations jobs in nonprofits are just as demanding and require just as much accountability as corporate jobs.

- If you work for a small business, you'll need to be much more of a generalist.

- It takes more than enthusiasm to keep up with the 24/7 ups and downs of public relations jobs in sports and entertainment.

- Your broader education is just as important as your public-relations-specific courses.

- Adaptability is a survival strategy for 21st-century learning—be ready to learn, unlearn and relearn.

SUMMARY

14.1 Identify different types of employers for public relations jobs.
All types of organizations can benefit from some form of public relations. Most public relations positions are with agencies, large businesses and corporations, nonprofits, NGOs, and military and government agencies. Some individuals work in public relations while also performing other core functions in small businesses, startups or self-owned operations.

14.2 Assess how different areas of specialization in public relations match your interests and consider the knowledge and skills that jobs in those areas require.
Major specialty areas of public relations are health, sports and entertainment, political and public affairs, financial and entrepreneurial, consumer, and international. This list is not exhaustive, and within each category are countless types of public relations jobs. Many of the jobs require some of the same skills.

14.3 Plan for your own continuing education in public relations including core competencies and evolving skills for a changing media environment.
Public relations degree programs offer a series of specific public relations courses designed to prepare students for entry into the field.

However, given the importance of relationship building, culture, persuasion, management, law, ethics, societal trends and research, a foundation in liberal arts, social sciences, business and language is also important to help you understand your role in society. Willingness to continually learn beyond school is also critical as media and society change rapidly.

14.4 Map a public relations career trajectory from entry level to executive.

Although specific job titles and tools may vary and change, the following five levels of professional growth still represent a general career progression in public relations: (1) technician, (2) supervisor, (3) manager, (4) director and (5) executive. Technicians primarily implement decisions of others, including writing and production of communication tactics. Managers become more responsible for developing strategy and participating in organizational decision-making, and they are held more accountable for program outcomes.

14.5 Discuss ethical dilemmas related to the professional values of competition and loyalty.

Competition is a key provision in the PRSA Code of Ethics. Ethical dilemmas may arise when loyalty to colleagues from prior jobs conflicts with responsibility for fair competition in a new job. For example, when working for a company that is accepting bids from agencies, you have to be careful not to give any unfair advantage to an agency for which you used to work. The goal is to promote fair competition and respect among professionals.

DISCUSSION QUESTIONS

1. Pick three organizations you would like to work for, and research their job openings. Do any of them list public relations or related jobs? If so, pick the one job that appeals to you most. (If you can't find a public-relations-related job opening, keep searching organizations that you like until you find one.) What are the primary duties of the position?

2. Which area of specialization (health, sports, entertainment, political, financial, etc.) appeals most to you, and why? How would a public relations job in that field be similar and different to other areas of specialization?

3. Find a specific job ad describing a position in public relations that you would like to have three to five years from now. Carefully review the qualifications. Which qualifications do you meet now? Which ones don't you meet? What, specifically, can you do in the next three to five years to make yourself competitive for that type of job?

4. Carefully observe an organization's social media accounts. In what ways are the people running those accounts serving a technician role? In what ways are they serving a management role?

5. Describe a time that you've been in a position (in games or school or work) where you were responsible for ensuring fair competition despite your loyalty to one of the competitors. Did competition trump loyalty? Why (or why not)? Would you use the same moral reasoning in a professional career in public relations?

KEY TERMS

Grassroots campaign   365
Grasstops campaign   365
Management role   372

Non-compete clause   376
Technician role   372

Universal Accreditation Board Competencies

DETAILED KNOWLEDGE, SKILLS AND ABILITIES TESTED ON THE COMPUTER-BASED EXAMINATION FOR ACCREDITATION IN PUBLIC RELATIONS (effective January 2016)		PERCENTAGE TESTED
Objective 1	**Researching, Planning, Implementing and Evaluating Programs**	**33%**
1.1	**Research (Concepts):** Understands and can apply primary and secondary, formal and informal, quantitative and qualitative methods. Decides on the population and sampling techniques. Understands instrument design. Develops a premise and research plan.	
1.2	**Research (Applications):** Uses a variety of research tools to gather information about the employer or client, industry and relevant issues. Investigates stakeholders' understanding of the product, organization and issues. Applies research findings.	
1.3	**Analytical skills:** Continuously analyzes the business environment that includes the client, stakeholders and employer. Objectively interprets data.	
1.4	**Strategic thinking:** Synthesizes relevant information to determine what is needed to position the client, organization, or issue appropriately in its market/environment, especially with regard to changing business, political, or cultural climates.	
1.5	**Planning:** Sets goals and objectives based on research findings. Distinguishes among goals, objectives, strategies and tactics. Distinguishes organizational/operational goals and strategies from communication goals and strategies. Aligns project goals with organizational mission and goals.	
1.6	**Audience identification:** Differentiates among publics, markets, audiences and stakeholders. Identifies appropriate audiences and the opinions, beliefs, attitudes, cultures, and values of each. Assesses interests of influential institutions, groups and individuals. Identifies appropriate communication channels/vehicles for reaching target audiences. Identifies communities formed through technologies. Understands varying needs and priorities of individual constituent groups (e.g., investors, governmental agencies, unions, consumers).	

1.7	**Diversity:** Identifies and respects a range of differences among target audiences. Researches and addresses the cultural preferences and/or needs and barriers to communication of target audiences. Develops culturally and linguistically appropriate strategies and tactics.	
1.8	**Implementation:** Understands sequence of events. Develops timelines and budget. Assigns responsibilities. Executes planned strategies and tactics.	
1.9	**Evaluation of programs:** Determines if goals and objectives of public relations program were met and the extent to which the results or outcomes of public relations programs have been accomplished. Uses evaluation results for future planning.	
Objective 2	**Applying Ethics and Law**	**13%**
2.1	**Integrity:** Conducts professional activities in a lawful and principled manner. Functions as the conscience of the organization.	
2.2	**Ethical behavior:** Understands and adheres to commonly accepted standards for professional behavior. Recognizes ethical dilemmas. Acts to remedy unethical acts.	
2.3	**First Amendment issues:** Understands First Amendment as a foundational principle for public relations. Distinguishes between political and corporate speech. Articulates conditions for libel and defenses thereof. Understands impact of digital record on status as public and private figure.	
2.4	**Privacy issues:** Understands federal law regarding privacy (e.g., HIPAA, FERPA, DPPA), identity protection, ethical implications and digital record. Effectively advises organization on strategic adoption and effective use of technology for listening to, communicating with and engaging priority publics.	
2.5	**Other legal issues:** Upholds applicable federal laws regarding disclosure, copyright, trademarks, fair use.	
Objective 3	**Managing Issues and Crisis Communications**	**13%**
3.1	**Issues and risk management:** Identifies potential or emerging issues that may impact the organization. Identifies potential risks to the organization or client. Analyzes probability and potential impact of risk. Ensures organization develops appropriate response plans. Designs and deploys a strategic public relations response.	
3.2	**Crisis management:** Understands the roles and responsibilities of public relations at the pre-crisis, crisis, and post-crisis phases. Communicates the implications of each of these phases and understands the messaging needs of each. Looks beyond current organizational mindset.	

3.3	**Counsel to management:** Understands the importance of providing counsel to the management team or client regarding issues, risks and crises. Looks beyond the current organizational mindset. Considers and accommodates all views on an issue or crisis. Factors views into communication strategy.	
Objective 4	**Understanding Communication Models, Theories and History of the Profession**	**8%**
4.1	**Communication/public relations models and theories:** Demonstrates familiarity with social science theories and research that guide planning, prioritizing audiences, developing messages, selecting spokespeople, establishing credibility and trust.	
4.2	**Barriers to communication:** Understands how messages and messengers are interpreted by different audiences. Understands barriers that prevent changes to knowledge, attitude and behavior. Understands how semantics, cultural norms, timing, context and related factors impact the practice.	
4.3	**Knowledge of the field:** Defines public relations and differentiates among related concepts (e.g., publicity, advertising, marketing, press agentry, public affairs, lobbying, investor relations, social networking, and branding). Identifies key figures who influenced the field and major trends in the development of public relations as it is practiced today.	
Objective 5	**Leading the Public Relations Function**	**18%**
5.1	**Business literacy:** Understands and explains how employers/clients generate revenue and how their operations are conducted. Identifies relevant business drivers and how they impact the business. Understands how the public relations function contributes to the financial success of the organization.	
5.2	**Resource management:** Takes into account human, financial and organizational resources. Prepares, justifies and controls budgets for departments, programs, clients or agencies. Understands what information needs to be collected, evaluated, disseminated, and retained. Is able to obtain information using innovative methods and appropriately store it, so that it can be retrieved easily for future use.	
5.3	**Organizational structure and resources:** Recognizes chain of command, including boards of directors, senior leadership, middle management, direct line supervision, line positions, and each level's distinctions. Knows how organizations are horizontally and vertically structured. Identifies which divisions within an organization that need to be involved in any communication program. Understands impact of organizational governance. Recognizes the relationships among PR, legal, finance and IT, as essential management functions.	

5.4	**Problem solving and decision-making:** Approaches problems with sound reasoning and logic. Distinguishes between relevant and irrelevant information. Evaluates opportunities for resolution. Devises appropriate courses of action based on context and facts. Makes sound, well-informed and objective decisions in a timely manner. Assesses the impact and implications of these decisions.	
5.5	**Leadership skills:** Influences others to achieve desired goals. Motivates and inspires others, builds coalitions and communicates vision. Influences overall organizational changes in policy, procedures, staffing and structure, as appropriate.	
5.6	**Organizational skills:** Integrates multiple dimensions of a public relations campaign. Integrates internal and external components, so that there is a synergy among the messages.	
Objective 6	**Managing Relationships**	**15%**
6.1	**Relationship building:** Understands consensus-building strategies and techniques to persuade key stakeholders to support a decision. Ensures discussions allow key stakeholders the opportunity to express opinions. Recognizes need for affected parties and stakeholders to find mutually acceptable solutions. Utilizes persuasion, negotiation and coalition building.	
6.2	**Reputation management:** Understands need for maintaining individual and organizational credibility with and among key constituents. Recognizes value of reputation, image, public trust and corporate-social responsibility.	
6.3	**Internal stakeholders:** Understands importance of internal relationships to the public relations function. Understands the importance of organizational culture and communicating key messages through frontline supervisors. Uses mediated and non-mediated channels of communication for effective engagement. Prioritizes internal audiences.	
6.4	**Media relations:** Understands definitions, strengths, weaknesses and needs of different media. Understands the relationships among public relations professionals, journalists and media organizations. Builds effective relationships with media based on mutual respect and trust. Analyzes current events and trends for opportunities and threats. Identifies appropriate controlled and un-controlled media channels and key influencers.	
6.5	**Networks:** Understands how different tactics can be used to establish and enhance relationships (e.g., electronic communications, special events, face-to-face communication, networking, social networking, word-of-mouth and third-party communication). Recognizes interconnectedness among various stakeholders. Considers broad/global relationships.	

PRSA Code of Ethics

Preamble

Public Relations Society of America Member Code of Ethics 2000

- Professional Values
- Principles of Conduct
- Commitment and Compliance

This Code applies to PRSA members. The Code is designed to be a useful guide for PRSA members as they carry out their ethical responsibilities. This document is designed to anticipate and accommodate, by precedent, ethical challenges that may arise. The scenarios outlined in the Code provision are actual examples of misconduct. More will be added as experience with the Code occurs.

The Public Relations Society of America (PRSA) is committed to ethical practices. The level of public trust PRSA members seek, as we serve the public good, means we have taken on a special obligation to operate ethically.

The value of member reputation depends upon the ethical conduct of everyone affiliated with the Public Relations Society of America. Each of us sets an example for each other—as well as other professionals—by our pursuit of excellence with powerful standards of performance, professionalism, and ethical conduct.

Emphasis on enforcement of the Code has been eliminated. But, the PRSA Board of Directors retains the right to bar from membership or expel from the Society any individual who has been or is sanctioned by a government agency or convicted in a court of law of an action that is not in compliance with the Code.

Ethical practice is the most important obligation of a PRSA member. We view the Member Code of Ethics as a model for other professions, organizations, and professionals.

PRSA Member Statement of Professional Values

This statement presents the core values of PRSA members and, more broadly, of the public relations profession. These values provide the foundation for the Member Code of Ethics and set the industry standard for the professional practice of public relations. These values are the fundamental beliefs that guide our behaviors and decision-making process. We believe our professional values are vital to the integrity of the profession as a whole.

ADVOCACY

We serve the public interest by acting as responsible advocates for those we represent. We provide a voice in the marketplace of ideas, facts, and viewpoints to aid informed public debate.

HONESTY

We adhere to the highest standards of accuracy and truth in advancing the interests of those we represent and in communicating with the public.

EXPERTISE

We acquire and responsibly use specialized knowledge and experience. We advance the profession through continued professional development, research, and education. We build mutual understanding, credibility, and relationships among a wide array of institutions and audiences.

INDEPENDENCE

We provide objective counsel to those we represent. We are accountable for our actions.

LOYALTY

We are faithful to those we represent, while honoring our obligation to serve the public interest.

FAIRNESS

We deal fairly with clients, employers, competitors, peers, vendors, the media, and the general public. We respect all opinions and support the right of free expression.

PRSA Code Provisions

FREE FLOW OF INFORMATION

Core Principle: Protecting and advancing the free flow of accurate and truthful information is essential to serving the public interest and contributing to informed decision-making in a democratic society.

INTENT:

> To maintain the integrity of relationships with the media, government officials, and the public.
>
> To aid informed decision-making.

GUIDELINES:

A member shall:

> Preserve the integrity of the process of communication.
>
> Be honest and accurate in all communications.

Act promptly to correct erroneous communications for which the practitioner is responsible.

Preserve the free flow of unprejudiced information when giving or receiving gifts by ensuring that gifts are nominal, legal, and infrequent.

EXAMPLES OF IMPROPER CONDUCT UNDER THIS PROVISION:

A member representing a ski manufacturer gives a pair of expensive racing skis to a sports magazine columnist, to influence the columnist to write favorable articles about the product.

A member entertains a government official beyond legal limits and/or in violation of government reporting requirements.

COMPETITION

Core Principle: Promoting healthy and fair competition among professionals preserves an ethical climate while fostering a robust business environment.

INTENT:

To promote respect and fair competition among public relations professionals.

To serve the public interest by providing the widest choice of practitioner options.

GUIDELINES:

A member shall:

Follow ethical hiring practices designed to respect free and open competition without deliberately undermining a competitor.

Preserve intellectual property rights in the marketplace.

EXAMPLES OF IMPROPER CONDUCT UNDER THIS PROVISION:

A member employed by a "client organization" shares helpful information with a counseling firm that is competing with others for the organization's business.

A member spreads malicious and unfounded rumors about a competitor in order to alienate the competitor's clients and employees in a ploy to recruit people and business.

DISCLOSURE OF INFORMATION

Core Principle: Open communication fosters informed decision-making in a democratic society.

INTENT:

To build trust with the public by revealing all information needed for responsible decision-making.

GUIDELINES:

A member shall:

Be honest and accurate in all communications.

Act promptly to correct erroneous communications for which the member is responsible.

Investigate the truthfulness and accuracy of information released on behalf of those represented.

Reveal the sponsors for causes and interests represented.

Disclose financial interest (such as stock ownership) in a client's organization.

Avoid deceptive practices.

EXAMPLES OF IMPROPER CONDUCT UNDER THIS PROVISION:

Front groups: A member implements "grass roots" campaigns or letter-writing campaigns to legislators on behalf of undisclosed interest groups.

Lying by omission: A practitioner for a corporation knowingly fails to release financial information, giving a misleading impression of the corporation's performance.

A member discovers inaccurate information disseminated via a website or media kit and does not correct the information.

A member deceives the public by employing people to pose as volunteers to speak at public hearings and participate in "grass roots" campaigns.

SAFEGUARDING CONFIDENCES

Core Principle: Client trust requires appropriate protection of confidential and private information.

INTENT:

To protect the privacy rights of clients, organizations, and individuals by safeguarding confidential information.

GUIDELINES:

A member shall:

Safeguard the confidences and privacy rights of present, former, and prospective clients and employees.

Protect privileged, confidential, or insider information gained from a client or organization.

Immediately advise an appropriate authority if a member discovers that confidential information is being divulged by an employee of a client company or organization.

EXAMPLES OF IMPROPER CONDUCT UNDER THIS PROVISION:

A member changes jobs, takes confidential information, and uses that information in the new position to the detriment of the former employer.

A member intentionally leaks proprietary information to the detriment of some other party.

CONFLICTS OF INTEREST

Core Principle: Avoiding real, potential or perceived conflicts of interest builds the trust of clients, employers, and the publics.

INTENT:

To earn trust and mutual respect with clients or employers.

To build trust with the public by avoiding or ending situations that put one's personal or professional interests in conflict with society's interests.

GUIDELINES:

A member shall:

Act in the best interests of the client or employer, even subordinating the member's personal interests.

Avoid actions and circumstances that may appear to compromise good business judgment or create a conflict between personal and professional interests.

Disclose promptly any existing or potential conflict of interest to affected clients or organizations.

Encourage clients and customers to determine if a conflict exists after notifying all affected parties.

EXAMPLES OF IMPROPER CONDUCT UNDER THIS PROVISION:

The member fails to disclose that he or she has a strong financial interest in a client's chief competitor.

The member represents a "competitor company" or a "conflicting interest" without informing a prospective client.

ENHANCING THE PROFESSION

Core Principle: Public relations professionals work constantly to strengthen the public's trust in the profession.

INTENT:

To build respect and credibility with the public for the profession of public relations.

To improve, adapt and expand professional practices.

GUIDELINES:

A member shall:

Acknowledge that there is an obligation to protect and enhance the profession.

Keep informed and educated about practices in the profession to ensure ethical conduct.

Actively pursue personal professional development.

Decline representation of clients or organizations that urge or require actions contrary to this Code.

Accurately define what public relations activities can accomplish.

Counsel subordinates in proper ethical decision-making.

Require that subordinates adhere to the ethical requirements of the Code.

Report practices not in compliance with the Code, whether committed by PRSA members or not, to the appropriate authority.

EXAMPLES OF IMPROPER CONDUCT UNDER THIS PROVISION:

A PRSA member declares publicly that a product the client sells is safe, without disclosing evidence to the contrary.

A member initially assigns some questionable client work to a non-member practitioner to avoid the ethical obligation of PRSA membership.

PRSA Member Code of Ethics Pledge

I pledge:

To conduct myself professionally, with truth, accuracy, fairness, and responsibility to the public; To improve my individual competence and advance the knowledge and proficiency of the profession through continuing research and education; And to adhere to the articles of the Member Code of Ethics 2000 for the practice of public relations as adopted by the governing Assembly of the Public Relations Society of America.

I understand and accept that there is a consequence for misconduct, up to and including membership revocation.

And, I understand that those who have been or are sanctioned by a government agency or convicted in a court of law of an action that is not in compliance with the Code may be barred from membership or expelled from the Society.

_____
Signature

_____
Date

The "IPRA Code of Conduct"

Adopted in 2011 the IPRA Code of Conduct is an affirmation of professional and ethical conduct by members of the International Public Relations Association and recommended to public relations practitioners worldwide.

The Code consolidates the 1961 Code of Venice, the 1965 Code of Athens and the 2007 Code of Brussels.

1. RECALLING *the Charter of the United Nations which determines "to reaffirm faith in fundamental human rights, and in the dignity and worth of the human person";*

2. RECALLING *the 1948 "Universal Declaration of Human Rights" and especially recalling Article 19;*

3. RECALLING *that public relations, by fostering the free flow of information, contributes to the interests of all stakeholders;*

4. RECALLING *that the conduct of public relations and public affairs provides essential democratic representation to public authorities;*

5. RECALLING *that public relations practitioners through their wide-reaching communication skills possess a means of influence that should be restrained by the observance of a code of professional and ethical conduct;*

6. RECALLING *that channels of communication such as the Internet and other digital media, are channels where erroneous or misleading information may be widely disseminated and remain unchallenged, and therefore demand special attention from public relations practitioners to maintain trust and credibility;*

7. RECALLING *that the Internet and other digital media demand special care with respect to the personal privacy of individuals, clients, employers and colleagues;*

In the conduct of public relations practitioners shall:

1. Observance
Observe the principles of the UN Charter and the Universal Declaration of Human Rights;

2. Integrity
Act with honesty and integrity at all times so as to secure and retain the confidence of those with whom the practitioner comes into contact;

3. Dialogue

Seek to establish the moral, cultural and intellectual conditions for dialogue, and recognise the rights of all parties involved to state their case and express their views;

4. Transparency

Be open and transparent in declaring their name, organisation and the interest they represent;

5. Conflict

Avoid any professional conflicts of interest and to disclose such conflicts to affected parties when they occur;

6. Confidentiality

Honour confidential information provided to them;

7. Accuracy

Take all reasonable steps to ensure the truth and accuracy of all information provided;

8. Falsehood

Make every effort to not intentionally disseminate false or misleading information, exercise proper care to avoid doing so unintentionally and correct any such act promptly;

9. Deception

Not obtain information by deceptive or dishonest means;

10. Disclosure

Not create or use any organisation to serve an announced cause but which actually serves an undisclosed interest;

11. Profit

Not sell for profit to third parties copies of documents obtained from public authorities;

12. Remuneration

Whilst providing professional services, not accept any form of payment in connection with those services from anyone other than the principal;

13. Inducement

Neither directly nor indirectly offer nor give any financial or other inducement to public representatives or the media, or other stakeholders;

14. Influence

Neither propose nor undertake any action which would constitute an improper influence on public representatives, the media, or other stakeholders;

15. Competitors

Not intentionally injure the professional reputation of another practitioner;

16. Poaching

Not seek to secure another practitioner's client by deceptive means;

17. Employment

When employing personnel from public authorities or competitors take care to follow the rules and confidentiality requirements of those organisations;

18. Colleagues

Observe this Code with respect to fellow IPRA members and public relations practitioners worldwide.

IPRA members shall, in upholding this Code, agree to abide by and help enforce the disciplinary procedures of the International Public Relations Association in regard to any breach of this Code.

Note: Adopted by the IPRA Board 5 November 2010.

IPR Ethical Standards and Guidelines for Public Relations Research and Measurement

Preface

This statement of ethical standards and guidelines for public relations research was developed by a team of the Institute for Public Relations Measurement Commission headed by Shannon Bowen, Ph.D, John Gilfeather and Brad Rawlins, Ph.D. This statement was approved by the IPR Measurement Commission on March 7, 2012. This is a discussion document that will be further developed in the near future as proposed interim standards for ethics in research and measurement.

Ethics Statement

The duty of professionals engaged in research, measurement, and evaluation for public relations is to advance the highest ethical standards and ideals for research. All research should abide by the principles of intellectual honesty, fairness, dignity, disclosure, and respect for all stakeholders involved, namely clients (both external and internal), colleagues, research participants, the public relations profession, and the researchers themselves.

This statement is based on and promotes the following Core Values:

- Autonomy
- Respondent rights
- Dignity
- Fairness
- Balance
- Duty
- Lack of bias
- Honesty
- Not using misleading information or "cherry picking" data
- Full disclosure
- Discretion
- Judgment
- Protection of proprietary data
- Public responsibility
- Intellectual integrity
- Good intention
- Valuing the truth behind the numbers
- Reflexivity (put self in other's place)
- Moral courage and objectivity

Notes

CHAPTER 1

1. James E. Grunig and Todd Hunt, *Managing Public Relations* (New York: Holt, Rinehart and Winston, 184), 6.
2. Glen M. Broom and Bey-Ling Sha, *Cutlip and Center's Effective Public Relations*, 11th ed. (Upper Saddle River, NJ: Prentice Hall, 2013), 5.
3. http://www.latimes.com/entertainment/tv/showtracker/la-et-st-kerry-washington-olivia-pope-scandal-role-model-20150805-story.html.
4. "21 Ridiculous Social Media Job Titles," Memeburn, accessed July 12, 2014, http://memeburn.com/2013/05/21-ridiculous-social-media-job-titles/.
5. "Public Relations Defined: A Modern Definition for the New Era of Public Relations," Public Relations Society of America, accessed July 12, 2014, http://prdefinition.prsa.org.
6. Stuart Elliott, "Redefining Public Relations in the Age of Social Media," *The New York Times*, November 20, 2011, accessed July 12, 2014, http://www.nytimes.com/2011/11/21/business/media/redefining-public-relations-in-the-age-of-social-media.html.
7. "Crowdsource," Oxford Dictionaries, accessed July 12, 2014, http://oxforddictionaries.com/us/definition/american_english/crowdsource?q=crowdsourcing.
8. "Snapshot: #PRDefined Word Cloud-Day 12," Public Relations Defined, accessed July 12, 2014, http://prdefinition.prsa.org/index.php/2011/12/02/snapshot-of-the-public-relations-defined-initaitve-submission-day12/.
9. "About Greenwashing," Greenwashing Index, accessed July 12, 2014. http://www.greenwashingindex.com/about-greenwashing/#score.
10. "Greenwashing Index," accessed July 12, 2014, http://www.greenwashingindex.com.
11. Pamela J. Brubaker, "Arthur W. Page: A Man of Vision, Valor, and Values," in *Words from a Page in History* (University Park, PA: Arthur W. Page Center for Integrity in Public Communication, 2011), 5–9.
12. Brad Rawlins, "Give the Emperor a Mirror: Toward Developing a Stakeholder Measurement of Organizational Transparency," *Journal of Public Relations Research* 21, no. 1 (2008): 71–99, 75.
13. Sarosh Waiz, "40+ Best Advertising Slogans of Modern Brands," Advergize, March 22, 2013, http://www.advergize.com/advertising/40-best-advertising-slogans-modern-brands/.
14. John Vernon Pavlik and Shawn McIntosh, *Converging Media: A New Introduction to Mass Communication* (New York: Oxford University Press, 2011), 365.
15. Anne Landman, "BP's 'Beyond Petroleum' Campaign Losing Its Sheen," The Center for Media and Democracy's PR Watch, May 3, 2010, accessed July 12, 2014, http://www.prwatch.org/node/9038.
16. Elizabeth Shogren, "BP: A Textbook Example of How Not to Handle PR," NPR.org, April 21, 2011, http://www.npr.org/2011/04/21/135575238/ bp-a-textbook-example-of-how-not-to-handle-pr.
17. Robert Kendall, *Public Relations Campaign Strategies*, 2nd ed. (New York: HarperCollins, 1996), 527.
18. "Edelman 2012 Trust Barometer Press Release," Edelman, accessed July 13, 2014, http://trust.edelman.com/trust-download/press-release/.
19. Tom Kelleher, "Conversational Voice, Communicated Commitment, and Public Relations Outcomes in Interactive Online Communication," *Journal of Communication* 59, no. 1 (2009): 172–188.
20. Arthur W. Page, "Speech Presented at the Bell Telephone System's General Manager Conference—May 1931," The Arthur W. Page Center at Penn State, accessed July 13, 2014, http://thepagecenter.comm.psu.edu/index.php?option=com_content&view=article&id=413:speech14&catid=36.
21. Harold Burson, "Is Public Relations Now Too Important to Be Left to Public Relations Professionals?," lecture delivered to the Institute for Public Relations, London, October 20, 2004.

22. "Ethics and Public Relations," Institute for Public Relations, accessed July 13, 2014, http://www.instituteforpr.org/topics/ethics-and-public-relations/.

23. Philip M. Seib and Kathy Fitzpatrick, *Public Relations Ethics* (Fort Worth, TX: Harcourt Brace College Publishers, 1995).

24. Kathy R. Fitzpatrick, "Ethical Decision-Making Guide Helps Resolve Ethical Dilemmas," Public Relations Society of America, accessed July 13, 2014, http://www.prsa.org/AboutPRSA/Ethics/documents/decisionguide.pdf.

25. "About Todd Defren," PR Squared, accessed July 13, 2014, http://www.pr-squared.com/index.php/about.

26. Todd Defren, "Tweeting Under False Circumstances: Social Media Ethical Dilemmas," PR Squared, accessed July 13, 2014, http://www.pr-squared.com/index.php/2010/01/tweeting-under-false-circumstances-social-media-ethical-dilemmas.

27. "About Enforcement," Public Relations Society of America, accessed July 13, 2014, http://www.prsa.org/AboutPRSA/Ethics/About Enforcement/index.html.

28. "PRSA Code of Ethics Preamble," Public Relations Society of America, accessed July 13, 2014, http://www.prsa.org/aboutprsa/ethics/codeenglish.

CHAPTER 2

1. James E. Grunig and Todd Hunt, *Managing Public Relations* (New York: Holt, Rinehart and Winston, 1984), 4.

2. James E. Grunig and Todd Hunt, *Managing Public Relations* (New York: Holt, Rinehart and Winston, 1984), 21.

3. Benjamin Reiss, "PT Barnum, Joice Heth and Antebellum Spectacles of Race," *American Quarterly* 51 (1999): 78–107.

4. Phineas Taylor Barnum, *Life of PT Barnum* (Buffalo, NY: The Courier Company Printers, 1886), 38.

5. http://brandchannel.com/2015/12/16/kfc-hong-kong-tvb-awards-121615/.

6. http://www.thewrap.com/ellen-degeneres-oscars-pizza-party-sparks-sales-surge-pizzeria/.

7. http://www.forbes.com/sites/lauraheller/2011/08/17/abercrombie-to-the-situation-stop-wearing-our-clothes/.

8. http://www.nytimes.com/2011/08/18/business/abercrombie-offers-jersey-shore-cast-a-paid-non-product-placement.html.

9. http://www.nytimes.com/2011/08/18/business/abercrombie-offers-jersey-shore-cast-a-paid-non-product-placement.html.

10. http://www.salon.com/2006/01/24/jeffries/.

11. http://mashable.com/2013/05/15/fitchthehomeless-abercrombie-fitch-homeless/.

12. http://www.relevantmagazine.com/reject-apathy/poverty/why-fitchthehomeless-backfires.

13. Scott M. Cutlip, *The Unseen Power: Public Relations, a History* (Hillsdale, NJ: Lawrence Erlbaum Associates, 1994), 40.

14. Ray Eldon Hiebert, *Courtier to the Crowd: The Story of Ivy Lee and the Development of Public Relations* (Ames: Iowa State University Press, 1966), 45.

15. Scott M. Cutlip, *The Unseen Power: Public Relations, a History* (Hillsdale, NJ: Lawrence Erlbaum Associates, 1994), 41.

16. Scott M. Cutlip, *The Unseen Power: Public Relations, a History* (Hillsdale, NJ: Lawrence Erlbaum Associates, 1994), 44.

17. Ray Eldon Hiebert, *Courtier to the Crowd: The Story of Ivy Lee and the Development of Public Relations* (Ames: Iowa State University Press, 1966), 48.

18. http://www.wired.com/wired/archive/15.04/wired40_ceo.html.

19. Scott M. Cutlip, *The Unseen Power: Public Relations, a History* (Hillsdale, NJ: Lawrence Erlbaum Associates, 1994), 53.

20. http://emilms.fema.gov/IS29/PIOsummary.htm.

21. Edward Bernays, *Biography of an Idea: Memoirs of Public Relations Counsel Edward L. Bernays* (New York: Simon and Schuster, 1965), 386.

22. Edward Bernays, *Biography of an Idea: Memoirs of Public Relations Counsel Edward L. Bernays* (New York: Simon and Schuster, 1965), 387.

23. Edward Bernays, *Biography of an Idea: Memoirs of Public Relations Counsel Edward L. Bernays* (New York: Simon and Schuster, 1965), 387.

24. Vanessa Murphree, "Edward Bernays's 1929 'Torches of Freedom' March: Myths and Historical Significance." American Journalism 32, no. 3 (2015): 258–281.

25. http://www.prmuseum.com/bernays/bernays_video_bacon.html.

26. James E. Grunig and Todd Hunt, *Managing Public Relations* (New York: Holt, Rinehart and Winston, 1984), 39.

27. Scott M. Cutlip, *The Unseen Power: Public Relations, a History* (Hillsdale, NJ: Lawrence Erlbaum Associates, 1994).

28. Arthur W. Page, "Speech to the Public Relations Conference of Chesapeake & Ohio Railway Company, October 27, 1939," accessed August 2, 2013, from http://thepagecenter.comm.psu.edu/index.php/research-resources/page-speeches/402-speech25.

29. James E. Grunig, "Two-Way Symmetrical Public Relations: Past, Present, and Future," in *Handbook of Public Relations*, ed. Robert L. Heath (Thousand Oaks, CA: Sage, 2001), 12.

30. http://www.bizjournals.com/pacific/news/2013/07/17/robbie-alm-leaving-hawaiian-electric.html.

31. http://www.hawaiibusiness.com/Hawaii-Business/April-2012/Talk-Story-with-Robbie-Alm/.

32. Robert E. Brown, "St. Paul as a Public Relations Practitioner: A Metatheoretical Speculation on Messianic Communication and Symmetry," *Public Relations Review* 29 (2003): 1–12.

33. Margaret Opdycke Lamme and Karen Miller Russell, "Removing the Spin: Toward a New Theory of Public Relations History," *Journalism & Communication Monographs* 11 (2010): 279–361.

34. Robert E. Brown, "St. Paul as a Public Relations Practitioner: A Metatheoretical Speculation on Messianic Communication and Symmetry," *Public Relations Review* 29 (2003): 232.

35. http://www.religioncommunicators.org/a-brief-history.

36. http://njop.org/resources/social-media-for-synagogues/jewish-treats-top-ten-jewish-influencer-awards/.

37. http://www.islamographic.com.

38. Margaret Opdycke Lamme and Karen Miller Russell, "Removing the Spin: Toward a New Theory of Public Relations History," *Journalism & Communication Monographs* 11 (2010): 279–361; Scott M. Cutlip, *Public Relations History: From the 17th to the 20th Century: The Antecedents* (Mahwah, NJ: Erlbaum, 1995).

39. Scott M. Cutlip, *Public Relations History: From the 17th to the 20th Century: The Antecedents* (Mahwah, NJ: Erlbaum, 1995).

40. Doug Newsom, J. Vanslyke Turk and D. Kruckeberg, *This Is PR: The Realities of Public Relations*, 8th ed. (Belmont, CA: Wadsworth/Thomson, 2004).

41. http://content.time.com/time/specials/packages/article/0,28804,2023831_2023829_2025198,00.html.

42. http://wcfcourier.com/news/local/govt-and-politics/nagle-howard-dean-was-the-godfather-of-today-s-online/.

43. http://www.jobvite.com/wp-content/uploads/2015/09/jobvite_recruiter_nation_2015.pdf.

44. Tom Kelleher and Kaye Sweetser, "Social Media Adoption Among University Communicators," *Journal of Public Relations Research* 24 (2012): 113.

45. Günter Bentele and Ivonne Junghänel, "Germany," in *Public Relations and Communication Management in Europe*, ed. Betteke Van Ruler and Dejan Verčič (Berlin: Mouton de Gruyter, 2004). Cited in Lamme and Russell, 288.

46. Karl Nessman, "Austria," in *Public Relations and Communication Management in Europe*, ed. Betteke Van Ruler and Dejan Verčič (Berlin: Mouton de Gruyter, 2004). Cited in Lamme and Russell, 288.

47. Paul F. Lazarsfeld and Robert K. Merton, "Mass Communication, Popular Taste and Organized Social Action," in *The Communication of Ideas*, ed. Lyman Bryson (New York: Harper & Bros, 1948). Reprinted in Paul Marris and Sue Thornham, *Media Studies: A Reader*, 2nd ed. (New York: NYU Press, 2000), 20.

48. http://www.npr.org/blogs/parallels/2013/05/14/183966785/for-palestinians-googles-small-change-is-a-big-deal.

49. Genevieve G. McBride, *On Wisconsin Women: Working for Their Rights from Settlement to Suffrage* (Madison: University of Wisconsin Press, 1993). Cited in Lamme and Russell.

50. http://www.nytimes.com/2012/02/06/technology/06iht-acta06.html?hpw=&pagewant.

51. http://www.avaaz.org/en/about.php.

52. Margaret Opdycke Lamme and Karen Miller Russell, "Removing the Spin: Toward a New Theory of Public Relations History." *Journalism & Communication Monographs* 11 (2010): 340.

53. Patrick Lee Plaisance, "Transparency: An Assessment of the Kantian Roots of a Key Element in Media Ethics Practice," *Journal of Mass Media Ethics* 22 (2007): 187–207.

54. James E. Grunig and Todd Hunt, *Managing Public Relations* (New York: Holt, Rinehart and Winston, 1984), p. 34.

55. http://www.oxforddictionaries.com/us/definition/american_english/objective?q=objective.

56. http://www.journalism.org/resources/principles-of-journalism/.

57. http://www.prsa.org/aboutprsa/ethics/codeenglish/.

58. http://www.spj.org/ethicscode.asp.

59. Genevieve McBride, "Ethical Thought in Public Relations History: Seeking a Relevant Perspective," *Journal of Mass Media Ethics* 4, no. 1 (1989): 5–20, p. 15.

60. *Lewiston Evening Journal*, July 12, 1934, p. 5 (via news.google.com).

CHAPTER 3

1. Henry Jenkins, *Convergence Culture: Where Old and New Media Collide* (New York: New York University Press, 2006), 14.

2. Henry Jenkins, *Convergence Culture: Where Old and New Media Collide* (New York: New York University Press, 2006), 14.

3. Henry Jenkins, "Convergence? I Diverge," *Technology Review* 104, no. 5 (2001): 93.

4. http://www.theglobalist.com/globalization-and-cultural-convergence/.

5. Henry Jenkins, *Convergence Culture: Where Old and New Media Collide* (New York: New York University Press, 2006), 18.

6. http://www.businessinsider.com/vladimir-putin-nyt-op-ed-ketchum-pr-2013-9.

7. http://www.thefreelibrary.com/Omnicom+Group+acquisition+of+Ketchum+Communications.-a017999670.

8. http://www.omnicomgroup.com/home.

9. http://adage.com/article/special-report-super-bowl/super-bowl-50-ad-chart-buying-big-game-commercials/301183/.

10. http://adage.com/article/special-report-super-bowl/super-bowl-50-ad-chart-buying-big-game-commercials/301183/.

11. http://www.marketingpower.com/AboutAMA/Pages/DefinitionofMarketing.aspx.

12. E. Jerome McCarthy, *Basic Marketing: A Managerial Approach* (Homewood, IL: Richard D. Irwin Inc., 1960).

13. http://www.electronichouse.com/eh/about_us.

14. http://www.wommapedia.org/#section1.

15. http://www.youtube.com/watch?v=Fz22PfPxoXI.

16. http://mashable.com/2013/07/08/facebook-promoted-posts-business/.

17. https://www.ae.com/aerie/stylegallery/.

18. Bob Lauterborn, "New Marketing Litany; Four P's Passe; C-Words Take Over," *Advertising Age* (1990, October 1): 26.

19. Henry Ford and Samuel Crowther, *My Life and Work* (Sydney: Cornstalk Publishing Company, 1922), 72.

20. *Portlandia*, "Is It Local?" Season 1, Episode 1, http://www.ifc.com/portlandia/videos/portlandia-is-it-local.

21. http://www.cluetrain.com/book/markets.html.

22. http://contentmarketinginstitute.com/what-is-content-marketing/.

23. http://mashable.com/2012/12/19/red-bull-content-marketing/.

24. http://www.shiftcomm.com/2013/11/2014-will-be-the-year-of-brand-journalism/.

25. http://www.commpro.biz/social-video/views-you-can-use/chrysler-group-vide/.

26. http://www.nytimes.com/2013/09/12/opinion/putin-plea-for-caution-from-russia-on-syria.html.

27. http://www.propublica.org/article/from-russia-with-pr-ketchum-cnbc.

28. http://www.buzzfeed.com/rosiegray/ketchum-placed-controversial-putin-op-ed.

29. http://www.prsa.org/aboutprsa/ethics/codeenglish/.

30. http://www.prweek.com/article/1337821/ketchum-calls-quits-russia-work.

CHAPTER 4

1. John A. Ledingham and Stephen D. Bruning (eds.), *Public Relations as Relationship Management: A Relational Approach to the Study and Practice of Public Relations* (New York: Routledge, 2000), xii–xiii.

2. Linda Childers Hon and James E. Grunig, "Guidelines for Measuring Relationships in Public Relations," The Institute for Public Relations, accessed July 21, 2014,

http://www.instituteforpr.org/wp-content/uploads/Guidelines_Measuring_Relationships.pdf.

3. Linda Childers Hon and James E. Grunig, "Guidelines for Measuring Relationships in Public Relations," The Institute for Public Relations, accessed July 21, 2014, http://www.instituteforpr.org/wp-content/uploads/Guidelines_Measuring_Relationships.pdf.

4. Elizabeth L. Toth, "From Personal Influence to Interpersonal Influence: A Model for Relationship Management," in *Public Relations as Relationship Management: A Relational Approach to the Study and Practice of Public Relations* (New York: Routledge, 2000), 205–219.

5. "Media," Oxford Dictionaries, accessed July 21, 2014, http://www.oxforddictionaries.com/us/definition/american_english/media?q=media#media.

6. Peter Himler, "Media Relations Is Dead. Long Live Media Relations," PRSAY, accessed July 22, 2014, http://prsay.prsa.org/index.php/2014/01/15/media-relations-is-dead-long-live-media-relations/.

7. "Worksheet 1.1: What Is Newsworthy?," PBS News Student Reporting Labs, accessed April 3, 2016, http://www.studentreportinglabs.com/sites/default/files/Worksheet%201.1.pdf.

8. "Rising Medical Solutions Named National Case Management Awards Finalist," PR Newswire, accessed July 22, 2014, http://www.prnewswire.com/news-releases/rising-medical-solutions-named-national-case-management-awards-finalist-250216211.html.

9. "C. Anthony Harris Achieves New Heights with ViSalus," PR Newswire, accessed July 22, 2014, http://www.prnewswire.com/news-releases/c-anthony-harris-achieves-new-heights-with-visalus-250217571.html.

10. Richard D., Waters, Natalie TJ Tindall and Timothy S. Morton, "Media Catching and the Journalist–Public Relations Practitioner Relationship: How Social Media Are Changing the Practice of Media Relations," *Journal of Public Relations Research* 22, no. 3 (2010): 241–264.

11. Jennifer G. Hanford, "5 Fantastic Examples of B2B Social Media Marketing," Social Media Today, accessed July 22, 2014, http://socialmediatoday.com/jenniferhanford/2094261/five-fantastic-examples-b2b-social-media-marketing.

12. "Best Companies to Work For 2014," Fortune, accessed July 22, 2014, http://money.cnn.com/magazines/fortune/best-companies/2014/methodology/index.html?iid=BC14_sp_method.

13. Nan S. Russell, "Reality Check: Do You Know the Impact of Trust?" *Psychology Today*, accessed July 22, 2014, http://www.psychologytoday.com/blog/trust-the-new-workplace-currency/201210/reality-check-do-you-know-the-impact-trust.

14. Taylor Short, "3 Ways Intel Gets Employees to Trust (and Adhere to) Their BYOD Security Program," accessed July 22, 2014, http://hello-operator.softwareadvice.com/3-ways-intel-gets-employees-to-trust-their-byod-program-1113/.

15. Linjuan Rita Men, "Engaging Employees: Effectiveness of Traditional vs. New Media Channels," Institute for Public Relations, accessed July 22, 2014, http://www.instituteforpr.org/2013/10/engaging-employees-effectiveness-traditional-vs-new-media-channels/.

16. http://www1.salary.com/Investor-Relations-Manager-Salaries.html; http://www.bloomberg.com/professional/blog/how-much-do-ir-professionals-earn/.

17. "About Us," National Investor Relations Institute, accessed July 22, 2014, http://www.niri.org/about/mission.cfm.

18. Alexander V. Laskin, "The Value of Investor Relations: A Delphi Panel Investigation," http://www.instituteforpr.org/wp-content/uploads/2007_Laskin.pdf, 21–22.

19. Julie O'Neil, "The Link Between Strong Public Relationships and Donor Support," *Public Relations Review* 33, no. 1 (2007): 99.

20. Richard D. Waters, "Measuring Stewardship in Public Relations: A Test Exploring Impact on the Fundraising Relationship," *Public Relations Review* 35, no. 2 (2009): 113–119.

21. Richard D. Waters, "Measuring Stewardship in Public Relations: A Test Exploring Impact on the Fundraising Relationship," *Public Relations Review* 35, no. 2 (2009): 116.

22. Kathleen S. Kelly, *Effective Fund-Raising Management* (Mahwah, NJ: Lawrence Erlbaum Associates, 1998), 441.

23. "Issue," Oxford Dictionaries, accessed July 22, 2014, http://www.oxforddictionaries.com/us/definition/american_english/issue?q=issue.

24. Larissa Grunig, "Activism: How It Limits the Effectiveness of Organizations and How Excellent Public Relations Departments Respond," in *Excellence in Public Relations and Communication Management*, ed. J. E. Grunig (Hillsdale, NJ: Lawrence Erlbaum, 2009), 504.

25. Mitch McNeil, "The Reality of Surfing in Chicago," The Inertia, accessed July 23, 2014, http://www.theinertia.com/surf/the-reality-of-surfing-in-chicago/.

26. "Surfing Information and Safety Awareness," Chicago Park District, accessed July 23, 2014, http://public.surfrider.org/files/Chicago_Surfing_Info_Safety.pdf.

27. Mark KonKol, "11-Time Surfing Champ Slater Says Chicago Regulates Waves 'Like a Police State,'" *Chicago Sun-Times*, January 19, 2012, accessed July 23, 2014, http://www.suntimes.com/news/metro/10110667-418/11-time-surfing-champ-slater-says-chicago-regulates-waves-like-a-police-state.html; Kelly Slater, January 18, 2012 (9:43 a.m.), commented on Twitter, "Surfing is not a crime," accessed July 23, 2014, https://twitter.com/kellyslater/status/159692314418225152.

28. "Lobbying Spending Database," OpenSecrets, accessed July 23, 2014, https://www.opensecrets.org/lobby/clientsum.php?id=D000000632.

29. "Interbrand-Best Global Brands," Interbrand, accessed July 25, 2014, http://www.interbrand.com/it/best-global-brands/2013/Coca-Cola.

30. "Are All Calories Created Equal?," Arthur W. Page Society, accessed July 25, 2014, http://www.awpagesociety.com/wp-content/uploads/2014/03/Coca-Cola_CaseStudy.pdf.

31. "Coca-Cola's Global Commitments to Help Fight Obesity," The Coca-Cola Company, accessed July 25, 2014, http://www.coca-colacompany.com/coming-together/infographic-illustrating-coca-colas-global-commitments-to-help-fight-obesity.

32. "About CSPI," Center for Science in the Public Interest, accessed July 25, 2014, http://www.cspinet.org/about/index.html.

33. CSPI, May 8, 2013 (12:55 p.m.), commented on Twitter, "Coca-Cola is desperately trying . . .," https://twitter.com/CSPI/status/332222216836087808.

34. http://www.nielsen.com/us/en/press-room/2015/consumer-goods-brands-that-demonstrate-commitment-to-sustainability-outperform.html.

35. "New Study Shows Strong CSR Boosts Profits," *Bulldog Reporter*, accessed July 25, 2014, http://www.bulldogreporter.com/dailydog/article/pr-biz-update/new-study-shows-strong-csr-boosts-profits-majority-of-companies-incre.

36. "Public Policy Engagement," The Coca-Cola Company, accessed July 25, 2014, http://www.coca-colacompany.com/investors/public-policy-engagement.

37. http://www.nytimes.com/2014/06/27/nyregion/city-loses-final-appeal-on-limiting-sales-of-large-sodas.html?_r=0.

CHAPTER 5

1. John E. Marston, *The Nature of Public Relations* (New York: McGraw-Hill, 1963).

2. Jerry Hendrix, Darrell Hayes and Pallavi Kumar, *Public Relations Cases* (Boston: Cengage Learning, 2013).

3. Sheila Clough Crifasi, as cited in Fraser P. Seitel, *The Practice of Public Relations*, 12th ed. (Upper Saddle River, NJ: Pearson, 2014).

4. "Silver Anvil Search," Public Relations Society of America, accessed April 4, 2016, http://www.prsa.org/Awards/SilverAnvil/Search.

5. Laurie J. Wilson and Joseph D. Ogden, *Strategic Communications Planning for Effective Public Relations & Marketing* (Dubuque, IA: Kendall Hunt, 2008).

6. "Silver Anvil Search," Public Relations Society of America, accessed September 21, 2014, http://www.prsa.org/Awards/SilverAnvil/Search.

7. http://www.traderjoes.com/our-story/timeline.

8. Tom Kelleher, "Conversational Voice, Communicated Commitment, and Public Relations Outcomes in Interactive Online Communication," *Journal of Communication* 59, no. 1 (2009): 172–188.

9. Kara Swisher, "Here's the Internal Yahoo No-Work-from-Home Memo for Remote Workers and Maybe More," All Things D,

accessed September 12, 2014, http://all thingsd.com/20130222/physically-together-heres-the-internal-yahoo-no-work-from-home-memo-which-extends-beyond-remote-workers/.

10. Kurt Lewin, *Field Theory in Social Science* (New York: Harper & Row, 1951), 169.

11. "Net Neutrality: What You Need to Know Now," Free Press, accessed September 12, 2014, http://www.savetheinternet.com/net-neutrality-101.

12. Reed Hastings, March 20, 2014 (2:00 p.m.), comment on Netflix US & Canada Blogs, "Internet Tolls and the Case for Strong Net Neutrality," accessed September 12, 2014, http://blog.netflix.com/2014/03/internet-tolls-and-case-for-strong-net.html.

13. https://www.fcc.gov/document/fcc-adopts-strong-sustainable-rules-protect-open-internet

14. http://www.freepress.net/press-release/106826/historic-win-internet-users.

15. Mieczysław Radochoński and Anna Radochońska, "Attitudes of the Polish University Students Toward Voluntary Blood Donation," *Rzeszow* 4 (2007): 329–334.

16. Lorenz Goette and Alois Stutzer, "Blood Donations and Incentives: Evidence from a Field Experiment," *IZA Discussion Papers*, no. 3580 (2008), accessed September 4, 2014, http://www.econstor.eu/bitstream/10419/35271/1/57333479X.pdf.

17. Don W. Stacks, *Primer of Public Relations Research* (New York: Guilford Press, 2010).

18. David Silverman, *Interpreting Qualitative Data: Methods for Analyzing Talk, Text and Interaction* (London: Sage, 2006).

19. David L. Morgan, *Focus Groups as Qualitative Research*, Vol. 16 (Thousand Oaks, CA: Sage, 1997), 11.

20. "About the Survey," National Survey on Drug Use and Health, accessed September 12, 2014, https://nsduhweb.rti.org/respweb/project_description.html.

21. "Underage Binge Alcohol Use Varies Within and Across States," The NSDUH Report, accessed September 12, 2014, http://www.samhsa.gov/data/2K14/NSDUH199/sr199-underage-binge-drinking-2014.pdf.

22. Dr. Joseph Sabia, "Minimum Wage and the Business Cycle: Does a Wage Hike Hurt More in a Weak Economy?" Employment Policies Institute, accessed September 18, 2014, http://www.epionline.org/study/minimum-wages-and-the-business-cycle-does-a-wage-hike-hurt-more-in-a-weak-economy/.

23. Kathleen Maclay, "Low-Wage Fast-Food Jobs Leave Hefty Tax Bill, Report Says," UC Berkeley News Center, accessed September 17, 2014, http://newscenter.berkeley.edu/2013/10/15/low-wage-fast-food-jobs-leave-hefty-tax-bill-report-says/.

24. Shannon A. Bowen and Don W. Stacks, "Understanding the Ethical and Research Implications of Social Media," in *Ethical Practice of Social Media in Public Relations*, ed. Marcia W. DiStaso and Denise Sevick Bortree (New York: Routledge, 2014), 219.

25. "Ethical Standards and Guidelines for Public Relations Research and Measurement 2012," Institute for Public Relations, accessed September 18, 2014, http://www.instituteforpr.org/wp-content/uploads/Ethical-standards-and-guidelines-for-public-relations-research-ver-1.1.pdf.

CHAPTER 6

1. Lucy Townsend, "How Much Has the Ice Bucket Challenge Achieved?," *BBC News Magazine*, September 1, 2014, http://www.bbc.com/news/magazine-29013707.

2. "The ALS Association Expresses Sincere Gratitude to Over Three Million Donors," The ALS Association, accessed February 8, 2015, http://www.alsa.org/news/media/press-releases/ice-bucket-challenge-082914.html.

3. "Goal Flow: Flow Analysis of Goals and Funnels," Google, accessed November 26, 2014, https://support.google.com/analytics/answer/1686005?hl=en.

4. Stuart Bruce, "The 10 Best Corporate Vine and Instagram Videos for PR," accessed November 26, 2014, http://stuartbruce.biz/2014/02/the-10-best-corporate-vine-and-instagram-videos-for-pr.html.

5. https://vine.co/tags/6secondscience.

6. Neil Patel, "The Marketer's Guide to Tumblr," KISSmetrics, accessed November 26, 2014, https://blog.kissmetrics.com/the-marketers-guide-to-tumblr/.

7. "About Us/Vision, Principles & Strategy," Water Supply & Sanitation Collaborative Council,

accessed November 26, 2014, http://www
.wsscc.org/about-us/mission-strategy-values.

8. Jelena Vucjic and Pavani K. Ram, *Handwashing Promotion: Monitoring and Evaluation Module*, UNICEF, accessed November 26, 2014, http://www.globalhandwashing.org/sites/default/files/UNICEF%20M%26E%20Toolkit%20Final%2011-24%20Low%20Res.pdf.

9. Jelena Vucjic and Pavani K. Ram, *Handwashing Promotion: Monitoring and Evaluation Module*, UNICEF, accessed November 26, 2014, http://www.globalhandwashing.org/sites/default/files/UNICEF%20M%26E%20Toolkit%20Final%2011-24%20Low%20Res.pdf, 8.

10. Jelena Vucjic and Pavani K. Ram, *Handwashing Promotion: Monitoring and Evaluation Module*, UNICEF, accessed November 26, 2014, http://www.globalhandwashing.org/sites/default/files/UNICEF%20M%26E%20Toolkit%20Final%2011-24%20Low%20Res.pdf.

11. Ronald D. Smith, *Strategic Planning for Public Relations* (Mahwah, NJ: Lawrence Erlbaum Associates, 2006), 240.

12. James Lukaszewski, "Finding Your First Job in Public Relations: How Agency Billing & Salaries Work," accessed November 26, 2014, http://www.e911.com/pr/PartII_HowAgencies Work.pdf.

13. Ameet Ranadive, "Demystifying Programmatic Marketing and RTB," Medium, accessed November 26, 2014, https://medium.com/@ameet/demystifying-programmatic-marketing-and-rtb-83edb8c9ba0f.

14. "Results of 4A's 2011 Television Production Cost Survey," American Association of Advertising Agencies, accessed November 26, 2014, http://www.aaaa.org/news/bulletins/pages/tvprod_01222013.aspx.

15. "Buy Instagram Followers," Foxfans, accessed November 26, 2014, http://foxfans.com/buy-instagram-followers/.

16. "Public Relations Society of America (PRSA) Member Code of Ethics," PRSA, accessed November 26, 2014, http://www.prsa.org/aboutprsa/ethics/codeenglish/.

CHAPTER 7

1. "Food with Integrity," Chipotle, accessed March 5, 2015, https://www.chipotle.com/en-US/fwi/fwi.aspx.

2. "We treat them like animals," Chipotle, accessed March 5, 2015, https://www.chipotle.com/en-US/fwi/animals/animals.aspx.

3. Matt Krantz, "How Chipotle Is Eating McDonald's Lunch," *USA Today*, January 22, 2015, http://americasmarkets.usatoday.com/2015/01/22/how-chipotle-is-eating-mcdonalds-lunch/.

4. Roberto A. Ferdman, "Why Chipotle's Pork Problem Is a Bad Sign for Its Future," *The Washington Post*, January 14, 2015, http://www.washingtonpost.com/blogs/wonkblog/wp/2015/01/14/why-chipotles-pork-problem-is-a-bad-sign-for-its-future/.

5. Erin Mosbaugh, "#Carnitasgate: Chipotle Not Serving Pork at One-Third of Its Restaurants," *First We Feast*, accessed March 5, 2015, http://firstwefeast.com/eat/carnitasgate-chipotle-not-serving-pork-at-one-third-of-its-restaurants/.

6. *APR Study Guide for the Examination for Accreditation in Public Relations*, Universal Accreditation Board, 2010, accessed March 5, 2015, http://www.praccreditation.org/resources/documents/apr-study-guide.pdf.

7. "Governor Masters Political Doublespeak," *CNN*, July 16, 2014, http://edition.cnn.com/videos/bestoftv/2014/07/16/ac-ridiculist-politician-avoids-question.cnn.

8. "LinkedIn Ads—Frequently Asked Questions," LinkedIn, accessed March 5, 2015, http://partner.linkedin.com/ads/info/Ads_faqs_updated_en_US.html.

9. Garett Sloane, "Snapchat Is Asking Brands for $750,000 to Advertise and Won't Budge," *Adweek*, accessed March 5, 2015, http://www.adweek.com/news/technology/snapchat-asks-brands-750000-advertise-and-wont-budge-162359.

10. "In Memoriam: John W. 'Jack' Felton, APR, Fellow PRSA," *Public Relations Tactics*, accessed March 5, 2105, http://www.prsa.org/Search Results/view/10186/105/In_Memoriam_John_W_Jack_Felton_APR_Fellow_PRSA.

11. Christopher Heine, "Arby's Dishes on Awesome Pharrell Williams Tweet," *Adweek*, accessed March 5, 2015, http://www.adweek.com/news/technology/arbys-dishes-awesome-pharrell-williams-tweets-156149.

12. Christopher Ratcliff, "A Look Inside GoPro's Dazzling YouTube Strategy," *Econsultancy*, accessed March 5, 2015, https://econsultancy.com/blog/64370-a-look-inside-gopro-s-dazzling-youtube-strategy.

13. Rosencratzinpants, Twitter post, November 22, 2011, https://twitter.com/PuppyOnTheRadio/status/138873729332686848.

14. Rob Taylor, "Epic Fail for Qantas Twitter Competition," *Reuters*, November 22, 2011, http://www.reuters.com/article/2011/11/22/us-qantas-idUSTRE7AL0HB20111122.

15. *APR Study Guide for the Examination for Accreditation in Public Relations*, Universal Accreditation Board, 2010, accessed March 5, 2015, http://www.praccreditation.org/resources/documents/apr-study-guide.pdf, 18.

16. "Search Engine Optimization," *Wikipedia, the Free Encyclopedia*, accessed March 5, 2015, http://en.wikipedia.org/w/index.php?title=Search_engine_optimization&oldid=648870961.

17. "Steps to a Google-Friendly Site," Google, accessed March 15, 2015, https://support.google.com/webmasters/answer/40349?hl=en.

18. Rebekah Iliff, "Why PR Is Embracing the PESO Model," *Mashable,* December 5, 2014, http://mashable.com/2014/12/05/public-relations-industry/.

19. Rebekah Iliff, "Why PR Is Embracing the PESO Model," *Mashable,* December 5, 2014, http://mashable.com/2014/12/05/public-relations-industry/.

20. Rebekah Iliff, "Why PR Is Embracing the PESO Model," *Mashable,* December 5, 2014, http://mashable.com/2014/12/05/public-relations-industry/.

21. Eric Deggans, "Diversity: The Gateway to Accuracy and Fairness in Media," in *Doing Ethics in Media: Theories and Practical Applications*, ed. Jay Black and Chris Roberts (New York: Taylor & Francis, 2011), 155.

22. "PRSA Member Code of Ethics," PRSA, accessed March 5, 2015, http://www.prsa.org/aboutprsa/ethics/codeenglish/.

23. "Agencies Must Find Answers for a Lack of Diversity," *PRWeek,* May 1, 2011, http://www.prweek.com/article/1264390/agencies-find-answers-lack-diversity.

24. Rosanna M. Fiske, "PRSA Committed to Increasing Diversity in Public Relations—PRWeek Letter to the Editor," PRSA, June 14, 2011, http://media.prsa.org/article_display.cfm?article_id=2136.

25. Jay Black and Chris Roberts (eds.), *Doing Ethics in Media: Theories and Practical Applications* (New York: Taylor & Francis, 2011), 151.

26. "Kimberly-Clark Names Sue Dodsworth Global Diversity Officer," Kimberly-Clark, November 1, 2010, http://investor.kimberly-clark.com/releasedetail.cfm?releaseid=525475.

27. Molly Petrilla, "How Analytics Helped Kimberly-Clark Solve Its Diversity Problem," *Fortune,* December 10, 2014, http://fortune.com/2014/12/10/kimberly-clark-dodsworth-diversity/.

28. Molly Petrilla, "How Analytics Helped Kimberly-Clark Solve Its Diversity Problem," *Fortune,* December 10, 2014, http://fortune.com/2014/12/10/kimberly-clark-dodsworth-diversity/.

29. "Kimberly-Clark Initiative Wins 2014 Catalyst Award," Kimberly-Clark, accessed January 29, 2014, http://investor.kimberly-clark.com/releasedetail.cfm?ReleaseID=821885.

CHAPTER 8

1. "PR Software, Marketing, and Media Relations Software and Services," Cision, accessed May 14, 2014, http://www.cision.com/us/.

2. "Say Goodbye to Media Monitoring and Hello to cliQ," iQ Media, accessed May 14, 2015, http://go.iqmediacorp.com/cliq.

3. "LexisNexis Newsdesk—Media Monitoring Solution," LexisNexis, accessed May 14, 2015, http://www.lexisnexis.com/en-us/products/newsdesk.page.

4. Andrew Rice, "Does BuzzFeed Know the Secret?," *New York Magazine,* April 7, 2013, http://nymag.com/news/features/buzzfeed-2013-4/.

5. Caroline Lees, "How Does Mashable Compete with New York Times?" *INMA Conference Blog,* March 26, 2015, http://www.inma.org/blogs/conference/post.cfm/how-does-mashable-compete-with-new-york-times-big-data.

6. Lisa Arthur, "What Is Big Data?," *Forbes,* August 15, 2013, http://www.forbes.com/sites/lisaarthur/2013/08/15/what-is-big-data/.

7. Seth Duncan, *Using Web Analytics to Measure the Impact of Earned Online Media on Business*

Outcomes: A Methodological Approach (Gainesville, FL: Institute for Public Relations), accessed May 14, 2015, http://www.instituteforpr.org/wp-content/uploads/Seth_Duncan_Web_Analytics.pdf.

8. Ashley Parker and Nick Corasaniti, "Data-Driven Campaigns Zero In on Voters, but Messages Are Lacking," *The New York Times*, October 31, 2014, http://www.nytimes.com/2014/10/31/us/politics/data-driven-campaigns-zero-in-on-voters-but-messages-are-lacking.html.

9. "Summit Agrees Framework of Global Programme Measurement Standard," International Association for Measurement and Evaluation of Communication, June 21, 2010, http://news.cision.com/amec/r/summit-agrees-framework-of-global-programme-measurement-standard,c498800.

10. "Barcelona Principles 2.0 Launched," International Association for Measurement and Evaluation of Communication, accessed September 3, 2015, http://amecorg.com/2015/09/barcelona-principles-2-0-launched-result-of-cross-industry-collaboration/.

11. "The Barcelona Declaration of Research Principles," Institute for Public Relations, June 18, 2010, http://www.instituteforpr.org/the-barcelona-declaration-of-research-principles/.

12. "Employee Engagement Survey Final Report," Charlotte-Mecklenburg Schools, October 8–25, 2012, http://www.cms.k12.nc.us/mediaroom/Documents/Employee Engagement Survey Final Report 2012.pdf.

13. "Google Brand Lift—Measuring Interest in Your Brand," Google, accessed November 21, 2014, https://www.youtube.com/watch?v=gYJQMRSbMlc.

14. "The Barcelona Declaration of Research Principles," Institute for Public Relations, June 18, 2010, http://www.instituteforpr.org/the-barcelona-declaration-of-research-principles/.

15. "Hiring Veterans and Military Spouses," Starbucks Coffee, November 5, 2013, https://www.youtube.com/watch?v=61aMc8tsAD4.

16. Joshua Williamson, "I am #TheSomebody who perseveres . . . ," April 21, 2015, https://twitter.com/ThatJoshuaDude/status/590676200344915968.

17. Lesley Wright, "I'm #TheSomebody who will be the first in my family . . . ," April 20, 2015, https://twitter.com/lesleyuf/status/590354132680237056.

18. Andre Manning and David Rockland, "Understanding the Barcelona Principles," *The Public Relations Strategist*, March 21, 2011, http://www.prsa.org/Intelligence/TheStrategist/Articles/view/9072/1028/Understanding_the_Barcelona_Principles.

19. Joel Best, *Damned Lies and Statistics: Untangling Numbers from the Media, Politicians, and Activists* (Berkeley: University of California Press, 2012).

20. Joel Best, *Damned Lies and Statistics: Untangling Numbers from the Media, Politicians, and Activists* (Berkeley: University of California Press, 2012), 5.

21. John Stauber and Sheldon Rampton, *Toxic Sludge Is Good for You: Lies, Damn Lies and the Public Relations Industry* (Monroe, ME: Common Courage Press, 1995).

22. "Public Relations Society of America (PRSA) Member Code of Ethics," Public Relations Society of America, accessed September 18, 2015, http://www.prsa.org/aboutprsa/ethics/codeenglish.

23. David Michaelson and Don W. Stacks, "Standardization in Public Relations Measurement and Evaluation," *Public Relations Journal* 5, no. 2 (2011): 1–22; Shannon A. Bowen and Don W. Stacks, "Toward the Establishment of Ethical Standardization in Public Relations Research, Measurement, and Evaluation," *Public Relations Journal* 7, no. 3 (2013): 1–28.

CHAPTER 9

1. http://thelisticles.net/simple-things-wrong/557598/.

2. http://www.cracked.com/article_20559_the-6-most-ridiculous-things-people-claimed-to-legally-own_p2.html.

3. "Listicle," *Wikipedia, The Free Encyclopedia*, accessed May 21, 2015, http://en.wikipedia.org/w/index.php?title=Listicle&oldid=659813869.

4. http://www.forbes.com/sites/stevedenning/2014/08/29/five-reasons-why-millennials-love-listicles/.

5. http://mag.uchicago.edu/arts-humanities/listicle-literary-form.

6. Craig E. Carroll, *The Handbook of Communication and Corporate Reputation* (Oxford, UK: Wiley-Blackwell, 2013), 4.

7. Brian Solis and Deirdre K. Breakenridge, *Putting the Public Back in Public Relations: How Social Media Is Reinventing the Aging Business of PR* (Upper Saddle River, NJ: FT Press, 2009), 102.

8. http://www.ncaa.org/champion/will-and-way.

9. William Zinsser, *On Writing Well: The Classic Guide to Writing Nonfiction* (New York: Harper-Perennial, 1998), 62.

10. http://www.ncaa.org/champion/will-and-way.

11. "Melissa Kleinschmidt, APR, on College Athletics, Strategy and Storytelling," *PR Tactics* 22, no. 3 (March 2015): 10.

12. Ann Wylie, "One More Phrase to Avoid: Enough Already with the 'At XX, We . . .' Construction," *PR Tactics* 22, no. 3 (March 2015): 7.

13. "Melissa Kleinschmidt, APR, on College Athletics, Strategy and Storytelling," *PR Tactics* 22, no. 3 (March 2015):10.

14. http://www.newyorker.com/magazine/2015/06/01/off-diamond-head-finnegan.

15. http://www.bbc.com/news/world-asia-32987622.

16. http://pages.instant.ly/bumble-bee-seafoods-testimonial.html.

17. https://twitter.com/marjoriemliu/status/606122784654299136.

18. https://twitter.com/mattbertz/status/606115220524662784.

19. Meta G. Carstarphen and Richard H. Wells, *Writing PR: A Multimedia Approach* (Boston: Pearson, 2004).

20. Meta G. Carstarphen and Richard H. Wells, *Writing PR: A Multimedia Approach* (Boston: Pearson, 2004), 192.

21. http://sanctuaries.noaa.gov/news/press/2015/independence-survey.html.

22. http://www.publicaffairs.noaa.gov/grounders/noaahistory.html.

23. http://sanctuaries.noaa.gov/about/.

24. http://sanctuaries.noaa.gov/maritime/contact_us.html.

25. Brian Solis and Deirdre K. Breakenridge, *Putting the Public Back in Public Relations: How Social Media Is Reinventing the Aging Business of PR* (Upper Saddle River, NJ: FT Press, 2009), 155.

26. http://www.merriam-webster.com/word-of-the-year/2004-word-of-the-year.htm.

27. http://blogs.law.harvard.edu/whatmakesaweblogaweblog.html.

28. http://mashable.com/2010/07/20/corporate-blogging-tips/.

29. http://www.cnn.com/2014/04/10/business/china-weibo-user-base/index.html.

30. http://www.edelman.com/post/friday5-twitter-vs-sina-weibo/.

31. "Search Engine Optimization," *Wikipedia, The Free Encyclopedia*, accessed March 5, 2015, http://en.wikipedia.org/w/index.php?title=Search_engine_optimization&oldid=648870961.

32. https://support.google.com/webmasters/answer/66358?hl=en.

33. http://goinswriter.com/seo-pages/.

34. https://support.google.com/webmasters/answer/40349?hl=en.

35. www.prsa.org/AboutPRSA/Ethics/CodeEnglish.

36. Jay Black and Chris Roberts, *Doing Ethics in Media: Theories and Practical Applications* (New York: Taylor & Francis, 2011).

37. Abel Meeropol, "Strange Fruit" (Commodore Records, 1939); Lewis Allan, *Strange Fruit* (New York: Edward B. Marks Music Corporation, 1940).

38. http://www.statesman.com/news/business/austin-pr-firm-changing-name-some-say-was-racially/njNHB/.

39. http://www.statesman.com/news/business/austin-pr-firm-changing-name-some-say-was-racially/njNHB/.

40. http://www.statesman.com/news/business/austin-pr-firm-changing-name-some-say-was-racially/njNHB/

CHAPTER 10

1. Patrick J. Lynch and Sarah Horton, *Web Style Guide*, 3rd ed., http://www.webstyleguide.com/.

2. http://www.forbes.com/sites/robertwynne/2014/01/20/how-to-write-for-public-relations/.

3. http://www.prdaily.com/Main/Articles/10798.aspx.

4. http://www.wsj.com/articles/in-photo-sharing-every-picture-tells-a-story-when-it-has-the-right-caption-1423007365.

5. http://www.cision.com/us/2014/07/pr-goes-pinterest-3-campaigns-to-inspire-you/.

6. James E. Grunig and Todd Hunt, *Managing Public Relations* (New York: Holt, Rinehart and Winston, 1984), 470.

7. http://www.prdaily.com/Main/Articles/5_creative_ways_brands_use_Snapchat_16717.aspx.

8. http://mashable.com/2014/02/24/snapchat-study-college-students/.

9. http://fortune.com/2015/08/25/social-media-brands-ignore/.

10. http://www.entrepreneur.com/article/238624.

11. http://infocus.gettyimages.com/post/new-embed-lets-you-share-tens-of-millions-of-images.

12. http://digg.com/originals/why-audio-never-goes-viral.

13. http://www.americanpressinstitute.org/publications/reports/survey-research/how-americans-get-news/.

14. http://www.journalism.org/2015/04/29/audio-fact-sheet/.

15. http://digg.com/originals/why-audio-never-goes-viral.

16. http://www.cbsnews.com/videos/new-hope-for-inmate-from-serial-podcast/.

17. http://www.cyberalert.com/blog/index.php/the-power-of-podcasts-for-public-relations-marketing/.

18. Scott M. Cutlip, H. Center Allen and M. Broom Glen, *Effective Public Relations*, 8th ed. (Englewood Cliffs, NJ: Prentice-Hall, 2000), 317.

19. https://www.youtube.com/yt/press/statistics.html.

20. http://www.bloomberg.com/news/articles/2016-04-28/snapchat-user-content-fuels-jump-to-10-billion-daily-video-views.

21. http://www.iab.net/media/file/GfKIAB-2014OriginalDigitalVideoReport.pdf.

22. http://www.ragan.com/Main/Articles/44483.aspx.

23. http://www.ragan.com/Main/Articles/44483.aspx.

24. http://www.prdaily.com/Main/Articles/3_ways_to_make_captivating_videos__18966.aspx.

25. https://www.brainshark.com/ideas-blog/2013/January/what-types-of-video-marketing-content-works-for-pinterest.

26. http://www.nytimes.com/2015/08/13/technology/personaltech/vertical-video-on-the-small-screen-not-a-crime.html.

27. http://www.nytimes.com/2015/08/13/technology/personaltech/vertical-video-on-the-small-screen-not-a-crime.html.

28. http://www.adweek.com/socialtimes/beyond-periscope-and-meerkat-the-state-of-live-streaming-video/620195.

29. https://www.elance.com/r/contractors/q-Video%20Production.

30. http://www.makerstudios.com/about.

31. http://www.comscore.com/Insights/Presentations-and-Whitepapers/2014/The-US-Mobile-App-Report.

32. https://www.snapchat.com/geofilters.

33. http://www.fritolay.com/company/media/media-article/2016/04/21/cracker-jack-popcorn-calls-play-ball-and-unveils-new-prize-inside.htm.

34. https://www.facebook.com/crackerjack/photos/a.138381416350587.1073741827.133794093475986/495572380631487/?type=3&comment_id=496069930581732&comment_tracking={%22tn%22%3A%22R%22}.

35. https://www.facebook.com/crackerjack/photos/a.138381416350587.1073741827.133794093475986/495571867298205/?type=3&comment_id=495714247283967&comment_tracking={%22tn%22%3A%22R0%22}.

36. http://www.chicagotribune.com/business/columnists/ct-rosenthal-cracker-jack-0501-biz-20160429-column.html.

37. J. G. Blumler, "The Role of Theory in Uses and GratificationsStudies," *Communication Research* 6, no. 1 (1979): 9–36.

38. Ruth Avidar, Yaron Ariel, Vered Malka and Eilat Chen Levy, "Smartphones and Young Publics: A New Challenge for Public Relations Practice and Relationship Building," *Public Relations Review* 39, no. 5 (2013): 603–605.

39. https://www.emarketer.com/public_media/docs/eMarketer_Cross_Device_Trends_Roundup.pdf.

40. http://www.prsa.org/AboutPRSA/Ethics/CodeEnglish/.

41. http://www.apple.com/watch/.

42. Jay Black and Chris Roberts, *Doing Ethics in Media: Theories and Practical Applications* (New York: Taylor & Francis, 2011), 242.

43. http://techcrunch.com/2015/06/02/apples-tim-cook-delivers-blistering-speech-on-encryption-privacy/.

CHAPTER 11

1. http://www.supremecourt.gov/opinions/12pdf/11-697_4g15.pdf.
2. http://www.justice.gov/usam/criminal-resource-manual-1854-copyright-infringement-first-sale-doctrine.
3. Stephen Breyer, *The Court and the World: American Law and the New Global Realities* (New York: Alfred A. Knopf, 2015), 4.
4. http://www.prsa.org/aboutprsa/ethics/codeenglish/.
5. http://www.nytimes.com/2015/08/16/technology/inside-amazon-wrestling-big-ideas-in-a-bruising-workplace.html.
6. https://medium.com/@jaycarney/what-the-new-york-times-didn-t-tell-you-a1128aa78931#.2loly3fay.
7. http://www.seattleweekly.com/home/961299-129/amazon-is-so-nice-to-employees.
8. http://fortune.com/2015/10/19/amazon-nyt-medium-carney/.
9. http://www.dmlp.org/sites/citmedialaw.org/files/2009-03-26-Simorangkir%20Complaint.pdf.
10. http://www.medialaw.org/topics-page/defamation-faqs.
11. https://www.law.cornell.edu/supremecourt/text/418/323.
12. https://www.law.cornell.edu/supremecourt/text/376/254.
13. https://www.law.cornell.edu/wex/patent
14. http://turnitin.com/en_us/what-we-offer/originality-checking.
15. http://memeburn.com/2015/09/top-south-african-instagrammer-accused-of-plagiarism/.
16. http://memeburn.com/2015/09/instagrammer-skye-grove-suspended-from-cape-town-partnership-pending-investigation/.
17. http://memeburn.com/2015/09/instagram-plagiarism-scandal-skye-grove-apologises-deletes-herself-off-internet/.
18. http://memeburn.com/2015/09/instagrammer-skye-grove-suspended-from-cape-town-partnership-pending-investigation/.
19. http://copyright.gov/fair-use/more-info.html.
20. http://www.nbcnews.com/news/us-news/twitter-suspends-deadspin-sbnation-accounts-over-copyright-n443306.
21. https://twitter.com/tos.
22. http://khn.org/syndication/.
23. http://archive.wired.com/techbiz/media/news/2002/06/53355.
24. http://cyber.law.harvard.edu/property99/metatags/1998futu.html.
25. http://louisville.edu/law/library/special-collections/the-louis-d.-brandeis-collection/other-peoples-money-chapter-v.
26. http://consumerist.com/2009/04/16/9-legal-drugs-with-extremely-disturbing-side-effects/.
27. http://www.fda.gov/Drugs/ResourcesForYou/Consumers/PrescriptionDrugAdvertising/ucm072077.htm#risk_disclosure.
28. https://www.ftc.gov/about-ftc.
29. http://www.holmesreport.com/latest/article/fitbit-brings-on-fleishmanhillard-burson-marsteller.
30. http://money.cnn.com/2015/06/18/investing/fitbit-ipo-stock-bounce/.
31. http://www.sec.gov/News/PressRelease/Detail/PressRelease/1365171484464.
32. https://www.law.cornell.edu/wex/invasion_of_privacy.
33. http://www.dmlp.org/legal-guide/elements-intrusion-claim.
34. http://usatoday30.usatoday.com/money/advertising/2011-07-21-kim-kardashian-old-navy_n.htm.
35. https://www.law.cornell.edu/wex/false_light.
36. http://www2.bloomberglaw.com/public/desktop/document/JENNIFER_E_PATTERSON_v_NATALIE_D_GRANTHERMS_No_M201300287COAR3CV_/1.
37. http://www2.bloomberglaw.com/public/desktop/document/JENNIFER_E_PATTERSON_v_NATALIE_D_GRANTHERMS_No_M201300287COAR3CV_/1.
38. https://www.prsa.org/AboutPRSA/Ethics/CodeEnglish/.
39. https://www.law.cornell.edu/wex/trade_secret.
40. http://www.wsj.com/articles/SB114835056149060280.
41. http://www.instituteforpr.org/social-media-account-really-guidelines-pr-practitioners-

organizations-determine-social-media-
ownership/.

42. http://comm.psu.edu/page-center/about/
arthur-w-page/the-page-principles.

CHAPTER 12

1. http://www.davecarrollmusic.com/music/
ubg/story/.
2. http://www.huffingtonpost.com/2009/07/24/
united-breaks-guitars-did_n_244357.html.
3. http://business.time.com/2013/09/03/
man-spends-more-than-1000-to-call-out-
british-airways-on-twitter/.
4. http://www.humansofnewyork.com/post/
43997717109/i-am-a-street-photographer-in-
new-york-city.
5. Amanda E. Cancel, Michael A. Mitrook and Glen
T. Cameron, "Testing the Contingency Theory of
Accommodation in Public Relations," *Public
Relations Review* 25, no. 2 (1999): 171–197;
Sarah Strasburg, Samuel M. Tham and Glen T.
Cameron, "Taming Contingency Theory: Creating a Quantitative Decision Tool Using Decision
Theory and Game Theory in Conflict Management," *Proceedings of the 18th International Public
Relations Research Conference* (2015): 331.
6. http://www.adn.com/article/20151112/
anchorage-restaurants-facebook-defense-
employee-wins-viral-support.
7. https://www.facebook.com/judyberrysinger/
posts/10206323203051973.
8. http://www.adn.com/article/20151112/
anchorage-restaurants-facebook-defense-
employee-wins-viral-support.
9. Elizabeth Dougall, "Issues Management,"
Institute for Public Relations, December 12,
2008, http://www.instituteforpr.org/
issues-management/.
10. Elizabeth Dougall, "Issues Management,"
Institute for Public Relations, December 12,
2008, http://www.instituteforpr.org/
issues-management/.
11. http://www.reuters.com/article/2015/09/22/
us-usa-volkswagen-emission-idUSKCN0RL2E
I20150922#0uoPtue9HzrAyxoo.97.
12. http://www.nytimes.com/2015/12/14/
business/the-engineering-of-volkswagens-
aggressive-ambition.html.
13. Michael Regester and Judy Larkin, *Risk Issues
and Crisis Management in Public Relations: A
Casebook of Best Practice*, 3rd ed. (London:
Kogan Page Publishers, 2005), 51.
14. www.nytimes.com/interactive/2015/10/23/
business/international/vw-scandal-timeline
.html.
15. http://www.bbc.com/news/business
-34324772.
16. http://www.wired.com/2015/11/vw-epa-3-liter-
audi-porsche-emissions/.
17. http://www.nytimes.com/2015/12/11/
business/international/vw-emissions-
scandal.html?_r=0.
18. http://money.cnn.com/2015/09/24/investing/
volkswagen-vw-emissions-scandal-stock/.
19. http://fortune.com/2015/10/08/volkswagen-
scandal-fallout/.
20. http://www.nytimes.com/2015/10/27/busi-
ness/lawyers-jostle-for-lead-position-in-
volkswagen-diesel-suits.html.
21. http://www.nytimes.com/2015/12/11/
business/international/vw-emissions-
scandal.html?_r=0.
22. Michael Regester and Judy Larkin, *Risk Issues
and Crisis Management in Public Relations: A
Casebook of Best Practice*, 3rd ed. (London:
Kogan Page Publishers, 2005).
23. http://www.nytimes.com/2016/06/28/
business/volkswagen-settlement-diesel-
scandal.html.
24. Michael Regester and Judy Larkin, *Risk Issues
and Crisis Management in Public Relations: A
Casebook of Best Practice*, 3rd ed. (London:
Kogan Page Publishers, 2005).
25. http://www.nytimes.com/2000/01/26/us/
anti-sweatshop-movement-is-achieving-gains-
overseas.html.
26. http://www.yourmembership.com/arti-
cles/166/How-Nonprofits-Turn-Seven-
Important-Issues-into-Opportunities.htm
27. http://www.cdc.gov/ecoli/2015/o26-11-15/
index.html.
28. http://www.bloomberg.com/news/arti-
cles/2015-12-04/chipotle-rescinds-16-
forecast-after-e-coli-scare-crushes-sales.
29. http://www.usatoday.com/story/money/
cars/2015/12/01/emissions-scandal-crushes-
volkswagen-sales-november/76605062/.
30. http://www.bloomberg.com/news/articles/
2015-12-04/chipotle-rescinds-16-forecast-
after-e-coli-scare-crushes-sales.

31. http://www.forbes.com/sites/jeannemeister/2012/06/07/corporate-social-responsibility-a-lever-for-employee-attraction-engagement/; http://www.thecro.com/topics/25115/how-to-recruit-and-retain-millennial/#sthash.KlguNCXg.dpuf.

32. http://www.instituteforpr.org/state-crisis-communication-evidence-bleeding-edge/.

33. W. Timothy Coombs and Sherry J. Holladay, *PR Strategy and Application: Managing Influence* (Chichester, UK: Wiley-Blackwell, 2010), 248.

34. http://www.foxnews.com/us/2013/09/28/chicago-tylenol-murders-remain-unsolved-after-more-than-30-years.html.

35. http://www.nytimes.com/2013/10/30/business/lawrence-g-foster-dies-at-88-helped-lead-tylenol-out-of-cyanide-crisis.html.

36. https://www.washingtonpost.com/archive/business/1982/10/11/tylenols-maker-shows-how-to-respond-to-crisis/bc8df898-3fcf-443f-bc2f-e6fbd639a5a3/.

37. http://www.govtech.com/social/Glendale-Calif-Takes-Head-on-Approach-to-Rumor-Control.html; http://www.latimes.com/local/political/la-me-pc-brown-lawn-bill-20150713-story.html.

38. http://usatoday30.usatoday.com/news/nation/2003-10-09-ghettopoly_x.htm.

39. https://www.washingtonpost.com/news/morning-mix/wp/2014/09/15/urban-outfitters-red-stained-vintage-kent-state-sweatshirt-is-not-a-smart-look-this-fall/.

40. http://fortune.com/2015/12/11/chipotle-ecoli-crisis-management/.

41. http://www.glendaleca.gov/government/departments/management-services/communications-community-relations/rumor-page.

42. http://www.reuters.com/article/us-oil-spill-bp-apology-idUSTRE6515NQ20100602.

43. http://adage.com/article/news/crisis-pr-assessing-domino-s-reaction-youtube-hubub/136086/.

44. https://www.youtube.com/watch?v=dem6eA7-A2I.

45. http://www.instituteforpr.org/crisis-management-communications/.

46. https://www.youtube.com/watch?v=dem6eA7-A2I.

47. http://adage.com/article/news/crisis-pr-assessing-domino-s-reaction-youtube-hubub/136086/.

48. http://money.cnn.com/2015/03/19/technology/security/target-data-hack-settlement/.

49. http://theconversation.com/spin-lance-armstrongs-confession-and-livestrongs-future-11616

50. http://www.prnewsonline.com/water-cooler/2013/05/30/livestrong-foundation-communications-team-struggles-to-overcome-negative-impact-of-lance-arm-strong/.

51. http://www.livestrong.org/who-we-are/.

52. FEMA, *The Crisis Plan: Organizational Roles and Responsibilities: Instructor Guide*, accessed December 21, 2015, https://www.training.fema.gov.

53. https://www.prsa.org/AboutPRSA/Ethics/CodeEnglish/.

54. Jay Black and Chris Roberts, *Doing Ethics in Media: Theories and Practical Applications* (New York: Taylor & Francis, 2011).

55. Ralph Barney, "Cases and Commentaries" *Journal of Mass Media Ethics* 1, no. 1 (1985): 80.

56. http://www.instituteforpr.org/crisis-management-communications/.

CHAPTER 13

1. http://www.dumplingemoji.org.

2. https://www.kickstarter.com/projects/657685639/where-is-the-dumpling-emoji/posts/1486619.

3. https://www.reddit.com/r/Fremont/comments/3cu15w/lets_bring_gigabit_internet_to_fremont/.

4. http://www.techtimes.com/articles/87039/20150923/more-than-half-the-worlds-population-still-doesnt-have-internet-access-says-un.htm.

5. http://nextcenturycities.org/.

6. http://nextcenturycities.org/about-ncc/.

7. http://www.pewglobal.org/2015/03/19/internet-seen-as-positive-influence-on-education-but-negative-influence-on-morality-in-emerging-and-developing-nations/technology-report-17/.

8. http://www.forbes.com/sites/saritharai/2016/01/06/india-just-crossed-1-billion-

mobile-subscribers-milestone-and-the-excitements-just-beginning/.

9. http://www.musicnotes.com/sheetmusic/mtd.asp?ppn=MN0056572.

10. http://one.laptop.org/about/mission.

11. https://www.ted.com/talks/nicholas_negroponte_on_one_laptop_per_child/transcript?language=en

12. http://www.bu.edu/writingprogram/journal/past-issues/issue-3/shah/.

13. Mark Warschauer and Morgan Ames, "Can One Laptop per Child Save the World's Poor?," *Journal of International Affairs* 64, no. 1 (2010): 33.

14. http://blog.al.com/spotnews/2010/07/study_shows_majority_of_birmin.html.

15. Mark Warschauer and Morgan Ames, "Can One Laptop per Child Save the World's Poor?" *Journal of International Affairs* 64, no. 1 (2010): 33.

16. http://www.businessweek.com/innovate/NussbaumOnDesign/archives/2007/09/its_time_to_cal.html.

17. http://www.nielsen.com/us/en/insights/news/2015/uncommon-sense-back-to-the-future-perspectives-on-thriving-in-2020.html.

18. http://www.peacecorps.gov/wws/lesson-plans/culture/.

19. http://www.geberit-aquaclean.com/en_uk/dusch_funktion/duschfunktion.html

20. www.iprn.com/project-of-the-year-2013-winner-turning-taboo-into-a-trend/

21. www.iprn.com/project-of-the-year-2013-winner-turning-taboo-into-a-trend/

22. http://heavy.com/entertainment/2014/11/squatty-potty-poop-toilet-stool-shark-tank-products-season-6-100th-episode/

23. https://www.youtube.com/watch?v=YbYWhdLO43Q

24. Edward Twitchell Hall, *Beyond Culture* (New York: Anchor, 1989), 91.

25. Edward Twitchell Hall, *Beyond Culture* (New York: Anchor, 1989), 91.

26. http://www.buzzfeed.com/katieheaney/the-one-thing-you-should-never-text-anyone-ever

27. www.brandingstrategyinsider.com/2015/08/behind-nikes-campaign.html.

28. Ilan Alon, Romie F. Littrell and Allan KK Chan, "Branding in China: Global Product Strategy Alternatives," *Multinational Business Review* 17, no. 4 (2009): 123–142.

29. http://adland.tv/ooh/nothing-sucks-electrolux-billboard-uk-1991.

30. https://www.youtube.com/watch?v=yZrQqnRhmZ0.

31. http://www.snopes.com/business/misxlate/nova.asp.

32. Marieke De Mooij, *Global Marketing and Advertising: Understanding Cultural Paradoxes* (Thousand Oaks, CA: Sage, 2013).

33. Geert Hofstede, *Culture's Consequences: Comparing Values, Behaviors, Institutions and Organizations Across Nations* (Thousand Oaks, CA: Sage, 2001).

34. http://web.evs.anl.gov/uranium/eis/whatiseis/index.cfm.

35. http://www.gamesforchange.org/play/never-alone-kisima-ingitchuna/.

36. http://www.gamesforchange.org/play/start-the-talk-underage-drinking/.

37. http://gamificationnation.com/friday-feminine-gamification-viewpoint-motivation-work/.

38. https://hbr.org/2004/10/cultural-intelligence.

39. https://hbr.org/2004/10/cultural-intelligence.

40. http://news.klm.com/abn-amro-new-partner-in-klms-corporate-biofuel-programme/.

41. http://time.com/2938225/klm-royal-dutch-airlines-gael-garcia-bernal-world-cup/.

42. http://www.prdaily.com/Main/Articles/16919.aspx.

43. https://twitter.com/PacoSaiso/status/483316208985337856?ref_src=twsrc%5Etfw.

44. Krishnamurthy Sriramesh and Dejan Vercic (eds.), *The Global Public Relations Handbook: Theory, Research, and Practice* (Mahwah, NJ: Lawrence Erlbaum), xxv.

45. http://www.climatechangenews.com/2015/12/12/cop21-ngos-react-to-prospective-un-paris-climate-deal/.

46. http://www.cop21.gouv.fr/en/partners/business-and-sponsors/.

47. Guy J. Golan, Dennis F. Kinsey and Sung-Un Yang (eds.), *International Public Relations and Public Diplomacy: Communication and Engagement* (New York: Peter Lang, 2014), 5.

48. http://www.dailymail.co.uk/news/article-2745875/War-Twitter-State-Department-releases-mock-ISIS-recruitment-film-bid-counter-terror-groups-online-pursuit-Westerners.html.

CHAPTER 14

1. http://www.payscale.com/research/US/ Job=Account_Coordinator/Salary.
2. http://www.payscale.com/research/US/ Job=Communications_Specialist/Salary.
3. https://www.wetfeet.com/articles/industry-overview-non-profit-and-government.
4. https://www.nonprofitadvancement.org/re-source/communications-public-relations-manager-salary-survey-sample-report.
5. Doug Newsom, Judy Turk and Dean Kruck-eberg, *Cengage Advantage Books: This Is PR: The Realities of Public Relations* (Boston: Cengage Learning, 2012).
6. https://www.sba.gov/sites/default/files/FAQ_March_2014_0.pdf.
7. https://www.census.gov/econ/susb/.
8. http://www.commpred.org/_uploads/report2-full.pdf.
9. http://www.commpred.org/_uploads/report1-full.pdf.
10. Alvin Toffler, *Future Shock* (New York: Bantam, 1990).
11. http://www.commpred.org/_uploads/industry-educator-summit-summary-report.pdf.
12. http://www.arikhanson.com/2012/06/12/ 10-skills-the-pr-pro-of-2022-must-have/.
13. http://www.arikhanson.com/2016/02/29/ 10-skills-the-pr-pro-of-the-future-will-need-revised/.
14. David M. Dozier, "The Organizational Roles of Communications and Public Relations Practi-tioners," in *Excellence in Public Relations and Communication Management*, ed. James Grunig (Mahwah, NJ: Lawrence Erlbaum, 1992), 327–355.
15. http://www.prsa.org/jobcenter/career_resources/resource_type/tools_tactics/ CareerGuidePRSAFoundation/Career_Guide.pdf.
16. https://medium.com/@taliajane/an-open-letter-to-my-ceo-fb73df021e7a#.c3m0iojso.
17. https://medium.com/@taliajane/an-open-letter-to-my-ceo-fb73df021e7.
18. http://www.buzzfeed.com/davidmack/ talia-jane-vs-yelp.
19. https://www.gofundme.com/Help-A-Yelper-EAT.
20. http://www.ranker.com/list/talia-jane-insta-gram-photos/ariel-kana.
21. http://qz.com/622232/the-yelp-employee-who-was-fired-after-her-incendiary-open-letter-to-the-ceo-speaks-out/.
22. www.forbes.com/sites/quora/2016/02/26/ does-talia-jane-deserve-the-backlash-from-her-open-letter-to-jeremy-stoppelman-yelps-ceo/.
23. http://money.cnn.com/2015/08/10/pf/ pay-raise/.
24. http://www.forbes.com/sites/cameronkeng/ 2014/06/22/employees-that-stay-in-companies-longer-than-2-years-get-paid-50-less/.
25. http://www.fastcompany.com/3055035/ the-future-of-work/you-should-plan-on-switching-jobs-every-three-years-for-the-rest-of-your-
26. http://www.cbsnews.com/news/ why-job-hoppers-make-the-best-employees/.
27. https://www.prsa.org/AboutPRSA/Ethics/ CodeEnglish/.
28. https://www.prsa.org/AboutPRSA/Ethics/ CodeEnglish/

Glossary

A/B testing Experiment in which one group of participants is randomly assigned to see one version of a message and another group is randomly assigned to see a second version. Results are then compared to test the effectiveness of message variations.

Access divide Gap between people with access to digital technology and those without access.

Accredited business communicator (ABC) Credential awarded by IABC to recognize communicators who have reached a globally accepted standard of knowledge and proficiency in their chosen field.

Accredited in public relations (APR) Credential awarded by PRSA and other UAB affiliates to those who have demonstrated competency in the knowledge, skills and abilities required to practice public relations effectively.

Active publics People who behave and communicate actively in response to a problem or issue.

Actual malice When a defamatory statement is made with knowledge of its falsity and reckless disregard for the truth.

Advertising Media space purchased by sponsors to persuade audiences; or the practice of planning and producing this service.

Advertising value equivalency (AVE) A calculation of the value of news or editorial coverage based on the cost of the equivalent amount of advertising space or time.

Advertorial Paid advertising that is presented in the form of editorial content.

Advocacy Public promotion of a cause, idea or policy.

Algorithm A formula or set of steps for solving a problem. A computer algorithm can be the series of steps used in automated message testing and placement.

Analytics Researching online data to identify meaningful patterns. In strategic communication, analytics often focus on how web traffic leads to behavioral results such as sharing information or making online purchases.

Anchor text Clickable text that provides a hyperlink.

Apology Act of taking responsibility for an issue or crisis and seeking forgiveness or understanding.

Associated Press (AP) style Rules of writing (including grammar, capitalization and punctuation) published by the Associated Press news agency.

Asymmetrical model Model of public relations in which communication is two-way but unbalanced, with the organization using research/feedback in an effort to persuade publics to change attitudes or behaviors.

Attitudinal Having to do with affect, emotion, favor or disfavor toward an organization, brand, product, service, idea or any other attitude object.

Authenticity The degree to which one communicates reliably, accurately and true to his or her own character and the character of the organization that he or she represents.

Automated copy testing Using computer programs to automate the process of testing digital messages such as promotional copy.

Autoplay Feature that enables automatic playing of videos or other multimedia elements on users' devices.

Aware publics People who recognize that they are affected by a problem or issue in their environment.

Backgrounder Writing tactic used to give depth and context as background information for news stories.

Backlinks Incoming links that direct web users to a web page from another web page.

Banner ads Advertisements on web pages designed to encourage users to click to reach an advertiser's site.

Behavioral Having to do with observable human action.

Benchmarking Process of setting a point for comparison with eventual program results in order to observe change over time. (Benchmarking can also be used to make performance comparisons with other organizations or industry standards.)

Big data Large amounts of data from traditional and digital sources that can be used for ongoing discovery and analysis of media content and human behavior.

Billable rate Amount that an agency or firm charges clients per hour of an employee's time.

Black box fallacy False notion that predicts most human communication needs will eventually be satisfied with a single device.

Blog Online post (or web log) with reflections, comments and often links provided by the writer.

Bolstering Attempting to offset reputational damage to an organization during a crisis by emphasizing the good work that the organization has done in the past.

Boomerang effect Unintended consequence of an apology or other attempt to create positive response that results instead in a negative response.

Bounce rate In online strategy, the percentage of visitors who visit a site but then leave the site instead of continuing toward other goals as defined by the strategist.

Brand journalism Application of journalistic skills to produce news content for an organization to communicate directly with its publics without going through a third-party news organization.

Brochureware Web pages that present essentially the same material as printed materials such as brochures.

Business to business (B2B) The relationship between a business and other businesses.

Business to consumer (B2C) The relationship between a business and the end users or consumers of its product or services.

Clear and present danger Circumstance that may limit rights to free speech in the interest of preventing "substantive evils."

Clickbait Promotional or sensational internet content designed primarily to entice users to visit another website.

Click-through rate Percentage of users who view an ad on the web and click on it to reach an advertiser's site.

Clipping services Businesses that monitor print and electronic media for mentions of clients in local, national or international outlets; see also **media monitoring services**.

Code-switching Alternating between two or more languages or cultural styles.

Cognitive Having to do with mental processes such as thinking, knowing, perceiving, learning and understanding.

Communal relationships Relationships in which each party gives benefits to the other and a primary motivation for each is the other's benefit.

Compensation Crisis response strategy of offering products, services or money to help make amends with publics.

Consequentialism Results-based system of ethics that holds that the best ethical decision is the one leading to the best outcomes or impacts.

Constraint recognition When people detect a problem or situation in their environment but perceive obstacles that limit their behavior to do anything about it.

Content analysis A systematic method for analyzing recorded information such as audio, video or text.

Content marketing Development and sharing of media content to appeal to consumers as part of an indirect marketing strategy in which consumers are drawn primarily to media content instead of directly to the product being marketed.

Contingency theory A theory that proposes that the best course of action in any situation depends on the specifics of the situation.

Control group A group of subjects or people in an experiment who do not receive or are not exposed to a treatment for the purpose of comparison.

Controlled media Channels of communication that allow public relations practitioners to write, edit, produce and distribute messages as they see fit.

Conversational voice An authentic, engaging and natural style of communication that publics perceive to be personable.

Conversion rate In online strategy, the number of goals reached divided by the number of unique visitors to a site.

Cookie A text file stored on a user's computer that is used to track and remember the user's activity online.

Copyright Claim to intellectual property rights of an original work of authorship including rights to reproduce, distribute, perform, display, license and so on.

Copyright infringement Use of protected works without proper permission from the copyright holder.

Corporate advertising Paid media designed to promote an organization as a whole rather than sell a particular service, product or product category (also sometimes called institutional advertising).

Corporate social responsibility (CSR) Company's commitment of resources to benefit the welfare of their workforce, local communities, society at large and the environment.

Cost per thousand (CPM) A measure of advertising reach that represents the cost of an advertisement relative to the estimated size of the audience.

Creative Commons Nonprofit organization that encourages fair and legal sharing of content by helping content creators make their work available with specific terms and conditions for sharing.

Crowdsource To obtain information or input into a particular task or project by enlisting the services of a number of people, either paid or unpaid, typically via the internet.

Cultural convergence When various forms of culture are exchanged, combined, converted and adapted. On a global scale, this phenomenon has accelerated with the growth of digital media.

Cultural intelligence Ability to adapt, communicate and interact effectively across cultures by learning and applying cognitive, emotional and behavioral skills.

Culture A shared system of beliefs, values, customs and so on that guides behavior of a particular group or public.

Customer relationship management (CRM) Process of tracking and forecasting customers' interactions with an organization, often leveraging data for sales support.

Dateline Text at beginning of news story that describes when and where a story occurred (e.g., "BEIJING, June 16—").

Deep link Hyperlink that bypasses an organization's home page and takes users directly to resources deeper in an organization's website structure.

Defamation False communication that injures someone's reputation.

Delayed lead A style of beginning a story in a way that entices readers to continue reading without summarizing the story's main points.

Demographic research Data describing objective characteristics of a population including age, level of income or highest educational degree obtained.

Deontological ethics System of decision-making that focuses on the moral principles of duty and rules.

Dialogic communication Exchanges involving people communicating their own views and backgrounds while remaining completely open to seeing the world as others do.

Digital divide Gap between those people with relatively little access and use of information and communication technologies and those people with greater access and usage.

Digital watermarking Information embedded into digital audio and video signals that can be used to track when and where the content is delivered.

Direct lead A style of beginning a news story that summarizes the story's main points (e.g., who, what, where, when, why, how) in the first sentence or two.

Distributed public relations Intentional practice of sharing public relations responsibilities among a broad cross section of an organization's members or employees, particularly in an online context.

Diversity Inclusion of different types of people and different types of views.

Dominant coalition Group of people with the greatest influence in determining how an organization operates and pursues its mission.

Economic convergence When various media organizations and functions are merged under a single ownership structure. This form of media convergence is different from the term economists use to describe trends in world economies.

End-user license agreements (EULA) Legal agreement between a software provider and the person using the software.

Ethics Moral principles that govern a person's or group's behavior.

Exchange relationships Relationships in which each party gives benefits to the other with the expectation of receiving comparable benefits in return.

Explainer video Video produced to demonstrate a product, service or process.

External publics Groups of people that exist mostly outside of an organization and have a relationship with the organization.

Eye tracking Process of measuring eye movements to determine where people are focusing; often used in website testing.

Fact sheet Short (often one-page) document that presents factual information in concise format.

Fair use An exception to copyright laws that allows for the use of otherwise copyrighted material for purposes such as educational use, criticism or commentary.

Feature story A story that explores some angle of an event, a person's life, an organization or a place.

Federal Trade Commission (FTC) U.S. federal agency responsible for regulating all types of consumer products and services, including the promotion of these products and services.

Feedback Information returned from the environment in response to an organization's action or communication that can be used for continuous adjustment and improvement of the organization.

First-party data Data on user or consumer behavior that is collected by an organization from the people who use the organization's websites or online services.

Flaming Hostile communication among internet users.

Flash mob When a group of people plans and executes a surprise public event or performance that is usually organized via electronic media and unanticipated by those who are not participants.

Food and Drug Administration (FDA) U.S. federal agency responsible for regulating food, drugs, and health-related products and services including the promotion of these products and services.

Formal research Research designed with clear rules and procedures for collection and analysis of information.

Formative research Research conducted at the beginning of the planning process, or during the implementation of a plan.

Framing When clickable material in a link is actual content from the site to which it links.

Freedom of Information Act (FOIA) U.S. federal law passed to ensure that the government makes its information accessible to citizens.

Freelancers People who work on a project-by-project basis instead of working more permanently for a single employer (e.g., freelance writers, photographers, video producers).

Frequency The average number of times people in an audience are exposed to a particular message in a defined period of time.

Functional magnetic resonance imaging (fMRI) Tests that use magnetic fields to generate images of brain activity, including responses to communication and media stimuli.

Funnel A model for tracking how people move from exposure and awareness to action, particularly in online marketing where the goal is to convert a large number of web page viewers to sales leads or purchases.

Gamification Strategy of applying rules and rewards of game playing (points, scoring, competition, collaboration, etc.) to other areas of behavior such as desired public relations outcomes.

General public A nonspecific term referring to everyone in the world, making the concept rather meaningless in strategic communication and relationship building.

Geofilter Feature of social media (particularly Snapchat) that encourages communication among users within a specified geographic area by allowing users to post images with location-specific overlays.

Geolocation Function of communication devices that identifies the specific geographic location of the device.

Glass ceiling Metaphor used to describe a barrier to promotion for women and minorities.

Goals Statements that indicate a desired result for public relations efforts. In strategic planning, goals are more specific than the organization's mission but more general than objectives.

Golden mean Ethical doctrine holding that the best courses of action are found between extremes.

Golden rule Ethic of reciprocity—treat others as you would like to be treated yourself.

Government relations Management of relationships between an organization and government officials who formulate and execute public policy.

Grassroots campaign A bottom-up campaign that focuses strategy on mass participation of citizens or political constituents in an effort to influence policy or legislation.

Grasstops campaign A campaign that focuses strategy on directly influencing opinion leaders and well-connected individuals such as donors or political party leaders.

Greenwashing When an organization spends more resources claiming to be "green" through publicity, advertising and marketing than actually implementing practices that minimize environmental impact.

Hashtag A word or phrase (with no spaces) preceded by the hash symbol (#) that users can include in posts to categorize information online. Many social media platforms allow users to search or filter news feeds for information identified with the tag.

High-context communication Exchanges in which most of the meaning conveyed between people lies in the context of the communication or is internal to the communicators.

Human interest A personal or emotional storytelling angle that focuses on the human condition.

Hyperlink A piece of text or an image online that can be clicked on to reach another resource online.

Impacts The broadest and furthest-reaching results of public relations efforts, often stated in terms of societal benefit.

Impression management Process in which people influence perceptions of themselves or their organizations by regulating and controlling information in social interactions.

Impressions A measure of how many people were exposed to a message.

In house When public relations people are employed directly within an organization rather than working for an external agency or contracted as independent consultants.

Inbound marketing Marketing strategy that focuses on tactics for attracting customers with useful, entertaining or valuable information that customers find on blogs, search results, and other forms of online and social media.

Independence In public relations ethics, the value of autonomy and accountability in providing objective counsel.

Individualism-collectivism Cultural dimension describing the difference between cultures that value loyalty to self and immediate family more and those that value loyalty to larger groups and society more.

Infographics Visual presentations designed to communicate information simply and quickly with combinations of images, charts, tables or text.

Informal research Research conducted without clear rules or procedures, which makes the findings difficult to replicate or compare to other research or situations.

Ingratiation A type of reinforcing crisis response strategy in which stakeholders are praised or thanked to win their good favor.

Initial public offering (IPO) Financial event in which a private company offers sale of stocks to public investors for the first time.

Insider trading When a company's employees or executives buy and sell stock in their own organization or share information with others who buy or sell before the information has been made public.

Integrated communication Communicating with publics consistently across organizational functions including public relations, advertising, marketing and customer service.

Integrated marketing communication Strategic coordination of communication functions such as marketing, advertising and publicity to achieve a consistent concept in consumers' minds.

Intellectual property Any product of the human mind that is protected by law from unauthorized use by others.

Intercultural public relations Management of relationships between organizations and publics of different cultures.

Internal publics Groups of people inside of an organization or groups of people that share an identity with the organization.

International public relations Management of relationships between organizations and publics of different nations.

Internet of things (IoT) Global network of physical objects that are connected to one another in a way that enables them to communicate with one another and the intenet at large.

Inverted pyramid A style of newswriting in which the most important information is presented at the broad top of a story and narrower supporting details are written below.

Investor relations Management of relationships between an organization and publics in the financial community—for example, investors, analysts, regulators.

Issue An important topic or problem that is open for debate, discussion or advocacy.

Issues management Systematic process whereby organizations work to identify and resolve issues before they become crises.

Landscape orientation Images or video framed so that width is greater than height, like traditional movies.

Latent publics People who are affected by a problem or issue but don't realize it.

Legislative relations Management of relationships between an organization and lawmakers, staffers and others who influence legislation.

Level of involvement The degree to which people feel or think that a problem or issue affects them.

Libel Written or otherwise recorded false communication that injures someone's reputation.

Likert-type items Questionnaire items that ask people to respond to statements with a range of defined response options such as the range from "strongly disagree" to "strongly agree."

Listening Deliberately paying attention to and processing what others are communicating. In public relations and organizational communication, this means processing feedback.

Listicle An online article presented in the format of a numbered or bulleted list.

Lobbying Working to influence the decisions of government officials on matters of legislation.

Long-term orientation Cultural dimension describing the difference between cultures that value long-held traditions more and cultures that value entrepreneurship and innovation more.

Low-context communication Exchanges in which most of the meaning of messages is stated explicitly in the messages and requires little understanding of context.

Loyalty A sense of obligation or support for someone or something, including both organizations and publics.

Management function Part of an organization involved in its overall leadership and decision-making, guiding how the organization operates in its environment, rather than merely following the instructions of others.

Management role Concept describing those in public relations who primarily develop strategy, participate in organizational decision-making and are held accountable for program outcomes.

Market skimming Marketing strategy that starts with higher prices for early adopters of unique products and services and then lowers prices later to sell to a broader base of consumers when competitors enter the market.

Marketing Business of creating, promoting, delivering and selling products and services.

Marketing mix Combination of product, price, place and promotion strategies in support of profitable exchange.

Masculinity-femininity Cultural dimension describing the difference between cultures that value competition, achievement and material success more and those that value care, collaboration and modesty more.

Mashups Media presentations created by combining two or more preexisting elements from different sources.

Material information Any information that could influence the market value of a company or its products.

Media catching When journalists post queries online inviting public relations people or others with relevant information or expertise to respond. Public relations people "catch" these opportunities rather than "pitching" story ideas to journalists.

Media gatekeepers People or processes that filter information by deciding which content is published, broadcasted, posted, shared or forwarded.

Media kits Packages of information assembled by public relations people for news media. Common contents include news releases, fact sheets, backgrounders, position papers, photos, graphics and so on.

Media monitoring services Vendors that assist public relations practitioners in the collection, analysis and reporting of media data for evaluation; see also **clipping services**.

Media planning Choosing media channels to achieve strategic communication goals and objectives. Media planning drives advertising purchases.

Mediated public diplomacy A nation's strategic use of media to promote its agenda abroad to foreign publics.

Meta tags Text used to describe a web page to search engines.

Microblog A shorter blog post limited by space or size constraints of the delivery platform.

Mission Overall reason an organization exists.

Mission statement A formal statement of an organization's steady, enduring purpose.

Monologic communication Communication in which one party attempts to impose its view on others.

Morgue Storage space for archived files of old stories, notes and media materials kept by news organizations.

Multimedia The combination of any two or more forms of media such as text, graphics, moving images and sounds.

Multipliers Formulae applied to circulation or other media reach numbers based on assumptions that more than one person will be exposed to each copy of a message or that being covered as part of a news story is more valuable than paid advertising in the same media space.

Native advertising Paid advertising that is presented in the form of the media content that surrounds it. Advertorials are a type of native advertising, as are promoted tweets, sponsored posts and so on. Native advertising should be labeled as "advertising," "paid content," "sponsored," etc.

Natural links Hyperlinks to a web page that are provided by other people who see value in the content of the page, as opposed to links that are posted for the primary purpose of manipulating search engines.

Net neutrality When data transmitted on the internet is treated equally by governments and service providers in a way that does not slow down, speed up or manipulate traffic to create a favorable business environment for some organizations or users over others.

News release A statement of news produced and distributed on behalf of an organization to make information public. Traditionally news releases (aka press releases) have been issued to news media with the intent of publicizing the information to the news organization's readers, listeners or viewers.

Newsworthiness Standard used to determine what is worth covering in news media.

Non-compete clause Part of an employment contract that restricts employees from working for competitors or sharing competitive information such as trade secrets even after they no longer work for the organization.

Nongovernmental organization (NGO) A group of people organized at the local, national or international level, often serving humanitarian functions and encouraging political participation. Many NGOs work closely with the United Nations.

Nonparticipant observation Research method in which the researcher avoids interaction with the environment or those being observed.

NSFW Shorthand for "not safe/suitable for work."

Objectives Statements that indicate specific outputs or outcomes desired. In strategic public relations, objectives are specific steps taken to achieve broader goals.

Objectivity State of being free from the influence of personal feelings or opinions in considering and representing facts.

Organic search results Search engine results that are generated because of their relevance to the search terms entered by users and not resulting directly from paid placement as advertising.

Organization A group of people organized in pursuit of a mission, including businesses, nonprofits, NGOs, clubs, churches, unions, schools, teams and government agencies.

Organizational crisis A major threat to an organization's operations or reputation.

Organizational culture The unique character of an organization comprised of beliefs, values, symbols and behaviors.

Original digital video Video that is recorded, produced and uploaded digitally for sharing online, as opposed to video originally produced for other channels like television or theaters.

Outcomes Observable results of public relations work.

Outputs Tasks or work attempted and completed, including communication tactics produced. Outputs can be completed without necessarily leading to meaningful results (i.e., outcomes).

Overhead expenses Costs of running a business that are not directly related to the product or services delivered.

Participant observation Research method in which the researcher deliberately interacts with the environment and those being observed.

Participatory culture A culture in which private citizens and publics are as likely to produce and share as they are to consume; commonly applied in mediated contexts in which consumers produce and publish information online.

Participatory media Media in which publics actively participate in producing and sharing content.

Patent Claim to intellectual property rights of an invention.

Pay per click Model of media sales in which advertisers, marketers or sponsors pay an online publisher or website owner for each time the sponsored message or advertisement is clicked.

Pitching When a public relations person approaches a journalist or editor to suggest a story idea involving the organization for which the public relations practitioner works.

Plagiarism Presenting someone else's words or ideas as one's own.

Planning Forethought about goals and objectives and the strategies and tactics needed to achieve them.

Post production Process in media production that occurs after raw audio, video or images have been recorded—includes editing, combining media elements, transitions and special effects.

Power-distance Cultural dimension describing the difference between cultures that value hierarchy and authority more and those that value equal distribution of power more.

Pre-roll advertising A commercial ad is displayed as online video before the desired video is shown.

Press agentry/publicity model Model of public relations in which communication is mostly one-way, initiated by an organization with little concern for accuracy or completeness in order to gain the attention of publics.

Primary publics Groups of people identified as most important to the success of a public relations campaign or program.

Primary research Systematic design, collection, analysis and application of original data or observation.

Pro bono Public relations work conducted as a public service without fee or payment.

Proactive A management style that is anticipatory, change-oriented, and self-initiated to improve the organization's environment and its future.

Problem or opportunity statement A concise written summary of the situation that explains the main reason for a public relations program or campaign.

Problem recognition When people detect a problem or situation in their environment and begin to think about it.

Professional convergence When various functions of professional communication such as publicity, advertising, online services and marketing are combined to improve strategy.

Programmatic media buying Automated media buying that is preprogrammed so that advertising purchases are completed when certain criteria set by buyers (marketers) and sellers (media) are met. Programmatic media buying commonly occurs via computer-run, real-time auctions.

Propaganda The spread of information used to promote or support a particular point of view. In modern use, the term usually refers to false, misleading or exaggerated information.

Proselytizing When members of publics advocate or promote to others the goals and objectives of a communication strategy. Proselytizing is a key part of campaigns going viral.

Pseudo-event An event organized primarily for the purpose of generating media coverage.

Psychographic research Data describing psychological characteristics of a population including interests, attitudes and behaviors.

Public affairs Management of policy-focused relationships between an organization, public officials and their constituents.

Public diplomacy Subset of international public relations that focuses on promoting national interests.

Public domain Works of intellectual property for which the copyright has expired, the creator has forfeited rights or copyright laws do not apply, making the works freely available for public use.

Public figure Someone "of general fame or notoriety in the community" who is subject to less protection in libel cases than a private individual.

Public information model Model of public relations in which communication is mostly one-way, initiated by an organization to inform publics with truthful and accurate information.

Public information officer (PIO) A public relations person, commonly working in a government position, whose job focuses on the dissemination of information to appropriate publics in an accurate and timely manner.

Public relations Management of communication between an organization and its publics, or the strategic communication process that builds mutually beneficial relationships between organizations and their publics.

Publicity Unpaid media coverage, or the practice of deliberately planning and producing information and activities to attract this coverage.

Publics Groups of people with shared interests. An organization's publics either have an effect on the organization, are affected by the organization, or both.

Pure accommodation Stance in issues management in which a public relations practitioner fully concedes to a public's demands.

Pure advocacy Stance in issues management in which a public relations practitioner firmly pleads an organization's case without compromise.

Qualitative research Research that results in in-depth description and understanding without relying on the use of numbers or statistics to analyze findings.

Quantitative research Research that results in numerical or statistical data and analysis.

Reach Percentage or number of people exposed to a message at least once via a specific communication channel during a defined period of time.

Reactive A management style that mainly responds to problems as they arise rather than anticipating them and averting them.

Relational maintenance strategies Ways of building and sustaining mutually beneficial relationships between organizations and publics.

Relational public diplomacy Engagement between a nation and its foreign publics in cultural exchange and two-way communication with the goal of achieving mutual benefits.

Reliability Consistency and precision of a particular research technique.

Replicability The ability to perform a research procedure or experiment repeated times to attain comparable results.

Reputation management Acting and communicating—often in writing—to influence an organization's reputation as part of a process that includes planning, analyzing feedback and evaluating.

Responsible supply chain management Careful monitoring of product production and distribution to ensure that generally high ethical standards of social and environmental responsibility are maintained.

Scapegoating Blaming an outside person or organization for a crisis.

Search advertising Paid placement of advertising on search-engine results pages. Ads are placed to appear in response to certain keyword queries.

Search engine optimization (SEO) Process of improving the position of a specific website in the organic search results of search engines.

Secondary publics Groups of people who are important to a public relations campaign or program because of their relationship with primary publics.

Secondary research Collection, summary, analysis or application of previously reported research.

Securities and Exchange Commission (SEC) U.S. federal agency responsible for regulating financial activities and investing.

Selective attention Process of filtering information by focusing on some stimuli in the environment while ignoring others.

Self-efficacy One's belief that he or she can perform certain behaviors to achieve certain outcomes.

Situation analysis A report analyzing the internal and external environment of an organization and its publics as it relates to the start of a campaign or program.

Situational crisis communication theory (SCCT) Theory that proposes effective crisis communication entails choosing and applying appropriate response strategies depending on how much responsibility for the crisis is attributed to the organization by key publics.

Situational theory of publics Theory that the activity of publics depends on their levels of involvement, problem recognition and constraint recognition.

Slander Oral communication that is false and injures someone's reputation.

Snackable content Easy-to-consume pieces of content that are available on the go.

Social media creators Influential social media users who are among the first to identify and post about crises online.

Social media crisis communication model (SMCC) Model describing the role of social media influencers, followers and inactives in spreading information in crisis situations.

Social media followers Social media users who receive crisis information from social media creators.

Social media inactives People who receive crisis information indirectly from social media via traditional media and offline word of mouth.

Social media release A news release that applies the conventions of social media and includes content designed for social media distribution and sharing.

Spambots Computer programs that automatically send unsolicited email or post comments in online forums.

Spin Disingenuous strategic communication involving skewed interpretation or presentation of information.

Status conferral When media pay attention to individuals and groups and therefore enhance their authority or bestow prestige to them.

Stealing thunder Crisis response strategy in which an organization exposes its own problems (and works to address those problems) before opponents have the opportunity to do so.

Stock images Images that are professionally produced for selling or sharing, commonly available in searchable databases.

Story placement The outcome of a successful pitch, when a story involving a public relations practitioner's organization or client is covered in the news media.

Strategic decision-making Daily management and communication decisions made with mindfulness of the objectives, goals and mission of the organization.

Strategy Underlying logic that holds a plan together and offers a rationale for why it will work.

Summative research Research conducted at the end of a campaign or program to determine the extent that objectives and goals were met.

Sunshine law State law that stipulates which documents and records must be open to the public and which meetings and events must be open.

SWOT analysis Description and discussion of an organization's internal strengths and weaknesses and its external opportunities and threats.

Symmetrical model Model of public relations in which two-way communication is mostly balanced, with the organization as likely to change attitudes or behavior as its publics.

Tactical decision-making Daily management and communication tactics implemented without consideration of the strategic objectives, goals and mission of the organization.

Tactics Specific actions taken and items produced in public relations.

Target audience Group of people strategically identified for their propensity to consume an organization's products, services or ideas.

Technician role Concept describing those in public relations who primarily implement decisions of others in an organization including writing, production and dissemination of communication tactics.

Technological convergence (aka digital convergence) When information of various forms such as sound, text, images and data are digitized, affording communication across common media.

Tertiary publics Groups of people who indirectly influence or are indirectly affected by a public relations campaign or program.

Third-party credibility Assumption that information delivered from an independent source is seen as more objective and believable than information from a source with a vested interest in persuasion.

Third-party data Data on user behavior that is collected or aggregated by one organization and sold to another organization.

Trade secret Business information that is not generally known to the public and not readily available to others who could profit from its disclosure or use.

Trademark Word, name, phrase, symbol or design used to distinguish a product or service from others in the competitive marketplace.

Transmedia storytelling Telling a story across multiple platforms like games, web pages, apps, social media and traditional media.

Transparency Deliberate attempt to make available all legally reasonable information for the purpose of enhancing the reasoning ability of publics.

Treatment group A group of subjects or people in an experiment who receive or are exposed to a treatment.

Two-way communication When both parties send and receive information in an exchange, as opposed to the one-way dissemination of information from an organization to its publics.

Uncertainty avoidance Cultural dimension describing the difference between cultures that are less comfortable with ambiguity (high uncertainty avoidance) and those that are more at ease with ambiguity.

Unconferences Meetings or conferences organized by their participants for active peer-to-peer exchange of ideas and information. Unconferences are less structured and more participatory (e.g., fewer one-to-many presentations) than traditional conferences.

Uncontrolled media Channels of communication that are outside of the control of public relations practitioners.

Usage divide (or second digital divide) Gap between people who use information and communication technologies for education, self betterment, civic engagement, etc. and those who use the technologies for less constructive reasons.

User-centered design Process by which media, messages and other products and services are developed with continuous and deliberate attention to how end users will experience them.

Uses and gratifications Approach to studying communication that focuses on how people use media and the gratifications they seek from media, as opposed to studying the effects of media on people as passive audiences.

Utilitarianism Principle that the most ethical course of action is the one that maximizes good and minimizes harm for people.

Validity Accuracy of a particular research technique in measuring or observing what the researcher intends to measure or observe.

Vertical video Video framed in an orientation in which height is greater than width.

Video news release A news release that provides broadcast journalists with pre-produced news packages including audio and video material.

Word-of-mouth promotion Passing of information and recommendations from person to person.

Credits

Name Index

Subject Index

Facebook (*Continued*)
  most-shared news articles on, 259
  recruitment via, 44
  reposting and, 288
Facebook Insights, 371
Facebook Live, 263
Fact sheets, 233, 234
Fairness, 386
Fair use, 284–86
Falk, Thomas J., 187
False light, portrayal in a, 295
Fast Company, 376
Fault, 281
FDA. *See* Food and Drug Administration
fda.gov, 291
Feature stories, 226–29
Federal Emergency Management Agency
  (FEMA), 33–34
Federalist Papers, The, 42
Federal Trade Commission (FTC), 290, 291
FedEx, 57
Feedback, 10, 152–53, 237
Felton, Jack, 177
FEMA. *See* Federal Emergency
  Management Agency
Female Moral Reform Society, 45
Fenton, 212, 213*t*
Fight for the Future, 122*p*
Financial field, PR careers in, 363–64
Financial information, 291–92
Finkelstein, Barry, 325–26
First Amendment, 277–80, 282, 284
First-party data, 198
"First sale" doctrine, 276
#FirstWorldProblems, 333
Fiske, Rosanna, 185–186
Fitbit, 292
#FitchTheHomeless, 30–31
Fitzpatrick, Kathy, 19–20
Flaherty, Rob, 370
Flaming, 12
Flash mobs, 34
Fleischman, Doris, 37, 38*p*, 48–49
FleishmanHillard, 292, 356
Florida Department of Citrus, 208
Florida Public Relations Association, 22
Focus groups, 127–28, 128*p*, 194
Focus Groups as Qualitative Research
  (Morgan), 128
Food and Drug Administration (FDA),
  290, 291
Foote Communications LLC, 242
Foote, Cornelius, 242–43
Forbes, 29, 188, 198, 221, 252
Forbes.com, 375
Ford, Henry, 69
Ford, Henry, II, 38
Ford Motor Company, 38–39, 169
Formal research, 129–32
Formative research, 112, 152–53
Forrester Research, 256
Fortune, 96, 187, 280, 319
Fort Worth Fire, 161

Fort Worth Star-Telegram, 161
Four C's of integrated marketing
  communication, 69–71, 94. *See also*
  Communication; Consumers;
  Convenience; Cost
Four P's of marketing, 63–67, 69. *See also*
  Place; Price; Product; Promotion
Four R's of stewardship, 100
Foxfans.com, 162
Framing, 288
Francis, Pope, 317
Fraser, Renee White, 292
Fraser Communications, 292
Freedom of Information Act (FOIA), 289
Free flow of information, 78–79, 386–87
Freelancers, 263
Free Press, 120–21, 122
Free speech, 277–78, 284
Frequency, 159
Frito Lay, 267
Frizzell, Roger, 114
FTC. *See* Federal Trade Commission
Functional magnetic resonance imaging
  (fMRI), 193
Funnel, 146, 203
Future Shock (Toffler), 370

G
Games for Change (gamesforchange.org), 344
Gamification, 344–45
Gamification Nation Ltd., 345
Gantt charts, 154, 155*f*
Gap, 70, 313, 315
Gartner Inc., 335
Gates, Robert, 204
Gawker, 227
General Electric (GE), 68, 147, 147*p*, 185,
  216, 364
General Motors, 73, 216, 342
General public, 2, 3
Geofilter service, 266, 266*p*
Geolocation functions, 266
German Football Association (DFB), 363*p*
Gertz v. Robert Welch, Inc., 281–82
Getty Images, 258
Ghettopoly (board game), 318
Gialopsos, P. J., 307, 307*p*
Glass ceiling, 187
Glendale, California (false rumor about),
  317, 319
Global Alliance for Public Relations and
  Communication Management, 19,
  204, 216
Global Citizen Festival, 86*p*
Global Handwashing Day, 148–51
Globalization, 346–47, 349
Global public relations, 331–54
  digital divide and, 333–38, 334*f*
  intercultural public relations in,
  338–40, 349
  international public relations in, 346–47
  public diplomacy in, 347–48
Global Strategy Group, 365

Global Technology Adoption Index (GTAI),
  182–84
GMMB, 270
Goals
  Barcelona Principles on, 200–202, 210
  defined, 148
  writing and, 222–23
Godiva Chocolatiers, 76
Godzilla story, 226, 227*p*, 229, 234
Goebbels, Joseph, 50
"Golden hours" (following a crisis), 323
Golan, Guy, 349
Golden mean, 104, 106
Golden rule, 244
Golin, 114*t*
Google, 44, 45, 62, 94, 104, 160, 182,
  185, 195, 203–4, 239, 332,
  336, 348
Google AdWords, 182, 199
Google alerts, 237
Google Analytics, 62, 146, 204, 371
Google Hangouts, 263
Google Places, 11
GoPro, 179, 179*p*
Government
  history of PR in, 42–43
  PR careers in, 359–60
  public information dissemination in,
  33–34
Government relations, 102–4
Grammys, 178–79
Grant-Herms, Natalie, 295
Grassroots campaigns, 364, 365
Grasstops campaigns, 364, 365
Great Place to Work Institute, 96
Greenpeace, 348
Greenwashing, 6–7, 20
"Greenwashing Index"
  (greenwashingindex.com), 7, 7*p*
Greiner, Lori, 340
Grey New York, 58
Grove, Skye, 283–84
Guardian, The, 304

H
Hale, Tony, 369*p*
Handwashing campaign, 140,
  148–51, 152
Harder, Heather, 103
HARO (Help a Reporter Out), 93
Harpers Weekly, 289
Harvard College, 42
Hashimoto, Krislyn, 375–76
Hashtags, 30, 238
Hawaiian Electric Co. (HECO), 3, 40
Hayward, Tony, 320, 320*p*
Headlines, 239–40
Healthcare, PR careers in, 361, 362
Heaney, Katie, 341
Hennessey, Amy, 205
Henry J. Kaiser Family Foundation, 287
Heth, Joice, 27–28, 27*p*
Hewlett-Packard Co., 3

Media relations, 66, 75, 88, 89
Media space, 60–61
Mediated public diplomacy, 348
Medium.com, 279, 280, 374
Memeburn, 4, 283
Menendez, Robert, 78
Merrill Lynch, 38
Message testing, 193–94
Meta tags, 240, 241*t*
MetLife, 76
Metrics, 197–99. *See also* Measurement
Mexican Association of Public Relations
    Professionals (PRORP), 22
Meyer, Marissa, 120
Miami Herald, The, 242
Michelin, 348
Microblogs, 237, 238
Microsoft, 119–20, 332
minimumwage.com, 135, 136*p*
Minimum wage issue, 134–35
Mission, 148
Mission statements, 117
MIT Media Lab, 336
Mixed media, 182
Mixed-motive model, 39
M&Ms, 369*p*
Mobile media, 264–67, 270, 271
    localization and, 266
    personalization of, 265–66
    snackable content on, 266–67
    social media and, 265
    uses and gratifications of, 268–69
Molinaro, Melissa, 294*p*
Monitoring (proactive issues management
    step), 312–13, 312*t*
Monologic communication, 350
Moore, Carissa, 63*p*, 72
Moore, Jeff, 72
Moran, Monty, 319
Morgue (news organization archives),
    233, 234
MSLGroup, 114*t*
MTV, 29, 185
Multimedia, 250–64, 270, 271
    audio in, 258–60
    career skills needed for, 370–71
    defined, 250
    images in, 255–58
    text in, 251–55
    video in (*see* Video)
Multipliers, 206, 216
Murphy, Eileen, 79
Myers, Cayce, 296–98

N

NAACP, 41, 49
Nadal, Rafael, 174*p*
Nandan, Amresh, 335
National Association of Black
    Journalists, 242
National Association of Minority Media
    Executives, 242

National Baseball Hall of Fame and
    Museum, 161
National Black Public Relations
    Association, 5
National Black Public Relations Society
    Inc., 242
National Do Not Call Registry, 291
National Employment Law Project, 135
National Health Service (U.K.), 359
National Hot Rod Association, 161
National Investor Relations Institute, 98
National Jewish Outreach Program, 42
National Kidney Foundation Serving North
    Texas, 242
National Oceanic and Atmospheric
    Administration (NOAA), 234–35
National Public Radio (NPR), 9, 45, 259,
    267, 288
National School Public Relations
    Association, 22
Native advertising, 177, 228
Natural links, 240
Nature Conservancy, 99
Nazis (Lee's work with), 32, 50
NBA, 256, 270
NBC News (television program), 304
NCAA, 220, 225, 226
Negroponte, Nicholas, 336–37
Nestlé, 58
Net neutrality, 110, 120–22
Never Alone (game), 344
News Corporation, 336
News-driven relationships, 88–93. *See also*
    Journalism
News media, writing for, 231–35
Newsom, Earl, 38, 169
Newspaper advertising, 159
News releases, 180, 243, 252
    defined, 29, 231
    social media, 232, 253*f*
    video, 232
    writing, 231–33
News stories
    accounts of publics in, 124
    writing, 229–30
Newsworthiness, 89–91, 90*t*, 231, 232, 233
Newton, Cam, 317, 318*p*
New Yorker, The, 226
New York Times, The, 5, 29, 78–79, 135, 183,
    197, 199, 262, 278–80, 309, 332
New York Times Co. v. Sullivan, 282
New York Times Magazine, The, 104
Next Century Cities movement, 333
NFL, 58, 285, 286, 317
Ng, Konrad, 360
NGOs. *See* Nongovernmental organizations
Nielsen Media Research, 106, 119, 193, 259
Nike, 313, 315, 316*f*, 322, 341–42, 347
nikeresponsibility.com, 315
90-10 rule, 8
Nissan North America, 76
"No More" (ad), 58

Non-compete clauses, 376–77, 377*p*
Nongovernmental organizations (NGOs), 348
    defined, 2
    gamification and, 344
    PR careers in, 358–59
Nonparticipant observation, 128
Nonprofit organizations, 39, 46, 203*f*
    gamification and, 344
    PR careers in, 358–59
    relationship management in, 99–100
Nordstrom, 94
NPR. *See* National Public Radio
NSFW, 255

O

Obama, Barack, 43, 78, 79*p*, 161, 360
Objectives, 147–48, 222–23. *See also*
    SMART objectives
Objectivity, 49–50, 215
Obscene material, 288–89
Ogilvy, 207
Ogilvy Interactive, 270
Ogilvy & Mather, 9
Ogilvy Public Relations Worldwide, 116
Oglethorpe, James, 44
Old Navy, 293–94
Olson, Bo, 279
Oman, 332
Omnicom, 57–58, 346, 347
One Laptop per Child program, 331,
    336–38, 337*p*
One-way communication, 34, 176, 222,
    350. *See also* Press agentry/publicity
    model; Public information model
Open Internet proceeding, 122
Openness, 85, 86
OpenSecrets.org, 102
Opponents (publics as), 123
Opportunities (SWOT analysis), 115
Opportunity statements. *See* Problem
    statements
Opportunity to *see* (OTS), 206
Oracle, 94, 332
Organic search results, 45
Organizational crises, 316
Organizational culture, 118
Organizations, 2–3
    Barcelona Principles on performance
        of, 203–4, 210
    defined, 2
    beyond offerings, 74–75
    as publics, 100–104
    research and, 117–18
Original digital video, 261
Oscars, 29
Outcomes
    attitudinal, 202
    Barcelona Principles on, 202–3, 210
    behavioral, 202
    cognitive, 202
    defined, 151
    measurement models, 212, 213*t*

Outputs, 151, 202–3, 210
Overhead expenses, 159
Owned media, 175–76, 182–84, 199, 228, 370–71